PRAISE FOR THE BEST RECIPE SERIES AND OTHER AMERICA'S TEST KITCHEN TITLES

"This tome definitely raises the bar for all-in-one, basic, must-have cookbooks. . . .Kimball and his company have scored another hit."
*PORTLAND OREGONIAN ON **THE AMERICA'S TEST KITCHEN FAMILY COOKBOOK***

"A foolproof, go-to resource for everyday cooking."
*PUBLISHERS WEEKLY ON **THE AMERICA'S TEST KITCHEN FAMILY COOKBOOK***

"For anyone looking for a lighter way of cooking, this book and its 300 recipes would be a most valuable resource."
*PROVIDENCE JOURNAL ON **THE BEST LIGHT RECIPE***

"Further proof that practice makes perfect, if not transcendent. . . . If an intermediate cook follows the directions exactly, the results will be better than takeout or mom's."
*THE NEW YORK TIMES ON **THE NEW BEST RECIPE***

"Exceptional renditions with thorough instruction…"
*PUBLISHERS WEEKLY ON **COOKING AT HOME WITH AMERICA'S TEST KITCHEN***

"Like a mini-cooking school, the detailed instructions and illustrations ensure that even the most inexperienced cook can follow these recipes with success."
*PUBLISHERS WEEKLY ON **BEST AMERICAN SIDE DISHES***

"Makes one-dish dinners a reality for average cooks, with honest ingredients and detailed make-ahead instructions."
*THE NEW YORK TIMES ON **COVER & BAKE***

"*Steaks, Chops, Roasts, & Ribs* conquers every question one could have about all things meat."
*THE SAN FRANCISCO CHRONICLE ON **STEAKS, CHOPS, ROASTS, & RIBS***

"The best instructional book on baking this reviewer has seen."
*LIBRARY JOURNAL (STARRED REVIEW) ON **BAKING ILLUSTRATED***

"A must-have for anyone into our nation's cooking traditions—and a good reference, too."
*LOS ANGELES DAILY NEWS ON **AMERICAN CLASSICS***

"If you've always wanted to make real Italian dishes as close to the Italian way as we can make them in America, here's a cookbook that shows you how."
*PITTSBURGH POST-GAZETTE ON **ITALIAN CLASSICS***

"*Cook's Illustrated* to the rescue. . . . *Perfect Vegetables* belongs on every cooking reference shelf. Here's to our health."
*PITTSBURGH TRIBUNE-REVIEW ON **PERFECT VEGETABLES***

WELCOME TO AMERICA'S TEST KITCHEN

THIS BOOK HAS BEEN TESTED, WRITTEN, AND edited by the folks at America's Test Kitchen, a very real 2,500-square-foot kitchen located just outside of Boston. It is the home of *Cook's Illustrated* magazine and *Cook's Country* magazine and is the Monday-through-Friday destination for more than two dozen test cooks, editors, food scientists, tasters, and cookware specialists. Our mission is to test recipes over and over again until we understand how and why they work and until we arrive at the "best" version.

We start the process of testing a recipe with a complete lack of conviction, which means that we accept no claim, no theory, no technique, and no recipe at face value. We simply assemble as many variations as possible, test a half dozen of the most promising, and taste the results blind. We then construct our own hybrid recipe and continue to test it, varying ingredients, techniques, and cooking times until we reach a consensus. The result, we hope, is the best version of a particular recipe, but we realize that only you can be the final judge of our success (or failure). As we like to say in the test kitchen, "We make the mistakes, so you don't have to."

All of this would not be possible without a belief that good cooking, much like good music, is indeed based on a foundation of objective technique. Some people like spicy foods and others don't, but there is a right way to sauté, there is a best way to cook a pot roast, and there are measurable scientific principles involved in producing perfectly beaten, stable egg whites. This is our ultimate goal: to investigate the fundamental principles of cooking so that you become a better cook. It is as simple as that.

You can watch us work (in our actual test kitchen) by tuning in to *America's Test Kitchen* (www.americastestkitchen.com) on public television or by subscribing to *Cook's Illustrated* magazine (www.cooksillustrated.com) or *Cook's Country* magazine (www.cookscountry.com), which are each published every other month. We welcome you into our kitchen, where you can stand by our side as we test our way to the "best" recipes in America.

THE BEST 30-MINUTE RECIPE

A BEST RECIPE CLASSIC

THE
BEST
30-MINUTE
RECIPE

A BEST RECIPE CLASSIC

BY THE EDITORS OF

COOK'S ILLUSTRATED

PHOTOGRAPHY

DANIEL J. VAN ACKERE

CARL TREMBLAY

ILLUSTRATIONS

JOHN BURGOYNE

AMERICA'S TEST KITCHEN

BROOKLINE, MASSACHUSETTS

America's Test Kitchen
17 Station Street
Brookline, MA 02445

ISBN-13: 978-0-936184-98-2
ISBN 10: 0-936184-98-1
Library of Congress Cataloging-in-Publication Data
The Editors of Cook's Illustrated

The Best 30-Minute Recipe
Want to serve your grandmother's chicken and roasted potatoes tonight but don't have a grandmother's schedule?
We streamlined this dish and 300 more to be on your table in 30 minutes or less.
1st Edition

ISBN-13: 978-0-936184-98-2
ISBN-10: 0-936184-98-1
(hardcover): U.S. $35; Can. $43.95
I. Cooking. I. Title
2006

Manufactured in the United States of America

Distributed by America's Test Kitchen, 17 Station Street, Brookline, MA 02445

Senior Editor: Lori Galvin
Senior Food Editor: Julia Collin Davison
Associate Editor: Keith Dresser
Assistant Editors: Charles Kelsey and Elizabeth Wray Emery
Test Cooks: Rachel Toomey and Diane Unger
Series and Jacket Designer: Amy Klee
Designer: Christian Steinmetz
Interior and Back Cover Photographers: Daniel J. van Ackere and Carl Tremblay
Interior and Back Cover Food Styling: Marie Piraino and Mary Jane Sawyer
Front Cover Photographer: Keller + Keller
Front Cover Food Styling: Mary Jane Sawyer
Illustrator: John Burgoyne
Senior Production Manager: Jessica Lindheimer Quirk
Copyeditor: Cheryl Redmond
Proofreader: Sally Sisson
Indexer: Cathy Dorsey

Pictured on front of jacket: Pan-Roasted Chicken Breasts with Potatoes (page 113)
Pictured on back of jacket: 30-Minute Chicken Provençal (page 73), Skillet Lasagna (page 137), Easy Asian Chicken Noodle Soup (page 47),
Skillet Beef Pot Pie (page 117), and Pan-Roasted Chicken Breasts with Potatoes (page 113)

Contents

PREFACE

BACK IN THE EARLY 60S, CHARLIE BENTLEY and I were walking along the town road after loading up the last hay wagon. A thunderstorm came in, so I started to run toward the barn. I looked back and asked Charlie why he wasn't hurrying. His answer (paraphrased from Benjamin Franklin) was, "I'm neither sugar nor salt, I won't melt."

That pretty much sums up country life. In my state of Vermont or elsewhere, you never see a farmer run, a cook rush around the kitchen, or a team of horses do much more than plod along, pulling a mower or a rake. Farmers also take their time speaking—to the point that long silences, even in a crowded parlor, are the norm.

What does all of this have to do with a cookbook containing 30-minute recipes? Actually, quite a lot. Two-hundred years ago, slow cooking was the essence of convenience. Much food was simmered slowly for hours while everyone was out working in the fields. Stews, pot roasts, and bean-hole suppers (the beans are cooked in a hole in the ground) suited the lifestyle of the age.

All of that has changed. Today's "lifestyles" (spoken of as if you could choose one in much the way you can choose a flavor of ice cream) demand speed and convenience. Do I think this is a good thing? Of course I don't. I still think that preparing dinner on a wood cookstove (which I do occasionally) is a vastly preferable approach. But I do admit that modern times offer less time to prepare meals. Since the alternative is either fast or convenience foods, I am all in favor of giving home cooks as many easy choices as possible, as long as we agree to start with wholesome ingredients.

A book of quick, 30-minute recipes includes, of course, recipes that are naturally quick: stir fries, simple pasta sauces, skillet recipes, salads, and egg dishes, for instance. No secrets there. After a while, though, people get tired of having the same old sandwich, omelet, or stir-fry for supper. How about a stew or some chili, or a lasagna, meatloaf, or barbecued chicken? That's where our

test kitchen had to get into high culinary gear.

After months of work, we did indeed find a way to make skillet lasagna, pork stew, chicken chili, Indian curry, gumbo, mini meatloaves, and oven-barbecued chicken all in 30 minutes. And, let's be clear, this includes preparation time, not just cooking time! Every test cook in the kitchen had to use a timer from start to finish; no one was allowed to break the half-hour rule. (We also sent recipes out to regular home cooks to make sure that they could get things done in 30 minutes or less.) We offer advice about what prep work can be done during lulls in the cooking process. We offer suggestions on how to boost the flavor of a recipe if you have even a few extra minutes to spare. And we offer lots of shopping suggestions based on years of taste tests. Starting with just the right ingredients is the first crucial step in quick cooking.

These days, now that I have reached the half-century mark, I don't run to the barn when it starts to pour. I have learned to enjoy a walk in the rain. And at our farm my family and I boil our own maple syrup, harvest our own honey, grow our own potatoes . . . the list goes on. But I do admit that I have a cell phone, use the Internet daily, and drive much too fast on occasion. I also love a good, quick recipe, especially when it tastes almost as good as the long-cooked version. Try the skillet lasagna and you'll know what I mean. It's easy, it's fast, and, in my opinion, it tastes fresher and lighter than the "real thing."

Sure, Charlie Bentley might say that a long slow walk in the rain isn't inconvenient—he's not likely to melt. And I would agree. But putting a home-cooked meal on the table in 30 minutes is not only convenient, it's also a worthy goal for any good cook. Especially when the food tastes good.

Christopher Kimball
Founder and Editor
Cook's Illustrated and *Cook's Country*

1

HEARTY EGG SUPPERS

HEARTY EGG SUPPERS

HEARTY SCRAMBLED EGGS ON TOAST 3
Prosciutto and Asparagus Scrambled Eggs with Porcini Butter
Chorizo and Bell Pepper Scrambled Eggs with Chipotle Butter
Smoked Salmon Scrambled Eggs with Chive Butter

FAMILY-SIZED OMELETS 6
Family-Sized Cheese Omelet
Family-Sized Tomato, Bacon, and Garlic Omelet
Family-Sized Arugula, Sun-Dried Tomato, and Provolone Omelet

THICK AND HEARTY FRITTATAS 8
Asparagus, Ham, and Gruyère Frittata
Leek, Prosciutto, and Goat Cheese Frittata
Broccoli Rabe, Sun-Dried Tomato, and Fontina Frittata

SKILLET STRATA 10
Skillet Strata with Cheddar and Thyme
Skillet Strata with Bacon, Scallions, and Pepper Jack Cheese
Skillet Strata with Sausage and Gruyère
Skillet Strata with Spinach and Smoked Gouda

CORNED BEEF HASH 11
Corned Beef Hash

SPANISH TORTILLA 12
Spanish Egg and Potato Tortilla
Roasted Red Pepper Aïoli

MIGAS 13
One-Minute Salsa
Migas

HUEVOS RANCHEROS 14
Huevos Rancheros

SKILLET EGG SUPPER 15
Eggs, Sausage, and Pepper Skillet Supper

EGGS HAVE LONG BEEN A QUICK AND convenient dinner option. Who doesn't have a carton of eggs in the fridge? Better yet, eggs are quick cooking, so no matter how tired you are after a long day, or how pressed for time on a busy weeknight, eggs can easily make a satisfying meal. Eggs also pair well with a variety of ingredients and flavors, making them so much more than a simple breakfast food—think softly scrambled eggs flavored with chipotle butter and cheddar cheese, a soufflé-like skillet strata with spinach and smoked Gouda, or an elegant, velvety Spanish egg and potato tortilla.

However you prepare your eggs, there are a few points to keep in mind. A good ovenproof nonstick skillet and a wooden or heatproof rubber spatula are necessities. These equipment choices will save you a lot of frustration, because they keep eggs from sticking to the pan. And using an ovenproof skillet makes it easy to go from the stovetop to the oven in recipes such as frittatas and skillet stratas. When it comes to add-ins, vegetables should typically be pre-cooked before mixing them with the eggs (so as to help evaporate excess moisture, which can lead to soggy eggs), and meats should have a low moisture content for the same reason. Finally, because eggs cook so quickly, it's a good idea to have all of your prep work done (in most cases) before you start cooking.

HEARTY SCRAMBLED EGGS ON TOAST

SCRAMBLED EGGS AND TOAST MAKE FOR a quick, light dinner but they can't help but feel like breakfast. We wanted to elevate scrambled eggs to supper status by introducing hearty, sophisticated flavors to this breakfast staple. And we didn't want this dish to be merely scrambled eggs with flavor add-ins and toast alongside—we wanted the entire dish to work together as a whole.

To start, we developed a quick savory butter, which involves simply mashing minced rehydrated porcini mushrooms and minced shallot with softened butter. Porcini mushrooms have a deep, woodsy flavor so we looked to complementary flavors to add to our eggs. Chopped prosciutto, sautéed asparagus, and freshly grated Parmesan fit the bill. To pull the dish together, we used some of the savory butter to cook our eggs and slathered the rest over thick slices of crusty toast. We piled the finished eggs on the buttered toast and all that was left to do was pick up a knife and fork and dig in. You can be sure that no one will mistake these eggs for breakfast. We also developed two other flavor variations: A Mexican-inspired dish that includes chorizo sausage, smoky chipotle chiles, and cheddar cheese; and one that features the classic duo of smoked salmon and chives.

TEST KITCHEN TIP: Scrambling Eggs
We learned that a folding method yielded the creamiest, softest scrambled eggs. If you push the eggs to and fro with a spatula instead of constantly stirring them (the more conventional method), you will end up with large, airy curds and very fluffy scrambled eggs.

1. Using a wooden spoon or plastic spatula, push the eggs from one side of the pan to the other.

2. As the curds form, lift and fold the eggs until they are clumped in a single mound.

Prosciutto and Asparagus Scrambled Eggs with Porcini Butter

SERVES 4 TO 6

If you don't have prosciutto on hand, use any good low-moisture ham. Round out the meal with a leafy green salad.

12	large eggs
6	tablespoons half-and-half
	Salt and ground black pepper
4	tablespoons unsalted butter, softened (see Kitchen Shortcut below)
1/4	ounce dried porcini mushrooms, rehydrated and minced (see below)
1	teaspoon minced shallot
1	teaspoon vegetable oil
1/2	bunch asparagus, trimmed and sliced thin on bias
1/2	cup grated Parmesan cheese
3	ounces thinly sliced prosciutto, chopped coarse
6	thick slices rustic white bread, toasted

MAKING THE MINUTES COUNT:
Rehydrate the porcini mushrooms first so they have ample time to soften.

1. COMBINE EGG MIXTURE AND PREPARE PORCINI BUTTER: Whisk eggs, half-and-half, ¾ teaspoon salt, and ¼ teaspoon pepper together and set aside. In separate bowl, mash butter, porcini, and shallot together and set aside.

2. COOK ASPARAGUS: Heat oil in 12-inch nonstick skillet over medium heat until shimmering. Add asparagus and cook until lightly browned and crisp-tender, 2 to 4 minutes; transfer to plate and set aside.

3. COOK EGGS: Wipe skillet clean with paper towels and return to medium heat. Add 1 tablespoon of porcini butter and melt, swirling to coat skillet, until foaming subsides. Following illustrations on page 3, add eggs and cook, using rubber spatula to push them back and forth, until curds begin to form. Continue to cook, lifting and folding curds from side to side, until they clump in single mound but are still very moist, about 3 minutes.

4. FINISH AND ASSEMBLE: Off heat, gently fold in Parmesan, prosciutto, and asparagus. Spread remaining porcini butter on toast and spoon eggs on top. Serve immediately.

KITCHEN SHORTCUT
SOFTENING BUTTER IN A HURRY

It can take a long time for chilled butter to soften on the counter. The microwave is a quick but sometimes imperfect solution. We like to cut the butter into tablespoon-sized pieces, which should soften in just 10 minutes—the time it takes to gather other ingredients or heat the oven.

REHYDRATING PORCINI MUSHROOMS

1. Rinse the mushrooms of any grit and place in a small bowl. Pour boiling water over them to cover and let stand until softened, about 5 minutes. Use a fork to lift the mushrooms from the liquid, leaving any additional grit behind. The mushrooms are ready to be minced and used as directed.

2. The soaking liquid is quite flavorful and can be used in other applications—simply strain the liquid through a coffee filter or a single sheet of paper towel to remove any grit.

Chorizo and Bell Pepper Scrambled Eggs with Chipotle Butter
SERVES 4 TO 6

Although chorizo, a Spanish-style pork sausage, is preferred here, andouille or linguiça can be substituted.

12	large eggs
6	tablespoons half-and-half
	Salt and ground black pepper
4	tablespoons unsalted butter, softened
	(see Kitchen Shortcut on page 4)
2½	teaspoons minced chipotle chiles in adobo sauce
1	small garlic clove, minced
1	teaspoon vegetable oil
8	ounces chorizo sausage, cut into ½-inch pieces
1	red bell pepper, cored and cut into ½-inch pieces
3	scallions, white and green parts separated and sliced thin
½	cup shredded sharp cheddar cheese
6	thick slices rustic white bread, toasted

MAKING THE MINUTES COUNT:
Because this dish comes together quickly, prep all your ingredients before you begin cooking.

1. COMBINE EGG MIXTURE AND PREPARE CHIPOTLE BUTTER: Whisk eggs, half-and-half, ¾ teaspoon salt, and ¼ teaspoon pepper together and set aside. In separate bowl, mash butter, chipotle, and garlic together and set aside.

2. COOK SAUSAGE AND VEGETABLES: Heat oil in 12-inch nonstick skillet over medium heat until shimmering. Add chorizo and cook until fat begins to render, about 2 minutes. Add bell pepper and scallion whites, and continue to cook until chorizo and peppers begin to brown, about 3 minutes. Transfer to small bowl and set aside.

3. COOK EGGS: Wipe skillet clean with paper towels and return to medium heat. Add 1 tablespoon chipotle butter and melt, swirling to coat skillet, until foaming subsides. Following illustrations on page 3, add eggs and cook, using rubber spatula to push them back and forth, until curds begin to form. Continue to cook, lifting and folding curds from side to side, until they clump in single mound but are still very moist, about 3 minutes.

4. FINISH AND ASSEMBLE: Off heat, gently fold in chorizo mixture, cheddar, and scallion greens. Spread remaining chipotle butter on toast and spoon eggs on top. Serve immediately.

Smoked Salmon Scrambled Eggs with Chive Butter
SERVES 4 TO 6

12	large eggs
6	tablespoons half-and-half
	Salt and ground black pepper
4	tablespoons unsalted butter, softened
	(see Kitchen Shortcut on page 4)
¼	cup minced fresh chives
2	ounces smoked salmon, minced
6	thick slices rustic white bread, toasted

EQUIPMENT: Nonstick Skillets
Nothing takes the challenge out of cooking delicate foods better than a slick nonstick skillet. The downside is that the nonstick coating is easily damaged, so we find it best to buy inexpensive nonstick skillets.

We tested nine 12-inch nonstick skillets ranging in price from $8.99 to $49.99. Our main criticisms focused on pan construction, because some of the pans turned out to be downright flimsy. However, the Cuisinart Chef's Classic Nonstick Hard Anodized Omelet Pan ($41.95) was our favorite, with the Wearever Collections Premium 12-inch Nonstick Aluminum Skillet ($8.99) coming in a close second.

THE BEST NONSTICK SKILLETS

The Cuisinart Chef's Classic Nonstick Hard Anodized Omelet Pan (left) and Wearever Collections Premium 12-inch Nonstick Aluminum Skillet (right) offer the best combination of nonstick performance and solid construction.

MAKING THE MINUTES COUNT:
Prep all your ingredients before you begin cooking.

1. COMBINE EGG MIXTURE AND PREPARE CHIVE BUTTER: Whisk eggs, half-and-half, ¾ teaspoon salt, and ¼ teaspoon pepper together and set aside. In separate bowl, mash butter and chives together.

2. COOK EGGS: Melt 1 tablespoon chive butter in 12-inch nonstick skillet over medium heat, swirling to coat skillet, until foaming subsides. Following illustrations on page 3, add eggs and cook, using rubber spatula to push them back and forth, until curds begin to form. Continue to cook, lifting and folding curds from side to side, until they clump in single mound but are still very moist, about 3 minutes.

3. FINISH AND ASSEMBLE: Off heat, gently fold in salmon. Spread remaining chive butter on toast and spoon eggs on top. Serve immediately.

A TEST KITCHEN CLASSIC

FAMILY-SIZED OMELETS

WE ALL THINK OF OMELETS AS A QUICK, last-minute dinner alternative, but the truth is that if you want to make more than one or two omelets, it's just not very practical (or quick). We set out to see if we could make one big omelet.

Our initial tests were disastrous, with runny eggs on top and burnt eggs underneath. Obviously, flipping a behemoth, eight-egg omelet was out of the question. Cooking the omelet over low heat was the key to avoiding scorched eggs on the bottom, but we still had to figure a way to cook the top of the omelet—and melt the cheese that is sprinkled on top of the eggs. Throwing the omelet under the broiler was a decent solution; however, we found it easiest to just cover the skillet with a tight-fitting lid, thus trapping the steam and cooking the top layer of eggs. This method also partially melted the cheese. Shaping this super-sized omelet was as simple as sliding it halfway out of

the pan and then folding it over onto itself—and the residual heat was also enough to perfectly finish melting the cheese.

Family-Sized Cheese Omelet
SERVES 4

Monterey Jack, colby, or any good melting cheese can be substituted for the cheddar.

8	large eggs
	Salt and ground black pepper
2	tablespoons unsalted butter
¾	cup shredded cheddar cheese

1. COMBINE EGG MIXTURE AND PREPARE SKILLET: Whisk eggs, ½ teaspoon salt, and ⅛ teaspoon pepper together. Melt butter in 12-inch nonstick skillet over medium heat, swirling to coat skillet, until foaming subsides.

2. COOK OMELET: Add eggs and cook, stirring gently in circular motion, until mixture is slightly thickened, about 1 minute. Following illustration on page 7, use rubber spatula to pull cooked edges of egg toward center of pan, tilting pan so uncooked egg runs to cleared edge of pan. Repeat until bottom of omelet is just set but top is still runny, about 1 minute. Cover skillet, reduce heat to low, and cook until top of omelet begins to set but is still moist, about 5 minutes.

3. FINISH WITH CHEESE AND SERVE: Remove pan from heat. Sprinkle cheese evenly over eggs, cover, and let sit until cheese partially melts, about 1 minute. Following illustration on page 7, slide half of omelet onto serving platter using rubber spatula, then tilt skillet so remaining omelet flips over onto itself, forming half-moon shape. Cut into wedges and serve immediately.

> **TEST KITCHEN TIP:**
> **Folding in the Fillings**
> In our omelet variations, we found that mixing the filling ingredients together with the egg mixture—rather than folding the omelet over the filling—makes this super-sized omelet easier to handle and allows for a cohesive mix of filling and egg in every bite.

➤ VARIATIONS

Family-Sized Tomato, Bacon, and Garlic Omelet

8	slices bacon, minced
1	large tomato, cored, seeded, and chopped fine
1/2	green bell pepper, cored and chopped fine
4	garlic cloves, minced
3/4	cup shredded pepper Jack cheese

MAKING THE MINUTES COUNT:
Prep your ingredients before you begin cooking.

Fry bacon in 12-inch nonstick skillet over medium-high heat until crisp, about 8 minutes. Stir in tomato and bell pepper and cook until vegetables are softened, about 6 minutes. Stir in garlic and cook until fragrant, about 30 seconds. Transfer mixture to paper towel–lined plate. Wipe skillet clean and follow Family-Sized Cheese Omelet recipe, adding bacon mixture to pan with eggs in step 2. Substitute pepper Jack cheese for cheddar in step 3.

Family-Sized Arugula, Sun-Dried Tomato, and Provolone Omelet

1	tablespoon olive oil
1/2	onion, minced
1/8	teaspoon red pepper flakes
5	ounces baby arugula, cut into 1/2-inch strips
1/4	cup oil-packed sun-dried tomatoes, minced
3/4	cup shredded provolone cheese

MAKING THE MINUTES COUNT:
Prep your ingredients before you begin cooking.

Heat oil in 12-inch nonstick skillet over medium-high heat until shimmering. Add onion and pepper flakes and cook until softened, about 5 minutes. Stir in arugula and sun-dried tomatoes and cook until arugula begins to wilt, about 1 minute. Transfer mixture to plate and set aside. Wipe skillet clean and follow recipe for Family-Sized Cheese Omelet, adding arugula mixture to pan with eggs in step 2. Substitute provolone for cheddar in step 3.

HOW TO MAKE AN OVERSIZED OMELET

Our eight-egg omelet calls for a special cooking method that requires a 12-inch nonstick skillet with a tight-fitting lid.

1. To cook the omelet evenly, pull the cooked edges of the egg mixture toward the center of the pan and allow the raw egg to run to the edges.

2. When the omelet is set on the bottom but still very runny on the top, cover the skillet and reduce the heat to low.

3. After the top of the omelet begins to set, remove the cover and sprinkle with the cheese. Let the omelet rest off the heat, covered, until the cheese has partially melted.

4. Use a rubber spatula to slide half of the omelet out onto a platter, then tilt the skillet so that the omelet folds over onto itself to make the traditional half-moon shape.

A TEST KITCHEN CLASSIC

THICK AND HEARTY FRITTATAS

A QUICK RECIPE BY DESIGN, FRITTATAS often end up dry, overstuffed, and overcooked. We wanted a frittata with a pleasing balance of egg to filling, firm yet moist eggs, and a supportive, browned exterior. Right away we found that 12 eggs mixed with 3 cups of cooked vegetables and meat provided the best balance of filling to eggs and nicely served 4 to 6 people for dinner. And of all the cooking methods we tried, the most promising was the traditional stovetop-to-broiler method: The eggs cook on the stovetop and then get a flash under the broiler to finish.

While this technique sounds easy, we found it can be a bit tricky to cook a frittata through evenly—with the eggs on the bottom, in the middle, and on the top all perfectly done. After lots of testing, we noted three key steps: First, set the eggs on the bottom using a quick blast of high heat on the stovetop. Second, slide the skillet under the broiler to cook the eggs on top (don't walk away from the broiler—some broilers cook quicker than others). Third, remove the frittata from the broiler when the eggs in the middle are still slightly wet and runny, so that the residual heat can finish cooking them through to their ideal doneness.

One last thing: Because the frittata is slid under the high heat of the broiler, you want to make sure that your nonstick skillet is ovensafe.

TEST KITCHEN TIP:
Tasty Bites of Cheese
When adding cheese, it's best to cut it into cubes (rather than shredding it) for nice little pockets of melted cheese throughout.

Asparagus, Ham, and Gruyère Frittata
SERVES 4 TO 6

Although we prefer the strong flavor of Gruyère in this recipe, you can substitute Swiss cheese.

12	large eggs
3	tablespoons half-and-half
	Salt and ground black pepper
3	ounces Gruyère cheese, cut into ¼-inch cubes
2	teaspoons olive oil
½	bunch asparagus, trimmed and sliced thin on bias
4	ounces thick-sliced deli ham, chopped small
1	shallot, minced

1. HEAT OVEN AND COMBINE EGG MIXTURE: Adjust rack about 5 inches from broiler element and heat broiler. Whisk eggs, half-and-half, ½ teaspoon salt, and ¼ teaspoon pepper together, then stir in cheese; set aside.

2. COOK ASPARAGUS, HAM, AND SHALLOT: Heat oil in 12-inch ovensafe nonstick skillet over medium heat until shimmering. Add asparagus and cook until lightly browned and crisp-tender, 2 to 4 minutes. Stir in ham and shallot and cook until shallot softens, about 2 minutes.

3. COOK FRITTATA: Add egg mixture to skillet and cook, using rubber spatula to stir and scrape bottom of skillet, until large curds form and spatula begins to leave wake but eggs are still very wet, about 2 minutes. Shake skillet to distribute eggs evenly and continue to cook without stirring to set bottom, about 30 seconds.

4. FINISH UNDER BROILER: Slide skillet under broiler and cook until surface is puffed and spotty brown, yet center remains slightly wet and runny when cut into with paring knife, 3 to 4 minutes.

5. LET STAND UNTIL SET: Remove skillet from broiler and let stand until eggs in middle are just set, about 5 minutes. Use rubber spatula to loosen frittata from skillet, then slide onto cutting board, slice into wedges, and serve.

Leek, Prosciutto, and Goat Cheese Frittata

SERVES 4 TO 6

Wash the leeks well to remove them of any grit. If desired, substitute any good low-moisture ham for the prosciutto.

2	tablespoons unsalted butter
2	medium leeks, white and light green parts, halved lengthwise, sliced thin and washed
	Salt and ground black pepper
12	large eggs
3	tablespoons half-and-half
3	ounces thinly sliced prosciutto, chopped
¼	cup minced fresh basil
½	cup crumbled goat cheese

1. HEAT OVEN AND COOK LEEKS: Adjust rack about 5 inches from broiler element and heat broiler. Melt butter in 12-inch ovensafe nonstick skillet over medium heat until foaming subsides. Stir in leeks and ¼ teaspoon salt. Cover, reduce heat to low, and cook, stirring occasionally, until softened, 8 to 10 minutes.

2. COMBINE EGG MIXTURE: Meanwhile, whisk eggs, half-and-half, ½ teaspoon salt, and ¼ teaspoon pepper together, then stir in prosciutto, basil, and half of goat cheese; set aside.

3. COOK FRITTATA: Add egg mixture to skillet and cook, using rubber spatula to stir and scrape bottom of skillet, until large curds form and spatula begins to leave wake but eggs are still very wet, about 2 minutes. Shake skillet to distribute eggs evenly and continue to cook without stirring to set bottom, about 30 seconds.

4. ADD CHEESE AND FINISH UNDER BROILER: Dot remaining goat cheese evenly over eggs. Slide skillet under broiler and cook until surface is puffed and spotty brown, yet center remains slightly wet and runny when cut into with paring knife, 3 to 4 minutes.

5. LET STAND UNTIL SET: Remove skillet from broiler and let stand until eggs in middle are just set, about 5 minutes. Use rubber spatula to loosen frittata from skillet, then slide onto cutting board, slice into wedges, and serve.

Broccoli Rabe, Sun-Dried Tomato, and Fontina Frittata

SERVES 4 TO 6

2	teaspoons olive oil
8	ounces broccoli rabe, trimmed and cut into 1-inch pieces
	Salt and ground black pepper
12	large eggs
3	tablespoons half-and-half
3	ounces Italian fontina cheese, cut into ¼-inch cubes
¼	cup oil-packed sun-dried tomatoes, minced
1	garlic clove, minced
⅛	teaspoon red pepper flakes

1. HEAT OVEN AND COOK BROCCOLI: Adjust rack about 5 inches from broiler element and heat broiler. Heat oil in 12-inch ovensafe nonstick skillet over medium heat until shimmering. Add broccoli rabe and ¼ teaspoon salt and cook until beginning to brown and soften, 6 to 8 minutes.

2. COMBINE EGG MIXTURE: Meanwhile, whisk eggs, half-and-half, ½ teaspoon salt, and ¼ teaspoon pepper together, then stir in cheese and sun-dried tomatoes; set aside.

3. COOK FRITTATA: Add garlic and pepper flakes to skillet and cook until fragrant, about 30 seconds. Add egg mixture and cook, using rubber spatula to stir and scrape bottom of skillet, until large curds form and spatula begins to leave wake but eggs are still very wet, about 2 minutes. Shake skillet to distribute eggs evenly and continue to cook without stirring to set bottom, about 30 seconds.

4. FINISH UNDER BROILER: Slide skillet under broiler and cook until surface is puffed and spotty brown, yet center remains slightly wet and runny when cut into with paring knife, 3 to 4 minutes.

5. LET STAND UNTIL SET: Remove skillet from broiler and let stand until eggs in middle are just set, about 5 minutes. Use rubber spatula to loosen frittata from skillet, then slide onto cutting board, slice into wedges, and serve.

SKILLET STRATA

STRATA IN ITS MOST BASIC FORM IS A layered brunch casserole comprising day-old bread, eggs, cheese, and milk. The result is a hearty, savory bread pudding. Typically, strata is made hours in advance, usually the night before serving, giving the dry bread enough time to soak up the custard; it then bakes for an hour or so. But we wanted a fast strata, one that would deliver the same cheesy richness in a fraction of the time. After numerous tests, we discovered a way to speed things up by using an ovensafe nonstick skillet.

Sautéing the filling ingredients is the first step. Then fresh bread (not stale) is added and cooked until lightly toasted—toasting the bread in the skillet is a crucial step because it gives the strata structure and prevents the bread from turning to mush. Finally, the custard is added to the skillet off the heat, and the strata is finished in the oven, producing a delicate, souffléed texture for an elegant main course in less than 30 minutes.

Skillet Strata with Cheddar and Thyme

SERVES 6 TO 8

Do not trim the crusts from the bread or the strata will be dense and eggy. Using a 10-inch skillet is crucial for the thickness and texture of this dish.

4	tablespoons unsalted butter
1	onion, minced
	Salt and ground black pepper
6	large eggs
1½	cups whole milk
1	teaspoon minced fresh thyme
1	cup shredded cheddar cheese
5	slices high-quality sandwich bread, cut into 1-inch squares

1. HEAT OVEN AND COOK ONION: Adjust oven rack to middle position and heat oven to 425 degrees. Melt butter in 10-inch ovensafe nonstick skillet over medium-high heat, swirling to coat skillet, until foaming subsides. Add onion and ½ teaspoon salt and cook until onion is softened and lightly browned, about 6 minutes.

2. COMBINE EGG MIXTURE: Meanwhile, in large bowl, whisk eggs, milk, thyme, and ¼ teaspoon pepper together, then stir in cheese; set aside.

3. TOAST BREAD: Add bread to skillet and, using rubber spatula, carefully fold bread into onion mixture until evenly coated. Cook bread, folding occasionally, until lightly toasted, about 3 minutes.

4. ADD EGG MIXTURE: Off heat, fold in egg mixture until slightly thickened and well combined with bread. Gently press on top of strata to help it soak up egg mixture.

5. FINISH IN OVEN: Bake until edges and center are puffed and edges have pulled away slightly from sides of pan, about 12 minutes, and serve.

EQUIPMENT: Rubber Spatulas

Heatproof rubber spatulas can be used in a variety of applications, from removing stuck-on bits in a hot skillet to scraping the last bits of cookie dough from a mixing bowl. We tested 10 brands to find the best models. Two came out on top: the Rubbermaid 13.5-inch High Heat Scraper ($17.50), which has a fairly conventional design. The blade is wide and flexible, though firm enough to stir the stiffest batter—a big plus. Its long, plastic handle is stiff and sits comfortably in the hand. The Le Creuset Heatproof 13-inch Spatula ($12.95) followed closely despite demerits for its thin wooden hand. Its blade, thicker than the Rubbermaid's, worked admirably and resisted wear well.

THE BEST RUBBER SPATULA

The Rubbermaid 13.5-inch High Heat Scraper (top) and the Le Creuset Heatproof 13-inch Spatula (bottom) are not only your best bets for folding and mixing, but because they're heatproof, they can also be used for stirring eggs in a skillet.

➤ VARIATIONS
Skillet Strata with Bacon, Scallions, and Pepper Jack Cheese

Substitute 4 slices bacon, chopped fine, for butter. Cook bacon in skillet over medium-high heat until fat begins to render, about 2 minutes, before adding onion in step 1. Omit thyme. Substitute 1 cup shredded pepper Jack cheese for cheddar and sprinkle with 2 scallions, sliced thin, before serving.

Skillet Strata with Sausage and Gruyère

Reduce butter to 1 tablespoon and add 8 ounces raw, crumbled breakfast sausage to skillet with onion in step 1. Substitute 1 cup shredded Gruyère or Swiss cheese for cheddar.

Skillet Strata with Spinach and Smoked Gouda

Removing the excess moisture from the spinach is crucial here. After thawing the spinach in the microwave, wrap it in paper towels and squeeze out as much liquid as possible.

After toasting bread in step 3, stir in 2 minced garlic cloves and cook until fragrant, about 30 seconds. Stir 1 (10-ounce) package frozen chopped spinach, thawed and squeezed dry, into skillet with eggs in step 4. Substitute 1 cup shredded smoked Gouda cheese for cheddar.

CORNED BEEF HASH

GREAT CORNED BEEF HASH REQUIRES TIME (and patience). How, we wondered, could we peel raw potatoes, cube them, then fry them until golden in rendered bacon fat, layer in the corned beef and poach the eggs in 30 minutes or less? We knew right away that we needed to conquer the longest-cooking element in the dish—the potatoes—to get this dish on the table quickly.

It was clear that partially cooking the potatoes first—before adding them to the pan—would be necessary. We tested some par-cooking techniques: Parboiling the potatoes quickened the overall cooking pace, but still took more time than we would have liked. And microwaving the

potatoes worked well, yet we still couldn't seem to keep the time under the 30-minute mark. Stumped, we headed to the supermarket to investigate the varieties of prepared potato products available. We discovered that making a quicker hash required the convenience of frozen precooked, cubed hash browns. It worked best if we parcooked the potatoes in the microwave before adding them to the pan, where they cooked up golden brown and crusty.

Eggs for hash are usually poached and placed on top of the hash just before serving, but we aimed to make this quick dish a one-pot affair. We found that we could "poach" the eggs in the same pan as the hash by nestling the eggs into indentations in the hash, covering the pan, and cooking them over low heat. The results were perfect: eggs with runny yolks, conveniently set in the hash and ready to be served.

Corned Beef Hash
SERVES 4

In the vast world of frozen potatoes the term "hash browns" can be used to describe several different varieties. We found the best results with cubed hash browns, which are sometimes labeled "Southern" style. They are often sold in 2-pound bags.

4	slices bacon, chopped
1	onion, minced
4	cups (20 ounces) frozen diced potatoes (see note)
1	tablespoon vegetable oil
	Salt and ground black pepper
2	garlic cloves, minced
1/2	teaspoon minced fresh thyme
1/3	cup heavy cream
1/4	teaspoon Tabasco
12	ounces thinly sliced corned beef, cut into 1/2-inch pieces
4	large eggs

1. **COOK BACON AND ONION:** Fry bacon in 12-inch nonstick skillet over medium-high heat until fat begins to render, about 2 minutes. Add onion and cook until softened and lightly

browned, about 8 minutes.

2. MICROWAVE POTATOES: Meanwhile, toss potatoes with oil, ½ teaspoon salt, and ¼ teaspoon pepper in medium microwave-safe bowl. Cover tightly with plastic wrap and microwave on high until potatoes are hot, about 5 minutes.

3. COOK HASH: Stir garlic and thyme into bacon-onion mixture and cook until fragrant, about 30 seconds. Stir in hot potatoes, cream, and Tabasco. Using back of spatula, gently pack potatoes into pan, and cook undisturbed for 2 minutes. Flip hash, one portion at a time, and lightly repack into pan. Repeat flipping process every few minutes until potatoes are nicely browned, 6 to 8 minutes.

4. ADD CORNED BEEF AND COOK: Stir in corned beef and lightly repack hash into pan. Make four shallow indentations (about 2 inches wide) in surface of hash.

5. ADD EGGS AND COOK: Crack 1 egg into each indentation and sprinkle eggs with salt and pepper. Reduce heat to medium-low, cover with tight-fitting lid, and continue to cook until eggs are just set, about 5 minutes. Serve immediately.

GOT EXTRA TIME?

If you want to use fresh potatoes (which will add an extra few minutes to the recipe for corned beef hash), substitute 1½ pounds russet potatoes (3 to 4 medium), scrubbed and cut into ½-inch pieces, for the frozen potatoes. Increase the microwave cooking time to 8 minutes, or until the potatoes are tender around the edges, shaking the bowl halfway through. Proceed as directed.

SPANISH TORTILLA

TRADITIONALLY, A SPANISH TORTILLA IS made by slow-cooking potatoes and onion in olive oil. Once the potatoes are cooked, beaten eggs are added. The whole mixture coalesces into a savory, velvety cake somewhat like an omelet or frittata, but with deep potato flavor. While wedges of tortilla are often served in Spain as tapas along with drinks, we thought they could also make it a quick dinner too—if we could overcome the lengthy potato-cooking part of the process.

Since olive oil is crucial to the recipe, lending the potatoes both flavor and texture, we couldn't microwave the potatoes and toss them into the skillet with the eggs. We found that cutting the potatoes into small cubes (¼-inch dice), then covering the skillet to allow the onion and potatoes to sweat and cook together until softened, produced moist, well-flavored potatoes. All that was left was to pour in the beaten eggs, allow the tortilla to set on the stove, then finish it in the oven for just 3 to 5 minutes. This tortilla is good served as is, or you can dress it up with our easy-to-make Roasted Red Pepper Aïoli (page 13).

Spanish Egg and Potato Tortilla
SERVES 4 TO 6

In a pinch, Yukon gold or red potatoes can be substituted for the russets. Serve the tortilla as is or, if you have extra time, with Roasted Red Pepper Aïoli on page 13.

¼	cup olive oil
1	pound russet potatoes (2 potatoes), peeled and cut into ¼-inch cubes
1	onion, minced
	Salt and ground black pepper
10	large eggs

1. HEAT OVEN AND COOK POTATOES AND ONION: Adjust oven rack to middle position and heat oven to 450 degrees. Heat oil in 10-inch ovensafe nonstick skillet over medium-high heat until shimmering. Add potatoes, onion, and ½ teaspoon salt. Cover and cook, stirring occasionally, until potatoes and onion are soft, 8 to 10 minutes.

2. ADD EGG MIXTURE AND COOK: Whisk eggs, ¼ teaspoon salt, and ¼ teaspoon pepper together. Add eggs to skillet and cook, using rubber spatula to stir gently in circular motion, until mixture is slightly thickened, about 1 minute.

3. FINISH IN OVEN: Bake until top is puffed and edges have pulled away slightly from sides of pan, 3 to 5 minutes. Use rubber spatula to loosen tortilla from skillet, then slide onto cutting board, slice into wedges, and serve.

GOT EXTRA TIME?

In Spanish tapas bars, it's not uncommon to find a creamy, potatoey wedge of tortilla served along with a small dollop of aïoli—the Provençal version of mayonnaise made with olive oil and fresh garlic. In thinking how to give our aïoli a bit of a Spanish flair, we added roasted red peppers to the food processor. The roasty, charred sweet flavor of the peppers—similar to the often hard-to-find Spanish piquillo pepper, added a good amount of complexity and depth.

Roasted Red Pepper Aïoli

MAKES ABOUT 1¼ CUPS

To finely mince the garlic, either press it through a garlic press or grate it on a rasp-style grater (Microplane). If you do not have regular olive oil, use a blend of equal parts extra-virgin olive oil and vegetable oil—using all extra-virgin olive oil will make the aïoli taste too bitter. Serve the aïoli with the tortilla or try it with roasted or grilled meats.

I	teaspoon finely minced garlic (see note)
2	large egg yolks
I	tablespoon fresh lemon juice
⅛	teaspoon sugar
	Salt and ground black pepper
	Pinch cayenne
¾	cup olive oil (see note)
2	medium jarred roasted red peppers, rinsed, patted dry, and chopped (½ cup)

Process garlic, yolks, lemon juice, sugar, ¼ teaspoon salt, pinch of black pepper, and cayenne in food processor until combined, about 10 seconds. With machine running, gradually add oil in slow, steady stream, about 30 seconds. Scrape down sides of bowl with rubber spatula. Add peppers and continue to process until smooth, about 1 minute. Season with salt and pepper to taste and serve with Spanish Egg and Potato Tortilla. (The aïoli will keep refrigerated in airtight container for up to 3 days.)

INGREDIENT:
Jarred Roasted Red Peppers

Roasting your own peppers isn't difficult, but when you're in a rush, why bother—especially when you can buy peppers already roasted? But are all brands of roasted red bell peppers created equal? To find out, we collected six brands from local supermarkets. The top two brands, Divina and Greek Gourmet, were preferred for their "soft and tender texture" (Divina) and "refreshing," "piquant," "smoky" flavor (Greek Gourmet). The other brands were marked down for their lack of "roasty flavor" and for the unpleasantly overpowering flavor of their brines. These peppers tasted as if they'd been "buried under brine and acid" or were thought to have a "sweet and acidic aftertaste." The conclusion? Tasters preferred peppers with a full, smoky, roasted flavor, a brine that was spicy but not too sweet, and a tender texture.

THE BEST JARRED ROASTED RED PEPPERS

Divina peppers (left) were the top choice of tasters. Greek Gourmet peppers (right) came in a close second.

MIGAS

POPULAR IN MEXICO, MIGAS IS USUALLY a combination of crushed tortillas and scrambled eggs cooked with onions, garlic, and chiles. Easy to prepare and delicious, it is a natural for the quick-cooking repertoire.

Most recipes we found in our search called for corn tortillas that are fried. But we wanted this to be a quick recipe and didn't want to fuss with frying tortillas, so we shifted our focus to store-bought tortilla chips. We tried several brands of chips and all worked just fine, yet tasters preferred baked tortilla chips because they didn't have the greasy flavor we noted with fried chips.

We then went on to develop the other flavors in the eggs. Onions and garlic were a given for their pungency. We also tried a variety of chiles and peppers. While tasters liked the mild flavors of Anaheim and poblano chiles, we had a hard time locating them at our local grocery store and felt it was better to go with widely available red bell pepper. To complement the sweet crunch of the red pepper, we added a jalapeño chile. With the addition of pepper Jack cheese for richness, we had a distinctive, satisfying dish that was easy to assemble and quick to get on the table. Migas is delicious on its own but can be enhanced with a spoonful of salsa served alongside—we provide a quick recipe that gets its heat from spicy chipotles.

Migas

SERVES 4

Serve with our One-Minute Salsa or your favorite store-bought brand.

8	large eggs
2	ounces baked tortilla chips, broken into ½-inch pieces (about 1 cup)
	Salt and ground black pepper
2	tablespoons unsalted butter
1	small red onion, minced
1	red bell pepper, cored and chopped fine
3	garlic cloves, minced
1	jalapeño chile, cored and minced
¾	cup shredded pepper Jack cheese
2	tablespoons minced fresh cilantro

1. **COMBINE EGG MIXTURE**: Mix eggs, tortilla chips, ¼ teaspoon salt, and pinch of black pepper together and set aside.

2. **COOK VEGETABLES**: Melt butter in 12-inch nonstick skillet over medium-high heat. Add onion and bell pepper and cook until softened, about 4 minutes. Stir in garlic and jalapeño and cook until fragrant, about 30 seconds.

3. **ADD EGG MIXTURE AND COOK**: Reduce heat to medium. Add egg mixture and cook, using rubber spatula to push mixture back and forth following illustrations on page 3, until curds begin to form. Continue to cook, lifting and folding curds from side to side, until they clump in single mound but are still very moist, about 3 minutes.

4. **FINISH AND SEASON**: Off heat, gently fold in cheese and cilantro and season with salt and pepper to taste. Serve.

HUEVOS RANCHEROS

HUEVOS RANCHEROS, OR "RANCHER-STYLE eggs," is a dish born of ease and convenience: a quick satisfying meal of crisp corn tortillas topped with a fried egg and melted cheese, and garnished with salsa. But most often, the basic subtleties of the rustic dish are lost under heaping piles of toppings (ground beef, shredded lettuce, sliced olives—think nachos gone wild). We headed into the test kitchen to return huevos rancheros to its simple roots.

Most authentic recipes call for fresh, handmade corn tortillas crisped up in oil. We were stuck with all-but-stale supermarket versions and didn't have time to heat up oil and fry tortillas in batches. We discovered, however, that when brushed lightly with oil, sprinkled with a little salt, and toasted until golden brown at 450 degrees, supermarket tortillas were crisp and dry—a perfect foil for beans and cheese. Toasting the tortillas in the oven also gave us a chance to multi-task and turn

---

⏱ GOT EXTRA TIME?

Canned diced tomatoes are the key to this quick salsa.

One-Minute Salsa

MAKES ABOUT 1 CUP

Half a minced jalapeño chile can be substituted for the chipotle.

¼	small red onion, chopped coarse
1	small garlic clove, minced
2	tablespoons fresh cilantro
2	teaspoon minced chipotle in adobo
2	teaspoons fresh lime juice
1	(14.5-ounce) can diced tomatoes, drained
	Salt and ground black pepper

Pulse all ingredients except tomatoes in food processor until minced, about 5 pulses, scraping sides of bowl as needed. Add tomatoes and continue to pulse until roughly chopped, about 2 pulses. Season with salt and pepper to taste.

our attention to frying the eggs while the tortillas crisped. Then, when the tortillas were out of the oven and cool enough to handle, we spread each one with a layer of beans and a sprinkling of cheese. We then returned the bean-and-cheese topped tortillas to the oven. There was no need to turn the oven on; the residual heat from toasting the tortillas was enough to gently warm the beans through and melt the cheese while we finished the eggs.

As for toppings, tasters were happy with a sprinkle of thinly sliced scallions and homemade salsa, drained of excess moisture to keep it from making our huevos rancheros soggy. In the end, some liked the addition of sour cream and/or guacamole; however, no one felt strongly that they were absolutely necessary additions.

Huevos Rancheros

SERVES 4 TO 6

To complete this recipe in 30 minutes, heat your oven before assembling your ingredients. Although you turn the oven off at the end of step 1, the residual heat in the oven will still be strong enough to melt the cheese in step 3.

8	(6-inch) corn tortillas
2	tablespoons vegetable oil
	Salt and ground black pepper
2	tablespoons unsalted butter
8	large eggs
1	(15-ounce) can refried beans
1½	cups shredded cheddar cheese
1	cup store-bought salsa, drained, or One-Minute Salsa (page 14), drained
2	scallions, sliced thin

1. **HEAT OVEN AND TOAST TORTILLAS**: Adjust oven rack to middle position and heat oven to 450 degrees. Lightly brush both sides of each tortilla with oil and sprinkle with salt. Spread tortillas out over baking sheet (some overlapping or hanging over edge is fine). Bake until tortillas are lightly golden on both sides, about 10 minutes, turning them over halfway through. Remove tortillas from oven and turn oven off.

2. **COOK EGGS**: While tortillas are crisping, preheat 10-inch nonstick skillet over lowest possible heat for 5 minutes. Add 1 tablespoon of butter to hot skillet and melt, swirling to coat pan. Crack 4 eggs into 2 small bowls. Following illustrations below, add eggs to pan. Season eggs with salt and pepper, cover, and cook until desired doneness—about 2 minutes for runny yolks, 3 minutes for soft but set yolks, and 4 minutes for firmly set yolks. (Slide eggs onto plate and cover with foil to keep warm.) Repeat with remaining 4 eggs. (While eggs cook, follow step 3.)

3. **TOP TORTILLAS AND RETURN TO OVEN**: Spread refried beans evenly over top of each crisped tortilla and sprinkle with cheddar. Return the tortillas to the oven for beans to heat through and cheddar to melt while you prepare second batch of eggs.

4. **ADD EGGS AND GARNISH**: Remove hot tortillas from oven, transfer to individual plates, and top each with fried eggs. Garnish with salsa and scallions before serving.

TEST KITCHEN TIP:
Perfect Fried Eggs

Cracking eggs one at a time into a hot skillet is a surefire way to produce at least one overcooked fried egg. Instead, follow our method to ensure all your eggs cook at the same rate—and come out perfectly every time.

Crack the eggs into two small bowls. Then add the eggs, sliding them into the hot skillet simultaneously from opposite sides of the pan.

SKILLET EGG SUPPER

THIS RECIPE IS BASED ON A FULL-flavored one-dish meal called *chakchouka*, found in the Middle East and parts of North Africa in countries such as Tunisia and Morocco. Typically, a sauce is built by simmering onions, garlic, peppers, tomatoes, and fresh chiles until soft and their flavors have blended together. Eggs are then added and lightly poached in the mixture. The egg is a soft, creamy counterpoint that tempers the spiciness of the sauce. Usually served as a light meal or appetizer alongside a stack of warm pita bread, we wanted our own version of this exotic dish to have a bit more heft.

A simple dish by design, we settled on the basic elements first: onion, garlic, bell peppers, and canned diced tomatoes. There was no getting around prepping the first three ingredients; however, tasters did prefer the flavor and convenience of canned diced tomatoes—the tomato juice worked as a good base for our sauce as well.

With the basics under our belt, we looked to the fresh chile component. We tested our recipe with a number of fresh chiles found in our local supermarket, but none of them seemed right. Without access to the bounty of complexly flavored fresh chiles available in the Middle East and North Africa, we headed to our pantry to see what spices we could use. Chili powder was in the running for a while, until tasters tried a mix of cumin and cayenne. Together, these fairly pedestrian spices found in most peoples' cupboards added the exotic complexity, depth, and judicious amount of spiciness we were after. As far as heft was concerned, we felt that the addition of chorizo sausage pushed our recipe into the supper category; tasters also liked its sweet-smoky flavor.

Skillet Egg, Sausage, and Pepper Supper

SERVES 4 TO 6

For a bit more color, use a mix of different colored bell peppers. Serve with warm pita bread or slices of toast.

2	tablespoons olive oil
8	ounces chorizo sausage, split in half and cut into 1/4-inch slices
1	onion, chopped
2	large bell peppers, cored and sliced into 1/4-inch strips
4	garlic cloves, minced or pressed through a garlic press
1	(14.5-ounce) can diced tomatoes
1	teaspoon ground cumin
1/4	teaspoon cayenne pepper
4–6	large eggs
	Salt and ground black pepper
2	tablespoons minced fresh cilantro

1. **BROWN SAUSAGE:** Heat 1 tablespoon of oil in 12-inch nonstick skillet over medium-high heat until shimmering. Add chorizo and cook until fat begins to render, about 2 minutes. Transfer chorizo to small bowl and set aside.

2. **COOK ONION AND PEPPERS:** Add remaining 1 tablespoon of oil to empty skillet and heat until shimmering. Add onion and cook until it starts to soften, about 3 minutes. Add peppers and cover skillet with lid. Cook until peppers are soft and lightly browned, about 10 minutes.

3. **ADD GARLIC, TOMATOES, AND SPICES:** Stir in garlic and cook until fragrant, about 1 minute. Reduce heat to medium and add tomatoes, cumin, and cayenne. Cook mixture until sauce is slightly thickened and flavors have melded, about 5 minutes. Stir in reserved chorizo.

4. **ADD EGGS, COOK, AND GARNISH:** Make four shallow indentations (about 2 inches wide) in surface of sauce. Crack an egg into each indentation and sprinkle egg with salt and pepper. Reduce heat to medium-low, cover with tight-fitting lid, and continue to cook until eggs are just set, about 5 minutes. Sprinkle with cilantro and serve.

2

SALAD FOR SUPPER

SALAD FOR SUPPER

QUICK BLENDER VINAIGRETTES   20
Basic Vinaigrette
Fresh Herb Vinaigrette
Dried Cranberry Vinaigrette
Miso-Ginger Vinaigrette
Cilantro-Lime Vinaigrette
Sun-Dried Tomato and Basil Vinaigrette
Orange-Sherry Vinaigrette
Bistro-Style Mustard Vinaigrette

QUICK CREAMY BLENDER DRESSINGS   23
Blue Cheese Dressing
Creamy Greek Dressing
Creamy Chipotle-Lime Dressing
Creamy Caesar Dressing

FAST AND FRESH CHICKEN SALADS   26
Chicken Caesar Salad
Romaine Salad with Chicken, Cheddar, Apple, and Spiced Pecans
Chinese Chicken Salad with Hoisin Vinaigrette

BUFFALO CHICKEN SALAD WITH BLUE CHEESE DRESSING   29
Buffalo Chicken Salad with Blue Cheese Dressing

CHEF'S SALADS   30
Chef's Salad
Italian-Style Chef's Salad with Artichokes and Asiago
California-Style Chef's Salad with Chicken, Spinach, and Gouda

TACO SALAD   32
Taco Salad

STEAK SALADS   33
30-Minute Steak and Potato Salad
Thai-Style Beef Salad

SALADS ARE A QUICK AND EASY WAY TO round out a meal, but when bulked up with vegetables and protein, they are a meal in themselves. The problem is that really good main course salads are far from quick. From cleaning greens and chopping vegetables to cooking protein and preparing a dressing, a main-course salad can require more work than many traditional main courses. Our challenge in this chapter was to develop fresh-flavored, hearty dinner salads that can be made in under 30 minutes.

We began by turning to the supermarket for salad shortcuts. If you don't mind spending a little extra money, you can skip washing your own greens and buy packaged pre-washed greens. However, it is important to carefully examine the package for bruised or wilted greens—and to check the sell-by date, too. Cleaned and trimmed green beans and other pre-cut vegetables are good options, as well. Pantry staples like tuna, jarred roasted red peppers, and canned beans are all reliable shortcuts.

As for dressings, the ever-expanding aisle of salad dressings offers plenty of options, but for the most part, their flavor just can't compare with that of homemade. So we decided to see if there were any shortcuts that would allow us to dispense with the time it took to mince garlic and shallots or chop fresh herbs. Our answer turned out to be the blender, which not only whisked our dressing together, but did all the chopping for us as well.

With fast dressings resolved, we turned our attention to cooking the protein for these quick salads. Cooking protein can push a main-course salad past the 30-minute prep mark. We found solutions in a combination of techniques and careful choices. For chicken, we used a half sautéing, half poaching method that yields moist, tender meat every time. For beef, we chose cuts that are naturally quick-cooking—steaks such as flank and top loin—and used a very hot skillet. Scallops add richness to salads and are a snap to cook, and precooked shrimp are a terrific option when you're short on time.

In addition to paring back our salad prep to fit the 30-minute model, we also wanted to provide lots of interesting choices. You'll find a combination of classic main-course salads such as Chicken Caesar Salad and Taco Salad along with satisfying new dishes like 30-Minute Steak and Potato Salad; Warm Spinach Salad with Scallops, Almonds, and Orange; and Bistro Bacon and Egg Salad.

And finally, because salads contain multiple components, timing is key. Read through the recipe before you start and follow our tips for making the minutes count—while one component is cooking, say chicken or beef, use the downtime to complete another task such as preparing the dressing, cutting vegetables, or toasting croutons. With these recipes, you'll find that satisfying, fresh-flavored salads really can be quick and easy.

QUICK BLENDER VINAIGRETTES

HOMEMADE VINAIGRETTES ARE FAR superior to bottled dressings, and they take little time to make. They can be stored in your refrigerator for about a week, ready to dress up a salad at a moment's notice. While the conventional method of bowl and whisk is fairly simple, we wanted to streamline the process even further, eliminating the need for any mincing of garlic, shallot, or herbs. To that end, we opted for a blender—first adding the garlic, shallot, or whatever needs to be minced finely, along with the vinegar and whirring it all for about 15 seconds. Then, we added the oil and continued to blend to emulsify the mixture. It's almost as easy as opening a bottle of store-bought vinaigrette, but tastes worlds better.

> **TEST KITCHEN TIP:**
> **Adding Vinegar**
> For simple salad dressings, we've found that the ideal ratio of oil to vinegar is 4 to 1. This ratio, however, can change depending on what type of vinegar you're using (some vinegars are sharper than others) and what other flavorings are in the dressing (such as sweet sun-dried tomatoes or spicy jalapeños). So when whipping up your own dressing, simply start with 4 parts oil to 1 part vinegar, then add extra vinegar as needed to taste.

Basic Vinaigrette

MAKES ABOUT 1 CUP

Champagne vinegar or herb-flavored vinegars also work nicely here. If you'd like to use balsamic vinegar, omit the Dijon.

3	tablespoons red or white wine vinegar
1	shallot, peeled
1	small garlic clove, peeled
2	teaspoons Dijon mustard
2	teaspoons fresh thyme
	Salt and ground black pepper
¾	cup extra-virgin olive oil

Process all ingredients except oil in blender until shallot and garlic are finely chopped, about 15 seconds. With blender running, add oil and continue to process until dressing is smooth and emulsified, about 15 seconds.

Fresh Herb Vinaigrette

MAKES ABOUT 1 CUP

The combination of fresh herbs is the secret to the flavor of this vinaigrette.

3	tablespoons red or white wine vinegar
1	shallot, peeled
1	small garlic clove, peeled
2	teaspoons Dijon mustard
1	teaspoon fresh thyme
	Salt and ground black pepper
10	fresh basil leaves
1	tablespoon fresh oregano, tarragon, chives, or parsley
¾	cup extra-virgin olive oil

Process vinegar, shallot, garlic, mustard, thyme, ½ teaspoon salt, and ¼ teaspoon pepper in blender until shallot and garlic are finely chopped, about 15 seconds. With blender running, add basil and oregano, then oil, and continue to process until dressing is smooth and emulsified, about 15 seconds.

Dried Cranberry Vinaigrette

MAKES ABOUT 1¼ CUPS

Raspberry vinegar gives this dressing a distinct fruity flavor; however, red wine vinegar can be substituted. If you don't have cranberry juice on hand, water can be used instead. If the dressing seems too thick, thin it out with additional cranberry juice or water.

¼	cup cranberry juice
¼	cup dried cranberries
¼	cup raspberry vinegar (see note)
1	shallot, peeled
1	small garlic clove, peeled
2	teaspoons fresh thyme
2	teaspoons Dijon mustard
	Salt and ground black pepper
¾	cup extra-virgin olive oil

1. **REHYDRATE CRANBERRIES:** Combine cranberry juice and dried cranberries in microwave-safe bowl, cover with plastic wrap, and microwave on high power until hot, about 1 minute.

2. **BLEND VINAIGRETTE:** Process hot cranberry mixture, vinegar, shallot, garlic, thyme, mustard, ½ teaspoon salt, and ½ teaspoon pepper in blender until shallot and garlic are finely chopped, about 15 seconds. With blender running, add oil and continue to process until smooth and emulsified, about 15 seconds.

KITCHEN SHORTCUT
PICKING THYME LEAVES

The fastest way to separate the thyme leaves from their woody stem is to slide the sprig between your forefinger and thumb.

Miso-Ginger Vinaigrette

MAKES ABOUT 1 CUP

Several types of fresh miso—fermented soybean paste—can be found in Asian markets and in the refrigerated section of some well-stocked supermarkets. We prefer the flavor of red miso paste in this dressing. Do not use powdered miso or the dressing will be overly salty and have a watery texture. In addition to greens, this vinaigrette works well tossed with blanched and cooled green beans.

5	tablespoons rice vinegar
2	tablespoons red miso paste
1	tablespoon soy sauce
1	(2-inch) piece fresh ginger, peeled
1	small garlic clove, peeled
1/4	teaspoon cayenne
3/4	cup peanut or vegetable oil
1	teaspoon toasted sesame oil

Process vinegar, miso, soy sauce, ginger, garlic, and cayenne in blender until ginger and garlic are finely chopped, about 15 seconds. With blender running, add oils and continue to process until smooth and emulsified, about 15 seconds.

Cilantro-Lime Vinaigrette

MAKES ABOUT 1 CUP

Freshly squeezed lime juice is key for flavor here.

5	tablespoons fresh lime juice
1	shallot, peeled
1	jalapeño chile, stemmed and seeded
1	small garlic clove, peeled
1	teaspoon sugar
1/2	teaspoon ground cumin
	Salt
1/2	cup fresh cilantro
3/4	cup extra-virgin olive oil

Process lime juice, shallot, jalapeño, garlic, sugar, cumin, and 1/2 teaspoon salt in blender until shallot and garlic are finely chopped, about 15 seconds. With blender running, add cilantro, then oil, and continue to process until smooth and emulsified, about 15 seconds.

Sun-Dried Tomato and Basil Vinaigrette

MAKES ABOUT 1 1/4 CUPS

Oil-packed sun-dried tomatoes have a much softer texture than plain dried tomatoes and work best in this dressing.

1/4	cup red wine vinegar
1/4	cup oil-packed sun-dried tomatoes, rinsed
1	shallot, peeled
1	small garlic clove, peeled
	Salt and ground black pepper
10	fresh basil leaves
3/4	cup extra-virgin olive oil

Process vinegar, sun-dried tomatoes, shallot, garlic, 1/2 teaspoon salt, and 1/2 teaspoon pepper in blender until shallot and garlic are finely chopped, about 15 seconds. With blender running, add basil, then oil, and continue to process until smooth and emulsified, about 15 seconds.

KITCHEN SHORTCUT
JUICING LEMONS

For juicing small quantities of citrus fruits, we find there's no need for a special juicing tool. Just use a fork. See another tip for juicing lemons on page 42.

1. Slice the fruit in half and poke the flesh a few times with a fork.

2. Stick the fork in the fruit and twist, just as you would with a reamer.

Orange-Sherry Vinaigrette

MAKES ABOUT I CUP

Sherry vinegar gives this vinaigrette a distinctive flavor that works well with the orange zest.

- ¼ cup sherry vinegar
- I shallot, peeled
- I small garlic clove, peeled
- 2 teaspoons Dijon mustard
- I teaspoon grated orange zest
   Salt and ground black pepper
- ¾ cup extra-virgin olive oil

MAKING THE MINUTES COUNT:

Use a Microplane grater and grate the zest from about half an orange right over the blender jar.

Process vinegar, shallot, garlic, mustard, orange zest, ½ teaspoon salt, and ½ teaspoon pepper in blender until shallot and garlic are finely chopped, about 15 seconds. With blender running, add oil and continue to process on high speed until smooth and emulsified, about 15 seconds.

Bistro-Style Mustard Vinaigrette

MAKES ABOUT I CUP

This is a classic French vinaigrette and works especially well with sturdier greens like romaine and escarole.

- 3 tablespoons red or white wine vinegar
- 3 tablespoons whole-grain mustard
- I shallot, peeled
- I small garlic clove, peeled
- 2 teaspoons fresh thyme
   Salt and ground black pepper
- ¾ cup extra-virgin olive oil

Process vinegar, mustard, shallot, garlic, thyme, ½ teaspoon salt, and ½ teaspoon pepper in blender until shallot and garlic are finely chopped, about 15 seconds. With blender running, add oil and continue to process until smooth and emulsified, about 15 seconds.

INGREDIENTS: White Wine Vinegar

All vinegar is the product of double fermentation. In the first round, yeast transforms a sugary or starchy substance (apples, grains, grapes) into alcohol (cider, malt, wine). In the second, the bacteria Acetobacter aceti transforms the alcohol into acetic acid, and vinegar (cider vinegar, malt vinegar, wine vinegar) is born. We tasted vinegars both raw and cooked in an effort to determine if we could find a vinegar that works well in every application. We first zeroed in on acid levels, which ranged from 5 percent to 7.5 percent, yet it was clear that acidity had little bearing on taster preference. Upon analyzing tasters' comments about raw vinegar, we came across repeated references to an off aroma reminiscent of "nail-polish remover." After further research we learned that when manufacturers adjust fermentation times, they essentially create a compound, ethyl acetate, which gives nail-polish remover its characteristic smell. The purpose of this process is to ramp up the vinegar's fruity notes, but obviously in increased amounts this process backfires. Therefore we determined it to be our goal to find a vinegar with only moderate amounts of ethyl acetate, yet enough fruit flavor to stand up to a rich, buttery sauce. Ultimately we were able to realize our preferences for a fruity floral vinegar with moderate ethyl acetate levels, selecting two that we considered the best all-purpose vinegars: Acetaia Bellei and Four Monks.

The Best All-Purpose White Wine Vinegars
Acetaia Bellei and Four Monks are the test kitchen favorites for their fruity and sweet flavors and their ability to perform well in both raw and cooked applications.

QUICK CREAMY BLENDER DRESSINGS

LIKE VINAIGRETTES, CREAMY DRESSINGS are a natural in the blender, coming together in less than a minute. We traditionally make our creamy dressings with buttermilk, mayonnaise, and sour cream, but the whirring action of the blender overworked our creamy dressing, turning it soupy. To combat this problem, we found that omitting the buttermilk and tweaking the amounts of mayonnaise and sour cream did the trick—we had the dressing we were looking for with a full, nicely rounded flavor and just enough tang. We also found that when preparing creamy dressings with cheese, it's important to add the cheese to the blender last and process with just a few short pulses—otherwise it will break down too much and give the dressing a grainy consistency. Creamy dressings can be made ahead and kept refrigerated for up to 4 days.

Process vinegar, garlic, sugar, ½ teaspoon salt, and ½ teaspoon pepper in blender until garlic is finely chopped, about 15 seconds. Add mayonnaise and sour cream, and continue to process until smooth, about 10 seconds. Add cheese and pulse until just incorporated, about 5 pulses. Thin dressing with water as needed to adjust consistency.

Blue Cheese Dressing

MAKES ABOUT 1½ CUPS

When buying blue cheese for this recipe, choose one with a mellow flavor, such as Stella or Danish blue. Pair this heavy dressing with sturdy lettuce that can support its weight, such as romaine, as in Buffalo Chicken Salad on page 29.

2	tablespoons white wine vinegar
I	small garlic clove, peeled
½	teaspoon sugar
	Salt and ground black pepper
¾	cup mayonnaise
¼	cup sour cream
½	cups crumbled blue cheese (see note)
	Water

Creamy Greek Dressing

MAKES ABOUT 1¾ CUPS

The flavors in this dressing work especially well with a leafy green salad with sliced cucumber and tomato.

3	tablespoons red wine vinegar
I	shallot, peeled
I	small garlic clove, peeled
I	tablespoon fresh oregano
2	teaspoons Dijon mustard
	Salt and ground black pepper
¾	cup mayonnaise
¼	cup sour cream
¾	cup crumbled feta cheese

EQUIPMENT: Blenders

At first glance, you might think all blenders are pretty much the same. But after testing nine inexpensive models (all priced under $50), we can tell you they are not. Pureed soup with stringy bits of broccoli, strawberry smoothies with hidden "icebergs," and pesto that refused to come together were just some of the problems we encountered in testing. Here's what we found:

Blade design, size, and sharpness are similar in all nine models; it's in the way the food reaches the blade that they differ. The best blenders leave no room for ingredients to hide and have a tapered, funnel-shaped jar that guides the ingredients into the blade.

It's worth spending a few extra dollars for a better blender that includes a heavy glass jar. Most cheap blenders we tested have plastic jars, which are prone to scratching. Those tiny scratches are more likely to retain color and odor over years of use.

Buttons, which clutter most base units, and the crevices surrounding them can be difficult, if not impossible, to clean. Dials wipe clean easily. Another drawback of the button design is that it's too easy to go straight for high speed; do so and you get an eruption of food. Patient cooks will punch their way up from low speed to high, but most won't and will pay a messy price. With the dial, you have no choice but to rev up through the speeds, a much easier and neater proposition.

Of all the blenders we tested, the Braun PowerMax ($49) best fit our criteria. The triangular jar funnels ingredients to the blade and keeps them moving, while dialing through the five speeds keeps things tidy.

The Best Blender

The Braun PowerMax MX2050 ($49) reduced ice cubes to a powder in less than 10 seconds and produced an ultra-smooth (nearly emulsified) pesto in 30 seconds. A smoothie passed the test of passing through a strainer cleanly, and pureed soup was almost—but not quite—perfect. The only blender we tested with all dishwasher-safe parts.

Process vinegar, shallot, garlic, oregano, mustard, ½ teaspoon salt, and ½ teaspoon pepper in blender until shallot and garlic are finely chopped, about 15 seconds. Add mayonnaise and sour cream, and continue to process until smooth, about 10 seconds. Add feta and pulse until just incorporated, about 5 pulses.

❧ Creamy Chipotle-Lime Dressing

MAKES ABOUT 1½ CUPS

To make this dressing spicy, use 2 teaspoons minced chipotle chiles in adobo sauce.

5	tablespoons fresh lime juice
1	shallot, peeled
1	small garlic clove, peeled
1–2	teaspoons minced chipotle chiles in adobo sauce
1	teaspoon sugar
½	teaspoon ground cumin
	Salt and ground black pepper
¾	cup mayonnaise
¼	cup sour cream
½	cup fresh cilantro

Process lime juice, shallot, garlic, chipotle, sugar, cumin, ½ teaspoon salt, and ½ teaspoon pepper in blender until shallot and garlic are finely chopped, about 15 seconds. Add mayonnaise, sour cream, and cilantro, and continue to process until smooth, about 15 seconds.

❧ Creamy Caesar Dressing

MAKES ABOUT 1½ CUPS

Take care not to overblend the dressing after the cheese has been added or the texture will be grainy.

3	tablespoons extra-virgin olive oil
2	tablespoons fresh lemon juice
3	anchovy fillets, rinsed
1	shallot, peeled
2	garlic cloves, peeled
4	teaspoons Dijon mustard
1	teaspoon Worcestershire sauce
	Salt and ground black pepper
¾	cup mayonnaise
½	cup grated Parmesan cheese

Process oil, lemon juice, anchovies, shallot, garlic, mustard, Worcestershire, ½ teaspoon salt, and ½ teaspoon pepper in blender until shallot and garlic are finely chopped, about 15 seconds. Add mayonnaise and continue to process until smooth, about 15 seconds. Add Parmesan and pulse until just incorporated, about 5 pulses.

INGREDIENTS:
Supermarket Extra-Virgin Olive Oil

When olives are pressed for oil, they go through the process several times. The first batch of oil that comes from the olives is labeled extra-virgin and is the most intensely flavored. Since vinaigrettes and dressings only contain a few ingredients, it is important to use a good-quality olive oil. And while it is easy to pay upwards of $30 for a bottle of extra-virgin olive oil at specialty food stores, we wondered if we could find a tasty, far less expensive bottle at the supermarket. The olive oils in our tasting were evaluated for color, clarity, viscosity, bouquet, depth of flavor, and persistence of flavor. The panel was quickly divided into those who liked boldly flavored oil and those who preferred a more mellow taste. Nonetheless, our tasters were able to wade through the myriad choices available in supermarkets, selecting one that we considered the best all-purpose oil: DaVinci Extra-Virgin Olive Oil.

The Best Supermarket Extra-Virgin Olive Oil
DaVinci Extra-Virgin Olive Oil is the test kitchen favorite among leading supermarket brands for its ripe, buttery, and complex flavor.

FAST AND FRESH CHICKEN SALADS

SURE YOU CAN MAKE A SALAD WITH leftover chicken, but it's worlds better if the chicken is fresh, tender, and moist. Could we find an easy way to quick-cook the chicken, so we could have fresh chicken at the ready whenever we wanted a salad? We found our solution in a quick-cooking method that half-sautés and half-poaches boneless skinless chicken breasts—yielding moist and flavorful meat every time and in under 12 minutes. While the chicken cooks we prep the other ingredients and make the dressing.

Here you'll find three distinctly different chicken salad recipes, all of which use this same technique to cook the chicken. Chicken Caesar Salad is far better than the Caesar "kits" you find at the supermarket. Romaine Salad with Chicken, Cheddar, Apple, and Spiced Pecans sports our favorite fall flavors pulled together with a tangy dried cranberry vinaigrette, and Chinese Chicken Salad with Hoisin Vinaigrette includes shredded cabbage, bean sprouts, and chow mein noodles in a lively Asian-inspired vinaigrette. Of course you can also design your own salad, but take a cue from our recipes and keep a few things in mind: Choose components that work well together in terms of flavor and texture, and choose a complementary dressing that pulls all the flavors together.

TEST KITCHEN TIP:

Chicken with Bias

Slicing cooked chicken on the bias is a good trick to know—it looks attractive and makes the chicken easier to fork.

With the knife held at an angle, slice the chicken on the bias into thin slices.

Chicken Caesar Salad

SERVES 4

If you have extra time, Garlic Croutons (page 27) go especially well with this salad.

1	pound boneless, skinless chicken breasts
	Salt and ground black pepper
1	tablespoon vegetable oil
½	cup water
1	recipe Creamy Caesar Dressing, page 25
1	large head romaine lettuce, torn into bite-sized pieces (10 cups)
2	cups store-bought croutons (see note)

MAKING THE MINUTES COUNT:
While the chicken cooks, make the vinaigrette.

1. **BROWN CHICKEN:** Pat chicken dry with paper towels and season with salt and pepper. Heat oil in 12-inch nonstick skillet over medium-high heat until just smoking. Add chicken and cook until browned on one side, about 3 minutes.

2. **POACH CHICKEN:** Flip chicken over, add water, and cover. Reduce heat to medium and continue to cook until thickest part of chicken registers 160 degrees on instant-read thermometer, 5 to 7 minutes longer. Transfer to carving board and cool slightly. (While chicken cooks, make dressing).

3. **DRESS AND ASSEMBLE SALAD:** Toss lettuce with ¾ cup of dressing. Divide salad among individual plates. Slice chicken on bias following illustration at left, and arrange over greens. Sprinkle with croutons. Spoon remaining dressing over chicken, or pass separately.

SHORTCUT INGREDIENT:
Pre-Cut Bagged Lettuce

These days, every supermarket produce section has a refrigerator case chock full of bags of prewashed leafy greens, from fancy mixed baby greens to pre-cut coleslaws. We gathered dozens of them from local supermarkets to evaluate whether they were worthy of our salad bowls. They are indeed. It does, however, pay to trust your own judgment in addition to the sell-by date when it comes to freshness. For the freshest greens, only careful visual inspection of the goods will do.

It's not difficult to make your own croutons, but it does require a few extra minutes. Here's our recipe.

Quick Homemade Croutons
MAKES 4 CUPS

Nearly any type of bread will make good croutons. Be careful, however, when using distinctly flavored breads such as pumpernickel, rye, and sourdough— their strong flavors might not work well in the variations. Leftovers will keep in an airtight container or zipper-lock bag for about one week.

- 3 tablespoons olive oil
  Salt
- 4 cups (½-inch) fresh bread cubes

Adjust oven rack to middle position and heat oven to 350 degrees. Whisk oil and ¼ teaspoon salt together in large bowl. Add bread cubes and toss until thoroughly coated.Spread bread onto baking sheet and bake until golden brown, 20 to 25 minutes. Let cool before adding to salad.

VARIATIONS
Garlic Croutons
These croutons are recommended with our Chicken Caesar Salad.

Whisk 2 minced garlic cloves into oil and salt.

Herb Croutons
If desired, omit the garlic.

Whisk ¼ teaspoon ground black pepper, 2 teaspoons minced fresh rosemary (or ½ teaspoon dried), and 2 teaspoons minced fresh thyme, sage, or dill (or ½ teaspoon dried) into oil with 2 minced garlic cloves and salt.

Parmesan Croutons
If desired, omit the garlic.

Increase amount of oil to 6 tablespoons and add 1 cup grated Parmesan cheese with oil, 2 minced garlic cloves, and salt.

Romaine Salad with Chicken, Cheddar, Apple, and Spiced Pecans
SERVES 4

Store-bought spiced pecans taste fine in this salad, but if you have a few extra minutes you can make your own (page 28).

- 1 pound boneless, skinless chicken breasts
  Salt and ground black pepper
- 1 tablespoon vegetable oil
- ½ cup water
- 1 recipe Dried Cranberry Vinaigrette, page 21
- 1 large head romaine lettuce, torn into bite-sized pieces (10 cups)
- 8 ounces sharp cheddar cheese, cut into ½-inch cubes
- 1 Granny Smith apple, cored and sliced thin (see page 28)
- 1 cup store-bought spiced pecans (see note)
- ½ red onion, sliced thin
- ¼ cup dried cranberries

MAKING THE MINUTES COUNT:
While the chicken cooks, make the vinaigrette.

1. **BROWN CHICKEN:** Pat chicken dry with paper towels and season with salt and pepper. Heat oil in 12-inch nonstick skillet over medium-high heat until just smoking. Add chicken and cook until browned on one side, about 3 minutes.

2. **POACH CHICKEN AND PREPARE VINAIGRETTE:** Flip chicken over, add water, and cover. Reduce heat to medium and continue to cook until thickest part of chicken registers 160 degrees on instant-read thermometer, 5 to 7 minutes longer. Transfer to carving board and cool slightly. (While chicken cooks, make vinaigrette).

3. **DRESS AND ASSEMBLE SALAD:** Toss lettuce, cheddar, apple, pecans, onion, and dried cranberries with ¾ cup of vinaigrette. Divide salad among individual plates. Slice chicken on bias following illustrations on page 26, and arrange over greens. Spoon remaining vinaigrette over chicken, or pass separately.

GOT EXTRA TIME?

While you can use store-bought spiced pecans in your salad, these homemade spiced pecans are easy to prepare and tasty—and on their own, also make a delicious snack.

Quick Spiced Pecans

MAKES ABOUT 2 CUPS

These nuts can be stored in a zipper-lock plastic bag at room temperature for up to 1 week. If adding to a salad, be sure to shake off any extra sugar first.

2	tablespoons unsalted butter
	Salt and ground black pepper
½	teaspoon ground cinnamon
⅛	teaspoon ground cloves
⅛	teaspoon ground allspice
2	cups pecan halves
1	tablespoon sugar

Melt butter in 12-inch nonstick skillet over medium-low heat. Stir in ½ teaspoon salt, ¼ teaspoon pepper, cinnamon, cloves, and allspice, then stir in pecans. Toast nuts, stirring often, until color of nuts deepens slightly, 6 to 8 minutes. Transfer to bowl, toss with sugar, then spread out on plate to cool.

KITCHEN SHORTCUT
APPLE SLICES IN A FLASH

Here is the quickest way to core and slice apples.

1. Cut the four sides of a peeled apple squarely from the core.

2. Slice the apple pieces into thin slices.

Chinese Chicken Salad with Hoisin Vinaigrette

SERVES 4

Chow mein noodles, often sold in 5-ounce canisters, can be found in most supermarkets with other Asian ingredients; La Choy is the most widely available brand. These Americanized noodles add a welcome crunch to this salad.

4	boneless, skinless chicken breasts
	Salt and ground black pepper
5	tablespoons vegetable oil
½	cup water
⅓	cup rice vinegar
3	tablespoons hoisin sauce
1½	tablespoons soy sauce
1	tablespoon grated fresh ginger
½	medium head napa cabbage, shredded (4 cups)
1	red bell pepper, cored and sliced thin
1	cup bean sprouts
2	scallions, sliced thin
1	cup chow mein noodles (see note)

1. **BROWN CHICKEN ON ONE SIDE**: Pat chicken dry with paper towels and season with salt and pepper. Heat 1 tablespoon of oil in 12-inch nonstick skillet over medium-high heat until just smoking. Add chicken and cook until browned on one side, about 3 minutes.

2. **POACH CHICKEN**: Flip chicken over, add water, and cover. Reduce heat to medium and continue to cook until thickest part of chicken registers 160 degrees on instant-read thermometer, 5 to 7 minutes longer. Transfer chicken to carving board and cool slightly.

3. **MAKE DRESSING**: While chicken cooks, whisk vinegar, remaining 4 tablespoons oil, hoisin sauce, soy sauce, and ginger together.

4. **SHRED CHICKEN AND ASSEMBLE SALAD**: Shred cooled chicken (see illustration on page 80) and toss with one-third of dressing. Toss cabbage, red pepper, sprouts, and scallions with remaining dressing. Divide salad among individual plates. Arrange chicken over cabbage mixture, sprinkle with chow mein noodles, and serve.

BUFFALO CHICKEN SALAD WITH BLUE CHEESE DRESSING

BUFFALO CHICKEN SALAD—BREADED CHICKEN strips (in lieu of wings) slathered in a spicy sauce with greens and blue cheese dressing—is a favorite offering on chain-restaurant menus around the country. Having sampled a few of these salads ourselves, we thought we could do better. Most versions we encountered (both in restaurants and in other cookbooks) suffered from lackluster, soggy chicken strips and overdressed greens, or took too long to make to prepare on a busy weeknight.

First we looked at the main element of the salad—the chicken. Instead of cutting and breading chicken, we turned to readily available (and pretty tasty) frozen breaded chicken strips, which only needed to be fried.

Next we turned to the hallmark spicy Buffalo sauce—a cinch to make with the aid of the microwave. We started with the traditional component for the Buffalo sauce, Frank's Hot Sauce, and added butter, brown sugar, and vinegar to brighten the flavors. To bump up the heat a little further, we turned to a more spicy hot sauce—Tabasco sauce. This added the kick we were looking for and made a perfect saucy coating for the crispy fried chicken.

For the greens, romaine or iceberg were top choices, and trademark celery and carrots, cut into sticks for easy dipping, added fresh crunch. And while we have our own recipe for blue cheese dressing (page 24), you can use your own favorite bottled version if you like.

GOT EXTRA TIME?

Tasters liked the flavor and speed of using frozen chicken tenders in this salad, but if you have an extra 25 minutes, you can also make your own—see Crispy Breaded Chicken Fingers on page 200.

Buffalo Chicken Salad with Blue Cheese Dressing

SERVES 4

Feel free to use 1½ cups of your favorite store-bought blue cheese dressing if you don't want to make homemade.

4–5	cups peanut or vegetable oil
I	recipe Blue Cheese Dressing, page 24
I	pound frozen breaded chicken strips
4	tablespoons unsalted butter
½	cup Frank's Red Hot Original Sauce
2	tablespoons Tabasco sauce
I	tablespoon dark brown sugar
2	teaspoons cider vinegar
I	large head romaine or iceberg lettuce, torn into bite-sized pieces (10 cups)
2	celery ribs, cut into sticks
2	carrots, cut into sticks

MAKING THE MINUTES COUNT:
While oil heats, prepare blue cheese dressing.

1. **HEAT OIL AND MAKE DRESSING:** Measure ½ inch oil into Dutch oven, and bring to 350 degrees over medium-high heat. (Use an instant-read thermometer that registers high temperatures or clip a candy/deep fat thermometer onto the side of the pan before turning on the heat.)

2. **FRY CHICKEN:** Fry half of chicken strips until golden brown on both sides, 3 to 5 minutes, flipping halfway through. Transfer to paper towel–lined plate. Repeat with remaining chicken.

3. **MAKE BUFFALO SAUCE:** Meanwhile, combine butter, hot sauces, brown sugar, and vinegar in large microwave-safe bowl and microwave on high power until butter is melted and sugar is dissolved, about 2 minutes.

4. **DRESS AND ASSEMBLE SALAD:** Toss lettuce with ¾ cup of dressing, and divide among individual plates. Toss fried chicken with Buffalo sauce and arrange over salads. Garnish salads with celery and carrots, and pass remaining dressing separately.

CHEF'S SALADS

A HEARTY GREEN SALAD TOPPED WITH deli meats, cheese, tomato, and hard-cooked egg, chef's salad is a delicious and satisfying supper when done right. The problem is that most recipes read like loose guidelines for cleaning out the fridge. Recycled sandwich meats and cheeses, topped with a haphazard array of vegetables and bottled dressing, leave much to be desired.

After dissecting ingredient lists in a variety of recipes, we chose components that we felt were crucial, and left the others behind. Key to a great chef's salad are the deli meats, and we found it best to have the meats sliced on the thick side—about ¼ inch thick, rather than the wafer-thin slices you'd pile into a sandwich. We preferred the slices cut into matchsticks, too, so they are easier to eat with a fork.

We also paid special attention to the vinaigrette—because the deli meats and cheese are so rich, they require a zestier dressing to balance them, so we added an extra tablespoon of vinegar to the vinaigrette. And while we like traditional chef's salad, we thought we'd come up with some flavor variations, just to keep things interesting—an Italian-style chef's salad with sliced fennel, artichoke hearts, and Asiago cheese; and a California-style chef's salad where we swap fresh spinach for the romaine and chicken for the deli meat, and add diced avocado. All of our chef's salads include homemade croutons, which are optional. If you're pressed for time, store-bought croutons work just fine too.

TEST KITCHEN TIP: Slice It Thick

Deli meat for a chef's salad should be cut thick enough to prevent clumping in the bowl, but thin enough to be easily incorporated into the salad. At the deli counter, ask for ham and turkey sliced about ¼ inch thick. At home, cut the deli meats into matchstick pieces.

Chef's Salad

SERVES 4

We like our Basic Vinaigrette in this salad, but any type of simply flavored vinaigrette can be used here. Buy good quality baked ham for this salad—avoid boiled ham, which often has a rubbery texture and little flavor. See page 38 for our tip on peeling hard-cooked eggs quickly.

4	large eggs
½	cup Basic Vinaigrette, page 21
1	tablespoon red or white wine vinegar
1	large head romaine lettuce, torn into bite-sized pieces (10 cups)
1	small cucumber, peeled and sliced thin
1	pint cherry tomatoes, halved
4	radishes, trimmed and sliced thin
8	ounces thick-sliced deli ham, cut into matchsticks
8	ounces thick-sliced deli turkey, cut into matchsticks
8	ounces sharp cheddar cheese, cut into matchsticks
2	cups Garlic Croutons (optional, page 27)

MAKING THE MINUTES COUNT:
Prep the salad components, including the croutons, while the eggs cook and chill.

1. HARDCOOK EGGS AND PREPARE VINAIGRETTE: Place eggs in medium saucepan, cover with 1 inch of water, and bring to boil over high heat. As soon as water reaches boil, remove pan from heat, cover, and let sit for 10 minutes. (While eggs cook, make vinaigrette.)

2. CHILL EGGS: Transfer eggs to ice water bath, chill for 5 minutes, then peel and quarter.

3. DRESS AND ASSEMBLE SALAD: Whisk vinaigrette with vinegar, then toss with lettuce, cucumber, tomatoes, and radishes. Divide salad among individual plates. Arrange ham, turkey, and cheddar over salads, and garnish with eggs and croutons (if using).

Italian-Style Chef's Salad with Artichokes and Asiago

SERVES 4

Use a mild, soft Asiago that crumbles easily; avoid aged Asiago that has a hard, dry texture.

1/2	cup Basic Vinaigrette, page 21
1	tablespoon red or white wine vinegar
1	large head romaine lettuce, torn into bite-sized pieces (10 cups)
1	fennel bulb, trimmed, cored, and sliced thin (see illustrations at right)
1	(8-ounce) jar roasted red peppers, rinsed and sliced 1/2 inch thick
1	(14-ounce) can water-packed artichoke hearts, drained and halved
8	ounces thick-sliced hard salami, cut into matchsticks
8	ounces thick-sliced deli turkey, cut into matchsticks
2	cups crumbled Asiago cheese
1/2	cup pitted Kalamata olives
2	cups Garlic Croutons (optional, page 27)

Whisk vinaigrette with vinegar, then toss with lettuce, fennel, red peppers, and artichoke hearts. Divide salad among individual plates. Arrange salami and turkey over salads, and garnish with Asiago, olives, and croutons (if using).

California-Style Chef's Salad with Chicken, Spinach, and Gouda

SERVES 4

Either regular or smoked Gouda can be used in this salad.

1/2	cup Basic Vinaigrette, page 21
1	tablespoon red or white wine vinegar
4	ounces baby spinach (5 cups)
1	small head radicchio, shredded
1	Belgian endive, cored and shredded
1/2	red onion, sliced thin
8	ounces thick-sliced deli chicken breast, cut into matchsticks
8	ounces Gouda cheese, cut into matchsticks
2	avocados, halved, pitted, and cut into 1/2-inch cubes (see page 32)

Whisk vinaigrette with vinegar, then toss with spinach, radicchio, endive, and red onion. Divide salad among individual plates. Arrange chicken and Gouda over salads, and garnish with avocado.

PREPARING FENNEL

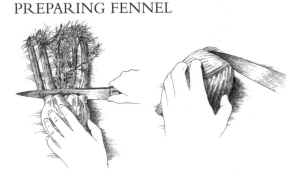

1. Cut off the stems and feathery fronds. (The fronds can be minced and used for a garnish, if desired.)

2. Trim a very thin slice from the base and remove any tough or blemished outer layers from the bulb.

3. Cut the bulb in half through the base. Use a small, sharp knife to remove the pyramid-shaped core.

4. Place the cored fennel on a work surface and, with the knife parallel to the cutting board, cut the fennel in half crosswise. With the knife perpendicular to the cutting board, cut the fennel pieces lengthwise into thin strips.

TACO SALAD

TACO SALADS APPEAR IN QUICK-COOKING books often—they're a great way to enjoy the flavors of a taco, but without the assembly usually required. Making your own tacos isn't difficult, but when you're trying to feed a family, especially children, you might not want them to be fussing with taco components at the table. This recipe makes things a bit more streamlined and less messy. We make a quick, well-seasoned ground beef mixture in a skillet—no seasoning packet required. While the beef mixture cooks and cools, you can make the Cilantro-Lime Vinaigrette; it's what really gives this salad zip. Romaine lettuce, diced tomato, cubed avocado, and shredded cheddar or Mexican blend cheese round out the salad—tortilla chips are all you need on the side.

KITCHEN SHORTCUT
DICING AN AVOCADO

This method is quick, easy, and saves your cutting board from getting messy.

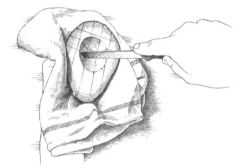

1. Use a dish towel to hold the halved avocado steady. Make ½-inch crosshatch incisions in the flesh of each avocado half with a dinner knife, cutting down to—but not through—the skin.

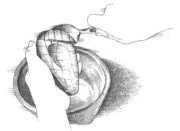

2. Separate the diced flesh from the skin, using a spoon inserted between the skin and the flesh. Then gently scoop out the avocado cubes.

Taco Salad
SERVES 4

Salsa, sour cream, and minced cilantro also taste great on this salad. Keep your eye on the beef mixture while it cooks, because it has a tendency to burn. Serve this salad with tortilla chips or in store-bought tortilla bowls.

I	tablespoon vegetable oil
I	onion, minced
2	tablespoons chili powder
4	garlic cloves, minced
I	pound 90 percent lean ground beef
I	(8-ounce) can tomato sauce
	Salt and ground black pepper
I	recipe Cilantro-Lime Vinaigrette, page 22
I	head romaine lettuce, torn into bite-sized pieces (10 cups)
2	tomatoes, cored and chopped medium
I	avocado, peeled, pitted, and cut into ½-inch cubes
I	cup shredded cheddar or Mexican cheese blend
	Tortilla chips (for serving)

1. **SAUTÉ AROMATICS:** Heat oil in 12-inch non-stick skillet over medium heat until shimmering. Add onion and chili powder and cook until onion is softened, 3 to 5 minutes. Stir in garlic and cook until fragrant, about 30 seconds.

2. **BROWN BEEF, ADD SAUCE, AND SIMMER:** Stir in beef and cook, stirring often, until lightly browned, 6 to 8 minutes. Stir in tomato sauce and simmer until slightly thickened, about 2 minutes. Season with salt and pepper to taste, and set aside to cool slightly. (While beef cools, make vinaigrette.)

3. **DRESS AND ASSEMBLE SALAD:** Toss lettuce with ½ cup of vinaigrette. Portion beef on top of salad and sprinkle with tomatoes, avocado, and cheese. Sprinkle remaining vinaigrette over top of salad, or pass separately. Serve with tortilla chips.

STEAK SALADS

MOST QUICK STEAK SALADS START WITH leftover steak which is then draped over mundane greens with a nondescript dressing. We knew we could do better, even in just 30 minutes. For our first salad we wanted freshly seared steak, well-dressed greens, and (because they go so well with steak) crispy potatoes to round out the meal. The secret was to microwave baby new potatoes and then, while they were cooking, sear two top loin steaks quickly in a hot skillet. To infuse the potatoes with meaty flavor, we browned them in the same skillet we had used for the steak while the steak was resting. A simple but flavorful mustard vinaigrette was all we needed to pull together the remaining ingredients, making this a fresh and easy dinner, rather than just another way to use up leftover steak.

Our second recipe, Thai-Style Beef Salad, is not a typical quick salad. The steak is usually marinated for hours, cooked, then allowed to rest and sliced on the bias. We came up with a far quicker method by mixing up the steps a bit. Instead of marinating the meat before cooking, we did so after, transferring the cooked steak right out of the skillet into the marinade to rest. In five minutes the steak absorbed the tangy flavors of the marinade and was ready to be served. And while the steak cooked, we prepped and assembled the lettuce, cucumber, and onion. The traditional garnish, chopped peanuts, provided the finishing touch.

TEST KITCHEN TIP:
Gristle and Grain

Top loin steaks (New York strip steaks) usually have some fat and gristle around the edges, which should be trimmed away before slicing and serving (no need to trim before cooking). Also, remember to slice the cooked steak against the grain, or the pieces will be chewy.

30-Minute Steak and Potato Salad

SERVES 4

Boneless rib-eye steaks (Delmonico steaks) are a good substitute for the top loin steaks (New York strip steaks), and most any simple vinaigrette can be used here.

1	pound red potatoes (3 medium), cut into ³/₄-inch-thick wedges
3	tablespoons vegetable oil
2	(8-ounce) top loin steaks, 1 inch thick (see note)
	Salt and ground black pepper
1	recipe Bistro-Style Mustard Vinaigrette, page 23
1	large head romaine lettuce, torn into bite-sized pieces (10 cups)
1	red onion, halved and sliced thin
	Parmesan cheese

MAKING THE MINUTES COUNT:
Prep the onion and lettuce while the potatoes are browning in the skillet.

1. MICROWAVE POTATOES: Toss potatoes with 2 tablespoons of oil in large microwave-safe bowl. Cover with plastic wrap and microwave on high until potatoes are tender, 5 to 10 minutes, shaking bowl halfway through.

KITCHEN SHORTCUT
QUICK PARMESAN SHAVINGS

To quickly achieve paper-thin slices of Parmesan, employ your vegetable peeler. Run the peeler over a block of Parmesan and use a light touch for thin shavings.

2. COOK STEAKS AND PREPARE VINAIGRETTE: Meanwhile, pat steaks dry with paper towels and season with salt and pepper. Heat remaining tablespoon of oil in 12-inch skillet over medium-high heat until just smoking. Brown steaks on first side, about 5 minutes, reducing heat if pan begins to scorch. Flip steaks over and continue to cook to desired doneness (see page 193), 3 to 6 minutes. (While steaks cook, make vinaigrette.)

3. BROWN POTATOES: Transfer steaks to carving board and tent with foil, leaving fat in skillet. Return skillet to high heat until just smoking. Add microwaved potatoes and cook until well browned, about 5 minutes. Season with salt and pepper to taste.

4. DRESS AND ASSEMBLE SALAD: Toss lettuce and red onion with ½ cup of vinaigrette and divide among individual plates. Arrange potatoes on salads, then shave several Parmesan shavings over top following illustration on page 33. Slice steak thin against grain, discarding any gristle, and lay on top of salads. Spoon remaining vinaigrette over steak, or pass separately.

Thai-Style Beef Salad
SERVES 4

The lettuce (which is not torn into pieces or tossed with a dressing) will catch plenty of the marinade and dressing from the meat and vegetables.

I	pound flank steak
	Salt and ground black pepper
3	tablespoons vegetable oil
¼	cup fresh lime juice
¼	cup fish sauce
4	teaspoons brown sugar
I	small cucumber, peeled and sliced thin
½	red onion, sliced thin
I	tablespoon minced fresh cilantro
I	tablespoon minced fresh mint
I	head Bibb lettuce, leaves separated
¼	cup chopped unsalted roasted peanuts

MAKING THE MINUTES COUNT:
Prep the lettuce and vegetables while the steak cooks.

I. COOK STEAK: Pat steak dry with paper towels and season with salt and pepper to taste. Heat 1 tablespoon of oil in 12-inch skillet over medium-high heat until just smoking. Brown steak on first side, about 5 minutes, reducing heat if pan begins to scorch. Flip steak over and continue to cook to desired doneness (see page 193), 3 to 6 minutes. Transfer to carving board, tent with foil, and let rest, 5 to 10 minutes.

2. PREPARE MARINADE AND TOSS WITH STEAK: Whisk lime juice, fish sauce, and brown sugar together until sugar is dissolved. Slice steak in half lengthwise; then following illustrations on page 33, slice steak halves thinly widthwise, against grain, on bias. Toss sliced steak with half of lime marinade and set aside for 5 minutes.

3. PREPARE VINAIGRETTE AND ASSEMBLE SALAD: Whisk remaining lime marinade with remaining 2 tablespoons of oil, and toss with cucumber, onion, cilantro, and mint. Divide lettuce leaves among individual plates and spoon vegetables with dressing over top. Remove steak from marinade (discarding marinade) and lay over salads. Sprinkle with peanuts before serving.

TEST KITCHEN TIP:
Marinate After Cooking
Marinating meat before you cook it not only takes hours, it also tends to make the meat mushy. We prefer to marinate steak after it has been cooked, for about five minutes—it's faster, the marinade flavors really come through, and the texture of the meat isn't compromised.

ARUGULA SALAD WITH SAUSAGE AND WHITE BEANS

YOU DON'T NEED FRESH VEGETABLES TO MAKE a quick salad—you can turn to pantry staples, like canned white beans and roasted red peppers. While canned beans don't taste exactly like fresh, it is possible to infuse them with terrific flavor.

Partner them with hearty sausage (precooked chicken or turkey sausage only requires browning) and peppery arugula, and you can have dinner on the table in no time. How did we do it? First we browned the sausage. Then we cooked the onion, olives, peppers, and the beans, along with a tangy mustard vinaigrette (mustard is a great pairing with sausage). After a quick simmer, our beans were as flavorful as if they'd simmered for hours. All that was left to do was add the arugula to the skillet, gently wilt it, slice the sausage, and arrange it over the salads, and we had a warm and satisfying main-course salad in under 30 minutes.

Arugula Salad with Sausage and White Beans

SERVES 4

Most supermarkets carry several brands and flavors of cooked chicken and turkey sausage (don't use pork sausage here—it's too fatty). Choose a sausage with flavors that will complement the salad, such as garlic or sun-dried tomato. If using raw poultry sausage, extend the covered cooking time by about five minutes.

4	teaspoons olive oil
1	pound cooked chicken or turkey sausage (see note)
½	cup water
1	recipe Bistro-Style Mustard Vinaigrette, page 23
1	(15-ounce) can cannellini beans, rinsed
1	red onion, sliced thin
1	(8-ounce) jar roasted red peppers, rinsed and sliced ½ inch thick
½	cup pitted Kalamata olives, chopped coarse
7	ounces bagged arugula (10 cups)

MAKING THE MINUTES COUNT:
Prepare the vinaigrette while the sausage cooks.

1. COOK SAUSAGE AND PREPARE VINAIGRETTE:
Heat 2 teaspoons of oil in 12-inch nonstick skillet over medium-high heat until just smoking. Brown sausage on one side, about 3 minutes. Turn sausage over, add water, and cover. Reduce heat to medium and continue to cook until sausage is

heated through, 3 to 5 minutes. (While sausage cooks, make vinaigrette.) Transfer sausage to carving board. Pour off remaining water in skillet and wipe dry with paper towels.

2. PREPARE BEAN MIXTURE: Add remaining 2 teaspoons oil to skillet and return to medium-high heat until shimmering. Add beans and onion and cook until onion begins to soften, about 3 minutes. Add peppers, olives, and ¾ cup of vinaigrette, bring to brief simmer, then remove from heat.

3. DRESS AND ASSEMBLE SALAD: Toss arugula with warm bean mixture, and divide among individual plates. Slice sausage thin on bias, and arrange over salads. Spoon remaining ¼ cup vinaigrette over sausage, or pass separately.

TEST KITCHEN TIP:
Cutting Citrus for Salads
Here is how to cut up any citrus fruit into bite-sized pieces that won't fall apart when tossing or serving.

1. Cut away the rind and pith from the orange using a paring knife.

2. Quarter the peeled orange, then slice each quarter crosswise into ½-inch-thick wedges.

WARM SPINACH SALAD WITH SCALLOPS

WARM WILTED SPINACH SALADS MAKE A wonderful starter, but add quick-cooking scallops and suddenly you have an elegant meal. There are, however, a few things to keep in mind. The first is to dry the scallops thoroughly with paper towels to prevent excess moisture from inhibiting the caramelization process. The second trick is not to overcrowd the scallops in the pan, which can also prevent the scallops from caramelizing. We found that a two-batch cooking method solves this problem. Cook the first batch of scallops until the undersides are golden brown, remove to a plate and keep warm, then cook the second batch of scallops until just browned. Flip the scallops and add the first batch back to the skillet (browned sides up) so that all the scallops finish cooking at once. Toasted almonds add crunch to this salad and red onion and oranges add zest and a citrusy brightness—perfect counterpoints to the rich scallops.

Warm Spinach Salad with Scallops, Almonds, and Orange

SERVES 4

For more information on how to buy, prepare, and pan-sear scallops, see page 218.

8	ounces baby spinach (10 cups)
2	oranges, peeled, quartered, and sliced crosswise 1/2 inch thick (see page 35)
1	cup sliced almonds, toasted
1/2	red onion, sliced thin
1 1/2	pounds sea scallops (16 to 20 large), tendons removed (see page 218)
	Salt and ground black pepper
4	tablespoons vegetable oil
1	recipe Orange-Sherry Vinaigrette, page 23

MAKING THE MINUTES COUNT:
Prep the vinaigrette and other salad ingredients before you begin to cook; this dish comes together quickly.

1. COMBINE SPINACH MIXTURE: Place spinach, oranges, almonds, and red onion together in large bowl and set aside.

2. DRY AND PREP SCALLOPS: Lay scallops out over paper towel–lined plate, then season with salt and pepper to taste. Press paper towel flush to surface of scallops and set aside.

3. BROWN SCALLOPS: Heat 2 tablespoons of oil in 12-inch nonstick skillet over high heat until just smoking. Add half of scallops to skillet and cook until evenly golden, 1 to 2 minutes (first few scallops will be close to golden when last scallop has been added to pan). Transfer scallops to large plate, browned side up, and set aside. Wipe out skillet with wad of paper towels. Add remaining 2 tablespoons of oil and return to high heat until just smoking. Add remaining scallops and cook until evenly golden, 1 to 2 minutes.

4. FINISH SCALLOPS: Reduce heat to medium, flip second batch of scallops over, and return first batch to skillet, browned side up. Continue to cook until sides of scallops have firmed up and all but middle third of scallop is opaque, 30 to 60 seconds longer. Transfer scallops to plate and cover with foil to keep warm.

5. SIMMER VINAIGRETTE; DRESS AND ASSEMBLE SALAD: Add 3/4 cup of vinaigrette to hot skillet, bring to brief simmer, then toss with spinach mixture. Divide salad among individual plates and arrange scallops over top. Spoon remaining vinaigrette over scallops, or pass separately.

TEST KITCHEN TIP: Toasting Nuts
Nuts will contribute the most flavor if they are toasted. To toast a small amount (under 1 cup) of nuts or seeds, put them in a dry skillet over medium heat. Simply shake the skillet occasionally to prevent scorching and toast until they are lightly browned and fragrant, 3 to 8 minutes. Watch the nuts closely because they can go from golden to burnt very quickly. To toast a large quantity of nuts, spread the nuts in a single layer on a rimmed baking sheet and toast in a 350-degree oven. To promote even toasting, shake the baking sheet every few minutes and toast until the nuts are lightly browned and fragrant, 5 to 10 minutes.

ASIAN SHRIMP AND SPINACH SALAD WITH MISO-GINGER VINAIGRETTE

PAIRING COLD SHRIMP WITH SALAD IS A nice change from the ordinary, and this Asian-inspired salad serves as the perfect foil to sweet, tender shrimp. But to peel, devein, poach, and properly cool down shrimp for a salad takes time. In order to finish this salad in 30 minutes, we turned to a product that the test kitchen had not previously considered: pre-cooked shrimp. Available fresh from the fishmonger or frozen at just about every supermarket, this time-saving convenience is the ideal solution for a recipe where cooked shrimp is needed. Paired with baby spinach, peppery radishes, and a robust miso dressing, shrimp is the centerpiece of a quick, fresh-flavored dinner. Toasted sesame seeds sprinkled over the top is the perfect garnish, lending their trademark toasty flavor as well as visual appeal.

Asian Shrimp and Spinach Salad with Miso-Ginger Vinaigrette
SERVES 4

One cup of any herbed vinaigrette can be substituted for the Miso-Ginger Vinaigrette. Sesame seeds can be toasted in a medium skillet over medium heat until golden, 3 to 5 minutes—but don't walk away from the skillet because they can easily burn.

- 8   ounces baby spinach (10 cups)
- 1   small cucumber, peeled, and sliced thin
- 8   radishes, sliced thin
- 1   recipe Miso-Ginger Vinaigrette, page 22
- 1   pound extra-large (21/25) pre-cooked shrimp, peeled
- 1   tablespoon sesame seeds, toasted (see note)

Toss spinach, cucumber, and radishes with ¾ cup of vinaigrette. Divide salad among individual plates and arrange shrimp over top. Spoon remaining vinaigrette over shrimp and sprinkle with sesame seeds.

SALADE NIÇOISE

LEAVE IT TO THE FRENCH TO TURN THE ordinary into something sophisticated: Canned tuna becomes much more than a sandwich filling when paired with hard-cooked eggs, potatoes, and green beans. While this salad is not difficult to prepare, it does pose challenges for the cook looking to get dinner on the table in 30 minutes. Classic salade niçoise has a laundry list of ingredients that require significant preparation. Potatoes have to be boiled, green beans blanched, eggs hard-cooked, and more than five garnishes gathered. We started by figuring out which components were vitally important to this salad, then focused on the quickest way to prepare them. First, the eggs are hard-cooked and quick-chilled in an ice bath. Steaming sliced potatoes, rather than boiling them whole, shaves eight minutes off the total cooking time. While the potatoes cook, prepare the vinaigrette. And once the potatoes are finished cooking, add the green beans to the same cooking water for a quick steaming. All that's left to do dress and assemble the salad—and dinner is ready.

INGREDIENTS: Tuna

After buying and tasting nearly every type of "canned" tuna sold at the supermarket, we can say with authority that brand, style of packaging, and price do matter. Our first place tuna is imported from Spain; however, it can be hard to find and its price tag is a little steep for everyday ($2.56 per ounce). For a more reasonably priced supermarket tuna, we prefer StarKist Solid White Tuna packed in a foil pouch (42 cents per ounce).

1ST CHOICE: Ortiz Bonito del Norte "Ventresca," $9.95 for a 3.88-ounce can. These small fillets blew all other contenders out of the water with their "silky texture" and "fresh flavor." Good for a special occasion.

2ND CHOICE: StarKist Solid White Tuna packed in a foil pouch, $2.99 for a 7.06-ounce pouch. While all brands of tuna sold in pouches ranked higher than their canned counterparts, StarKist was the clear favorite. This is our pick for the best balance of flavor and texture to price.

Salade Niçoise

SERVES 4

4	large eggs
1	pound red potatoes (3 medium), sliced 1/8 inch thick
1	recipe Fresh Herb Vinaigrette, page 21
1	pound green beans
2	(7-ounce) foil pouches tuna
8	ounces mesclun (10 cups)
1	pint cherry tomatoes, halved
1/2	cup niçoise olives, pitted (see note at right)
8	anchovy fillets, rinsed and patted dry (optional)

MAKING THE MINUTES COUNT:
Prep the potatoes while the potato water comes to a boil.

1. HARD-COOK AND CHILL EGGS: Place eggs in medium saucepan, cover with 1 inch water, and bring to boil over high heat. As soon as water reaches boil, remove pan from heat, cover, and let sit for 10 minutes. Transfer eggs to ice-water bath, chill for 5 minutes, then peel and quarter.

2. STEAM POTATOES AND MAKE VINAIGRETTE: Meanwhile, place steaming basket in large pot, add water until it touches bottom of basket, and bring to boil over high heat. Add potatoes to basket, cover, and steam until potatoes are tender, 6 to 8 minutes. (While potatoes cook, make vinaigrette.) Transfer potatoes to medium bowl and toss with 1/4 cup of vinaigrette.

3. STEAM GREEN BEANS: Return steamer basket to pot, add water as needed until it touches bottom of rack, and return to boil. Add green beans, cover, and cook until green beans are bright green and just tender, 5 to 7 minutes. Transfer beans to bowl with potatoes and toss to combine.

4. DRESS AND ASSEMBLE SALAD: Toss 1/4 cup of vinaigrette with tuna, gently flaking tuna apart with fork. Toss mesclun with remaining 1/2 cup of vinaigrette and divide among individual plates. Arrange potatoes and beans, tuna, eggs, tomatoes, olives, and anchovies (if using) over greens.

KITCHEN SHORTCUT
PITTING OLIVES QUICKLY

Removing the pits from tiny niçoise olives (or any size olive for that matter) by hand is not all that quick and easy. To speed things up a bit, cover a cutting board with a clean kitchen towel and spread the olives on top, spacing them about one inch apart. Place a second clean towel over the olives. Using a mallet, pound all of the olives firmly, being careful not to split the pits. Remove the top towel and, using your fingers, press the pit out of each olive.

KITCHEN SHORTCUT
PEELING EGGS FAST

1. After draining the hot water from the pot used to cook the eggs, shake the pot back and forth to crack the shells.

2. Add enough ice water to cover the eggs and let cool. The water seeps under the broken shells, allowing them to be slipped off without a struggle.

BISTRO SALAD

EVERYONE AGREES THAT BACON AND EGGS are a great fallback for a quick dinner, but they're not something you would think of as salad components. As unusual as it sounds, the concept has been common in French bistros for years, and it's easy to make.

While it's traditional to use lardons (French-style diced bacon), we use thick-sliced American bacon. We start by cooking chopped bacon until crisp; while the bacon cooks, we make the mustard vinaigrette. Many recipes for bistro bacon and egg salad call for the eggs to be poached, but we found frying the eggs to be less daunting and fussy. We were able to fry four eggs at once, in a large non-stick skillet, then separate them with a spatula for easy serving. Once the greens and bacon are tossed with the vinaigrette, we portion the mixture onto plates, perch an egg on top, and serve with toasts slathered with garlicky Boursin cheese.

Bistro Bacon and Egg Salad

SERVES 4

Heat the oven for the toasts before you begin cooking or even gathering your ingredients. Feel free to substitute frisée for some of the mesclun for added bitterness and texture. Any good quality herbed cheese spread, or even goat cheese, can be substituted for the Boursin.

12	(½-inch-thick) baguette slices
2	tablespoons extra-virgin olive oil
1	cup Boursin cheese spread (see note)
8	slices thick-cut bacon, chopped coarse (see note at right)
½	cup Bistro-Style Mustard Vinaigrette, page 23
1	tablespoon unsalted butter
4	large eggs, cracked into 2 small bowls Salt and ground black pepper
8	ounces mesclun (10 cups)

MAKING THE MINUTES COUNT:
Make the vinaigrette while the bacon cooks.

1. HEAT OVEN AND PREPARE TOASTS: Adjust oven rack to middle position and heat oven to 400 degrees. Arrange bread in single layer on large baking sheet. Bake until bread is dry and crisp, about 10 minutes, flipping slices over halfway through. Drizzle one side of toasts with olive oil, then spread with even layer of Boursin.

2. COOK BACON AND PREPARE VINAIGRETTE: Meanwhile, fry bacon in 10-inch nonstick skillet over medium heat until crisp, about 8 minutes. Transfer bacon to paper towel–lined plate. (While bacon cooks, make vinaigrette).

3. COOK EGGS: Pour off bacon fat and wipe out skillet with wad of paper towels. Add butter to skillet and melt over low heat until foaming subsides. Following illustrations on page 15, add eggs to pan. Season eggs with salt and pepper, cover, and cook until desired doneness, about 2 minutes for runny yolks, 3 minutes for soft but set yolks, and 4 minutes for firmly set yolks.

4. DRESS AND ASSEMBLE SALAD: While eggs are cooking, toss mesclun and bacon with vinaigrette, and divide among individual plates. Using rubber spatula, separate eggs and carefully slice one egg on top of each salad. Arrange toasts around edge of each plate and serve immediately.

KITCHEN SHORTCUT
CHOPPING BACON QUICKLY

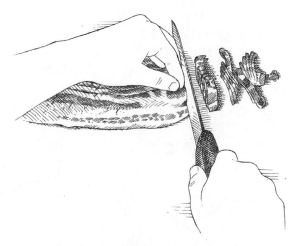

Trim the time it takes to chop the bacon from five minutes to just one, by leaving the bacon in its shingled stack (as it is in the package), and simply slicing it widthwise into roughly ⅓-inch-wide pieces.

Pre-Cooked Bacon

Full-cooked packaged bacon is now commonly available in most supermarkets. Could it be any good, we wondered? After a quick shopping trip, we came up with three brands of shelf-stable bacon: Oscar Mayer, Hormel, and a generic house brand from a Boston-area supermarket. We conducted a blind tasting of these bacons in two applications: BLT (bacon, lettuce, and tomato) sandwiches and spinach salad with bacon dressing. As a point of comparison, we included in the mix one of our recommended brands of supermarket bacon—Boar's Head Naturally Smoked Sliced Bacon—to see if our panel of tasters would be fooled.

Straight out of the package, the pre-cooked bacon ranged from thin and pale with a substantial amount of white fat to dark and crispy looking with spotty black sections and salt crystals. Although all three brands had been fully cooked, they still needed some manner of reheating and had to be refrigerated once opened.

Tasters overwhelmingly preferred the crisp-chewy texture and rich, meaty, salty-smoky flavor of the fresh Boar's Head bacon over any of the pre-cooked varieties. Placing a distant second, the Oscar Mayer pre-cooked bacon was mild in flavor, salty but not smoky, and "flaccid" in the BLT sandwich. When diced and added to the salad, it was alternately described as "meaty and smoky," "flavorless," and having "a strong bacon flavor, but tastes frozen." Not horrible—but not quite a glowing recommendation. The Hormel and the generic brand both came up short across the board, thanks to their chewy texture and "stale," "one-dimensional" flavor.

Our verdict? Aside from the advantages of being ready to eat in half the time of "raw" bacon and being convenient for camping (or stockpiling in the pantry), we don't see much justification for buying these expensive strips.

PASTA SALADS

PASTA SALAD IS NORMALLY SERVED AS A picnic side dish, but it also makes for an easy main course when bulked up with ingredients like shrimp, meat, cheese, and vegetables. We're not talking about the unappetizing looking pasta salads drenched in mayonnaise that are featured in most deli cases across America, with mushy pasta, drab olive-green vegetables, and lackluster flavor. For these main-course salads we aimed to marry perfectly tender pasta with bright vinaigrettes, and customized each with a different pasta shape (cheese-filled tortellini, fusilli, and farfalle) and a variety of hearty proteins, fresh vegetables, and flavorings.

To cut through the richness of these somewhat fatty ingredients, we found that we needed a highly acidic vinaigrette, which we tossed with the still-hot pasta. As the pasta cooled it soaked up flavor and seasonings from the vinaigrette.

For our salad combinations we chose ingredients that require minimal preparation, like cherry tomatoes with baby arugula and pine nuts combined with hearty cheese-filled tortellini. Thick-sliced salami with provolone and baby spinach works with the fusilli. And cooked shrimp pairs well with fennel, feta, arugula, and farfalle. You can, of course, cook your own shrimp, but in the interest of time we found that pre-cooked shrimp works just fine here. In just 30 minutes, these pasta salads offer a satisfying and refreshing summer supper.

MINCING SHALLOTS

1. Place the peeled bulb flat-side down on a work surface and slice crosswise almost to (but not through) the root end.

2. Make a number of parallel cuts through the top of the shallot down to the work surface.

3. Make very thin slices perpendicular to the lengthwise cuts made in step 2.

Shrimp and Pasta Salad with Fennel and Feta

SERVES 4 TO 6

We like to use medium-sized shrimp in this dish; however, extra-large shrimp (21/25) can be substituted.

6	tablespoons extra-virgin olive oil
½	cup finely crumbled feta cheese
¼	cup red wine vinegar
1	shallot, minced
1	garlic clove, minced
1½	teaspoons minced fresh oregano
	Salt and ground black pepper
1	pound farfalle pasta
1	fennel bulb, trimmed, cored, and sliced thin (see page 31)
1½	pounds medium (31/40) pre-cooked shrimp, peeled
1½	ounces baby arugula (2 cups)
½	cup pitted Kalamata olives, sliced

1. **BOIL WATER FOR PASTA**: Bring 4 quarts water to boil in large pot.

2. **MAKE DRESSING**: Meanwhile, whisk olive oil, feta, vinegar, shallot, garlic, oregano, ½ teaspoon salt, and ½ teaspoon pepper together in bowl large enough to hold entire pasta salad.

3. **COOK FARFALLE**: Add farfalle and 1 tablespoon salt to boiling water, and cook, stirring often, until tender. Drain, shaking off excess water.

4. **MARINATE PASTA**: Add hot, drained farfalle, fennel, and shrimp to bowl with dressing and toss. Cover and refrigerate until cooled, about 15 minutes.

5. **FINISH**: Just before serving, stir in arugula and olives and season with salt and pepper to taste.

Fusilli Salad with Salami, Provolone, and Sun-Dried Tomato Vinaigrette

SERVES 4 TO 6

Pepperoni can be substituted for the salami. Nearly any small, curly-shaped pasta will work here; however, we really like how the corkscrew shape of the pasta traps the sun-dried tomato dressing.

6	tablespoons extra-virgin olive oil
1	(8-ounce) jar oil-packed sun-dried tomatoes, drained and minced
¼	cup red wine vinegar
2	tablespoons minced fresh basil or parsley
1	garlic clove, minced
	Salt and ground black pepper
1	pound fusilli pasta
8	ounces thickly sliced salami, cut into matchsticks
1½	ounces baby spinach (2 cups)
8	ounces thickly sliced provolone, cut into matchsticks
½	cup pitted Kalamata olives, sliced

1. **BOIL WATER FOR PASTA**: Bring 4 quarts water to boil in large pot.

2. **MAKE DRESSING**: Meanwhile, whisk olive oil, sun-dried tomatoes, vinegar, basil, garlic, ½ teaspoon salt, and ½ teaspoon pepper together in bowl large enough to hold entire pasta salad.

3. **COOK FUSILLI**: Add fusilli and 1 tablespoon salt to boiling water and cook, stirring often, until tender. Drain, shaking off excess water.

4. **MARINATE FUSILLI**: Add hot, drained fusilli and salami to bowl with dressing and toss. Cover and refrigerate until cooled, about 15 minutes.

5. **FINISH**: Just before serving, stir in spinach, provolone, and olives, and season with salt and pepper to taste.

KITCHEN SHORTCUT
SHREDDING BASIL

To shred basil or other leafy herbs and greens, simply stack several leaves on top of one another, roll them up, and slice. In the case of basil, we have found that rolling the leaves tip to tail minimizes bruising.

Tortellini Salad with Cherry Tomatoes, Arugula, and Pine Nuts

SERVES 4 TO 6

We prefer the more delicate texture and flavor of fresh tortellini (found in the refrigerator section of most supermarkets); however, frozen tortellini can be substituted.

6	tablespoons extra-virgin olive oil
3	tablespoons fresh lemon juice
½	cup shredded fresh basil
1	shallot, minced
1	garlic clove, minced
	Salt and ground black pepper
2	(9-ounce) packages fresh cheese tortellini (see note)
1	pint cherry tomatoes, halved
1½	ounces baby arugula (2 cups)
½	cup grated Parmesan cheese
¼	cup pine nuts, toasted

1. BOIL WATER FOR PASTA: Bring 4 quarts water to boil in large pot.

2. MAKE DRESSING: Meanwhile, whisk olive oil, lemon juice, basil, shallot, garlic, ½ teaspoon salt, and ½ teaspoon pepper together in bowl large enough to hold entire pasta salad.

3. COOK TORTELLINI: Add tortellini and 1 tablespoon salt to boiling water and cook, stirring often, until tender. Drain tortellini, shaking off excess water.

4. MARINATE TORTELLINI: Add hot, drained tortellini and cherry tomatoes to bowl with dressing and toss. Cover and refrigerate until cooled, about 15 minutes.

5. FINISH: Just before serving stir in arugula, Parmesan, and pine nuts, and season with salt and pepper to taste.

KITCHEN SHORTCUT
SQUEEZING LEMONS

If you don't happen to have a small enough strainer for small jobs (such as straining the juice of one or two lemons) and would rather not haul out your large strainer, try this method:

1. First, start by rolling the lemon on a hard surface, pressing down firmly with the palm of your hand to break the membranes inside the fruit. Cut the lemon in half.

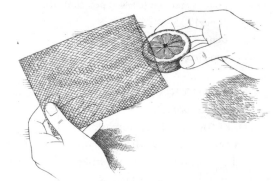

2. Save the leftover mesh bags from small produce items (such as shallots or new potatoes). After cleaning the bag well, drop in a lemon half.

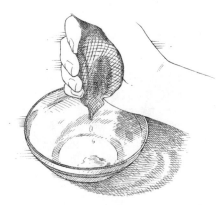

3. Squeeze as much juice as needed. All of the seeds and pith will be trapped in the mesh bag.

3

SOUP FOR DINNER

Soup For Dinner

CHICKEN SOUPS   46
Chicken Noodle Soup
Chicken and Rice Soup
Asian Chicken Noodle Soup
Chicken Soup with Potatoes, Green Beans, and Leeks
Tortilla Soup
Mulligatawny Soup
Thai Chicken and Coconut Soup

TORTELLINI SOUP   51
Tortellini Soup

CLAM CHOWDER   52
New England-Style Pantry Clam Chowder
Fish Chowder

QUICK CORN CHOWDER   53
Quick Corn Chowder

BLACK BEAN SOUP   54
Black Bean Soup

WHITE BEAN SOUP   55
Tuscan White Bean Soup

RED LENTIL SOUP   55
Indian-Style Red Lentil Soup with Coconut

MOROCCAN-STYLE CHICKPEA SOUP   57
Moroccan-Style Chickpea Soup

CREAM OF VEGETABLE SOUPS   58
Cream of Vegetable Soup
Cream of Asparagus Soup with Leek and Tarragon
Cream of Broccoli Soup with Bacon and Cheddar
Cream of Green Pea Soup with Prosciutto and Parmesan

HEARTY SOUPS CAN MAKE A SATISFYING one-dish meal. But for the busy cook, soups are often not an option—and when they are, their flavor often falls short because quick versions lack the depth and richness of the long-simmered original. Our goal was to develop recipes for soups that were both quick to prepare and intensely satisfying. We found that the key to developing richly flavored 30-minute soup is a well-designed flavor base, which begins with the broth.

A flavorful broth is essential for great tasting soup—be it quick or not. Homemade broth would obviously not be an option for 30-minute soup. We have used store-bought broth many times in the test kitchen and found that with a little doctoring, it is a perfectly acceptable shortcut. Enhancing store-bought broth involves simmering ingredients such as herbs, garlic, and aromatic spices in the broth. This step imparts a long-cooked flavor in a matter of minutes.

In addition to an enhanced broth, we experimented with other flavor-boosting ingredients, such as bacon, chipotle chiles, and rich spice mixes like garam masala—each adds a complex flavor boost in a short period of time. Almost every recipe in this chapter contains one or two of these flavor intensifiers.

In building delicious soup in 30 minutes, it became necessary for us to multi-task. While our doctored broth was brought to a simmer, we worked on prepping the other elements in our soup. We added ingredients that took almost 30 minutes to cook—such as potatoes, rice, and lentils—to the broth right away, so that they could start cooking along with the broth as it was brought to a boil. By doing so, we were able to use the full 30-minute cooking time to ensure that these ingredients were fully cooked and tender.

Used together, these ingredients and techniques allowed us the capacity and flexibility to create a number of "one pot meals" that taste like they've been simmering all day, even though they spend only 30 minutes on the stove. With some crusty bread and perhaps a wedge of cheese, these soups make a hearty meal any time of year.

CHICKEN SOUPS

MOST RECIPES FOR FAST HOMEMADE chicken soups are the same: chunks of chicken and vegetables are dumped into store-bought chicken broth and hastily boiled. This cooking method yields not only a weak-flavored broth but also dry, flavorless cubes of chicken. Our goal was twofold—to build a flavorful broth and to produce a variety of chicken soups with tender, flavorful pieces of chicken.

Addressing the bland broth was our first task. Since we were relying on canned broth, we had to find a way to augment its dull flavor. The answer was to simmer the broth with bay leaves and thyme. These two simple ingredients helped enliven the broth and lent it a homemade flavor. We also found it important to start simmering the doctored broth before anything else, so that the broth spends the maximum amount of time becoming infused with flavor.

Now that we had a flavorful broth, we focused on the chicken. Boneless skinless breasts were the obvious choice because of their short cooking time, but in our experience simply simmering cubes of meat in broth often leads to tough, dry nuggets of chicken. We avoided this problem by browning whole chicken breasts in the pot and then poaching them whole in the broth. Once the chicken was cooked through, we shredded it into bite-sized pieces and returned it to the broth. By cooking the chicken this way, we ensured that the chicken remained moist and tender. As an added benefit, we found that browning the chicken left behind flavorful browned bits. These bits, called fond, along with some caramelized onion, helped us build a complex and rich broth.

These techniques work with a whole range of similar chicken broth–based soups like Tortilla Soup and Mulligatawny Soup (see page 49). After the initial steps of building the broth, we found that we could alter the vegetables, noodles or rice, spices, and flavorings to create a host of soups that have long-simmered flavor in just 30 minutes.

Chicken Noodle Soup

SERVES 6

Use thin egg noodles in this soup because they cook more quickly and are easier to eat with a spoon.

6	cups low-sodium chicken broth
1	teaspoon fresh thyme, or 1/4 teaspoon dried
2	bay leaves
1	pound boneless, skinless chicken breasts
	Salt and ground black pepper
1	tablespoon vegetable oil
1	onion, minced
2	carrots, sliced 1/4 inch thick
1	celery rib, sliced 1/4 inch thick
4	ounces thin egg noodles (2 cups)
2	tablespoons minced fresh parsley

MAKING THE MINUTES COUNT:

While the chicken browns, prep the onion. While the onion browns, prep the carrots and celery.

1. HEAT BROTH MIXTURE: Bring broth, thyme, and bay leaves to boil, covered, in large saucepan and set aside.

2. SEASON AND BROWN CHICKEN: Meanwhile, pat chicken dry with paper towels, then season with salt and pepper. Heat oil in large Dutch oven over medium-high heat until just smoking. Add chicken and cook until lightly browned on both sides, about 5 minutes. Transfer chicken to plate.

3. BROWN ONION: Add onion and 1/2 teaspoon salt to fat left in Dutch oven and cook over medium-high heat until lightly browned, about 5 minutes.

4. ADD BROTH MIXTURE, VEGETABLES, AND CHICKEN: Turn heat to low and stir in hot broth mixture, scraping up any browned bits. Add carrots, celery, and browned chicken. Cook, covered, until chicken is cooked through and no longer pink in center, about 10 minutes.

5. REMOVE CHICKEN AND COOK NOODLES: Remove chicken from pot and stir in noodles. Increase heat to medium-high and cook until noodles are just tender, about 5 minutes.

6. SHRED CHICKEN AND FINISH: While noodles cook, shred chicken into bite-sized pieces. Off heat, remove bay leaves and stir in shredded chicken and parsley. Season with salt and pepper to taste and serve.

VARIATION

Chicken and Rice Soup

Omit egg noodles and add 1½ cups long-grain rice to pot with browned chicken in step 4. After removing chicken in step 5, increase heat to medium-high and cook until rice is tender, about 5 minutes.

Asian Chicken Noodle Soup

SERVES 6

Keep the bok choy greens and stalks separate after they've been prepped, because they are added to the soup at different times.

6	cups low-sodium chicken broth
1	(2-inch) piece ginger, chopped coarse
2	garlic cloves, chopped coarse
2	tablespoons dry sherry
2	tablespoons soy sauce
1	pound boneless, skinless chicken breasts
	Salt and ground black pepper
1	tablespoon vegetable oil
1	onion, minced
1	small head bok choy, greens sliced thin and stalks chopped medium
1	(3-ounce) bag ramen noodles, seasoning packet discarded
2	scallions, sliced thin

MAKING THE MINUTES COUNT:

While the chicken browns, prep the onion. While the onion browns, prep the bok choy.

> **TEST KITCHEN TIP:**
>
> **Tender Chicken**
>
> While poaching the browned chicken breasts has two advantages (a more flavorful broth and moister chicken), it's important to watch the simmering level. Don't let the broth simmer too vigorously or the chicken will toughen.

1. HEAT BROTH MIXTURE: Bring broth, ginger, garlic, sherry, and soy sauce to boil, covered, in large saucepan and set aside.

2. SEASON AND BROWN CHICKEN: Meanwhile, pat chicken dry with paper towels, then season with salt and pepper. Heat oil in large Dutch oven over medium-high heat until just smoking. Brown chicken lightly on both sides, about 5 minutes total. Transfer chicken to plate.

3. BROWN ONION: Add onion and ¼ teaspoon salt to fat left in Dutch oven and cook over medium-high heat until lightly browned, about 5 minutes.

4. ADD BROTH MIXTURE AND COOK: Turn heat to low and strain broth into Dutch oven, scraping up any browned bits. Add bok choy stalks and browned chicken. Cook, covered, until chicken is cooked through and no longer pink in center, about 10 minutes.

5. REMOVE CHICKEN AND ADD NOODLES: Remove chicken from the pot and stir in noodles. Increase heat to medium-high and cook until noodles are just tender, about 3 minutes.

6. SHRED CHICKEN AND FINISH: While noodles are cooking, shred chicken into bite-sized pieces. Stir in bok choy greens and cook until just wilted, about 1 minute. Off heat, stir in shredded chicken and scallions. Season with salt and pepper to taste and serve.

GOT EXTRA TIME?

If you've got an extra 15 minutes to spare, we found the chicken flavor in the soup tasted a little deeper when we substituted 2 split bone-in chicken breasts (about 12 ounces each), cut in half (see above), for the boneless, skinless chicken. Let them brown for an extra 3 minutes on the skin side in step 2, and let them simmer for an extra 12 minutes in step 4. Discard the skin and bones when shredding the meat in step 6.

Chicken Soup with Potatoes, Green Beans, and Leeks
SERVES 6

If using dried tarragon, place the full amount in with the broth in step 1. See page 66 for some tips on washing leeks.

6	cups low-sodium chicken broth
1	pound red potatoes (3 medium), cut into 1-inch chunks
1	tablespoon minced fresh tarragon, or 1 teaspoon dried
2	bay leaves
	Salt and ground black pepper
1	pound boneless, skinless chicken breasts
1	tablespoon vegetable oil
2	leeks, white and light green parts, halved lengthwise and sliced thin
6	garlic cloves, minced
2	cups frozen cut green beans

MAKING THE MINUTES COUNT:
Wash and slice the leeks while the chicken browns.

1. HEAT BROTH MIXTURE: Bring broth, potatoes, 1 teaspoon tarragon, bay leaves, and ½ teaspoon salt to boil, covered, in large saucepan. Reduce to simmer and continue to cook, covered, until needed in step 4.

2. SEASON AND BROWN CHICKEN: Meanwhile, pat chicken dry with paper towels, then season with salt and pepper. Heat oil in large Dutch oven over medium-high heat until just smoking. Add chicken and cook until lightly browned on both sides, about 5 minutes. Transfer chicken to plate.

3. ADD LEEKS AND GARLIC: Add leeks and ¼ teaspoon salt to fat left in Dutch oven and cook over medium-high heat until lightly browned, about 5 minutes. Stir in garlic and cook until fragrant, about 30 seconds.

4. ADD BROTH MIXTURE AND CHICKEN: Turn heat to low and stir in broth mixture, scraping up any browned bits. Add browned chicken, cover, and continue to cook until chicken is cooked through and no longer pink in center, about 10 minutes.

5. REMOVE CHICKEN AND ADD BEANS: Remove chicken from pot and stir in green beans. Increase heat to medium-high and cook until potatoes are tender, about 5 minutes.

6. SHRED CHICKEN AND FINISH: While potatoes are cooking, shred chicken into bite-sized pieces. Off heat, remove bay leaves and stir in shredded chicken and remaining 2 teaspoons tarragon. Season with salt and pepper to taste and serve.

Tortilla Soup
SERVES 6

Chipotle chiles, which are smoked jalapeños, can be found packed in adobo sauce in the international aisle of most supermarkets.

6	cups low-sodium chicken broth
I	pound boneless, skinless chicken breasts
	Salt and ground black pepper
I	tablespoon vegetable oil
I	onion, minced
I	tablespoon minced chipotle chiles in adobo sauce
2	teaspoons tomato paste
2	garlic cloves, minced
2	tablespoons fresh lime juice
4	ounces tortilla chips, crushed into large pieces (4 cups)
3	plum tomatoes, cored, seeded, and chopped
I	ripe avocado, pitted and cut into 1/2-inch cubes (see page 32)
1/2	cup fresh cilantro leaves

MAKING THE MINUTES COUNT:
Mince the onion while the chicken browns. Prepare the garnishes (tortilla chips, tomatoes, avocado, and cilantro) while the soup simmers.

I. HEAT BROTH: Bring broth to boil, covered, in large saucepan and set aside.

2. SEASON AND BROWN CHICKEN: Meanwhile, pat chicken dry with paper towels, then season with salt and pepper. Heat oil in large Dutch

oven over medium-high heat until just smoking. Add chicken and cook until lightly browned on both sides, about 5 minutes. Transfer chicken to plate.

3. BROWN ONION AND ADD SEASONINGS: Add onion and 1/2 teaspoon salt to fat left in Dutch oven and cook over medium-high heat until lightly browned, 3 to 5 minutes. Stir in chipotle, tomato paste, and garlic and cook until fragrant, about 1 minute.

4. ADD BROTH AND POACH CHICKEN: Turn heat to low and stir in hot broth, scraping up any browned bits. Add browned chicken. Cook, covered, until chicken is cooked through and no longer pink in center, about 10 minutes. Remove chicken from pot. Increase heat to medium-high and cook to meld flavors, 5 minutes.

5. SHRED CHICKEN, SEASON, AND FINISH: While soup is simmering, shred chicken into bite-sized pieces. Off heat, stir in lime juice and season with salt and pepper to taste. Divide tortilla chips, shredded chicken, tomatoes, and avocado among individual bowls. Ladle broth over each bowl, sprinkle with cilantro, and serve.

Mulligatawny Soup
SERVES 6

Mulligatawny is a highly spiced soup from southern India consisting of chicken and vegetables flavored with curry, ginger, and coconut.

6	cups low-sodium chicken broth
1/2	cup shredded unsweetened coconut
I	pound boneless, skinless chicken breasts
	Salt and ground black pepper
I	tablespoon vegetable oil
I	onion, minced
I	tablespoon grated fresh ginger
4	garlic cloves, minced
I	tablespoon curry powder
2	carrots, grated
I	very ripe banana, peeled and cut into 1-inch pieces
3/4	cup plain yogurt
2	tablespoons minced fresh cilantro

MAKING THE MINUTES COUNT:
Mince the onion and garlic and grate the ginger while the chicken browns.

1. HEAT BROTH MIXTURE: Bring broth and coconut just to boil, covered, in large saucepan and set aside.

2. SEASON AND BROWN CHICKEN: Meanwhile, pat chicken dry with paper towels, then season with salt and pepper. Heat oil in large Dutch oven over medium-high heat until just smoking. Add chicken and cook until lightly browned on both sides, about 5 minutes. Transfer chicken to plate.

3. BROWN ONION AND ADD SEASONINGS: Add onion and ½ teaspoon salt to fat left in Dutch oven and cook over medium-high heat until lightly browned, 3 to 5 minutes. Stir in ginger, garlic, and curry powder and cook until fragrant, about 1 minute.

4. ADD BROTH MIXTURE, CARROTS, AND BANANA; POACH CHICKEN: Turn heat to low and stir in hot broth mixture, scraping up any browned bits. Add carrots, banana, and browned chicken. Cook, covered, until chicken is cooked through and no longer pink in center, about 10 minutes.

5. REMOVE CHICKEN AND INCREASE HEAT: Remove chicken from pot. Increase heat to medium-high and cook until carrots are tender, about 5 minutes.

6. SHRED CHICKEN, PUREE SOUP, SEASON, AND GARNISH: While soup is simmering, shred chicken into bite-sized pieces. Puree soup in batches in blender until smooth. Return pureed soup to pot, stir in chicken, and return to brief simmer to heat through. Season with salt and pepper to taste. Dollop yogurt over individual bowls of soup, sprinkle with cilantro, and serve.

Thai Chicken and Coconut Soup

SERVES 6

Keep the bok choy greens and stalks separate after they've been prepped, because they are added to the soup at different times. If you prefer your soup less spicy, use the lesser amount of curry paste. For more information on fish sauce, see page 100. Be sure to use light coconut milk here, or the soup will be too rich.

INGREDIENTS: Supermarket Chicken Broth

Which chicken broth should you reach for when you haven't got time for homemade? We recommend choosing a mass-produced, lower-sodium brand and checking the label for evidence of mirepoix ingredients, such as carrots, celery, and onion. In a tasting of all the widely available brands, Swanson Certified Organic was a clear winner. And if you don't mind adding water, Better Than Bouillon Chicken Base came in a very close second and was the favorite of several tasters. Swanson's less expensive "Natural Goodness" Chicken Broth was just about as good as the winner, though some tasters thought it tasted "overly roasted."

Swanson Certified Organic Free Range Chicken Broth
Swanson's newest broth won tasters over with "very chickeny, straightforward, and honest flavors," a hearty aroma, and restrained "hints of roastiness."

Better Than Bouillon Chicken Base
We're not ready to switch to a concentrated base for all our broth needs (you have to add water), but the 18-month refrigerator shelf life means it's a good replacement for dehydrated bouillon.

Swanson "Natural Goodness" Chicken Broth
Swanson's standard low-sodium broth was full of chicken flavor, but several tasters noted an out-of-place overly roasted flavor.

4   cups low-sodium chicken broth

3   tablespoons fish sauce

1   tablespoon light brown sugar

1   pound boneless, skinless chicken breasts
    Salt and ground black pepper

1   tablespoon vegetable oil

2   tablespoons grated fresh ginger

3–4 teaspoons red curry paste

1   small head bok choy, greens sliced thin and
    stalks chopped medium

2   (14-ounce) cans light coconut milk

8   ounces sliced white mushrooms

3   tablespoons fresh lime juice

1/2 cup fresh cilantro leaves

MAKING THE MINUTES COUNT:
Prepare the ginger and bok choy while the chicken browns. Slice the mushrooms and prepare the garnishes while the soup simmers.

1. HEAT BROTH MIXTURE: Bring broth, fish sauce, and brown sugar to boil, covered, in large saucepan and set aside.

2. SEASON AND BROWN CHICKEN: Meanwhile, pat chicken dry with paper towels, then season with salt and pepper. Heat oil in large Dutch oven over medium-high heat until just smoking. Add chicken and cook until lightly browned on both sides, about 5 minutes. Transfer chicken to plate.

3. ADD SEASONINGS AND COOK: Add ginger, curry paste, and ½ teaspoon salt to fat left in Dutch oven and cook over medium heat until fragrant, about 1 minute.

4. ADD BROTH MIXTURE AND BOK CHOY STALKS; POACH CHICKEN: Turn heat to low and stir in hot broth mixture, scraping up any browned bits. Add bok choy stalks and browned chicken. Cook, covered, until chicken is cooked through and no longer pink in center, about 10 minutes. Remove chicken and set aside.

5. ADD COCONUT MILK AND MUSHROOMS: Stir in coconut milk and mushrooms. Increase heat to medium-high and cook until mushrooms soften slightly, about 5 minutes.

6. SHRED CHICKEN; ADD BOK CHOY GREENS, SEASON, AND FINISH: While soup is simmering, shred chicken into bite-sized pieces. Stir in bok choy greens and cook until wilted, about 1 minute. Off heat, stir in shredded chicken and lime juice. Season with salt and pepper to taste. Sprinkle bowls with cilantro leaves before serving.

TORTELLINI SOUP

TORTELLINI SOUP IS NATURALLY QUICK AND simple and features tortellini and greens (often spinach) gently simmered in chicken broth. The key to a really good tortellini soup is a rich broth, so when you're in a hurry and there is no time to make broth from scratch, infuse store-bought broth with as much flavor as possible.

The trick is to simmer the broth with some aromatics while you prepare the other ingredients, giving it time to become enriched with their flavors. Also, as with our Chicken Noodle Soup (see page 47), lightly browned onions provide some rich meaty flavor to the soup. The choice of tortellini and spinach also makes a big difference in this soup. Fresh tortellini (often found in the deli section of the supermarket) was much preferred over frozen tortellini. As for the spinach, while bagged, prewashed baby spinach was convenient, tasters found that a bunch of sturdier leaf spinach was a better option in terms of both texture and flavor.

Tortellini Soup
SERVES 6

Be sure to rinse the bunched spinach thoroughly of excess grit before adding it to the soup.

8   cups low-sodium chicken broth

1   teaspoon fresh thyme, or ¼ teaspoon dried

3   bay leaves

1   tablespoon vegetable oil

1   onion, minced
    Salt and ground black pepper

3   garlic cloves, minced

2   (9-ounce) packages fresh cheese tortellini

1   bunch flat-leaf spinach (1 pound), stemmed

MAKING THE MINUTES COUNT:
While the tortellini cooks, trim and rinse the spinach.

1. HEAT BROTH MIXTURE: Bring broth, thyme, and bay leaves to boil, covered, in large saucepan and set aside.

2. BROWN ONION: Meanwhile, heat oil in large saucepan over medium heat until shimmering. Add onion and ½ teaspoon salt, increase heat to medium-high, and cook until lightly browned and softened, about 5 minutes.

3. ADD GARLIC, BROTH MIXTURE, TORTELLINI, AND COOK: Stir in garlic and cook until fragrant, about 30 seconds. Stir in broth mixture, scraping up any browned bits. Add tortellini and cook until tender, 3 to 6 minutes.

4. ADD SPINACH AND SEASON: Stir in spinach and cook until wilted, about 2 minutes. Off heat, remove bay leaves, season with salt and pepper to taste, and serve.

CLAM CHOWDER

THE IDEA OF A QUICK CLAM CHOWDER using canned clams is nothing new. The problem is that most quick clam chowders are overly thick, sometimes gloppy; and even worse, they lack the sweet, briny flavor of clams. Instead, they taste like cream or milk and potatoes—and little else. To build a better chowder, we started with 4 cans of minced clams and 3 bottles of clam juice—a mixture that lends full-bodied clam flavor. To give the chowder a rounded flavor, we relied on a generous amount of bacon and a couple cloves of garlic. These full-flavored ingredients helped boost the chowder's flavor without adding substantial preparation or cooking time. Finishing the chowder with just a cup of cream smoothed out the clam flavor and gave the broth a silky texture, providing us with what we were looking for—a smooth, lush chowder that tastes distinctly of clams. We then turned to creating a fish chowder based on the same method, swapping cod for clams and adding white wine for brightness.

New England-Style Pantry Clam Chowder

SERVES 6 TO 8

Both canned clams and bottled clam juice are often salty, so be careful when seasoning the soup.

4	(6.5-ounce) cans minced clams
3	(8-ounce) bottles clam juice
1½	pounds red potatoes (5 medium), cut into ½-inch chunks
1	teaspoon fresh thyme, or ¼ teaspoon dried
2	bay leaves
4	slices bacon, chopped fine
1	onion, minced
	Salt and ground black pepper
2	garlic cloves, minced
¼	cup unbleached all-purpose flour
1	cup heavy cream
2	tablespoons minced fresh parsley

1. HEAT BROTH MIXTURE: Drain clams, reserving juice; set clams aside. Add bottled clam juice to reserved clam juice to measure 5 cups (if necessary, add water). Bring clam juice, potatoes, thyme, and bay leaves to boil, covered, in large saucepan. Reduce to simmer and continue to cook, covered, until needed in step 2.

2. COOK BACON AND ONION: Cook bacon in large Dutch oven over medium-high heat until fat is partially rendered, about 2 minutes. Add onion and ¼ teaspoon salt and continue to cook, stirring occasionally, until softened and slightly browned, about 8 minutes.

3. ADD GARLIC, FLOUR, AND BROTH MIXTURE: Stir in garlic and cook until fragrant, about 30 seconds. Stir in flour and cook until lightly

> **TEST KITCHEN TIP:**
> **Tender, Not Tough Clams**
> Canned minced clams can become tough and bland if simmered for an extended amount of time. To avoid this, we found it best to add the clams to the chowder at the end of the cooking time. Cooking the clams for just two minutes ensured that they remained tender and full of flavor.

browned, about 1 minute. Slowly stir in broth mixture, scraping up any browned bits. Bring to simmer and cook until potatoes are tender, 7 to 10 minutes.

4. ADD CLAMS, CREAM, AND SEASONINGS: Stir in clams, cream, and parsley. Return to simmer and cook for 2 more minutes. Off heat, remove bay leaves, season with salt and pepper to taste, and serve.

➤ VARIATION
Fish Chowder

Cod is the best choice of fish for this chowder, but any firm-fleshed white fish, such as haddock or hake, can be substituted.

Omit minced clams and add ½ cup white wine and 1 cup water to saucepan in step 1. Stir 1 pound of cod, cut into 1-inch cubes, into pot in step 4 and increase simmering time to 5 minutes.

QUICK CORN CHOWDER

TRADITIONAL CORN CHOWDERS REQUIRE the cook to shuck ears of corn, strip the kernels from the cobs, and then simmer the cobs in broth or milk before even lifting a finger to make the actual chowder itself. Admittedly, this process builds a lot of flavor, but it is also very time consuming. Could we build a flavorful corn chowder without these laborious steps? We had learned from our clam chowder that browned onions and bacon provide a flavorful start, but the real challenge was the corn flavor. Bags of frozen corn were the obvious starting point, but simply simmering the corn kernels in milk with a few

---

TEST KITCHEN TIP:
Corny But True
Most people think that all frozen vegetables taste the same. However, we find a big disparity between budget or store brands of corn and widely available national brands. While the national brands might cost a little more, we found their corn to be more consistent in taste and texture.

---

potatoes produced a runny chowder that lacked the desired richness as well as sweet corn flavor. After some testing, we discovered that a blender was the simple key to the best quick corn chowder. Processing half of the corn kernels with the milk produced a smooth, creamy mixture and let loose the intense flavor trapped in the kernels. This puree, along with the remaining kernels, resulted in a chowder with a wonderfully thick consistency and fresh corn flavor.

Quick Corn Chowder
SERVES 6 TO 8

3	cups low-sodium chicken broth
1	pound red potatoes (3 medium), cut into ½-inch chunks
1	teaspoon fresh thyme, or ¼ teaspoon dried
2	bay leaves
	Salt and ground black pepper
2	slices bacon, chopped fine
1	onion, minced
2	pounds frozen corn, thawed
1½	cups whole milk
2	garlic cloves, minced

MAKING THE MINUTES COUNT:
Process the corn in the blender while the onion and bacon brown.

1. HEAT BROTH MIXTURE: Bring broth, potatoes, thyme, bay leaves, and ½ teaspoon salt to boil, covered, in large saucepan. Reduce to simmer and continue to cook, covered, until needed in step 4.

2. COOK BACON: Cook bacon in large Dutch oven over medium-high heat until fat is partially rendered, about 2 minutes. Stir in onion and ¼ teaspoon salt and cook, stirring occasionally, until softened and slightly browned, about 8 minutes.

3. PUREE CORN: Meanwhile, puree half of corn with milk in food processor until smooth.

4. SAUTÉ GARLIC; ADD BROTH MIXTURE AND CORN PUREE: Stir garlic into Dutch oven and cook until fragrant, about 30 seconds. Stir in broth mixture and pureed corn, scraping up any browned bits. Bring to simmer and cook until potatoes are almost tender, about 5 minutes.

5. ADD CORN AND SEASON: Stir in remaining corn. Return to a simmer and cook until corn is warmed through and potatoes are tender, about 2 minutes. Off heat, remove bay leaves, season with salt and pepper to taste, and serve.

BLACK BEAN SOUP

TRADITIONAL BLACK BEAN SOUP IS TYPICAL of a long-simmered soup that delivers big flavor. The soup begins with dried beans that are usually soaked hours ahead of cooking. Then, the beans are simmered with a ham hock and aromatic vegetables like onion, garlic, and bell peppers. Next a sofrito—a combination of finely diced garlic, onion, and pepper—is slowly cooked down in a separate pot until the flavors are concentrated. The sofrito is added to the bean mixture and the soup is cooked further to allow the flavors to meld. How could we streamline this laborious soup?

First, we swapped spicy chorizo sausage for the ham hock and sautéed it to provide smoky, meaty flavor to the soup. This worked like a charm. Next we tried simmering drained and rinsed canned beans with sautéed chopped aromatics (we skipped the mincing to save on time), but the beans simply didn't absorb the vegetables' flavor. Stuck, we looked for a way to mince the vegetables quickly and thought of the food processor. The processed vegetables and their juices let off more flavor in a shorter period of time, cooked down more quickly, and yielded a far more intense flavor. In addition, we found it necessary to use a heavy hand with the garlic—a whopping 6 cloves for big flavor. And hauling out the food processor to mince the vegetables wasn't a big deal at all, considering it would be necessary to puree the beans. Oregano, cumin, cayenne, and Tabasco lent the soup requisite spice and heat while cilantro and a squeeze of lime brightened the flavors considerably.

Black Bean Soup
SERVES 6

Don't bother washing the food processor bowl or blade after processing the vegetables—you will need to use them again to puree the beans.

3	cups low-sodium chicken broth
6	ounces chorizo sausage, diced medium
1	onion, chopped coarse
1	red bell pepper, cored and chopped coarse
6	garlic cloves, chopped coarse
	Salt
4	(15-ounce) cans black beans, rinsed
1	cup water
1	tablespoon minced fresh oregano, or
	1 teaspoon dried
1/2	teaspoon ground cumin
1/2	teaspoon cayenne
1/2	cup minced fresh cilantro
	Tabasco sauce
2	limes, quartered (for serving)

1. HEAT BROTH: Bring broth to boil, covered, in large saucepan and set aside.

2. COOK CHORIZO: Meanwhile, cook chorizo in large Dutch oven over medium heat until browned and fat is rendered, about 5 minutes.

3. PROCESS AROMATICS: While chorizo cooks, pulse onion, bell pepper, and garlic in food processor until finely minced, 20 to 30 seconds, scraping down sides of bowl as needed.

4. COOK SOFRITO AND PUREE BEANS: Stir processed vegetables and 1/2 teaspoon salt into Dutch oven and cook until vegetables are dry and beginning to brown, 6 to 8 minutes. While vegetables cook, puree 4 cups of beans and water together in food processor until smooth.

5. TOAST SPICES, ADD BROTH AND BEANS, AND FINISH: Stir oregano, cumin, and cayenne into Dutch oven and cook until fragrant, about 1 minute. Stir in broth, pureed beans, and remaining whole beans. Bring to simmer and cook until whole beans have warmed through, about 5 minutes. Off heat, stir in cilantro and season with salt and Tabasco to taste. Serve with lime wedges.

WHITE BEAN SOUP

ITALIAN COOKING IS KNOWN FOR ITS straightforward simplicity. Tuscan White Bean Soup is a recipe that highlights this simplicity. With just a handful of ingredients, this soup traditionally relies on long cooking to build its flavor, and we knew that creating a flavorful white bean soup within our time limit would be a challenge. The key to a rich white bean soup was to bring the beans to simmer in a strongly flavored broth before we proceeded with anything else. This technique enabled the beans to absorb as much flavor from the broth as possible in just 30 minutes. It also helped to rid the beans of their "canned" flavor. We infused the broth with a plump sprig of rosemary and a couple of bay leaves, both robust tastes commonly found in Tuscan bean soups. Beyond simmering the beans in a flavorful broth, we liked the smokiness and sweetness that browned bacon and onions added—a must for this style of hearty bean soup. Also, a healthy dose of minced garlic provided a flavorful backdrop for the beans. To finish the dish, we drizzled each bowl with fruity extra-virgin olive oil for a hint of richness and a little balsamic vinegar to accent the beans' mild flavor.

Tuscan White Bean Soup

SERVES 6

We prefer the texture of small white beans in this soup. However, the more traditional cannellini beans can be substituted.

4	cups low-sodium chicken broth
3	(15.5-ounce) cans small white beans, rinsed
1	sprig fresh rosemary
2	bay leaves
	Salt and ground black pepper
4	slices bacon, chopped fine
1	tablespoon extra-virgin olive oil, plus extra for serving
1	onion, minced
4	garlic cloves, minced
2	tablespoons minced fresh parsley
	Balsamic vinegar

1. **HEAT BROTH MIXTURE:** Bring broth, beans, rosemary, bay leaves, and ½ teaspoon salt to boil, covered, in large saucepan and set aside.

2. **COOK BACON AND ONION:** Meanwhile, cook bacon and oil in large Dutch oven over medium-high heat until fat starts to render, about 2 minutes. Stir in onion and ¼ teaspoon salt and cook, stirring occasionally, until softened and slightly browned, about 8 minutes.

3. **ADD GARLIC AND BROTH MIXTURE:** Stir garlic into Dutch oven and cook until fragrant, about 30 seconds. Stir in broth mixture, scraping up any browned bits. Bring to a simmer and cook until beans are fully tender and flavors have melded, 15 minutes.

4. **ADD PARSLEY, SEASON, AND FINISH:** Stir in parsley. Off heat, remove bay leaves and rosemary sprig and season with salt and pepper to taste. Serve soup drizzled with olive oil and vinegar.

RED LENTIL SOUP

LENTILS ARE POPULAR IN QUICK-COOKING recipes because of their short cooking time and because they don't require soaking before cooking. Red lentils are our favorite for soup because unlike other types of lentils, they only take about 20 minutes to cook. Moreover, once cooked they form a smooth thick puree—perfect for a hearty, satisfying soup. To maximize the efficiency of this dish, it was necessary to start cooking the lentils before preparing anything else, allowing time to build a flavorful base, before marrying the broth and base together. When flavoring the soup, we kept in mind the lentil's popularity in India and used flavor combinations common to this cuisine. In addition to the staples of onion, ginger, and garlic, we also used garam masala, a spice blend consisting of coriander, cardamom, cumin, cinnamon, and cloves, which provides complex flavor without a lot of effort. Beyond the aromatics, the soup benefited from the addition of coconut milk. The fragrant milk adds a deep, rich flavor to the soup, helping to draw the other flavors together with a creamy texture and a slight sweetness.

Indian-Style Red Lentil Soup with Coconut

SERVES 6

Garam masala is a flavorful spice blend popular in Indian cooking. It can be quite mild, so if you prefer spicy foods add a pinch of cayenne. You can also make your own homemade garam masala blend—see our recipe at right.

4	cups low-sodium chicken broth
2	cups water
2	cups split red lentils
	Salt and ground black pepper
1	tablespoon vegetable oil
1	onion, minced
4	garlic cloves, minced
1	tablespoon grated fresh ginger
1½	teaspoons garam masala
1	(14-ounce) can light coconut milk
½	cup minced fresh cilantro
3	plum tomatoes, cored, seeded, and chopped coarse

MAKING THE MINUTES COUNT:

Mince the garlic and grate the ginger while the onion cooks. Prep the garnishes while the soup simmers.

TEST KITCHEN TIP:
Coconut Milk Versus Cream of Coconut

Make sure to purchase coconut milk, not cream of coconut—they are vastly different products. Coconut milk comes in regular and light versions. It is made from shredded coconut meat steeped in water, which is then strained, pressed and mashed to release as much liquid as possible. Cream of coconut is a sweet and thick concoction that is used in cocktails, not soups.

1. HEAT BROTH MIXTURE: Bring broth, water, lentils, and ½ teaspoon salt to boil, covered, in large saucepan. Reduce to simmer and continue to cook, covered, until needed in step 3.

2. COOK ONION: Meanwhile, heat oil in large saucepan over medium-high heat until shimmering. Add onion and ¼ teaspoon salt and cook until softened and lightly browned, 3 to 5 minutes.

GARAM MASALA

GARAM MASALA IS A UNIQUE SPICE BLEND customarily used in Indian cooking. While this spice mixture can be found in many supermarkets, its flavor varies widely—depending on the brand, it can include up to 12 different spices. We wanted to concoct our own homemade version to have on hand. Our goal was to pare back the mixture's many spices without losing its aromatic personality. Once we identified cardamom as garam masala's most prominent flavor, we narrowed down our choices to spices that were neither too sweet nor overly spicy. Just a few spices—cinnamon, cloves, coriander, and cumin—added the flavor elements we desired, creating a balanced, warm, and fragrant spice mixture.

Garam Masala

MAKES ABOUT ¼ CUP

1	tablespoon ground cinnamon
1	tablespoon ground cardamom
1	tablespoon ground coriander
1	tablespoon ground cumin
¼	teaspoon ground cloves

In a small bowl, mix spices together until evenly blended. The mixture can be stored in an airtight container for up to 1 month.

3. COOK AROMATICS; ADD BROTH MIXTURE AND COCONUT MILK: Stir in garlic, ginger, and garam masala and cook until fragrant, about 1 minute. Stir in broth mixture and coconut milk, scraping up any browned bits. Bring to a simmer and cook until lentils are tender and soup is thickened, about 15 minutes.

4. SEASON AND GARNISH: Off heat, stir in cilantro and season with salt and pepper to taste. Sprinkle individual bowls of soup with chopped tomatoes before serving.

MOROCCAN–STYLE CHICKPEA SOUP

IN THE PAST WE'VE TRIED A NUMBER OF recipes for quick vegetable soups and have always been disappointed. The soups are either thin and watery or they employ dozens of vegetables (and countless minutes of prep time) to create a muddy mish-mash of flavors. This was until we tried a Moroccan soup composed of chickpeas and vegetables in a spicy tomato broth. This soup, similar to *harira* (a traditional Moroccan meat and vegetable soup that is eaten during the holy month of Ramadan), is a complex and exotically flavored dish that appeared to be the vegetable-rich one-pot meal we were looking for. The real challenge that faced us was trying to replicate this soup using a limited amount of ingredients.

Chickpeas (canned, of course), canned diced tomatoes, and store-bought chicken broth along with onion and a substantial amount of garlic provided us with a good flavor base. To give the soup more texture and fresh vegetal flavor, we added some diced zucchini. The squash was easily prepared while the onions cooked and its mild, slightly sweet flavor paired well with the other ingredients in the soup. As for flavoring the soup, we tinkered with a number of different spices and settled on the trio of saffron, ginger, and cumin. The saffron lent the soup a distinct aroma and rich color, while the cumin and ginger add a pungent kick that would fool anyone into thinking this soup was cooked for hours.

Moroccan-Style Chickpea Soup
SERVES 6

This soup can be made vegetarian by substituting vegetable broth for the chicken broth. You can also substitute yellow summer squash for the zucchini, if desired.

3	cups low-sodium chicken broth
2	(15.5-ounce) cans chickpeas, rinsed
1	(14.5-ounce) can diced tomatoes
1/4	teaspoon saffron threads, crumbled
	Salt and ground black pepper
2	tablespoons unsalted butter
1	onion, minced
4	garlic cloves, minced
1/2	teaspoon ground ginger
1/2	teaspoon ground cumin
2	zucchini, cut into 1/2-inch pieces
2	tablespoons minced fresh cilantro
2	lemons, quartered (for serving)

MAKING THE MINUTES COUNT:
While the onion browns, prep the zucchini and cilantro.

1. HEAT BROTH MIXTURE: Bring broth, chickpeas, tomatoes, saffron, and 1/2 teaspoon salt to boil, covered, in large saucepan and set aside.

2. SAUTÉ ONION: Meanwhile, melt butter in large saucepan over medium-high heat. Stir in onion and 1/4 teaspoon salt and cook until softened and slightly browned, 3 to 5 minutes.

3. SAUTÉ AROMATICS; ADD BROTH MIXTURE AND ZUCCHINI: Stir garlic, ginger, and cumin into pan and cook until fragrant, about 30 seconds. Stir in broth mixture and zucchini, scraping up any browned bits. Bring to a simmer and cook until zucchini is tender, about 10 minutes.

4. SEASON: Stir in cilantro. Off heat, season with salt and pepper to taste. Serve with lemon wedges.

CREAM OF VEGETABLE SOUPS

WHEN IT COMES TO FULL VEGETABLE FLAVOR, most quick cream of vegetable soups miss the mark. Whether it's broccoli, pea, or asparagus, the soup's vegetable flavor is eclipsed by the cream. This blandness derives from the fact that most quick recipes for cream of vegetable soup employ frozen vegetables.

Admittedly, the idea of simply tearing open a bag of vegetables is attractive. But except for frozen peas, which work well in soup, the lack of flavor in other frozen vegetables disappointed us. Frozen vegetables also extended the cooking time (think about the effect of adding ice to boiling water). Instead, we learned that using fresh vegetables and coarsely chopping them into small pieces greatly improved the flavor while adding only a few minutes to the preparation time. The small chop of the vegetable kept the cooking time short, which in turn helped to preserve the fresh flavors of the vegetables.

Now that we had a soup base with a strong vegetable presence, we could focus on the ingredients that would support and accentuate the vegetables. Since we didn't want to overpower the soup's delicate taste, it was important to use mildly flavored ingredients. In the end, we relied on a combination of thyme, shallots, and a splash of white wine to round out the soup's flavor. We also found that the soup tasted fuller and better balanced with a combination of vegetable and chicken broth, as opposed to all vegetable or all chicken broth. This step made our cream of vegetable soup better than any we've tasted.

TEST KITCHEN TIP: A Smoother Soup

To ensure the smoothest soup, spend a minute to properly prepare your vegetables. If using broccoli, be sure to trim the fibrous exterior from the stems before chopping. If using asparagus, be sure to snap off the tough ends before chopping.

Preparing Broccoli For Soup

1. Place the head of broccoli upside down on a cutting board. Using a large knife, trim off the florets very close to their heads and chop coarsely.

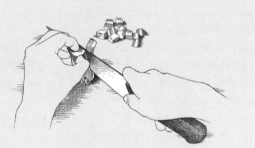

2. Stand each stalk up on the cutting board and square it off with a large knife to remove the outer ⅛ inch, which is quite tough. Cut the stalk in half lengthwise and chop coarsely.

Preparing Asparagus For Soup

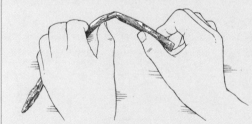

1. Remove just one asparagus spear from the bunch (leave the remaining bunch tied by the rubber bands), and snap off its tough end.

2. Using this piece of asparagus as a guide, trim off the remaining ends of asparagus in the bunch using a chef's knife. Remove rubber bands and chop coarsely.

Cream of Vegetable Soup

SERVES 6

This recipe can be made with broccoli, asparagus, or peas, but for best flavor, don't mix them.

2   cups low-sodium chicken broth
2   cups low-sodium vegetable broth
¼   cup white wine
1   teaspoon fresh thyme, or ¼ teaspoon dried
2   bay leaves
2   tablespoons unsalted butter
2   large shallots, minced
    Salt and ground black pepper
2   tablespoons all-purpose flour
2   pounds fresh broccoli or asparagus, chopped coarse, or 1½ pounds frozen peas
½   cup half-and-half

1. HEAT BROTH MIXTURE: Bring broths, wine, thyme, and bay leaves to boil, covered, in large saucepan.

2. SAUTÉ SHALLOTS: Meanwhile, melt butter in large saucepan over medium heat. Add shallots and ½ teaspoon salt and cook until softened, about 3 minutes. Stir in flour and cook for 1 minute.

3. ADD BROTH MIXTURE AND VEGETABLES: Slowly stir in broth mixture. Add vegetables, bring to simmer, and cook until vegetables are tender yet retain their green color, about 5 minutes. Remove bay leaves.

4. PUREE, FINISH, AND SEASON: Puree soup in batches in blender until smooth. Return pureed soup to pot and stir in half-and-half. Return soup to brief simmer, then remove from heat. Season with salt and pepper to taste and serve.

VARIATIONS

Cream of Asparagus Soup with Leek and Tarragon

Leeks can be very gritty—see page 66 for instructions on cleaning them.

2   cups low-sodium chicken broth
2   cups low-sodium vegetable broth
¼   cup white wine
2   bay leaves
2   tablespoons unsalted butter
1   leek, sliced thin
    Salt and ground black pepper
2   tablespoons all-purpose flour
2   pounds asparagus, chopped coarse
½   cup half-and-half
2   teaspoons minced fresh tarragon

1. HEAT BROTH MIXTURE: Bring broths, wine, and bay leaves to boil, covered, in large saucepan.

2. SAUTÉ LEEK: Meanwhile, melt butter in large sauce oven over medium heat. Add leek and ½ teaspoon salt and cook until softened, about 3 minutes. Stir in flour and cook for 1 minute.

3. ADD BROTH MIXTURE AND VEGETABLES: Slowly stir in broth mixture. Add asparagus, bring to simmer, and cook until tender and still green, about 5 minutes. Remove bay leaves.

4. PUREE, FINISH, AND SEASON: Puree soup in batches in blender until smooth. Return pureed soup to pot and stir in half-and-half. Return soup to brief simmer, then remove from heat. Stir in tarragon, season with salt and pepper to taste, and serve.

PUREEING SOUP SAFELY

Many vegetable soups are best pureed in a blender to create a smooth texture. Blending hot soup can be dangerous, though. To prevent mishaps, don't fill the blender jar past the halfway point, and hold the lid in place with a folded kitchen towel.

Cream of Broccoli Soup with Bacon and Cheddar

Because bacon is salty, you may not need to season the soup with additional salt.

2	cups low-sodium chicken broth
2	cups low-sodium vegetable broth
¼	cup white wine
1	teaspoon fresh thyme, or ¼ teaspoon dried
2	bay leaves
2	slices bacon, chopped fine
2	large shallots, minced
	Salt and ground black pepper
2	tablespoons all-purpose flour
2	pounds fresh broccoli, chopped coarse
1½	cups shredded cheddar cheese

1. HEAT BROTH MIXTURE: Bring broths, wine, thyme, and bay leaves to boil, covered, in large saucepan.

2. COOK BACON AND SAUTÉ SHALLOTS: Meanwhile, fry bacon in Dutch oven over medium-high heat until crisp, about 8 minutes. Leaving fat in pan, transfer bacon to paper towel–lined dish. Add shallots and ½ teaspoon salt to pan and cook until softened, about 3 minutes. Stir in flour and cook for 1 minute.

3. ADD BROTH MIXTURE AND BROCCOLI: Slowly stir in broth mixture. Add broccoli, bring to simmer, and cook until tender yet still green, about 5 minutes. Remove bay leaves.

4. PUREE, FINISH, AND SEASON: Puree soup in batches in blender until smooth. Return pureed soup to pot and stir in 1 cup cheddar cheese. Return soup to brief simmer, then remove from heat. Season with salt and pepper to taste. Sprinkle individual bowls with reserved bacon bits and remaining ½ cup cheddar cheese and serve.

THE SIMPLEST (AND FASTEST) GREEN SALAD

A GREEN SALAD IS THE PERFECT WAY TO round out any soup-based dinner. The following steps show the easiest way to make a green salad that takes no measuring or whisking, and virtually no time.

The Simplest Green Salad

Plan on about two cups of lightly packed greens per serving.

1. Pile washed and dried greens, torn into bite-sized pieces, into prepared bowl.

2. Holding your thumb over the mouth of the olive oil bottle to control flow, slowly drizzle greens with small amount of extra-virgin olive oil.

3. Toss greens very gently and repeat this drizzling and tossing as needed until greens are lightly coated and just glistening.

4. Finally, sprinkle greens with small amounts of vinegar, salt, and pepper and continue to toss gently until salad tastes just right. If you like, sprinkle in croutons—store bought or see our recipe on page 27.

KITCHEN SHORTCUT
GARLIC FLAVOR—FAST

The fastest way to add garlic flavor to your salad is to rub the bowl with a cut garlic clove before adding the greens.

Cream of Green Pea Soup with Prosciutto and Parmesan

Because prosciutto is salty, you may not need to season the soup with additional salt. If you like, garnish individual servings with Quick Homemade Croutons (page 27).

2	cups low-sodium chicken broth
2	cups low-sodium vegetable broth
1/4	cup white wine
1	teaspoon fresh thyme, or 1/4 teaspoon dried
2	bay leaves
1	tablespoon vegetable oil
2	ounces prosciutto, thinly sliced
2	large shallots, minced
	Salt and ground black pepper
2	tablespoons all-purpose flour
1 1/2	pounds frozen peas
1 1/4	cups finely grated Parmesan cheese

1. **HEAT BROTH MIXTURE:** Bring broths, wine, thyme, and bay leaves to boil, covered, in large saucepan.

2. **COOK PROSCIUTTO AND SAUTÉ SHALLOTS:** Meanwhile, heat oil and prosciutto in large saucepan over medium-high heat. Fry until crisp, about 8 minutes. Leaving fat in pan, transfer prosciutto to paper towel–lined dish. Add shallots and 1/2 teaspoon salt to pan and cook until softened, about 3 minutes. Stir in flour and cook for 1 minute.

3. **ADD BROTH MIXTURE AND VEGETABLES:** Slowly stir in broth mixture. Add peas, bring to simmer, and cook until peas are tender yet retain their green color, about 5 minutes. Remove bay leaves.

4. **PUREE, FINISH, AND SEASON:** Puree soup in batches in blender until smooth. Return pureed soup to pot and stir in 1 cup Parmesan. Return soup to brief simmer, then remove from heat. Season with salt and pepper to taste. Sprinkle individual bowls with reserved fried prosciutto bits and remaining 1/4 cup Parmesan and serve.

CURRIED CAULIFLOWER SOUP

AMONG VEGETABLE SOUPS, ONE OF OUR favorites is curried cauliflower. While not distinctly an Indian dish, this soup incorporates two popular ingredients in Indian cooking—curry and cauliflower. Once we had a successful cream of vegetable soup recipe, we figured we could easily substitute the cauliflower for the green vegetable and have a perfectly good soup. But when directly substituted, the denser cauliflower failed to cook within our 30-minute window. We solved this problem by adding the cauliflower to the broth before it was brought up to a simmer. Combining the cooking of the cauliflower with that of the broth gave the cauliflower a head start. By the time this mixture was added to the sautéed onion and spice mixture, the cauliflower only required a few minutes to simmer with the base of the soup.

We had a finished soup in the time required, but many tasters remarked that it tasted rather plain and unexciting. After some trial and error, we settled on a small amount of curry powder and ginger. In addition to the onion, the sweet pungent flavor of these two ingredients complemented the earthiness of the cauliflower. Finished with some tangy yogurt, this soup tasted as if it had come from our favorite Indian take-away.

Curried Cauliflower Soup
SERVES 6

If you buy cauliflower by the head, rather than bagged florets, you will need a 2½-pound head of cauliflower.

3	cups low-sodium chicken broth
1 1/2	pounds cauliflower florets, chopped coarse (5 cups—see note)
2	tablespoons unsalted butter
1	onion, minced
	Salt and ground black pepper
1	tablespoon grated fresh ginger
2	teaspoons curry powder
1/2	cup plain yogurt
1/2	cup whole milk
1	tablespoon minced fresh cilantro

1. **HEAT BROTH MIXTURE**: Bring broth and cauliflower to boil, covered, in large saucepan and set aside.

2. **SAUTÉ ONION**: Meanwhile, melt butter in large saucepan over medium heat. Add onion and ½ teaspoon salt and cook until softened, 3 to 5 minutes.

3. **SAUTÉ SPICES AND ADD BROTH MIXTURE**: Stir in ginger and curry powder and cook until fragrant, about 1 minute. Stir in broth mixture. Bring to simmer and cook until cauliflower is tender, 10 to 13 minutes.

4. **PUREE, FINISH, AND SEASON**: Puree soup in batches in blender until smooth. Return pureed soup to pot and stir in yogurt and milk. Return to brief simmer, then remove from heat. Season with salt and pepper to taste. Sprinkle with cilantro before serving.

CARROT GINGER SOUP

WE ENJOY THE SMOOTH, SILKY TEXTURE OF creamed carrot soup, but we often find the flavor lacking. This is especially true of quick carrot soups that, in the name of convenience, use those dry, tasteless "baby" carrots. Starting with fresh whole carrots, we set out to develop a flavorful yet quick carrot soup. Once we had discovered the secret of cream of cauliflower soup (cooking the vegetable in the broth), we easily transferred the technique to cream of carrot soup. As with the cauliflower soup, the major hurdle (other than shortening the cooking time) was to create a soup that had robust flavor. Carrots and ginger are a classic flavor combination, so ginger was a natural choice for deepening the flavor of this soup. Two tablespoons of grated fresh ginger provided the soup with a spicy punch while keeping the carrot flavor intact. In addition, we found that supplementing the milk with orange juice lent the soup a citrusy freshness that other quick soups often lack.

EQUIPMENT: Large Saucepans

In the test kitchen (and at home), most of us reach for a 3- to 4-quart saucepan more than any other because its uses go beyond boiling water. Which begs an obvious question: Does the brand of pan matter? In order to answer this question, we tested eight models, all between three and four quarts in size, from well-known cookware manufacturers.

The tests we performed were based on common cooking tasks and designed to highlight specific characteristics of the pans' performance. Sautéing minced onions illustrated the pace at which the pan heats up and sautés. Cooking white rice provided a good indication of the pan's ability to heat evenly as well as how tightly the lid sealed. Making pastry cream showed us how user-friendly the pan was—was it shaped such that a whisk could reach into the corners without trouble, was it comfortable to pick up, and could we pour liquid from it neatly? These traits can make a real difference when you use a pan day in and day out.

While none of the pans failed these tests outright, we found that pans that were sturdily constructed and had a solid heft for even heat distribution performed the best. We also found that overall weight made a difference. Heavier pans protect against burning and lighter pans require closer monitoring to prevent scorching. The ideal was about three pounds; pans near this weight balanced cooking efficiency with easy maneuverability.

So which pan should you buy? That depends largely on two things: your budget and your attention span. Based on our tests, we'd advise against really inexpensive pans—those that cost less than $50. For between $50 and $100, you can get a competent pan such as the Sitram. The only caveat is that you may have to watch them carefully; they offer less room for error than our favorite pan, made by All-Clad.

The Best Large Saucepan

The All-Clad Stainless Steel Saucepan (left) took top honors but, at $150, it was on the pricey side. The Sitram Profiserie Stainless Steel Saucepan (right) costs about $50 and worked nearly as well as the All-Clad.

Carrot Ginger Soup

SERVES 6

3	cups low-sodium chicken broth
1½	pounds carrots, peeled and chopped coarse (5 cups)
2	tablespoons unsalted butter
1	onion, minced
	Salt and ground black pepper
2	tablespoons grated fresh ginger
¾	cup whole milk
¼	cup orange juice
1	tablespoon minced fresh chives

1. **HEAT BROTH MIXTURE:** Bring broth and carrots to boil, covered, in large saucepan and set aside.

2. **SAUTÉ ONION:** Meanwhile, melt butter in large saucepan over medium heat. Add onion and ½ teaspoon salt and cook until softened, 3 to 5 minutes.

3. **SAUTÉ GINGER AND ADD BROTH MIXTURE:** Stir in ginger and cook until fragrant, about 1 minute. Stir in broth mixture. Bring to simmer and cook until carrots are tender, 10 to 13 minutes.

4. **PUREE SOUP, FINISH, AND SEASON:** Puree soup in batches in blender until smooth. Return pureed soup to pot and stir in milk and orange juice. Return to brief simmer, then remove from heat. Season with salt and pepper to taste. Sprinkle with chives before serving.

CREAM OF TOMATO SOUP

MAKING CREAM OF TOMATO SOUP IN LESS than 30 minutes is no problem—simply open a can, heat, and serve. But if you want a flavorful cream of tomato soup (rather than the tinny-flavored, overly sweet variety), time is definitely an issue. In the past, when making cream of tomato soup, we found it's important to roast whole canned tomatoes to rid them of excess water and intensify their flavor. (Think of the flavor difference between a fresh tomato and a sun-dried tomato and you'll understand what we're talking about.) The problem is that this one step takes 30 minutes. Still wanting to rid our tomatoes of excess juices, but not having the time to roast them, we turned to sautéing them. We began by sautéing canned diced tomatoes (instead of whole tomatoes to save on time) along with minced onion. This step gave the tomatoes a chance to dry out and begin to caramelize, which in turn gave the soup the intense tomato flavor we wanted. A touch of brown sugar and tomato paste also helped deepen the tomato flavor. To finish the soup, we called on a splash of sherry and a pinch of cayenne. These two ingredients gave the soup a lively note. In all, a few simple steps added only minutes to the preparation and cooking times, but the results were immeasurable.

Cream of Tomato Soup

SERVES 6

Serve Cheese Toasts (page 64) with this soup.

3	(14.5-ounce) cans diced tomatoes
3	cups low-sodium chicken broth
2	bay leaves
2	tablespoons unsalted butter
1	onion, minced
1	tablespoon light brown sugar
1	tablespoon tomato paste
	Salt
2	tablespoons all-purpose flour
½	cup heavy cream
2	teaspoons dry sherry
	Pinch of cayenne

1. **HEAT BROTH MIXTURE:** Drain tomatoes, reserving juice. Add broth to reserved tomato juice to measure 5 cups (if necessary, add water). Bring broth mixture and bay leaves to boil, covered, in large saucepan and set aside.

2. **SAUTÉ TOMATO MIXTURE:** Meanwhile, melt butter in large Dutch oven over high heat. Add drained tomatoes, onion, brown sugar, tomato

paste, and ½ teaspoon salt, and cook until tomatoes are dry and beginning to brown, 11 to 13 minutes. Stir in flour and cook for 1 minute.

3. ADD BROTH MIXTURE: Slowly stir in broth mixture. Bring to simmer and cook for 5 minutes. Remove bay leaves.

4. PUREE, FINISH, AND SEASON: Puree soup in batches in blender until smooth. Return pureed soup to pot and stir in cream and sherry. Return to brief simmer, then remove from heat. Season with salt and cayenne to taste and serve.

CHEESE TOASTS

NOTHING GOES BETTER WITH A BOWL OF cream of tomato soup (or any soup for that matter) than a grilled cheese sandwich. We admit grilled cheese sandwiches don't take very long to prepare, but we've come up with an even quicker interpretation. Our cheese toasts are essentially open-faced grilled cheese sandwiches that are made under the broiler while the soup simmers away on the stovetop.

In addition to their simplicity, cheese toasts can also be easily varied. Any good melting cheese can be used; our favorites are cheddar, colby, and Swiss. Also, before sprinkling with cheese, try spreading the bread with whole-grain mustard or adding slices of tomato, strips of roasted red pepper, or thin slices of ham or turkey.

For cheese toasts, brown ½-inch-thick slices of hearty bread on both sides under a preheated broiler, 1 to 2 minutes per side. Sprinkle each toast with ⅓ cup of your favorite shredded cheese. Return the toast to the broiler and cook until the cheese is melted and bubbly, 2 to 4 minutes.

PASTA E FAGIOLI

PASTA E FAGIOLI IS A RUSTIC BEAN AND PASTA soup made throughout Italy. Most recipes call for dozens of ingredients to lend a full flavor, including dried beans, which are notoriously long-cooking and sometimes need to be soaked for hours ahead of time. Our challenge for a quick pasta e fagioli was to infuse quick-cooking canned beans with flavor and to pare back the often-daunting ingredient list to the essentials—without any loss in flavor. After rinsing the beans to rid them of any tinny taste, we brought them to a simmer with the broth, tomatoes, and aromatics such as bay leaves and oregano. This served a double purpose, flavoring both the broth and the beans. It also gave us time to cook the bacon, onion, and garlic in a separate pan and add their juices and tasty browned bits to the soup. Chopped carrots and frozen cut green beans rounded out the vegetable elements, and a small-shaped pasta like ditalini enriched and thickened our soup. And a few gratings of Parmesan cheese just before serving finished this hearty, flavorful meal.

FASTEST DINNER ROLLS

WHILE THERE ARE MANY BRANDS OF "brown and serve" rolls at the market, we've always been put off by their unpronounceable ingredients and disappointed by their artificial flavors. The answer to our predicament was prepared pizza dough. Many supermarkets and pizzerias sell their dough for just a few dollars a pound and the dough can be easily frozen. Using prepared pizza dough, you can shape and bake fresh rolls that taste like homemade in a matter of minutes.

Cut one pound of dough into 8 even pieces and roll each into a ball. Arrange the rolls on a well-oiled baking sheet. Brush the top of each roll lightly with extra-virgin olive oil, and sprinkle with ½ teaspoon salt and ½ teaspoon ground black pepper. Bake at 400 degrees until golden brown, about 20 minutes. Cool 5 minutes on a wire rack.

Pasta e Fagioli
SERVES 6

Ditalini, orzo, and stellini are all small pastas that would work well in this soup.

6   cups low-sodium chicken broth
1   (19-ounce) can cannellini beans, rinsed
1   (14.5-ounce) can diced tomatoes, drained
2   bay leaves
2   teaspoons minced fresh oregano, or ½ teaspoon dried
    Salt and ground black pepper
4   slices bacon, chopped fine
1   onion, minced
4   garlic cloves, minced
2   carrots, chopped fine
½   cup small pasta, any shape (see note)
1   cup frozen cut green beans
    Grated Parmesan cheese (for serving)

MAKING THE MINUTES COUNT:
Mince the onion while the bacon cooks. Chop the carrot while the onion cooks.

1. HEAT BROTH MIXTURE: Bring broth, beans, tomatoes, bay leaves, oregano, and ½ teaspoon salt to boil, covered, in large saucepan and set aside.

2. COOK BACON AND ONION: Meanwhile, cook bacon in large saucepan over medium-high heat until fat is partially rendered, about 2 minutes. Stir in onion and ¼ teaspoon salt and cook until softened and slightly browned, about 8 minutes.

3. ADD GARLIC, BROTH MIXTURE, CARROTS, AND PASTA: Stir in garlic and cook until fragrant, about 30 seconds. Stir in broth mixture, carrots, and pasta. Bring to simmer and cook until carrots and pasta are tender, 9 to 11 minutes.

4. ADD GREEN BEANS AND SEASON: Stir in green beans and cook until heated through, about 2 minutes. Off heat, remove bay leaves and season with salt and pepper to taste. Serve, passing grated Parmesan separately.

RUSTIC POTATO LEEK SOUP

MOST PEOPLE THINK OF POTATO LEEK SOUP in its more formal guise of vichyssoise, a creamy French classic made with potatoes and leeks that is pureed and served cold. We found a number of recipes for quick vichyssoise but they invariably suffered from two problems. The first was a lack of leek flavor. These soups were more akin to thin mashed potatoes with some leeks thrown in as a garnish. The second problem was that these quick potato leek soups were too refined. That might be okay when you're serving soup as a first course (with more courses to follow), but we wanted our soup to be the main event—thick and satisfying.

To start we cooked down 3 pounds of leeks in a covered pot until they were meltingly tender with a sufficient concentration of sweet onion flavor. We left the leeks in fairly large pieces in order to create a soup with more textural interest. For the potato component, we favored red-skinned potatoes. The red potatoes held their texture better than other varieties of potatoes and didn't become waterlogged during cooking. To make the soup heartier, we also increased the amount of potatoes. Our final step was to mash some of the potatoes against the side of the pot before serving in order to give the soup a more substantial texture. With more potatoes and a chunky texture, this soup makes a tasty, satisfying dinner.

Rustic Potato Leek Soup
SERVES 6

5   cups low-sodium chicken broth
1½   pounds red potatoes (4 to 5 medium), cut into ½-inch chunks
1   teaspoon fresh thyme, or ¼ teaspoon dried
2   bay leaves
    Salt and ground black pepper
4   tablespoons unsalted butter
3   pounds leeks (8 medium), white and light green parts, halved and sliced thin
2   garlic cloves, minced

MAKING THE MINUTES COUNT:
Be sure to prep the leeks before you begin cooking. See instructions below.

I. HEAT BROTH MIXTURE: Bring broth, potatoes, thyme, bay leaves, and ½ teaspoon salt to boil, covered, in large saucepan. Reduce to simmer and continue to cook, covered, until needed in step 3.

2. COOK LEEKS AND GARLIC: Meanwhile, melt butter in large Dutch oven over medium-high heat. Stir in leeks, garlic, and ¼ teaspoon salt, cover, and cook until leeks are wilted and softened, about 10 minutes.

3. ADD BROTH MIXTURE: Stir in broth mixture. Bring to simmer and cook until potatoes are tender, 4 to 7 minutes.

4. FINISH AND SEASON: Off heat, remove bay leaves and mash some potatoes against side of pot to thicken soup to desired consistency. Season with salt and pepper to taste and serve.

TEST KITCHEN TIP:

A Better Mushroom

For Mushroom and Rice Soup, we prefer cremini mushrooms, which are immature portobellos, because they have a more intense flavor and slightly denser texture than the more commonly available white button mushroom. If creminis are unavailable, you can substitute white mushrooms. The soup, however, will have slightly less flavor.

MUSHROOM AND RICE SOUP

MUSHROOM AND BARLEY SOUP IS A popular soup that is often overlooked by home cooks because most quick versions lack any sort of convincing mushroom flavor. Our task was to solve this lack of flavor while creating a hearty "meal in a pot" soup.

We tried dozens of ingredients and found the key to building the mushroom flavor was threefold. First we sautéed the mushrooms with the onion until they were dry and beginning to brown. This rid the mushrooms of their high moisture content and concentrated their flavor. Second, we steeped dried porcinis in the broth. One-quarter of an ounce of dried mushrooms developed as much deep mushroom flavor as a basketful of fresh mushrooms and complemented the flavor of the fresh ones. Third, we added a healthy dose of soy sauce to reinforce the mushroom flavor and give the broth a deep brown hue.

Now that we had developed a soup with a strong mushroom flavor, we could focus on the barley component. No matter what we tried, the cooking time for the barley surpassed our time limit, but we liked the idea of a grain to round out the soup. Eschewing barley, we made the soup with a number of regular and quick-cooking grains and settled on long-grain rice. Like barley, the rice gave the soup body and made for a very satisfying and quick meal.

KITCHEN SHORTCUT: PREPARING LEEKS

1. Trim and discard the roots and the dark green leaves.

2. Slice the trimmed leek in half lengthwise, then cut it into ½-inch pieces.

3. Rinse the cut leeks thoroughly to remove dirt and sand.

Mushroom and Rice Soup
SERVES 6

6   cups low-sodium chicken broth
½   cup long-grain rice
2   tablespoons soy sauce
¼   ounce dried porcini mushrooms, rinsed (see illustrations on page 4) and minced
2   bay leaves
2   teaspoons fresh thyme, or ¼ teaspoon dried
    Salt and ground black pepper
2   tablespoons unsalted butter
1   onion, minced
1   pound cremini mushrooms, quartered
2   carrots, chopped medium

MAKING THE MINUTES COUNT:
Prep the carrots while the mushrooms cook.

1. **HEAT BROTH MIXTURE:** Bring broth, rice, soy sauce, dried porcini, bay leaves, thyme, and ¼ teaspoon salt to boil, covered, in large saucepan. Reduce heat and simmer until needed in step 2.

2. **COOK ONION AND MUSHROOMS:** Meanwhile, melt butter in large Dutch oven over high heat. Add onion, cremini mushrooms, and ¼ teaspoon salt and cook until all moisture has evaporated and mushrooms begin to brown, about 10 minutes.

3. **ADD BROTH MIXTURE AND CARROTS:** Stir in broth mixture and carrots, and bring to simmer. Cook until carrots and rice are tender, 7 to 10 minutes. Off heat, remove bay leaves, season with salt and pepper to taste, and serve.

⏱ GOT EXTRA TIME?

If you have extra time you can easily turn this soup into traditional mushroom barley soup. Simply substitute ½ cup of pearl barley for the long-grain rice and increase the chicken broth to 7 cups. Let the soup simmer an additional 15 minutes in step 3.

CALDO VERDE

CALDO VERDE IS A HEARTY PORTUGUESE soup made with greens, potatoes, and sausage. While this soup has readily assimilated into the world of quick-cooking soups, most versions are, on average, pretty bad. The problem is that when this soup is made quickly it tastes of its individual components and not like a cohesive and melded whole.

To make our soup flavorful, we started the potatoes in the broth with bay leaves and oregano. This allowed the potatoes to absorb the flavor of these pungent herbs as they cooked. While the broth simmered with the potatoes, we built the soup's base with onion and a lot of garlic. After combining the broth and potato mixture with the aromatic base, we added the kale and chorizo and let these ingredients simmer together. This simmering time brought out the spicy, garlicky flavors of the chorizo and the slightly sweet cabbage flavor of the kale. Because these central ingredients simmered together for the entire cooking time, the soup developed the deepest possible flavor in the shortest amount of time.

Caldo Verde
SERVES 6

Linguiça, a Portuguese pork sausage made with garlic and paprika, is traditional in this recipe. We, however, preferred the bold spicy flavor of chorizo. That said, if you cannot find chorizo, linguiça or smoked kielbasa can be substituted in a pinch.

6   cups low-sodium chicken broth
1   pound red potatoes (3 medium), cut into 1-inch chunks
1   teaspoon fresh minced oregano, or ¼ teaspoon dried
2   bay leaves
    Salt and ground black pepper
1   tablespoon olive oil
1   onion, minced
4   garlic cloves, minced
8   ounces chorizo sausage, sliced ¼ inch thick
1   bunch kale, stemmed, leaves shredded ¼ inch wide

MAKING THE MINUTES COUNT:
Prep the chorizo and kale while the onion cooks.

1. HEAT BROTH-POTATO MIXTURE: Bring broth, potatoes, oregano, bay leaves, and ½ teaspoon salt to boil, covered, in large saucepan. Reduce to simmer and continue to cook, covered, until needed in step 3.

2. COOK ONION: Meanwhile, heat oil in large saucepan over medium-high heat until shimmering. Add onion and ¼ teaspoon salt and cook until softened, 3 to 5 minutes.

3. ADD GARLIC, BROTH-POTATO MIXTURE, CHORIZO, AND KALE: Stir in garlic and cook until fragrant, about 30 seconds. Stir in broth mixture, chorizo, and kale, and bring to simmer. Cook until potatoes are tender, 7 to 10 minutes.

4. THICKEN AND SEASON: Off heat, remove bay leaves and mash some potatoes against side of pot to thicken soup to desired consistency. Season with salt and pepper to taste and serve.

FREEZING SOUPS IN SINGLE-SERVING PORTIONS

If you happen to have leftover soup, freeze it in easy-to-microwave single-serving portions.

Set out as many 10- or 12-ounce paper cups (for hot beverages) as you need and fill each with a portion of cooled soup (but not all the way to the top). Label, wrap in plastic wrap, and freeze each cup. Whenever you want a quick cup of soup, remove a cup from the freezer and microwave until hot.

TEST KITCHEN TIP:
Storing and Reheating Soups

While most soups can be cooled, then reheated without harm, some will suffer, especially in terms of texture. Soups with rice, pasta, and potatoes are best eaten immediately; when refrigerated, these ingredients become mushy and bloated as they absorb the liquid in the soup. Typically, soups with seafood also fail to hold up well when stored. For instance, clams will almost always overcook and become tough when reheated. Anticipate serving seafood soups as soon as they are done. And, pureed soups made from green vegetables will look their best if served immediately upon completion. Reheating breaks down the chlorophyll in some green vegetables (asparagus is especially prone to this problem). A soup that is bright green can turn drab army green if stored for several hours and then reheated. These soups will still taste delicious, but their visual appeal will be greatly diminished.

For those soups that can be stored and reheated without any loss in flavor and texture, there are a few things to keep in mind. Cool the soup to lukewarm and refrigerate (or freeze) promptly in an airtight container (or see our tip at left for freezing single-serving portions). When ready to serve, reheat only as much soup as you need at that time. You can reheat soup in the microwave or in a covered saucepan set over medium-low heat. Because the microwave heats unevenly, this method is best for single servings. Just heat the soup right in the cup, serving bowl, or mug. Larger quantities of soup are best reheated on the stovetop.

You may find that the soup has thickened in the refrigerator or freezer. (As soups cool, liquid evaporates in the form of steam.) Simply thin out the soup with a little water to achieve the proper texture.

4

RETHINKING BRAISES, STEWS, AND CHILIS

Rethinking Braises, Stews, and Chilis

STEWS, BRAISES, AND SIMILAR LONG-cooking dishes like curries and chilis might seem out of place in a quick-cooking book. After all, these dishes rely on a slow simmer over low heat to tenderize tough cuts of meat like beef chuck and pork shoulder or to develop complex flavors. While we knew that we couldn't make a traditional stew in under 30 minutes, we wondered if we could mimic what's so appealing about them: tender chunks of meat and well-flavored vegetables in a rich, well-seasoned sauce.

From the outset, we knew we'd need to choose cuts of meat that would cook in our 30-minute time limit. Chicken was one obvious choice so we tackled recipes such as white chicken chili and maque choux (the Cajun corn and bell pepper stew), where chicken breasts are shredded after being cooked and then returned to the pot to soak up the flavorful broths. Chicken thighs, however, proved a challenge. Many stews rely on the rich flavor and moist texture of chicken's dark meat, but we found it impossible to cook chicken thighs in under 30 minutes—until we thought of the microwave. We used the microwave to partially cook the thighs, then we finished them on the stovetop. This was just the jump start we needed to produce a host of richly flavored chicken stews.

And we didn't just limit our stews and braises to chicken. Cubes of pork tenderloin worked very well in our pozole, which is traditionally made with pork shoulder. We also developed another pork stew in the French style, with prunes, brandy, and cream, as well as an interpretation of the spicy Indian dish, pork vindaloo.

What about beef? Yes, we were able to make a spicy, well-seasoned ground beef chili, but when it came to beef stew, we made a decision not to include a recipe. Sure, other quick cookbooks have made 30-minute beef stews, but most of them rely on beef tenderloin. Traditionally, beef stew (to serve 6 to 8) is made with 3 pounds of beef chuck at about $5 per pound—about $15 altogether. Swapping in beef tenderloin at $15 per pound (and that's on the low end of the price scale) elevated the cost of our Tuesday night dinner to a grand total of $45! We could have used less meat and more vegetables, but then it's just not beef

stew anymore. Instead, if you have a hankering for tender pieces of beef in a rich gravy, see our recipe in Skillet Suppers for Skillet Beef Pot Pie. Because beef pot pie has a pastry crust and traditionally contains lots of vegetables, we were able to use just one pound of tenderloin, making it a more reasonable choice for a weeknight meal.

We also included fish stews in this chapter. Even though fish is naturally quick cooking, we have been disappointed time and time again by the weak flavors of so many fish stews. We incorporated lively additions like tomatoes, fennel, garlic, olives, and peppers that not only complement the flavor of the fish, but are also delicious soaked up with bread or spooned over rice.

In addition to choosing the right ingredients for our dishes, we found technique equally important to their success. The deep flavor of so many stews and braises is attained through slow cooking; therefore, it was more important than ever to maximize our 30-minute cooking time. One approach involves simply doubling our pots—which essentially resulted in halving our cooking time. This technique was essential to our beef chili. By using two pots, we were able to build a rich, flavorful tomato-bean broth in one, while we cooked the aromatics and beef in another. Sure there's an extra pot to wash, but once you taste the layers of flavor in this chili, you'll be hooked. We successfully applied this same method to shrimp and sausage gumbo by cooking the roux, the foundation of gumbo, in one pot, while we handled the sausage and vegetables in another.

As we've done throughout this book, we've chosen ingredients that minimize the work for the cook, such as flavorful store-bought curry paste in our Thai red curry and smoky chipotle chiles in adobo sauce for our chilis. And in order to achieve complex flavor in a short time, we weren't shy about using boldly flavored ingredients like garlic, olives, bacon, and sausage.

Because the recipes in this chapter go so well with starchy side dishes, we've provided a few recipes for those, too. We show you how to add flavor and character to normally bland quick-cooking couscous and instant polenta, as well as how to successfully cook long-grain white rice in the microwave.

CHICKEN BRAISES

BRAISING IS A MOIST-HEAT COOKING METHOD that involves slowly simmering meat in liquid. Most braises start with tough but flavorful pieces of meat that are browned and then simmered for hours in liquid until they're meltingly tender with concentrated flavor. While we couldn't shorten braising time for tough pieces of meat, we could apply the method to more tender meat, like chicken, to elicit the most concentrated flavor in a shorter amount of time.

We began by testing a variety of chicken parts. Whole chicken breasts, both boneless and bone-in, weren't as moist and flavorful as we would have liked for a braise. Bone-in thighs cooked evenly and tasted moist and rich, but they exceeded our time constraints. Boneless thighs were quicker and brought the same texture and flavor, but the cooking time still exceeded our 30-minute mark. We were determined to make this chicken braise work, and if we could do it, flavorful, boneless thighs would be our meat of choice.

We admit that we were a bit stymied at how to reduce the cooking time. We couldn't simmer the meat more briskly—it would toughen if we did so. With no other traditional cooking options in sight, we thought of the microwave. If we skipped browning the meat, and instead used that time in the microwave to get a jump start on the braise, maybe we could make this dish work. It was important for us to cover the chicken with plastic wrap so that it didn't dry out. After trying a variety of powers and cooking times, we found that 50 percent power for 15 minutes gave us what we were looking for. There was, however, one drawback to using the microwave: We lost the flavorful bits that are created when browning the chicken. To replace this flavor, we sautéed the aromatics in the pot we would be using for the braise while the chicken cooked in the microwave. We also found that browning a slice of diced bacon with the aromatics added the deep meaty flavor we lost by not browning the meat.

Once the chicken was out of the microwave, it was time for the actual braise. For the cooking liquid we chose both wine and chicken broth, which together produced the most concentrated flavor. A little flour helped thicken the liquid into a savory sauce that clung to the chicken. Some braises contain vegetables (in addition to aromatics like onions and garlic), and we found that we could easily change them as well as other flavor components depending on the dish.

30-Minute Chicken Provençal

SERVES 4

Chicken Provençal is a rustic French dish of chicken simmered with tomatoes, garlic, herbs, and olives. Serve this braise with soft polenta, rice, or crusty bread. Note that the dish of chicken will be very hot coming out of the microwave—be sure to set it on a clean, dry surface or trivet, and be careful of hot steam when removing the plastic wrap.

2	pounds boneless, skinless chicken thighs
	Salt and ground black pepper
1	slice bacon, minced
1	tablespoon vegetable oil
1	onion, minced
4	garlic cloves, minced
2	tablespoons unbleached all-purpose flour
1/2	cup dry white wine
1/2	cup low-sodium chicken broth
1	(14.5-ounce) can diced tomatoes
1	tablespoon minced fresh oregano, or
	1 teaspoon dried
1/2	cup pitted Kalamata olives, chopped coarse
2	tablespoons minced fresh parsley

MAKING THE MINUTES COUNT:
Immediately start the chicken in the microwave, then mince the bacon and onion. Measure out the flour, wine, and broth while the bacon and onion cook.

1. MICROWAVE CHICKEN: Season chicken with salt and pepper and arrange in single layer in microwave-safe casserole dish following illustration on page 75. Cover tightly with plastic wrap and microwave on 50 percent power for 15 minutes.

2. SAUTÉ BACON AND AROMATICS: While chicken cooks, sauté bacon with oil in large Dutch oven over medium-high heat until bacon fat begins to render, about 2 minutes. Stir in onion and ¼ teaspoon salt and cook until softened, about 5 minutes. Stir in garlic and cook until fragrant, about 30 seconds.

3. BUILD SAUCE: Stir in flour and cook until lightly browned, about 1 minute. Slowly stir in wine, scraping up any browned bits. Stir in broth, tomatoes, and oregano, and bring to simmer.

4. SIMMER CHICKEN: Reduce heat to low and add microwaved chicken with any accumulated juices. Cover and continue to cook until chicken is tender, about 10 minutes.

QUICK POLENTA
SERVES 4

While we prefer the flavor and texture of traditional slow-cooked polenta, 30 minutes isn't enough time to properly prepare it. Fortunately, quick-cooking polenta, which can be found in most supermarkets, is a close second to the real thing. Instead of following the back-of-the-box directions, follow our method for far better flavor.

4	cups water
	Salt and ground black pepper
I	cup instant polenta
2	tablespoons unsalted butter
¼	cup grated Parmesan cheese

Bring water and 1 teaspoon salt to simmer in large saucepan over medium-high heat. Very slowly, pour polenta into simmering liquid while stirring constantly. Reduce heat to lowest setting and cover. Cook, stirring occasionally, until soft and smooth, about 5 minutes. Off heat, stir in butter and Parmesan. Season with salt and pepper to taste. Serve immediately.

---

5. FINISH STEW: Stir in olives and parsley and season with salt and pepper to taste. Serve.

30-Minute Chicken Paprikash
SERVES 4

Buttered egg noodles are our favorite accompaniment to this simple Hungarian stew. To keep the sour cream from curdling, make sure to stir some of the hot stew liquid into the sour cream before adding it to the pot. The dish of chicken will be very hot coming out of the microwave—be sure to set it on a clean, dry surface or trivet, and be careful of hot steam when removing the plastic wrap.

2	pounds boneless, skinless chicken thighs
	Salt and ground black pepper
I	slice bacon, minced
I	tablespoon vegetable oil
I	onion, minced
I	red bell pepper, cored and chopped medium
4	garlic cloves, minced
2	tablespoons unbleached all-purpose flour
½	cup dry white wine
½	cup low-sodium chicken broth
I	(14.5-ounce) can diced tomatoes
¼	cup sour cream
2	tablespoons minced fresh parsley

MAKING THE MINUTES COUNT:
Immediately start the chicken in the microwave, then mince the bacon and onion. Measure out the flour, wine, and broth while the bacon and onion cook.

1. MICROWAVE CHICKEN: Season chicken with salt and pepper and arrange in single layer in microwave-safe casserole dish following illustration on page 75. Cover tightly with plastic wrap and microwave on 50 percent power for 15 minutes.

2. SAUTÉ BACON AND AROMATICS: While chicken cooks, sauté bacon with oil in large Dutch oven over medium-high heat until bacon fat begins to render, about 2 minutes. Stir in onion, bell pepper, and ¼ teaspoon salt and cook until softened and lightly browned, about 8 minutes.

Stir in garlic and cook until fragrant, about 30 seconds.

3. BUILD SAUCE: Stir in flour and cook until lightly browned, about 1 minute. Slowly stir in wine, scraping up any browned bits. Stir in broth and tomatoes, and bring to simmer.

4. SIMMER CHICKEN: Reduce heat to low and add microwaved chicken with any accumulated juices. Cover and continue to cook until chicken is tender, about 10 minutes.

5. FINISH STEW: Off heat, stir ½ cup of sauce into sour cream to temper, then stir mixture back into pot. Stir in parsley and season with salt and pepper to taste. Serve.

30-Minute Country Captain
SERVES 4

Country captain is a spicy, sweet, and fragrant dish that consists of chicken, onions, tomatoes, green peppers, and curry powder. It is traditionally served over rice and garnished with toasted almonds. The dish of chicken will be very hot coming out of the microwave—be sure to set it on a clean, dry surface or trivet, and be careful of hot steam when removing the plastic wrap.

2	pounds boneless, skinless chicken thighs
	Salt and ground black pepper
1	slice bacon, minced
1	tablespoon vegetable oil
1	onion, minced
1	green bell pepper, cored and chopped medium
1	tablespoon curry powder
¼	teaspoon cayenne
4	garlic cloves, minced
2	tablespoons unbleached all-purpose flour
½	cup low-sodium chicken broth
1	(14.5-ounce) can diced tomatoes
½	cup Major Grey's chutney
2	tablespoons fresh lime juice

MAKING THE MINUTES COUNT:
Immediately start the chicken in the microwave, then mince the bacon and onion. Measure out the flour and broth while the bacon and onion cook.

1. MICROWAVE CHICKEN: Season chicken with salt and pepper and arrange in single layer in microwave-safe casserole dish following illustration below. Cover tightly with plastic wrap and microwave on 50 percent power for 15 minutes.

2. SAUTÉ BACON AND AROMATICS: While chicken cooks, sauté bacon with oil in large Dutch oven over medium-high heat until bacon fat begins to render, about 2 minutes. Stir in onion, bell pepper, curry powder, cayenne, and ¼ teaspoon salt and cook until softened and lightly browned, about 8 minutes. Stir in garlic and cook until fragrant, about 30 seconds.

3. BUILD SAUCE: Stir in flour and cook until lightly browned, about 1 minute. Slowly stir in broth, scraping up any browned bits. Stir in tomatoes and chutney and bring to simmer.

4. SIMMER CHICKEN: Reduce heat to low and add microwaved chicken with any accumulated juices. Cover and continue to cook until chicken is tender, about 10 minutes.

5. FINISH STEW: Off heat, stir in lime juice and season with salt and pepper to taste. Serve.

TEST KITCHEN TIP:

The Dish on the Dish

When microwaving boneless, skinless chicken thighs for these 30-minute braises, we found it easiest to nestle them into a single layer in a small square casserole dish or a pie plate. This ensures that they will cook evenly (compared to being piled into a bowl) and that you can easily contain the flavorful cooked chicken juices—if you use a dinner plate, they could easily spill over and make a mess of your microwave.

30-Minute Chicken Fricassee with Mushrooms

SERVES 4

The dish of chicken will be very hot coming out of the microwave—be sure to set it on a clean, dry surface or trivet, and be careful of hot steam when removing the plastic wrap. Serve the fricassee with rice or crusty bread.

2	pounds boneless, skinless chicken thighs
	Salt and ground black pepper
1	slice bacon, minced
1	tablespoon vegetable oil
1	onion, minced
10	ounces white mushroom, quartered
4	garlic cloves, minced
2	tablespoons unbleached all-purpose flour
½	cup dry white wine
¾	cup low-sodium chicken broth
½	cup heavy cream
2	tablespoons minced fresh parsley

MAKING THE MINUTES COUNT:

Immediately start the chicken in the microwave, then mince the bacon and onion. Measure out the flour, wine, and broth while the bacon and onion cook.

1. MICROWAVE CHICKEN: Season chicken with salt and pepper and arrange in single layer in microwave-safe casserole dish following illustration on page 75. Cover tightly with plastic wrap and microwave on 50 percent power for 15 minutes.

2. SAUTÉ BACON, AROMATICS, AND MUSHROOMS: While chicken cooks, sauté bacon with oil in large Dutch oven over medium-high heat until bacon fat begins to render, about 2 minutes. Stir in onion, mushrooms, and ¼ teaspoon salt and cook until lightly browned, 8 to 10 minutes. Stir in garlic and cook until fragrant, about 30 seconds.

3. BUILD SAUCE: Stir in flour and cook until lightly browned, about 1 minute. Slowly stir in wine, scraping up any browned bits. Stir in broth and bring to simmer.

4. SIMMER CHICKEN: Reduce heat to low and add microwaved chicken with any accumulated juices. Cover and continue to cook until chicken is tender, about 10 minutes.

5. FINISH STEW: Stir in cream and parsley and return to brief simmer. Season with salt and pepper to taste. Serve.

EQUIPMENT: Dutch Ovens

Despite its misleading name, a Dutch oven is a large, squat pot sometimes referred to as a French oven, casserole, or stockpot. Traditionally, Dutch ovens were used to cook food buried in a campfire's embers, but nowadays they are generally employed for indoor use for making soups, stews, and braises.

We found that a Dutch oven should have a capacity of at least six quarts to be useful. Eight quarts is even better. As we used the pots, we came to prefer wider, shallower Dutch ovens—it's easier to see and reach inside them and they offer more bottom surface area to accommodate larger batches of meat for browning. This reduces the number of batches required to brown a given quantity of meat and, with it, the chances of burning the flavorful pan drippings. Ideally, the diameter of a Dutch oven should be twice as great as its height. The bottom should be thick—so that it maintains moderate heat and prevents food from scorching—and the lid should fit tightly to prevent excessive moisture loss.

Our test kitchen is stocked with many of our favorite Dutch ovens, made by All-Clad, but some of us are reluctant to shell out the $200 it takes to buy one. So we tested four Dutch ovens in the $50 to $100 range and came up with an alternative to the expensive brands. The Tramontina Sterling II 7-Quart Dutch Oven performed nearly as well as the more expensive models.

The Best Dutch Ovens

Our favorite pot is the 8-quart All-Clad Stainless Stockpot (left). Despite the name, this pot is a Dutch oven. Expect to spend nearly $200 for this piece of cookware. A less expensive alternative is the Tramontina Sterling II 7-Quart Dutch Oven (right), which costs about $60.

30-Minute Chicken Fricassee with Artichokes and Leeks

SERVES 4

This flavorful fricassee relies on fuss-free frozen artichoke hearts, which only require a quick thaw in the microwave. The dish of chicken will be very hot coming out of the microwave—be sure to set it on a clean, dry surface or trivet, and be careful of hot steam when removing the plastic wrap. Shake any excess water off the leek before adding it to the pan to ensure that the sauce thickens properly. Serve this fricassee over rice or egg noodles.

2	pounds boneless, skinless chicken thighs
	Salt and ground black pepper
I	slice bacon, minced
I	tablespoon vegetable oil
I	(9-ounce) box frozen artichoke hearts, thawed (see note)
I	leek, white and light green parts, halved and sliced thin
4	garlic cloves, minced
I	tablespoon unbleached all-purpose flour
1/2	cup dry white wine
3/4	cup low-sodium chicken broth
1/2	cup heavy cream
2	tablespoons minced fresh tarragon

MAKING THE MINUTES COUNT:
Immediately start the chicken in the microwave. Slice the leek and let soak in water to wash (see page 66) while cooking the bacon and artichokes.

I. MICROWAVE CHICKEN: Season chicken with salt and pepper and arrange in single layer in microwave-safe casserole dish following illustration on page 75. Cover tightly with plastic wrap and microwave on 50 percent power for 15 minutes.

2. SAUTÉ BACON, AROMATICS, AND VEGETABLES: While chicken cooks, sauté bacon with oil in large Dutch oven over medium-high heat until bacon fat begins to render, about 2 minutes. Stir in artichokes and cook until lightly browned, about 5 minutes. Stir in leek and cook until softened, about 5 minutes. Stir in garlic and cook until fragrant, about 30 seconds.

3. BUILD SAUCE: Stir in flour and cook until lightly browned, about 1 minute. Slowly stir in wine, scraping up any browned bits. Stir in broth and bring to simmer.

4. SIMMER CHICKEN: Reduce heat to low and add microwaved chicken with any accumulated juices. Cover and continue to cook until chicken is tender, about 10 minutes.

5. FINISH STEW: Stir in cream and tarragon and return to brief simmer. Season with salt and pepper to taste. Serve.

30-Minute Chicken Tagine

SERVES 4

Tagines are meat stews that feature a blend of sweet and savory ingredients. The dish of chicken will be very hot coming out of the microwave—be sure to set it on a clean, dry surface or trivet, and be careful of hot steam when removing the plastic wrap. See page 56 for information on garam masala. Serve the tagine over couscous or rice.

2	pounds boneless, skinless chicken thighs
	Salt and ground black pepper
2	tablespoons vegetable oil
I	onion, minced
2	teaspoons garam masala (see note)
4	garlic cloves, minced
2	tablespoons unbleached all-purpose flour
I	cup low-sodium chicken broth
I	(14.5-ounce) can diced tomatoes
1/2	cup dried apricots, quartered
I	(15-ounce) can chickpeas, rinsed
2	tablespoons minced fresh cilantro

MAKING THE MINUTES COUNT:
Immediately start the chicken in the microwave, then mince the onion. Measure out the flour and broth and chop the apricots while the onion cooks.

I. MICROWAVE CHICKEN: Season chicken with salt and pepper and arrange in single layer in microwave-safe casserole dish following illustration on page 75. Cover tightly with plastic wrap and microwave on 50 percent power for 15 minutes.

2. SAUTÉ AROMATICS: While chicken cooks, heat oil in large Dutch oven over medium-high heat until shimmering. Stir in onion, garam masala, and ¼ teaspoon salt and cook until softened, about 5 minutes. Stir in garlic and cook until fragrant, about 30 seconds.

3. BUILD SAUCE: Stir in flour and cook until lightly browned, about 1 minute. Slowly stir in broth, scraping up any browned bits. Stir in tomatoes, apricots, and chickpeas, bring to simmer, and cook until apricots begin to soften, about 5 minutes.

4. SIMMER CHICKEN: Reduce heat to low and add microwaved chicken with any accumulated juices. Cover and continue to cook until chicken is tender, about 10 minutes.

5. FINISH: Stir in cilantro and season with salt and pepper to taste. Serve.

SIMPLE COUSCOUS
SERVES 4

The mild flavor of couscous goes with most any stew, especially highly spiced stews like 30-Minute Chicken Tagine. While most recipes for couscous yield a bland, sometimes pasty dish, we've developed a quick recipe that highlights the nutty flavor of the couscous and keeps the grains separate and distinct.

2	tablespoons olive oil
1½	cups couscous
½	teaspoon salt
2¼	cups water

I. SAUTÉ COUSCOUS: Heat oil in medium saucepan over medium-high heat until shimmering. Add couscous and cook, stirring occasionally, until lightly browned, 3 to 5 minutes.

2. ADD WATER, BRING TO BOIL, AND FINISH: Stir in salt and water and bring to boil. Cover and remove from heat. Let stand for 5 minutes. Fluff couscous with fork before serving.

WHITE CHICKEN CHILI

WHITE CHILI WAS BORN IN THE Southwestern food craze of the 1980s. More brothy than its conventional red cousin, this chili usually contains chicken and hominy (dried corn kernels treated with lime) and is vibrantly flavored with a variety of fresh chiles and spices. The problem with this dish is a long ingredient list and significant cooking time. We sought to simplify this chili while retaining its rich, lively flavors.

We started with the choice of chicken part. For chili, the meat would need to be cut in bite-sized pieces or better yet, shredded. We thought of using boneless thighs, as in our chicken braises (for more information see page 73), but in keeping to our 30-minute mark, there wouldn't be enough time to cook and then shred the thighs. We then turned to boneless breasts, which are quicker cooking.

First, we brought the broth to a simmer. At the same time, we added the hominy to the broth, which allowed the two flavors to unify. While the mixture came to a simmer we browned the chicken.

For the aromatic base of the soup, we wanted to limit the amount of ingredients for efficiency's sake (and chilis often contain an endless list of aromatics). We sought just a few key ingredients that would pack a flavorful punch. Onions and garlic were a given, as they provide depth and richness. Tasters also liked the pungency of a couple teaspoons of cumin. For the chiles, we settled on a combination of Anaheim chiles and jalapeños. The Anaheim chiles lent the stew sweetness and depth while the jalapeño added a robust spiciness.

Even with the ingredients in place, we still had a problem. Chopping the aromatics was taking too much time. Relying on a trick we used in our Black Bean Soup (page 54), we tossed the vegetables into a food processor. The processed vegetables gave up more flavor in a shorter period of time and left us with a far more pungent chili.

After sautéing the aromatics, we returned the chicken to the pot, and then added the broth and hominy mixture. Tasters, however, felt the chili was a bit too brothy, so we decided to thicken it with some flour. Just after sautéing the aromatics, we added flour to the pot and stirred it until lightly toasted. At this point, we added the broth and hominy, which thickened nicely, and returned the chicken to the pot to cook through. We then removed the chicken, shredded it, and returned it to the pot. No one missed the chicken thighs—shredded into pieces, the breast meat, bathed in the heartily flavored broth, tasted rich and flavorful. All we needed to finish our chili was fresh lime juice and cilantro.

Quick White Chicken Chili

SERVES 4 TO 6

Both yellow hominy and white hominy will work in this chili; however, we prefer the deeper flavor of white hominy here. If you like your chili spicy, include some of the jalapeño seeds. If desired, serve with sour cream, shredded cheddar or Monterey Jack, chopped tomato, and sliced scallions.

4	cups low-sodium chicken broth
1	(14-ounce) can white hominy, rinsed
	Salt and ground black pepper
1½	pounds boneless, skinless chicken breasts
2	tablespoons vegetable oil
1	onion, peeled and cut into large chunks
3	Anaheim chiles, cored and cut into large chunks
1	jalapeño chile, seeded and cut into rough pieces
3	garlic cloves, peeled
2	teaspoons ground cumin
2	tablespoons unbleached all-purpose flour
2	tablespoons fresh lime juice
2	tablespoons minced fresh cilantro

MAKING THE MINUTES COUNT:
Prepare and process the vegetables while the chicken browns.

1. HEAT BROTH MIXTURE: Bring broth, hominy, and ¼ teaspoon salt to boil, covered, in large saucepan, and set aside.

2. BROWN CHICKEN: Meanwhile, pat chicken dry with paper towels and season with salt and pepper. Heat 1 tablespoon of oil in large Dutch oven over medium-high heat until just smoking.

Brown chicken lightly on both sides, about 5 minutes total. Transfer chicken to plate and set aside.

3. PROCESS VEGETABLES: While chicken browns, pulse onion, Anaheim chiles, jalapeño, and garlic in food processor until roughly chopped, about 10 pulses, scraping down sides of bowl as needed.

4. SAUTÉ PROCESSED VEGETABLES: Add remaining tablespoon oil to Dutch oven and return to medium-high heat until shimmering. Add processed vegetables and ½ teaspoon salt and cook until vegetables are dry and beginning to brown, 6 to 8 minutes. Stir in cumin and cook until fragrant, about 30 seconds.

5. BUILD SAUCE AND SIMMER CHICKEN: Stir in flour and cook until lightly browned, about 1 minute. Stir in broth mixture, scraping up any browned bits. Reduce heat to low and add browned chicken with any accumulated juices. Cover and cook until thickest part of chicken registers 160 degrees on instant-read thermometer, about 10 minutes.

6. SHRED CHICKEN AND FINISH CHILI: Remove chicken from pot and shred, following illustrations on page 80. Meanwhile, continue to simmer chili, uncovered, to thicken sauce slightly. Off heat, stir in shredded chicken, lime juice, and cilantro, and season with salt and pepper to taste. Serve.

KITCHEN SHORTCUT
EASY PEELING

Peel garlic cloves easily and quickly by covering the clove with the concave side of a wooden spoon and pressing down hard. The cup of the spoon prevents the garlic clove from shooting out across the work surface.

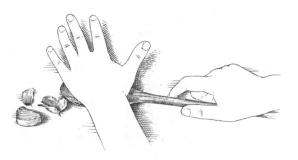

MAQUE CHOUX

FEW PEOPLE OUTSIDE OF LOUISIANA HAVE ever heard of maque choux, a Cajun side dish of corn, peppers, and onions similar to succotash. Although it's normally served as an accompaniment to a main dish, we found several recipes that incorporated chicken and sausage with the vegetables to transform it into a satisfying, one-pot dinner. In this form, maque choux seemed to be an ideal candidate for a quick-cooking stew.

The challenge in this recipe lay not in the cooking method, which follows a traditional procedure for stew (brown meat and vegetables then simmer in a broth). The challenge, instead, was in developing the corn flavor of the dish—the cornerstone of maque choux. Because there are so many other strongly flavored ingredients—red pepper, garlic, and kielbasa—the corn flavor can be easily and unfortunately diluted. Increasing the amount of whole corn kernels seemed the obvious response, but doing so didn't produce the desired effect. Trying a trick we learned from our Quick Corn Chowder (page 53), we pureed half of the corn with chicken broth. This created a broth that was smooth and creamy with an intense corn flavor. This broth, along with the remaining whole kernels, yielded a rich stew with a wonderfully hearty texture.

Maque Choux with Chicken and Kielbasa

SERVES 4 TO 6

Serve over rice with plenty of hot sauce.

I	pound boneless, skinless chicken breasts
	Salt and ground black pepper
2	tablespoons vegetable oil
½	pound kielbasa, cut into ½-inch pieces
I	onion, minced
I	red bell pepper, cored and chopped medium
I	pound frozen corn, thawed
2	cups low-sodium chicken broth
2	garlic cloves, minced
I	teaspoon minced fresh thyme, or ¼ teaspoon dried
2	tablespoons minced fresh parsley

MAKING THE MINUTES COUNT:
Chop the kielbasa, onion, and pepper while the chicken browns. Blend the corn while the vegetables cook.

I. **BROWN CHICKEN**: Pat chicken dry with paper towels and season with salt and pepper. Heat 1 tablespoon of oil in large Dutch oven over medium-high heat until just smoking. Brown chicken lightly on both sides, about 5 minutes total. Transfer chicken to plate and set aside.

2. **SAUTÉ KIELBASA AND AROMATICS**: Add remaining tablespoon oil to pot and return to medium-high heat until shimmering. Add kielbasa, onion, bell pepper, and ½ teaspoon salt to pot and cook over medium-high heat until lightly browned, about 8 minutes.

3. **PUREE HALF OF CORN WITH BROTH**: While the kielbasa cooks, puree half of corn with broth in blender until smooth.

4. **MAKE SAUCE AND SIMMER CHICKEN**: Stir garlic and thyme into pot and cook until fragrant, about 30 seconds. Stir in pureed corn mixture, scraping up browned bits. Reduce heat to low and add browned chicken with any accumulated juices. Cover and cook until thickest part of chicken registers 160 degrees on instant-read thermometer, about 10 minutes.

5. **SHRED CHICKEN AND FINISH STEW**: Remove chicken from pot and stir in remaining whole corn kernels. Increase heat to medium-high and cook

SHREDDING CHICKEN

Hold one fork in each hand, with the prongs down and facing each other. Insert the prongs into the chicken meat and gently pull the forks away from each other, breaking the meat apart into long, thin strands.

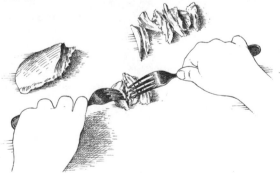

until corn is warmed through, about 2 minutes. Meanwhile, shred chicken following illustrations on page 80. Off heat, stir in shredded chicken and parsley. Season with salt and pepper to taste. Serve.

POZOLE

POZOLE IS THE MEXICAN NAME FOR BOTH hominy (dried corn kernels that have been treated with lime) and the rich, flavorful stew that is made with hominy and pork. While there are many versions of pozole, the one unifying theme is the pork shoulder, which is simmered for hours until it is meltingly tender and easily shredded. Given our 30-minute time constraint, we knew we couldn't replicate traditional pozole, but we hoped to create a stew that had a similar long-cooked flavor.

Our main concern was finding a cut of pork that had the right combination of flavor and tenderness—without a long cooking time. The best choice turned out to be tenderloin. Small pieces of tenderloin remained moist and tender, as if they had been stewed a long time, but actually only required 10 minutes of cooking time.

Even after finding a suitable replacement for the pork shoulder, we still were faced with building enough flavor within our given time limit. After a variety of tests, we found that a two-pan approach allowed us to build the flavor we wanted in just 30 minutes. In one pan we brought the broth, tomatoes, and hominy to a simmer with aromatic oregano. In a second pan, we browned the pork, then removed it to a bowl while we sautéed the onion, garlic, and chili powder. Once the aromatics were softened, we added in a bit of flour and stirred until lightly browned and toasted. (The flour acts as a thickener.) We then added the broth and hominy mixture to the aromatics and let them simmer briefly until thickened. At this point we added the pork to heat through and tossed in a few tablespoons of minced fresh cilantro to complete the dish. This two-pot method allowed us to maximize the time the individual ingredients cooked with one another, which melded their flavors into one cohesive and flavorful stew.

Quick Pozole
SERVES 4 TO 6

Serve with lime wedges and warm flour tortillas.

4	cups low-sodium chicken broth
1	(14.5-ounce) can diced tomatoes
2	(14-ounce) cans white hominy, rinsed
1	tablespoon minced fresh oregano, or
	1 teaspoon dried
	Salt and ground black pepper
1½	pounds pork tenderloin, cut into
	½-inch cubes
2	tablespoons vegetable oil
1	onion, minced
1	tablespoon chili powder
5	garlic cloves, minced
2	tablespoons unbleached all-purpose flour
2	tablespoons chopped fresh cilantro

MAKING THE MINUTES COUNT:
Mince the onion and garlic while the pork browns.

1. HEAT BROTH MIXTURE: Bring broth, tomatoes, hominy, oregano, and ¼ teaspoon salt to boil, covered, in large saucepan, and set aside.

2. BROWN PORK: Meanwhile, pat pork dry with paper towels and season with salt and pepper. Heat 1 tablespoon of oil in large Dutch oven over medium-high heat until just smoking. Brown pork lightly, about 6 minutes. Transfer pork to clean bowl and set aside.

3. SAUTÉ AROMATICS: Add remaining tablespoon oil to Dutch oven and return to medium-high heat until shimmering. Add onion, chili powder, and ½ teaspoon salt and cook until softened, about 5 minutes. Stir in garlic and cook until fragrant, about 30 seconds.

> **TEST KITCHEN TIP: Pozole**
> Pozole, also known as hominy, can normally be found with the canned beans at your supermarket. Both yellow and white varieties are sold, and while both will work in this stew, we prefer the deeper flavor of the white variety.

4. ADD BROTH MIXTURE AND SIMMER: Stir in flour and cook until lightly browned, about 1 minute. Slowly stir in broth mixture, scraping up any browned bits. Bring to simmer and cook until hominy is tender and warmed through, about 5 minutes.

5. ADD PORK AND FINISH STEW: Stir in pork with any accumulated juices and return to brief simmer. Off heat, stir in cilantro and season with salt and pepper to taste. Serve.

FRENCH-STYLE PORK STEW

ENCOURAGED BY OUR SUCCESS WITH THE pozole recipe, we looked for other pork stew recipes that we could adapt to our newly developed two-pan cooking technique. After some research, we came across a rustic French dish of braised pork combined with carrots, prunes, brandy and a touch of cream. Intrigued by these flavors, we set about incorporating these ingredients into a new quick pork stew.

As with the pozole, the key to success lay with the two-pan method. With this particular recipe, we simmered the carrots and prunes in the broth as we seared the meat. By starting these ingredients early in the cooking process, we found that at the end of 30 minutes the carrots were extremely tender and the prunes had partially dissolved, leaving the stew with a silky texture and distinct sweetness.

Brandy, a key ingredient, enhances the sweetness of the prunes. After we sautéed the aromatics and stirred in and toasted the flour, we added ½ cup of brandy to deglaze the pan. The brandy provided a distinct, sophisticated flavor to the stew, but tasters felt it could be more pronounced. So, to finish, we stirred in an additional tablespoon of brandy (along with the cream), which gave our rich pork stew a more lively finish.

30-Minute Pork Stew with Prunes and Brandy
SERVES 4

Most of the prunes dissolve during cooking, giving this stew a silky texture and rich, slightly sweet flavor. This stew is great served with crusty bread, but rice is also a good accompaniment.

2	cups low-sodium chicken broth
3	carrots, sliced ¼ inch thick
½	cup pitted prunes, halved
1	teaspoon minced fresh thyme, or ¼ teaspoon dried
	Salt and ground black pepper
1½	pounds pork tenderloin, cut into ½-inch cubes
2	tablespoons vegetable oil
1	onion, minced
2	garlic cloves, minced
2	tablespoons unbleached all-purpose flour
½	cup plus 1 tablespoon brandy
½	cup heavy cream
2	tablespoons chopped fresh parsley

MAKING THE MINUTES COUNT:
Mince the onion and garlic while the pork browns.

1. HEAT BROTH MIXTURE: Bring broth, carrots, prunes, thyme, and ¼ teaspoon salt to boil, covered, in large saucepan. Reduce to simmer and continue to cook until needed in step 4.

2. BROWN PORK: Meanwhile, pat pork dry with paper towels and season with salt and pepper. Heat 1 tablespoon of oil in large Dutch oven over medium-high heat until just smoking. Brown pork lightly, about 6 minutes. Transfer pork to clean bowl and set aside.

3. SAUTÉ AROMATICS: Add remaining tablespoon oil to Dutch oven and return to medium-high heat until shimmering. Add onion and ½ teaspoon salt and cook until softened, about 5 minutes. Stir in garlic and cook until fragrant, about 30 seconds.

4. ADD BROTH MIXTURE AND SIMMER: Stir in flour and cook until lightly browned, about 1 minute. Remove pot from heat and slowly stir in ½ cup of brandy, scraping up any browned bits. Return pot to medium-high heat and stir in broth mixture. Bring to simmer and cook until carrots are tender and prunes are softened, 10 to 12 minutes.

5. ADD PORK AND FINISH STEW: Stir in pork with any accumulated juices and cream, and return to brief simmer. Off heat, stir in remaining tablespoon brandy and parsley and season with salt and pepper to taste. Serve.

PORK VINDALOO

VINDALOO IS AN INDIAN STEW OF Portuguese ancestry that is full of flavors—hot, sweet, and tangy—that come together in a tantalizing dish. Given our success with pork stews, we considered combining our 30-minute technique with the traditional slow-cooked flavors of vindaloo.

Spices are the cornerstone of this stew. Traditional recipes use numerous spices to achieve its distinct flavor, but we didn't want to clutter up our ingredient list with a half dozen spices. We wondered if we could produce a tasty stew with just a few.

We brought tomatoes, mustard seeds, and chicken broth to a simmer in one pan for a flavorful, brothy base. While that simmered, we sautéed the pork tenderloin with onions, garlic, hot paprika, and garam masala. Because garam masala is a blend of spices (cumin, cardamom, cloves, and cinnamon, to name a few), this single ingredient packs a complex punch. Cooked with this spice blend and the other aromatics, the pork became substantially seasoned by the time we combined it with the broth mixture in the other pan. To provide the vindaloo its classic tanginess, we finished the dish with a splash of red wine vinegar and stirred in chopped fresh cilantro. Served over rice, this dish is intensely satisfying and intensely flavorful, but made in minutes.

30-Minute Pork Vindaloo
SERVES 4
Serve this highly spiced stew over rice.

2 cups low-sodium chicken broth
1 (14.5-ounce) can diced tomatoes
2 teaspoons mustard seeds
  Salt and ground black pepper
1½ pounds pork tenderloin, cut into
  ½-inch cubes
2 tablespoons vegetable oil
1 onion, minced
1½ teaspoons garam masala
1 teaspoon hot paprika
4 garlic cloves, minced
1 tablespoon unbleached all-purpose flour
1 tablespoon red wine vinegar
2 tablespoons chopped fresh cilantro

MAKING THE MINUTES COUNT:
Mince the onion and garlic while the pork browns.

1. HEAT BROTH: Bring broth, tomatoes, mustard seeds, and ¼ teaspoon salt to boil, covered, in large saucepan and set aside.

2. BROWN PORK: Meanwhile, pat pork dry with paper towels and season with salt and pepper. Heat 1 tablespoon of oil in large Dutch oven over medium-high heat until just smoking. Brown pork lightly, about 6 minutes. Transfer pork to clean bowl and set aside.

3. SAUTÉ AROMATICS: Add remaining tablespoon oil to Dutch oven and return to medium-high heat until shimmering. Add onion, garam masala, paprika, and ½ teaspoon salt and cook until softened, 5 minutes. Stir in garlic and cook until fragrant, about 30 seconds.

4. ADD BROTH AND SIMMER: Stir in flour and cook until lightly browned, about 1 minute. Slowly stir in broth and tomato mixture, scraping up any browned bits. Bring to simmer and cook until flavors have melded, about 10 minutes.

5. ADD PORK AND FINISH STEW: Stir in pork with any accumulated juices and return to brief simmer. Off heat, stir in vinegar and cilantro and season with salt and pepper to taste. Serve.

CHILI

LOOK IN ANY QUICK-COOKING COOKBOOK and you are bound to find a recipe for ground beef chili that boasts a long-cooked flavor. Curious to see if any of these claims were true, we tested a number of different recipes. More often than not, what we found was a bland collection of chilis that were nothing more than spiced tomato soup enriched with ground beef.

The complex flavor of chili is achieved through a series of steps. Aromatics need to be sautéed, spices need to toast, meat needs to brown, and then the whole is simmered. Recipes for quick chilis usually brown the meat and aromatics, throw everything else into the pot, and heat it through. We knew we'd need to take a more thoughtful approach.

We decided to start with a flavorful base and tackled the tomatoes first. We found that the type of canned tomatoes we used made a big difference. Tomato puree was too thick and sweet for the chili, while diced tomatoes in juice were just too chunky. Crushed tomatoes worked best, but unfortunately we found some dramatic textural differences among the various brands, which seriously affected the quality of the chili. In the end, we decided that spending an extra minute to puree a can of diced tomatoes with its juice into a loose, crushed-like consistency in a food processor was best. We simmered the tomatoes, canned beans that had been rinsed, and smoky chipotle chiles in a pot while we assembled the other ingredients of the dish. (Many chilis start with fresh jalapeños, but we didn't have time to sauté them properly. So instead we decided on canned chipotle chiles, which are jalapeños that have been smoked and packed in a tangy, vinegary sauce.) Off the bat, this step infused our chili with great flavor.

As these elements cooked together and their flavors melded, we sautéed onions, chili powder, cumin, and garlic in a separate pan. By slowly cooking the onions and spices in oil on their own for five minutes, we gave their flavors a chance to bloom and become more developed. Once the onions and spices were cooked through, we added the ground beef, breaking it up with a wooden spoon. Once the beef had lost its pink color, we transferred the tomato and bean mixture to the pot with the ground beef. Then we simmered all the components together for the last 15 minutes, finalizing the intermingling of flavors and producing a chili that tasted like it had been simmering all day.

We decided to use the identical technique to transform this meat chili into a tasty vegetarian chili. We increased the amount of beans that simmered with the tomatoes and then added frozen corn kernels and finished it with fresh cilantro. The addition of the corn and the zesty cilantro gave the vegetarian version a depth that is often lacking with meatless dishes.

✦

Fast All-American Beef Chili

SERVES 4 TO 6

The texture of the pureed diced tomatoes with their juice is very important here—do not substitute crushed tomatoes or tomato puree.

I	(28-ounce) can diced tomatoes
I	(15-ounce) can dark red kidney beans, rinsed
2–3	teaspoons minced chipotle chiles in adobo sauce
2	teaspoons sugar
	Salt and ground black pepper
2	tablespoons vegetable oil
I	onion, minced
3	tablespoons chili powder
2	teaspoons ground cumin
3	garlic cloves, minced
1½	pounds 85 percent lean ground beef

> **TEST KITCHEN TIP: I'm Crushed**
> We tested our chili with canned crushed tomatoes, canned pureed tomatoes, and canned diced tomatoes. Some chilis turned out soupy, some were too thick, some were too chunky, and some had a "canned" flavor. Crushed tomatoes were especially disappointing because they varied from brand to brand in terms of flavor and thickness. After a lot of testing, we came to the conclusion that canned diced tomatoes, pureed in the food processor, gave us the best combination of flavor and texture.

1. **PUREE TOMATOES**: Pulse tomatoes and their juice in food processor until slightly chunky, about 5 pulses.

2. **HEAT TOMATOES WITH BEANS**: Bring tomatoes, beans, chipotle chile, sugar, and ½ teaspoon salt to boil, covered, in large saucepan. Reduce to simmer and continue to cook until needed in step 5.

3. **SAUTÉ AROMATICS**: Heat oil in large Dutch oven over medium heat until shimmering. Add onion, chili powder, cumin, and ¼ teaspoon salt and cook until softened, about 5 minutes. Stir in garlic and cook until fragrant, about 30 seconds.

4. **ADD BEEF**: Increase heat to medium-high and add beef. Cook, breaking up beef with spoon, until no longer pink, about 3 minutes.

5. **ADD TOMATOES AND SIMMER**: Stir in tomato-bean mixture, scraping up any browned bits. Bring to simmer and cook until slightly thickened, about 15 minutes. Season with salt and pepper to taste before serving.

Easy Vegetarian Bean Chili

SERVES 4 TO 6

We prefer to use a combination of pinto, black, and dark red kidney beans in this chili. The texture of the pureed diced tomatoes with their juice is very important here—do not substitute crushed tomatoes or tomato puree.

1	(28-ounce) can diced tomatoes
2	(15-ounce) cans beans (see note), rinsed
2–3	teaspoons minced chipotle chiles in adobo sauce
2	teaspoons sugar
	Salt and ground black pepper
2	tablespoons vegetable oil
1	onion, minced
3	tablespoons chili powder
2	teaspoons ground cumin
3	garlic cloves, minced
1½	cups frozen corn, thawed
2	tablespoons minced fresh cilantro

1. **PUREE TOMATOES**: Pulse tomatoes and their juice in food processor until slightly chunky, about 5 pulses.

2. **HEAT TOMATOES WITH BEANS**: Bring tomatoes, beans, chipotle chile, sugar, and ½ teaspoon salt to boil, covered, in large saucepan. Reduce to simmer and continue to cook until needed in step 5.

3. **SAUTÉ AROMATICS**: Heat oil in large Dutch oven over medium heat until shimmering. Add onion, chili powder, cumin, and ¼ teaspoon salt and cook until softened, about 5 minutes. Stir in garlic and cook until fragrant, about 30 seconds.

4. **COMBINE AND SIMMER**: Stir in tomato-bean mixture, scraping up any browned bits. Bring to simmer and cook until slightly thickened, about 15 minutes.

5. **FINISH CHILI**: Stir in corn and cilantro and return to brief simmer. Season with salt and pepper to taste. Serve.

THAI CURRY

THERE IS NO DISH THAT EXEMPLIFIES the blend of flavors and textures of Thai cuisine better than a Thai curry. Crunchy vegetables and tender meats are bathed in a sauce made with coconut milk, salty fish sauce, and aromatic curry paste. Considering that Thai curries contain numerous hard-to-find ingredients and can employ some intricate techniques, we sought to develop a recipe that would simplify and streamline the process of making Thai curry at home.

We first sought to determine what ingredients were crucial to forming the base of the dish. Traditional curries usually start with a curry paste, which entails the laborious process of grinding a dozen aromatic ingredients into a fine paste. Luckily, we found that good red curry pastes are now available in most supermarkets, so we wouldn't have to labor over our own. To coax the most flavor out of the curry paste, we sautéed it in a little oil and then added light coconut milk—which, to our surprise, we preferred to its full-fat cousin because it didn't mute the complex flavors of the curry paste. To finish our curry base, we added fish sauce (also found in most supermarkets), which provided the dish with its distinct salty Thai flavor. We also added brown sugar to temper the spiciness of the curry paste.

In lieu of adding meat to our curry, we opted to use tofu. While not traditional, we thought that the subtle flavor of the tofu would be a nice complement to the richly flavored curry. In the course of testing, we found that dredging the tofu in flour and coating it in lightly beaten egg before browning not only boosted the flavor of the tofu but also gave it a handsome golden crust.

Once we prepared the tofu, we removed it to a dish and covered it to keep it warm. We then prepared the curry base in the same pan and added quick-cooking snap peas and strips of red pepper. Both provided a crispness that complemented the texture of the tofu and gave the dish vibrant color. Once the vegetables were crisp-tender, we removed the pan from the heat and added the browned tofu. After adding a healthy dose of fresh basil, we found that we had an exotic and satisfying meal—in no time.

Thai Red Curry with Tofu
SERVES 4

Serve over plain rice with lime wedges. If you like your food spicy, use 2 teaspoons of curry paste.

½	cup unbleached all-purpose flour
2	large eggs
1	(14-ounce) package tofu, sliced crosswise into ½-inch-thick slabs
	Salt and ground black pepper
3	tablespoons vegetable oil
1–2	teaspoons red curry paste (see note)
1	(13.5-ounce) can light coconut milk
2	tablespoons fish sauce
1	tablespoon brown sugar
1	red bell pepper, cored and sliced thin
½	pound snap peas, trimmed
½	cup coarsely chopped fresh basil

INGREDIENTS: Long-Grain Rice

The beauty of white rice resides in its neutral flavor, which makes it good at carrying other flavors. But is all long-grain white rice created equal? We set up a taste test to find out.

We rounded up a converted rice, three standard supermarket options, and an organic white rice available in bulk from a natural foods store. The most noticeable difference was an unpredictable variance in cooking time. According to the U.S. Rice Producers Association, the age of the rice, its moisture content, and the variety used can affect the rate of water uptake. Inconsistent cooking times are barely noticeable in plain rice, but they can become more apparent when other ingredients—such as aromatics and vegetables—are added to the pot.

All rices but one were noted for being "clean" and "like rice should be." The exception was Uncle Ben's, a converted rice that failed to meet our standards on all fronts. Converted rice is processed in a way that ensures separate grains, a firm texture, and more pronounced flavor. Those "round," "rubbery" grains and the telltale yellowish tint immediately brought back not-so-fond memories of "dining hall rice." Tasters agreed that some "stickiness" and minor "clumping" make for more natural-looking and better-tasting rice. The recommended brands were universally liked and are listed here alphabetically.

The Best Long-Grain Rice

The flavor of Canilla Extra Long (left) was likened to that of jasmine rice, and tasters found Carolina Extra Long Grain Enriched Rice (center) to be a good, clean slate on which to add flavor. Sem-Chi Organically Grown Florida Long Grain Rice (right) was rated the chewiest, with roasted and nutty flavors.

MAKING THE MINUTES COUNT:
While the sauce simmers, slice the bell pepper and remove the strings from the snap peas. While the vegetables cook, chop the basil.

1. PREPARE TOFU: Spread flour into shallow dish. Whisk egg in separate shallow dish. Pat tofu dry with paper towels and season with salt and pepper. Dredge tofu, one piece at a time, in flour to coat and shake off excess.

2. COAT AND COOK TOFU: Heat 2 tablespoons of oil in 12-inch nonstick skillet over medium-high heat until just smoking. Dip floured tofu in egg, allowing excess to drip off, then add to skillet. Brown tofu well on both sides, about 6 minutes total. Transfer tofu to plate and set aside.

3. MAKE SAUCE: Add remaining tablespoon oil and curry paste to oil left in skillet and cook over medium-hot heat until fragrant, about 1 minute. Whisk in coconut milk, fish sauce, and brown sugar and simmer until thickened, about 5 minutes.

4. SIMMER VEGETABLES: Stir in bell pepper and peas and simmer until vegetables are crisp-tender, about 5 minutes.

5. ADD TOFU AND FINISH: Off heat, stir in basil and season with salt and pepper to taste. Nestle tofu into sauce and serve.

RINSING RICE

Before cooking rice or grains, it's best to rinse them. This washes away any excess starch and prevents the final dish from turning out sticky or gummy. Simply place the rice or grain in a fine-mesh strainer and rinse under cool water until the water runs clear, occasionally stirring the rice or grains around lightly with your hand. Set the strainer of rinsed rice or grains over a bowl and let drain until needed.

MICROWAVED LONG-GRAIN RICE
SERVES 4

There are a number of quick-cooking and par-cooked rice products available at the market, and we use them throughout this book in a variety of dishes. But when served plain as a side dish, they're lacking in both flavor and texture. While you can make rice the old-fashioned way, there is a convenient alternative: cook the rice in the microwave right in the serving bowl. This microwave method frees up a little room on the stove for other things, eliminates the chance of scorching, and means that you'll have one less pot to wash because the rice cooks right in the serving dish. The dish of rice will be very hot coming out of the microwave—be sure to set it on a clean, dry surface or trivet, and be careful of hot steam when removing the plastic wrap.

1	cup long-grain white rice, rinsed
2	cups water
1	tablespoon oil
1/4	teaspoon salt

1. MICROWAVE RICE ON FULL POWER: Combine rice, water, oil, and salt in large microwave-safe serving bowl. Cover tightly with plastic wrap and microwave on 100 percent power until water begins to boil, 5 to 10 minutes.

2. MICROWAVE RICE ON HALF POWER: Reduce microwave heat to 50 percent power and continue to microwave until rice is tender, 10 to 15 minutes.

3. FLUFF RICE AND LET STAND: Remove bowl from microwave and fluff rice with fork. Re-cover bowl with plastic wrap, poke several vent holes with tip of paring knife, and let rice stand until completely tender before serving, about 5 minutes.

INDIAN CURRY

HAVING TACKLED A QUICKER, MORE streamlined approach to Thai curry, we turned to Indian curry, its richer, more highly spiced cousin. Of the quick recipes we tried, most were either dull and watery or harshly spiced and heavy. We were looking for a one-dish Indian curry with a complex, authentic flavor and a streamlined preparation that succumbed to neither of these faults.

We tinkered with several cooking methods and found that a technique similar to our stir-fry recipes (pages 95–102) worked the best. The first step was to sear the chicken (in this dish almost any type of meat worked well) in a small amount of oil. After removing the par-cooked chicken from the pan, we built the aromatic base of the curry. This base was composed of onion, curry powder, garlic, and fresh ginger. We sautéed these ingredients in oil in order to extract the maximum amount of flavor. To complete the base we added chicken broth mixed with a little bit of cornstarch. This mixture added a hint of richness and gave the sauce a little body.

For vegetables, we chose cauliflower, potatoes, and peas. These vegetables, which are often found in Indian curries, provided a flavorful, almost sweet contrast to the spices in the dish. They also made for a substantial meal. Once the vegetables were cooked, we added the chicken back to the pan and let it cook through. To finish, we stirred in ½ cup of yogurt, which tempered the flavors in the curry and added richness and body. A handful of chopped cilantro, stirred in just before serving, gave the curry a fresh flavor that all the other quick-cooking curries we tried in our research seemed to miss.

TEST KITCHEN TIP: Curry Powders
Curry powder is not a single spice but rather a blend of spices. Most supermarkets carry curry powder. Depending on the brand, some curry powders can be mild and sweet, while others are quite spicy. In addition to regular curry powder, there is madras curry powder, which is a sweeter and hotter blend. Unless you are familiar with a certain brand, we suggest you try several until you find one to your liking.

Chicken Curry with Potatoes and Cauliflower

SERVES 4

Thinly sliced pork loin or tenderloin, extra-large (21/25) shrimp, or diced extra-firm tofu can be substituted for the chicken.

1	pound boneless, skinless chicken breasts, cut into thin strips (see page 98)
	Salt and ground black pepper
2	tablespoons vegetable oil
1	onion, minced
2	teaspoons curry powder
4	garlic cloves, minced
1	tablespoon grated fresh ginger
1½	cups low-sodium chicken broth
1	tablespoon cornstarch
¾	pound red potatoes, cut into ½-inch chunks
¾	pound cauliflower florets (2 cups)
½	cup frozen peas, thawed
½	cup plain yogurt
¼	cup minced fresh cilantro

MAKING THE MINUTES COUNT:
While the chicken browns, mince the onion. While the onion and spices cook, cut the cauliflower and potatoes.

1. SAUTÉ CHICKEN: Season chicken with salt and pepper. Heat 1 tablespoon of oil in 12-inch nonstick skillet over medium-high heat until just smoking. Add chicken and cook, stirring occasionally and breaking up clumps, until lightly browned, about 3 minutes. Transfer chicken to clean bowl and set aside.

2. SAUTÉ AROMATICS: Add remaining tablespoon oil to skillet and return to medium-high heat until shimmering. Add onion, curry powder, and ½ teaspoon salt and cook until softened, about 5 minutes. Stir in garlic and ginger and cook until fragrant, about 30 seconds.

3. MAKE SAUCE AND COOK VEGETABLES: Whisk broth and cornstarch together to dissolve cornstarch, then stir into skillet. Add potatoes and cauliflower. Reduce heat to medium-low, cover, and cook until vegetables are tender, 7 to 10 minutes.

4. ADD CHICKEN AND FINISH CURRY: Stir in chicken with any accumulated juices and peas, and return to brief simmer. Off heat, stir in yogurt and cilantro and season with salt and pepper to taste. Serve.

GUMBO

GUMBO IS A THICK, DARK, STEW-LIKE DISH that is full of complex flavors and textures. Most traditional gumbo recipes call for several hours of preparation in order to develop a truly rich flavor. But what if you don't have several hours? With some testing, we hoped to develop a 30-minute recipe for gumbo that would taste (almost) like it was made in Louisiana.

The distinctive flavor, color, and aroma of gumbo stems from the trademark dark roux. Traditionally, a roux is used to thicken stews, but in the case of gumbo the dark roux loses most of its thickening ability and simply gives the stew a roasted, nutty flavor. But most recipes for gumbo suggest cooking the roux over low heat from anywhere from 40 to 60 minutes—not exactly quick cooking. Increasing the heat to medium, we found that we could achieve a dark roux in about 15 minutes. But this didn't leave much time to complete the gumbo. The solution was to build the roux in one pot while we cooked the vegetables and protein of the gumbo in a second pot. This allowed us to take our time and develop flavors simultaneously and then merge the two pots together.

For the liquid base of the gumbo, we tried chicken broth, clam juice, and water. While all three worked satisfactorily, we found the clam juice tied all the flavors of the dish together and added the most depth of flavor.

For our aromatics, we chose onion, red bell pepper, and celery—found in most gumbo recipes we researched. When it came to seasoning, we tried a number of combinations and settled on garlic, thyme, and a Creole spice mixture. The Creole spice mixture, a combination of pepper, herbs, and spices, was particularly important because it packed a complex punch in one ingredient. The last question that we addressed was the type of protein to use. Gumbos usually include some combination of seafood, poultry, small game, and sausage. For simplicity's sake, we chose a combination of andouille sausage (a garlicky sausage typical of Creole cooking) and quick-cooking shrimp. The sausage added an authentic, meaty complexity that was a welcome addition to our quick gumbo, and the shrimp required just a few minutes of simmering in the broth toward the end of our 30-minute cooking time.

Shrimp and Sausage Gumbo
SERVES 4 TO 6

Kielbasa can be substituted for the andouille. Be sure to look at the ingredient list of the spice mixture before using; many mixtures have a high proportion of salt, which may make additional seasoning unnecessary.

3	tablespoons plus 2 teaspoons vegetable oil
6	tablespoons unbleached all-purpose flour
2	(8-ounce) bottles clam juice
I	cup water
½	pound andouille sausage, cut into ½-inch pieces
I	onion, minced
I	red bell pepper, cored and chopped fine
I	celery rib, chopped fine
2	teaspoons Creole spice mixture (see below)
I	teaspoon minced fresh thyme, or ¼ teaspoon dried
	Salt and ground black pepper
4	garlic cloves, minced
I	pound extra-large (21/25) shrimp, peeled and deveined
3	scallions, sliced thin

TEST KITCHEN TIP: Going Creole
This gumbo gets much of its zesty flavor from a Creole or Cajun spice mixture in lieu of using a variety of different spices. You can usually find several brands of these blends (including Zatarain's and Emeril's) in the spice aisle of the supermarket.

MAKING THE MINUTES COUNT:
Prepare the sausage, onion, bell pepper, and celery while the roux browns. Place your cutting board near the stove, so you can keep an eye on the roux. If this isn't possible, prep the sausage and vegetables ahead.

1. **MAKE ROUX AND SAUCE:** Whisk 3 tablespoons of oil and flour together in small saucepan over medium heat. Cook, whisking occasionally, until mixture is color of an old copper penny, about 15 minutes. Slowly whisk in clam juice and water and bring to simmer. Continue to simmer until needed in step 3.

2. **SAUTÉ SAUSAGE AND VEGETABLES:** While roux cooks, heat remaining 2 teaspoons oil in large Dutch oven over medium-high heat. Add andouille, onion, bell pepper, celery, Creole spice mixture, thyme, and ¼ teaspoon salt and cook until lightly browned, about 7 minutes. Stir in garlic and cook until fragrant, about 30 seconds.

3. **ASSEMBLE GUMBO:** Slowly stir roux mixture into vegetables, scraping up any browned bits. Simmer until vegetables are tender, 5 to 7 minutes.

4. **COOK SHRIMP:** Stir in shrimp and continue to simmer until shrimp are cooked through, about 3 minutes. Off heat, season with salt and pepper to taste. Sprinkle with scallions before serving.

➤ VARIATION

Shrimp and Sausage Gumbo with Okra
Stir 1 (10-ounce) bag frozen okra, thawed, into skillet with vegetables in step 2.

MEDITERRANEAN FISH STEW

THERE ARE COUNTLESS RECIPES FOR quick-cooking fish stews that are based on the popular tomato-based stews of the Mediterranean. However, many of these stews have one unfortunate common denominator—their flavor is dull. We sought a deeply flavorful, hearty fish stew, redolent of garlic and laced with a bit of spice. The

obvious question was how we could prepare this flavorful stew in 30 minutes.

The challenge, we found, lies in building an intensely flavored broth in which to simmer the fish. The problem is that most recipes don't spend the time to develop this broth. Considering that small cubes of fish only take several minutes to cook, we thought that we had plenty of time to construct a good broth.

Our first step was to sauté a heap of vegetables in several tablespoons of fruity extra-virgin olive oil. A trio of onion, red pepper, and fennel provided us with an aromatic base. Along with the vegetables, we also added a half pound of chorizo sausage (a highly spiced smoked pork sausage), a heavy dose of garlic, and some hot red pepper flakes. These three potent ingredients lent the broth an intense, spicy flavor. To this pungent base, we stirred in canned diced tomatoes, a splash of white wine for brightness, and a bottle of clam juice to enhance the stew's fish flavor. With all the ingredients together, we simmered the broth for 10 minutes, allowing the components to meld and mellow. The final step was to add the fish and let it gently simmer for five minutes until just cooked through.

EASY GARLIC TOASTS
MAKES 12
Fresh bread is a great accompaniment to our fish stew, but these toasts are effortless and can be baked while the stew simmers.

12	½-inch-thick slices baguette
1	garlic clove, peeled
	Extra-virgin olive oil
	Salt and ground black pepper

Adjust oven rack to middle position and heat oven to 400 degrees. Arrange bread in single layer on large baking sheet. Bake until bread is dry and crisp, about 10 minutes, flipping slices over halfway through. Gently rub one side of each toast with garlic clove. Drizzle toasts lightly with oil and season with salt and pepper.

Hearty Mediterranean-Style Fish Stew with Chorizo Sausage

SERVES 4 TO 6

Serve this saucy stew with Easy Garlic Toasts (page 90), crusty bread, or over rice.

2	tablespoons extra-virgin olive oil
1	onion, minced
1	fennel bulb, trimmed, cored, and cut into thin strips (see page 31)
1	red bell pepper, cored and sliced thin
½	pound chorizo sausage, cut into ½-inch pieces
¼	teaspoon red pepper flakes
	Salt and ground black pepper
6	garlic cloves, minced
½	cup dry white wine
2	(14.5-ounce) cans diced tomatoes
1	(8-ounce) bottle clam juice
1½	pounds cod fillets, cut into 2-inch pieces

MAKING THE MINUTES COUNT:
Cut the cod while the stew simmers in step 2.

1. SAUTÉ SAUSAGE AND VEGETABLES: Heat oil in large Dutch oven over medium-high heat until shimmering. Add onion, fennel, bell pepper, chorizo, red pepper flakes, and ½ teaspoon salt and cook until vegetables are softened, about 7 minutes.

2. MAKE SAUCE: Stir in garlic and cook until fragrant, about 30 seconds. Stir in wine, scraping up any browned bits. Stir in tomatoes and clam juice. Bring to simmer and cook to blend flavors, 10 minutes.

3. COOK FISH AND FINISH STEW: Pat cod dry with paper towels and season with salt and pepper. Nestle cod into pan and spoon sauce over fish. Cover and cook over low heat until fish flakes apart when gently prodded with paring knife, about 5 minutes. Season with salt and pepper to taste and serve.

A TEST KITCHEN CLASSIC

FISH BRAISES

WHILE BRAISING IS USUALLY RESERVED FOR cooking tough pieces of meat over a long period of time, we found it to be a great way to add complexity to mild-flavored fish or to mellow the potency of stronger-tasting fish.

We aimed to develop our first fish braise around the spicy flavors popular in the Mexican region of Veracruz. We first built a tomato-based broth using drained diced tomatoes. (We drained the tomatoes so that we could enrich our sauce with white wine for brightness.) We also incorporated onion, garlic, pimiento-stuffed green olives, and chili powder. We then nestled pieces of fish into the sauce, covered the skillet, and let the fish braise. This method trapped the heat so the fish partially steamed and partially simmered in this aromatic stew of vegetables and spice. The aroma was delightful, not fishy. The result was tender, moist, flavor-packed fish that took less than 30 minutes to get on the table.

For our second fish braise, we looked to incorporate the flavors of the Italian dish, *peperonata,* or stewed bell peppers. Along with the bell peppers, we added fresh basil and balsamic vinegar. The combination nicely complemented the fish and was delicious sopped up with some crusty bread.

KITCHEN SHORTCUT
QUICK MINCED GARLIC

When you need to mince a large amount of garlic, it makes sense to use a garlic press. Add the cloves to the hopper and squeeze. The flesh is forced the through holes of the press, producing finely minced garlic quickly and easily.

Braised Cod Veracruz
SERVES 4

Halibut, snapper, tilapia, bluefish, monkfish, or sea bass fillets are all good substitutions for the cod. If desired, drizzle with extra-virgin olive oil before serving. Rice makes a nice accompaniment to this dish.

2	tablespoons olive oil
1	onion, halved and sliced thin
2	teaspoons chili powder
	Salt and ground black pepper
4	garlic cloves, minced
1	(14.5-ounce) can diced tomatoes, drained
1/4	cup pimiento-stuffed green olives, sliced thin
1/2	cup dry white wine
1	teaspoon minced fresh thyme
4	skinless cod fillets, 1 inch thick
2	tablespoons minced fresh cilantro

MAKING THE MINUTES COUNT:
While the onion cooks, prepare the garlic, olives, and thyme. Mince the cilantro while the fish cooks.

1. SAUTÉ AROMATICS: Heat oil in 12-inch non-stick skillet over medium heat until shimmering. Add onion, chili powder, and ½ teaspoon salt and cook until softened, about 5 minutes. Stir in garlic and cook until fragrant, about 30 seconds.

2. MAKE SAUCE: Stir in tomatoes, olives, wine, thyme, and ¼ teaspoon pepper, and bring to simmer.

3. POACH FISH: Pat cod dry with paper towels and season with salt and pepper. Nestle cod into pan and spoon sauce over fish. Cover and cook over low heat until fish flakes apart when gently prodded with paring knife, about 10 minutes.

4. FINISH SAUCE: Transfer fish to individual plates. Stir cilantro into sauce and season with salt and pepper to taste. Spoon sauce over fish and serve.

Braised Cod with Peperonata
SERVES 4

Halibut, snapper, tilapia, bluefish, monkfish, or sea bass fillets are all good substitutions for the cod. If desired, drizzle with extra-virgin olive oil before serving. Smoked paprika (often found in specialty spice markets) is a nice substitution for the paprika here. Serve with soft polenta or crusty bread.

2	tablespoons olive oil
2	red bell peppers, cored and sliced thin
1	onion, halved and sliced thin
2	teaspoons paprika (see note)
	Salt and ground black pepper
4	garlic cloves, minced
1	(14.5-ounce) can diced tomatoes, drained
1/2	cup dry white wine
1	teaspoon minced fresh thyme
4	skinless cod fillets, 1 inch thick
2	tablespoons coarsely chopped fresh basil
2	teaspoons balsamic or sherry vinegar

MAKING THE MINUTES COUNT:
While the peppers and onion cook, mince the garlic and thyme. Chop the basil while the fish cooks.

1. SAUTÉ AROMATICS: Heat oil in 12-inch non-stick skillet over medium heat until shimmering. Add bell peppers, onion, paprika, and ½ teaspoon salt and cook until softened, about 7 minutes. Stir in garlic and cook until fragrant, about 30 seconds.

2. MAKE SAUCE: Stir in tomatoes, wine, thyme, and ¼ teaspoon pepper, and bring to simmer.

3. POACH FISH: Pat cod dry with paper towels and season with salt and pepper. Nestle cod into pan and spoon sauce over fish. Cover and cook over low heat until fish flakes apart when gently prodded with paring knife, about 10 minutes.

4. FINISH SAUCE: Transfer fish to individual plates. Stir basil and vinegar into sauce and season with salt and pepper to taste. Spoon sauce over fish and serve.

5

MIX AND MATCH STIR-FRIES

Mix and Match Stir-Fries

FASTER STIR-FRIES

STIR-FRIES COOK IN JUST MINUTES, BUT IT'S all the preparation that can make them so laborious and time-consuming. Sure, you can use pre-cut meat labeled "for stir-fry," bags of frozen vegetables, and bottled stir-fry sauces, but they don't taste very good. The mystery meat has the texture of shoe leather, the frozen vegetables turn mushy, and the bottled sauces taste harsh and salty.

So how could we cut corners and still have a flavorful stir-fry? There are lots of fresh, pre-cut vegetables available at supermarket salad bars as well as bagged varieties in the produce section. And we think these taste pretty good. We also like some canned vegetables, like baby corn, water chestnuts, and bamboo shoots in stir-fries. As for the meat and the sauce, cutting up your own meat is well worth the five minutes it takes, as is spending two minutes to make your own sauce. We came up with a few easy, quick-prep sauces that you can mix and match to create your own stir-fries.

As for technique, using high heat is essential when stir-frying, and we find that a skillet, with its flat bottom, maximizes the heat output from a burner much better than a wok, with its wide, sloped sides. A 12-inch nonstick skillet is our stir-frying pan of choice. Also, it is important to cook the meat and vegetables separately, before combining them with the sauce to finish. If you brown your meat (or shrimp or tofu) first, then cook the vegetables, you can better ensure that every component is properly cooked. We've broken out the vegetables most commonly used in stir-fries into groups according to how long they need to cook and whether you need to add water to the pan to steam-cook them. It's also important to take care when stir-frying aromatics (such as garlic and ginger), which can easily burn—we take the precaution of stir-frying aromatics last, rather than first as most recipes do. Our hope is that once you understand the core technique for building a stir-fry, you will be able to mix and match all the components yourself, given your own preferences (and what you have on hand).

KITCHEN SHORTCUT
GRATING GINGER

Why bother mincing ginger when it's so much faster and easier to grate it? Be sure to follow this method to avoid scraping your fingers on the grater's sharp teeth: Peel a small section of a large piece of ginger. Then grate the peeled portion, using the rest of the ginger as a handle to keep your fingers safely away from the grater.

Stir-Fry Vegetables

Although we like to use pre-cut vegetables to save time, we've found that they sometimes benefit from a little extra trimming—either to make the pieces more uniform in size, or to trim off any browned edges. For very tough vegetables (listed below), it is necessary to cook them in the skillet with some water (about ½ cup) to help them steam and soften.

VERY TOUGH VEGETABLES (REQUIRE STEAMING DURING COOKING) 3 TO 6 MINUTES	Broccoli, Cauliflower, Green beans
LONGER-COOKING VEGETABLES I TO 6 MINUTES	Asparagus, Bell peppers, Bok choy, Carrots, Baby corn, Frozen shelled edamame, Fennel, Mushrooms, Red onions, Water chestnuts
FASTER-COOKING VEGETABLES 30 TO 60 SECONDS	Bean sprouts, Cabbage, Celery, Tender greens, Frozen peas, Scallion greens, Snow peas, Tomatoes

Stir-Fried Beef and Broccoli with Orange-Sesame Sauce

SERVES 4

Be sure to slice the beef thin against the grain (see illustration on page 98) to prevent it from becoming tough. Any kind of bell pepper will work here.

- 1   pound flank steak, cut into thin strips
- 2   teaspoons soy sauce
- 2   tablespoons vegetable oil
- 1   recipe Orange-Sesame Sauce, page 102
- 8   ounces bite-sized broccoli florets (3 cups)
- ½   cup water
- 1   bell pepper, cored, seeded, and sliced
- 1   (8-ounce) can water chestnuts, drained
- 3   garlic cloves, minced
- 1   tablespoon grated fresh ginger

MAKING THE MINUTES COUNT:

Prepare the sauce while the beef cooks. Mince the garlic and grate the ginger while the vegetables cook.

1. STIR-FRY BEEF AND PREPARE SAUCE: Toss steak with soy sauce. Heat 2 teaspoons of oil in 12-inch nonstick skillet over high heat until just smoking. Add beef and cook, stirring occasionally and breaking up clumps, until lightly browned, about 3 minutes. (While beef cooks, prepare sauce.) Transfer beef to clean bowl.

2. STIR-FRY VEGETABLES: Add 1 more tablespoon of oil to pan and return to high heat until shimmering. Add broccoli and water to pan, cover, and cook until bright green and slightly tender, about 2 minutes. Remove lid, add bell pepper and water chestnuts, and continue to cook until vegetables are tender, about 3 minutes.

3. COMBINE AND SIMMER: Clear center of pan and add remaining 1 teaspoon oil, garlic, and ginger. Cook, mashing garlic mixture into pan with back of spatula, until fragrant, about 30 seconds. Stir in cooked beef. Whisk sauce to recombine, add to pan, and bring to simmer. Cook sauce until thickened, 1 to 2 minutes. Serve immediately.

Stir-Fried Pork and Snow Peas with Sweet-and-Sour Sauce

SERVES 4

Canned pineapple works fine in this recipe but you can also use fresh pineapple, which is often available already cut into chunks.

- 1   pound pork tenderloin, cut into thin strips (see page 98)
- 2   teaspoons soy sauce
- 2   tablespoons vegetable oil
- 1   recipe Sweet-and-Sour Sauce, page 102
- 1   red onion, sliced thin (1 cup)
- 6   ounces snow peas, strings removed (1 cup)
- 1   (20-ounce) can diced pineapple, drained
- 3   garlic cloves, minced
- 1   tablespoon grated fresh ginger

MAKING THE MINUTES COUNT:

Prepare the sauce while the pork cooks. Mince the garlic and grate the ginger while the vegetables cook.

1. STIR-FRY PORK AND PREPARE SAUCE: Toss pork with soy sauce. Heat 2 teaspoons of oil in 12-inch nonstick skillet over high heat until just smoking. Add pork and cook, stirring occasionally and breaking up clumps, until lightly browned, about 3 minutes. (While pork cooks, prepare sauce.) Transfer pork to clean bowl.

2. STIR-FRY VEGETABLES AND PINEAPPLE: Add 1 more tablespoon of oil to pan and return to high heat until shimmering. Add onion and snow peas and cook, stirring frequently, until softened, about 3 minutes. Add pineapple and cook until warmed through.

3. COMBINE AND SIMMER: Clear center of pan and add remaining 1 teaspoon oil, garlic, and ginger. Cook, mashing garlic mixture into pan with back of spatula, until fragrant, about 30 seconds. Stir in cooked pork. Whisk sauce to recombine, add it to pan, and bring to simmer. Cook until sauce thickens, 1 to 2 minutes. Serve immediately.

Stir-Fried Chicken and Vegetables with Spicy Thai Basil Sauce

SERVES 4

Any type of bell pepper can be used here.

1	pound boneless, skinless chicken breasts, cut into thin strips (see page 98)
2	teaspoons soy sauce
2	tablespoons vegetable oil
1	recipe Spicy Thai Basil Sauce, page 102
1	8-ounce package sliced button mushrooms
4	ounces thinly sliced or julienned carrots (1 ½ cups)
1	bell pepper, cored, seeded, and sliced (1 ½ cups)
3	garlic cloves, minced
1	tablespoon grated fresh ginger

MAKING THE MINUTES COUNT:
Prepare the sauce while the chicken cooks. Mince the garlic and grate the ginger while the vegetables cook.

1. STIR-FRY CHICKEN AND PREPARE SAUCE: Toss chicken with soy sauce. Heat 2 teaspoons of oil in 12-inch nonstick skillet over high heat until just smoking. Add chicken and cook, stirring occasionally and breaking up clumps, until lightly browned, about 3 minutes. (While chicken cooks, prepare sauce.) Transfer chicken to clean bowl.

2. STIR-FRY VEGETABLES: Add 1 more tablespoon of oil to pan and return to high heat until shimmering. Add mushrooms and cook, stirring occasionally, until lightly browned, about 6 minutes. Stir in carrots and bell pepper and cook until tender, about 3 minutes.

3. COMBINE AND SIMMER: Clear center of pan and add remaining 1 teaspoon oil, garlic, and ginger. Cook, mashing garlic mixture into pan with back of spatula, until fragrant, about 30 seconds. Stir in cooked chicken. Whisk sauce to recombine, add to pan, and bring to simmer. Cook until sauce thickens, 1 to 2 minutes. Serve immediately.

Stir-Fried Shrimp and Snow Peas with Coconut-Curry Sauce

SERVES 4

Any type of bell pepper will work here.

1	recipe Coconut-Curry Sauce, page 102
1	pound extra-large (21/25) shrimp, peeled and deveined, page 173
2	teaspoons soy sauce
2	tablespoons vegetable oil
1	bell pepper, cored, seeded, and sliced (1 ½ cups)
8	ounces snow peas, strings removed (1 ½ cups)
1	cup bean sprouts
3	garlic cloves, minced
1	tablespoon grated fresh ginger

MAKING THE MINUTES COUNT:
Mince the garlic and grate the ginger while the vegetables cook.

1. PREPARE SAUCE AND STIR-FRY SHRIMP: Prepare sauce and set aside. Toss shrimp with soy sauce. Heat 2 teaspoons of oil in 12-inch nonstick skillet over high heat until just smoking. Add shrimp and cook, stirring occasionally and breaking up clumps, until curled and lightly browned, about 1½ minutes. Transfer shrimp to clean bowl.

2. STIR-FRY VEGETABLES: Add 1 more tablespoon of oil to pan and return to high heat until shimmering. Add bell pepper and cook, stirring occasionally, until crisp-tender, about 2 minutes. Stir in snow peas and bean sprouts and cook for 1 minute.

3. COMBINE AND SIMMER: Clear center of pan and add remaining 1 teaspoon oil, garlic, and ginger. Cook, mashing garlic mixture into pan with back of spatula, until fragrant, about 30 seconds. Stir in cooked shrimp. Whisk sauce to recombine, add to pan, and bring to simmer. Cook until sauce thickens, 1 to 2 minutes. Serve immediately.

Stir Fry 101

Stir-fries are naturally quick cooking. The key is to have all your meat and vegetables prepped before you begin cooking. They should be cut into even pieces so they all cook at the same rate. A vibrantly flavored sauce (see page 102) brings all the elements together.

SLICING MEAT FOR STIR-FRIES

The meat (and vegetables) should be cut into even pieces so they all cook at the same rate. It is better to take five minutes and cut up your own meat rather than to buy packages labeled "for stir-fry," since this can be any type or cut of meat, merely cut into small pieces. The right type of meat makes all the difference between tender bites and pieces that resemble shoe leather. To make it easier to cut meat thin, place it in the freezer for 15 minutes.

BEEF

We like to use flank steak because is easy to find, relatively lean, and has a big beefy flavor that can stand up to the potent flavors in a stir-fry.

1. Place the partially frozen steak on a clean, dry work surface. Using a sharp chef's knife, slice the steak lengthwise into 2-inch-wide pieces.

2. Cut each 2-inch piece of flank steak against the grain into very thin slices.

PORK

Although some stir-fry recipes call for ground pork or thinly sliced boneless chops, we find that strips cut from a pork tenderloin are the most tender and flavorful option.

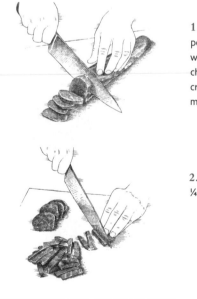

1. Place the partially frozen pork tenderloin on a clean, dry work surface. Using a sharp chef's knife, slice the pork crosswise into ¼-inch-thick medallions.

2. Slice each medallion into ¼-inch-wide strips.

CHICKEN

Boneless, skinless breasts work best for stir-fries and are easy to cut into ½-inch-wide strips. In the world of stir-frying, chicken requires a fairly long time to cook through and brown slightly—at least three or four minutes.

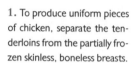

1. To produce uniform pieces of chicken, separate the tenderloins from the partially frozen skinless, boneless breasts.

2. Slice the breasts across the grain into ½-inch-wide strips that are 1½ to 2 inches long. Center pieces need to be cut in half so they are approximately the same length as the end pieces.

3. Cut tenderloins on the diagonal to produce pieces about the same size as the strips of breast meat.

STICKY WHITE RICE FOR STIR-FRIES

MAKES 5 CUPS

This traditional Chinese cooking method yields sticky rice that works well as an accompaniment to a stir-fry (and makes rice that is easier to eat with chopsticks).

2	cups long-grain white rice
3	cups water
½	teaspoon salt

1. Bring rice, water, and salt to boil in medium saucepan. Cook, uncovered over medium-high heat, until water level drops below top surface of rice and small holes form in rice, about 10 minutes.

2. Reduce heat to very low, cover, and continue to cook until rice is tender, about 15 minutes longer.

ESSENTIAL TOOLS FOR STIR-FRYING SUCCESS

Stir-frying requires only a couple of pieces of basic equipment (you probably already own them). Woks are the traditional cooking vessel for stir-frying in China. Conically shaped, woks rest in cylindrical pits containing the fire. Flames lick the bottom and sides of the pan so that food cooks remarkably quickly. A wok, however, is not designed for stovetop cooking, where heat only comes from the bottom. Therefore, we prefer a 12- or 14-inch nonstick skillet for stir-frying. This pan requires a minimum of oil and prevents food from burning onto the surface as it stir-fries. We tested major brands of nonstick skillets (see page 5), and particularly liked pans that were sturdy, but not overly heavy, with a good nonstick performance.

Our second choice for stir-frying is a regular 12- or 14-inch traditional skillet (see page 110 for our testing of traditional skillets). Without the nonstick coating, you will need to use slightly more oil. However, this pan will deliver satisfactory results. If you do not own a large skillet of any kind, do not substitute a smaller size. A 10-inch skillet is not large enough to accommodate all the ingredients in a stir-fry recipe for four. The ingredients will steam rather than stir-fry.

Chinese cooks use long-handled metal shovel-like spatulas to move food around woks. The same tool works well in a nonstick skillet, although to protect the pan's surface, you should use only plastic or wooden implements. We prefer large shovels with a wide, thin blade and long, heat-resistant handle.

STIR-FRYING STEP-BY-STEP

Here are the four key steps to making a stir-fry. (Be sure to use a 12-inch nonstick skillet and cook over high heat.)

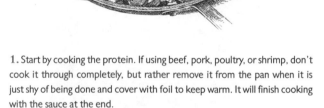

1. Start by cooking the protein. If using beef, pork, poultry, or shrimp, don't cook it through completely, but rather remove it from the pan when it is just shy of being done and cover with foil to keep warm. It will finish cooking with the sauce at the end.

2. Next, cook the vegetables in batches, adding the tougher vegetables first and the more delicate vegetables later (see Stir-Fry Vegetables on page 95). This ensures that each vegetable will be perfectly cooked.

3. Push the vegetables to the edges of the skillet, clearing a spot in the middle. Add the garlic, ginger, and a little oil to the cleared spot and cook, mashing them into the hot pan using a spatula until they are fragrant, about 30 seconds.

4. Return the cooked protein to the skillet, add the sauce, and toss to combine. Continue to cook until the sauce has thickened and the meat (if using) is fully cooked, 1 to 2 minutes.

ASIAN INGREDIENTS

With the increased interest in authentic Asian cooking, supermarkets are carrying a wider array of Asian ingredients. The following list includes common Asian ingredients that you'll find in some of our recipes.

ASIAN CHILI SAUCE:

Used both in cooking and as a condiment, this sauce comes in many different forms, each with varying degrees of heat. You'll find jars of chili sauce labeled "sambal oelek," "sriracha," and "chili garlic sauce" in the international aisle of larger supermarkets. You can use them interchangeably whenever a recipe calls for Asian chili sauce—just remember, a little goes a long way with these fiery sauces. Consisting of chiles, sugar, vinegar, salt, and sometimes garlic, Asian chili sauce will keep indefinitely when refrigerated.

COCONUT MILK:

Coconut milk is widely available in cans. It adds richness and a mild coconut flavor to soups, curries, and stir-fries. Be sure to shake the can well before using to distribute the coconut cream that will have solidified at the top of the can. Do not confuse coconut milk with cream of coconut, which is much sweeter.

FISH SAUCE:

Fish sauce, or *nam pla* or *nuoc cham,* is a salty, amber-colored liquid made from fermented fish. It is used both as an ingredient and a condiment in many Asian cuisines, most commonly in the foods of Southeast Asia. Used in very small amounts, it adds a well rounded, salty flavor to sauces, soups, and marinades. Fish sauce will keep indefinitely without refrigeration.

HOISIN SAUCE:

Also called Peking sauce, hoisin sauce is a mixture of soybeans, garlic, chile peppers, and spices, the most predominant of which is five-spice powder. This thick, dark brown sauce has a complex flavor that forms the base of many stir-fries. It is also used as a table condiment, much like ketchup. This sauce will keep indefinitely when refrigerated.

MIRIN:

Mirin is a sweet rice wine used for cooking. Made from glutinous rice, some mirin can contain corn syrup, water, alcohol, and salt. Typically used in Japanese cooking, we use mirin to brighten the flavor of stir-fries, teriyaki, and other Asian dishes. If you cannot find mirin, substitute 1 tablespoon white wine and ½ teaspoon sugar for every 1 tablespoon of mirin.

RICE VINEGAR:

Rice vinegar is made from fermented rice, sugar, and water. Because of its sweet-tart flavor, rice vinegar is used to accentuate many Asian dishes. It comes in two varieties: seasoned and unseasoned. We prefer the clean flavor of unseasoned. Rice vinegar will keep indefinitely without refrigeration. If you don't find rice vinegar with other Asian ingredients in the supermarket, look for it with the other vinegars.

SESAME OIL:

Raw sesame oil, which is very mild and light in color, is used mostly for cooking, while toasted sesame oil, which has a deep amber color, is primarily used for seasoning because of its intense, nutty flavor. For the biggest hit of sesame flavor, we prefer to use toasted sesame oil. Just a few drops of this oil will give stir-fries or noodle dishes a deep, nutty flavor—but too much will be overpowering.

SOY SAUCE:

Available everywhere, soy sauce is made from fermented soybeans with roasted wheat or barley added. We prefer naturally brewed soy sauces to synthetic sauces, which are very salty (and include hydrolyzed vegetable protein in their ingredient lists). "Lite" or lower sodium soy sauces are widely available and may be used in any recipe. Tamari is a Japanese soy sauce that contains no wheat, and is typically richer and stronger in flavor than regular soy sauce.

Stir-Fried Tofu and Vegetables with Orange-Sesame Sauce

SERVES 4

Be sure to use only firm or extra-firm tofu for this recipe. To save time, buy bagged pre-cut carrots.

1	(14-ounce) package extra-firm tofu, patted dry and cut into ½-inch cubes
2	teaspoons soy sauce
2	tablespoons vegetable oil
1	recipe Orange-Sesame Sauce, page 102
4	ounces julienned or thinly sliced carrots (1½ cups)
7	ounces frozen shelled edamame beans (1½ cups)
1	(15-ounce) can baby corn, rinsed
3	garlic cloves, minced
1	tablespoon grated fresh ginger

MAKING THE MINUTES COUNT:

Prepare the sauce while the tofu cooks. Mince the garlic and grate the ginger while the vegetables cook.

1. STIR-FRY TOFU AND PREPARE SAUCE: Toss tofu with soy sauce. Heat 2 teaspoons of oil in 12-inch nonstick skillet over high heat until just smoking. Add tofu and cook, stirring occasionally, until lightly browned, about 5 minutes. (While tofu cooks, prepare sauce.) Transfer tofu to clean bowl.

2. STIR-FRY VEGETABLES: Add 1 more tablespoon of oil to pan and return to high heat until shimmering. Add carrots, edamame, and corn, and cook until carrots are crisp-tender and beans are warmed through, about 4 minutes.

3. COMBINE AND SIMMER: Clear center of pan and add remaining 1 teaspoon oil, garlic, and ginger. Cook, mashing garlic mixture into pan with back of spatula, until fragrant, about 30 seconds. Stir in cooked tofu. Whisk sauce to recombine, add to pan, and bring to simmer. Cook until sauce thickens, 1 to 2 minutes. Serve immediately.

Create-Your-Own Stir-Fry

SERVES 4

Using freshly grated ginger is crucial for flavor.

1	pound protein such as flank steak, pork tenderloin, boneless, skinless chicken breasts, or tofu (cut into small, even pieces) or 1 pound shrimp (peeled and deveined)
2	teaspoons soy sauce
2	tablespoons vegetable oil
1	recipe stir-fry sauce, page 102
1½	pounds prepared vegetables, cut into small pieces and divided into batches based on cooking times (see page 95)
3	garlic cloves, minced
1	tablespoon grated fresh ginger

MAKING THE MINUTES COUNT:

Assemble the sauce while the protein cooks. Mince the garlic and grate the ginger while the vegetables cook.

1. STIR-FRY PROTEIN AND PREPARE SAUCE: Toss protein with soy sauce. Heat 2 teaspoons of oil in 12-inch nonstick skillet over high heat until just smoking. Add protein and cook, stirring occasionally and breaking up clumps, until lightly browned, 1½ to 5 minutes. (While protein cooks, prepare stir-fry sauce.) Transfer protein to clean bowl.

2. STIR-FRY VEGETABLES: Add 1 more tablespoon of oil to pan and return to high heat until shimmering. If using very tough vegetables, add to skillet with ½ cup water, cover, and steam over high heat for about 2 minutes; uncover. Add longer-cooking vegetables and cook, stirring occasionally, until crisp-tender, 1 to 5 minutes. Add faster-cooking vegetables and cook until vegetables are crisp-tender, 30 to 60 seconds.

3. COMBINE AND SIMMER: Clear center of pan and add remaining 1 teaspoon oil, garlic, and ginger. Cook, mashing garlic mixture into pan with back of spatula, until fragrant, about 30 seconds. Stir in cooked protein. Whisk sauce to recombine, add to pan, and bring to simmer. Cook sauce until thickened, 1 to 2 minutes. Serve immediately.

STIR-FRY SAUCES

STRONGLY FLAVORED SAUCES ARE THE KEY to vibrant stir-fries. In our testing, we found that too much cornstarch (many recipes call for 1 tablespoon or more) makes sauces thick and gloppy. We prefer the cleaner flavor and texture of sauces made with a minimum of cornstarch—no more than 2 teaspoons for a typical stir-fry. With so little cornstarch, it is necessary to limit the amount of liquid ingredients in the sauce—about 1 cup in the recipes that follow. We found that the yield of some stir-fry sauces are somewhat skimpy, so we made sure our yields were a bit more generous. About one cup of sauce will nicely coat the ingredients in our standard stir-fry, plus there will be enough to moisten your rice.

Orange-Sesame Sauce

MAKES ENOUGH FOR I STIR-FRY RECIPE

The citrus flavor is this sauce is especially good with chicken and seafood.

½	cup orange juice
¼	cup low-sodium chicken broth
¼	cup soy sauce
2	teaspoons toasted sesame oil
2	teaspoons cornstarch

Combine ingredients in medium bowl and use as directed in stir-fry recipes.

Spicy Orange Sauce

MAKES ENOUGH FOR I STIR-FRY RECIPE

Add more red pepper flakes to taste for even more heat.

I	cup orange juice
2	tablespoons hoisin sauce
2	teaspoons cornstarch
¼	teaspoon red pepper flakes

Combine ingredients in medium bowl and use as directed in stir-fry recipes.

Coconut-Curry Sauce

MAKES ENOUGH FOR I STIR-FRY RECIPE

This velvety sauce coats food especially well.

I	cup coconut milk
I	tablespoon fish sauce
I–2	teaspoons red curry paste
I	teaspoon light brown sugar
I	teaspoon cornstarch

Combine ingredients in medium bowl and use as directed in stir-fry recipes.

Sweet-and-Sour Sauce

MAKES ENOUGH FOR I STIR-FRY RECIPE

The flavors in this sauce are good with chicken, pork, and seafood.

6	tablespoons red wine vinegar
6	tablespoons orange juice
6	tablespoons sugar
3	tablespoons ketchup
I	teaspoon cornstarch
½	teaspoon salt

Combine ingredients in medium bowl and use as directed in stir-fry recipes.

Spicy Thai Basil Sauce

MAKES ENOUGH FOR I STIR-FRY RECIPE

Fish sauce gives this stir-fry sauce its authentic Thai flavor. This sauce goes well with meat, poultry, or seafood. It's good with tofu, too.

I	cup basil leaves, chopped coarse
¾	cup low-sodium chicken broth
2	tablespoons fish sauce
I	tablespoon Asian chili sauce
2	teaspoons brown sugar
2	teaspoons cornstarch

Combine ingredients in medium bowl and use as directed in stir-fry recipes.

PAN-ROASTED CHICKEN BREASTS WITH POTATOES **PAGE 113**

CORNMEAL FRIED FISH AND SUCCOTASH **PAGE 126**

ITALIAN SAUSAGE, PEPPER, AND ONION HOAGIES **PAGE 122**

30-MINUTE STEAK AND POTATO SALAD **PAGE 33**

SKILLET LASAGNA **PAGE 137**

BAKED ZITI **PAGE 140**

SIMPLE SAUTÉED CHICKEN BREASTS **PAGE 191** WITH WARM CHERRY TOMATO RELISH **PAGE 198**

ASIAN CHICKEN NOODLE SOUP **PAGE 47**

SHRIMP CURRY WITH POTATOES AND CAULIFLOWER **PAGE 88**

SKILLET STRATA WITH SPINACH AND SMOKED GOUDA **PAGE 11**

SPAGHETTI WITH GARLIC, OLIVE OIL, AND ARTICHOKES **PAGE 165**

SKILLET BEEF POT PIE **PAGE 117**

BEEF TERIYAKI **PAGE 205**

SIMPLIFIED PAD THAI **PAGE 180**

6

SKILLET SUPPERS

Skillet Suppers

QUICK COOKING ISN'T JUST ABOUT THE time it takes to cook a meal. It can also involve dealing with multiple pots and pans, which each require attention. A complete meal often means pulling out one pan for the meat, at least one for the vegetables, another for the starch, and so on. In this chapter, however, we decided to reduce the number of pans we use to the bare essentials—primarily just a skillet. In some cases, we use a two-track approach, relying on a skillet and a baking dish. In these cases, we start by pan-searing meat in the skillet and then we transfer it to the oven to finish cooking. Why? Because this frees up the skillet for cooking side dishes, allowing us to develop a wider variety of meals. The microwave also comes in handy in quick-cooking. A short spell in the microwave, followed by a finish on the stovetop or in the oven, gives long-cooking foods such as potatoes a head start so that they too can be part of a 30-minute meal.

That said, skillet suppers do pose particular challenges. Since they are meant to be a one-dish meal complete with a protein, a starch, and vegetables, we were faced with ingredients that often have very different cooking times. Orchestrating these different ingredients in and out of the skillet so that they were hot and properly cooked all at the same time proved to be quite a challenge. For example, when developing a recipe for paella, we had to figure out how to cook the rice, shrimp, and peas (ingredients with very disparate cooking times) in the same skillet, while avoiding sticky rice, rubbery shrimp, and mushy peas. After much trial and error (and many a bland and overcooked dish), we learned not only how to pair the ingredients in these recipes but also the order in which they should be added to the skillet. The recipes in this chapter aim to choreograph these sorts of issues while delivering tasty one-dish meals in just 30 minutes.

And while we adapted some unmistakable skillet classics, like fajitas and sloppy Joes, we found that rotating ingredients in and out of the skillet freed us to be more inventive when developing recipes. This flexibility enabled us to create dishes like Chicken and Couscous with Fennel and Orange and Cornmeal Fried Fish and Succotash.

The recipes in this chapter require a 12-inch skillet (many also require a cover); a smaller skillet will not work. In most cases, you can use a traditional skillet, but a few recipes do require a nonstick skillet for best results. See page 110 for the results of our testing of traditional skillets and page 5 for the results of our testing of nonstick skillets.

A TEST KITCHEN CLASSIC

CHICKEN AND RICE

MOST QUICK RECIPES FOR CHICKEN AND RICE rely on boneless chicken breasts, instant rice, and canned soup. The chicken comes out dry, the rice mushy, and the sauce tastes, well, canned. We knew we could do better on all fronts. We wanted fresh-tasting chicken and rice that resembled the traditional version, but could be on the table in 30 minutes.

We started with the chicken. Because chicken breasts are so lean, they do require special treatment to prevent the meat from drying out. We found that dredging the chicken breasts in flour protected their exterior, giving the chicken a golden brown crust, which ensures juicy meat. And because this is a 30-minute recipe, we relied on quick-cooking instant rice (see page 107). The texture of instant rice can often be mushy, so we made some modifications in cooking it. We sautéed it first (in butter or oil) with aromatics, and then added the cooking liquid. This step not only gave the rice a deeper flavor, but it kept the grains a bit more distinct and creamy, instead of mushy. As for the canned soup, forget it. There are some convenience products we find acceptable in certain applications (instant rice, for one), but canned soup just doesn't make the cut. Instead, we built our own quick broth in the same pan we used to sauté our chicken. We simply sautéed aromatic vegetables along with the browned bits left in the pan from the chicken, then added chicken broth, creating a rich tasting, deeply flavorful liquid.

To boost our fresher flavors even further, we added red pepper flakes and stirred lemon juice and scallions into the rice before serving. We also created a number of variations with bold flavor combinations like broccoli and cheddar, coconut milk and pistachios, curry and raisins, and saffron and chorizo.

SHORTCUT INGREDIENT:
Instant Rice

Essentially, white rice is brown rice made convenient. Developed thousands of years ago, the technique of stripping the germ and bran layers from brown rice to get white rice saves 30 minutes in cooking time. In today's busy world, that can make a big difference; but, even still, white rice needs at least 30 minutes to cook. Fortunately, rice manufacturers have made cooking long-grain white rice even more of a snap with five-minute instant varieties, boil-in-bag options, and even packaged fully-cooked rice. Here in the test kitchen, we set out to understand the differences in these products, and see how they would work in our quick recipes.

Some people mistake converted rice for shorter-cooking rice—not true. Converted rice is unmilled rice that is soaked in hot water, then steamed and dried in the husk. The primary advantage of this processing is that the rice remains firmer and more separate when it's cooked. The problem: it can take even longer than white rice to cook—not an option for our recipes.

Boil-in-bag products are a modern innovation made by precooking converted rice, and then drying it and packaging it in a perforated bag for quick and easy cooking. The idea is that the parboiling will create rice grains that will remain firm and separate during the 10-minute final cooking. Though tasters liked boil-in-bag rice when cooked on its own as a side dish, it did not fare as well in our recipes, as the grains remained too separate and firm.

And then there is instant rice. To make it, milled rice is fully precooked and then dried very fast. Usually in the test kitchen we are not impressed with instant rice, but we found that in certain applications, like Chicken and Rice (page 106) and Skillet Paella (page 131), where the rice is slightly creamy and sticky, it works well.

At the end of the spectrum is fully cooked rice, which is coated with oil to keep the grains distinct, and packaged in convenient microwavable pouches. Surprisingly, tasters didn't mind this product in our Simple Fried Rice (page 258), though in other applications like paella and jambalaya, where the rice needed to be cooked for longer amounts of time, it didn't fare as well.

Chicken and Rice with Peas and Scallions
SERVES 4

Be sure to use chicken breasts that are roughly the same size to ensure even cooking. To use long-grain rice, see "Got Extra Time?" below.

4	boneless, skinless chicken breasts
	Salt and ground black pepper
1/2	cup unbleached all-purpose flour
2	tablespoons vegetable oil
2	tablespoons unsalted butter
1	onion, minced
1 1/2	cups instant white rice
3	garlic cloves, minced
	Pinch red pepper flakes
1 1/2	cups low-sodium chicken broth
1	cup frozen peas
5	scallions, sliced thin
2	tablespoons fresh lemon juice

MAKING THE MINUTES COUNT:
While the chicken browns, mince the onion and garlic.

1. SEASON AND BROWN CHICKEN: Pat chicken dry with paper towels and season with salt and pepper. Dredge chicken in flour to coat and shake off excess. Heat oil in 12-inch nonstick skillet over medium-high heat until just smoking. Brown chicken well on one side, about 5 minutes. Transfer chicken to plate and set aside.

GOT EXTRA TIME?

If you don't have instant rice on hand or if you would like to use long-grain rice, follow this method for Chicken and Rice with Peas and Scallions.

Substitute 1½ cups long-grain rice and increase broth to 4½ cups. When transferring chicken to plate in step 4, brush any rice off chicken back into skillet, then cover and continue to cook rice over medium-low heat, stirring occasionally, until liquid has been absorbed and rice is tender, about 15 minutes. Then add peas off heat and continue with recipe as directed.

2. SAUTÉ AROMATICS AND RICE: Add butter to skillet and return to medium heat until melted. Add onion and ½ teaspoon salt and cook until softened, about 5 minutes. Stir in rice, garlic, and red pepper flakes, and cook until fragrant, about 30 seconds.

3. ADD BROTH; COOK CHICKEN AND RICE: Stir in broth, scraping up any browned bits. Nestle chicken into rice, browned-side up. Cover and cook over medium-low heat until liquid is absorbed and thickest part of chicken registers 160 degrees on instant-read thermometer, about 10 minutes.

4. REST CHICKEN AND FINISH RICE: Transfer chicken to clean plate. Off heat, sprinkle peas over rice, cover, and let warm through, about 2 minutes. Add scallions and lemon juice and gently fold into rice. Season with salt and pepper to taste and serve with chicken.

Chicken and Rice with Broccoli and Cheddar

SERVES 4

To use long-grain rice, see "Got Extra Time?" at right.

4	boneless, skinless chicken breasts
	Salt and ground black pepper
½	cup unbleached all-purpose flour
3	tablespoons vegetable oil
1	onion, minced
1½	cups instant white rice
3	garlic cloves, minced
1½	cups low-sodium chicken broth
1	(10-ounce) package frozen broccoli florets, thawed
1	cup shredded cheddar cheese
1	teaspoon Tabasco

MAKING THE MINUTES COUNT:
While the chicken browns, mince the onion and garlic.

1. SEASON AND BROWN CHICKEN: Pat chicken dry with paper towels and season with salt and pepper. Dredge chicken in flour to coat and shake off excess. Heat 2 tablespoons of oil in 12-inch nonstick skillet over medium-high heat until just smoking. Brown chicken well on one side, about 5 minutes. Transfer chicken to plate and set aside.

2. SAUTÉ AROMATICS AND RICE: Add remaining tablespoon oil to skillet and return to medium-high heat until shimmering. Add onion and ½ teaspoon salt and cook until softened, about 5 minutes. Stir in rice and garlic and cook until fragrant, about 30 seconds.

3. ADD BROTH; COOK CHICKEN AND RICE: Stir in broth, scraping up any browned bits. Nestle chicken into rice, browned side up. Cover and cook over medium-low heat until liquid is absorbed and thickest part of chicken registers 160 degrees on instant-read thermometer, about 10 minutes.

4. REST CHICKEN AND FINISH RICE: Transfer chicken to clean plate. Off heat, gently fold broccoli, ½ cup of cheddar, and Tabasco into rice and season with salt and pepper to taste. Sprinkle remaining ½ cup cheddar over top, cover, and let sit until cheese melts, about 2 minutes. Serve with chicken.

GOT EXTRA TIME?

If you don't have instant rice on hand or if you would like to use long-grain rice, follow this method for Chicken and Rice with Broccoli and Cheddar:

Substitute 1½ cups long-grain rice and increase broth to 4½ cups. When transferring chicken to plate in step 4, brush any rice off chicken back into skillet, then cover and continue to cook rice over medium-low heat, stirring occasionally, until liquid has been absorbed and rice is tender, about 15 minutes. Then add broccoli and cheddar off heat and continue with recipe as directed.

TEST KITCHEN TIP: Is It Done?
When cooking boneless chicken breasts or other chicken parts, simply lift the piece of meat with tongs and insert an instant-read thermometer sideways through the thickest part of the meat. When chicken breasts are done, the thermometer should read 160 degrees.

Chicken and Rice with Coconut Milk and Pistachios

SERVES 4

Garam masala is an Indian spice blend, and can often be found in well-stocked supermarkets or Indian markets (see page 56 for a recipe to make your own). We use light coconut milk here; full-fat coconut milk is simply too rich for this dish. To use long-grain rice, see "Got Extra Time?" below.

4	boneless, skinless chicken breasts
	Salt and ground black pepper
½	cup unbleached all-purpose flour
3	tablespoons vegetable oil
1	onion, minced
1½	teaspoons garam masala (see note)
1½	cups instant white rice
3	garlic cloves, minced
1	(13.5-ounce) can light coconut milk (see note)
1	cup frozen peas
½	cup chopped pistachios
½	cup minced fresh cilantro

MAKING THE MINUTES COUNT:

While the chicken browns, mince the onion and garlic. When the chicken is returned to the pan to finish cooking in step 3, chop the pistachios and cilantro.

1. SEASON AND BROWN CHICKEN: Pat chicken dry with paper towels and season with salt and pepper. Dredge chicken in flour to coat and shake off excess. Heat 2 tablespoons of oil in 12-inch nonstick skillet over medium-high heat until just smoking. Brown chicken well on one side, about 5 minutes. Transfer chicken to plate and set aside.

2. SAUTÉ AROMATICS AND RICE: Add remaining tablespoon oil to skillet and return to medium-high heat until shimmering. Add onion, garam masala, and ½ teaspoon salt and cook until softened, about 5 minutes. Stir in rice and garlic and cook until fragrant, about 30 seconds.

3. ADD COCONUT MILK; COOK CHICKEN AND RICE: Stir in coconut milk, scraping up any browned bits. Nestle chicken into rice, browned side up. Cover and cook over medium-low heat until liquid is absorbed and thickest part of chicken registers 160 degrees on instant-read thermometer, about 10 minutes.

4. REST CHICKEN AND FINISH RICE: Transfer chicken to clean plate. Off heat, sprinkle peas over rice, cover, and let warm through, about 2 minutes. Add pistachios and cilantro and gently fold into rice. Season with salt and pepper to taste and serve with chicken.

GOT EXTRA TIME?

If you don't have instant rice on hand or if you would like to use long-grain rice, follow this method for Chicken and Rice with Coconut Milk and Pistachios:

Substitute 1½ cups long-grain rice and add 2¾ cups low-sodium chicken broth to skillet with coconut milk. When transferring chicken to plate in step 4, brush any rice off chicken back into skillet, then cover and continue to cook rice over medium-low heat, stirring occasionally, until liquid has been absorbed and rice is tender, about 15 minutes. Then add peas off heat and continue with recipe as directed.

TEST KITCHEN TIP:

Tender, But Not Mushy, Rice

Plain instant white rice has little character and can be very bland, but we found that sautéing the rice first in butter and aromatics, before adding the liquid, gives the rice a creamy, more distinct character and infuses it with more flavor than if it had been simply prepared per package instructions.

Curried Chicken and Rice

SERVES 4

The spice level of curry varies from brand to brand. If your curry powder is very spicy, you may need to reduce the amount listed. To use long-grain rice, see "Got Extra Time?" below.

4	boneless, skinless chicken breasts
	Salt and ground black pepper
½	cup unbleached all-purpose flour
3	tablespoons vegetable oil
I	onion, minced
I	tablespoon curry powder
I½	cups instant white rice
3	garlic cloves, minced
I½	cups low-sodium chicken broth
I	cup frozen peas
¼	cup raisins
¼	cup minced fresh cilantro

MAKING THE MINUTES COUNT:

While the chicken browns, mince the onion and garlic. When the chicken is returned to the pan to finish cooking in step 3, mince the cilantro.

I. SEASON AND BROWN CHICKEN: Pat chicken dry with paper towels and season with salt and pepper. Dredge chicken in flour to coat and shake off excess. Heat 2 tablespoons of oil in 12-inch nonstick skillet over medium-high heat until just smoking. Brown chicken well on one side, about 5

GOT EXTRA TIME?

If you don't have instant rice on hand or if you would like to use long-grain rice in Curried Chicken and Rice, follow this method:

Substitute 1½ cups long-grain rice and increase broth amount to 4½ cups. When transferring chicken to a plate in step 4, brush any rice off chicken back into the skillet, then cover and continue to cook rice over medium-low heat, stirring occasionally, until liquid has been absorbed and rice is tender, about 15 minutes. Then add peas and raisins off heat and continue with recipe as directed.

minutes. Transfer chicken to plate and set aside.

2. SAUTÉ AROMATICS AND RICE: Add remaining tablespoon oil to skillet and return to medium-high heat until shimmering. Add onion, curry powder, and ½ teaspoon salt and cook until softened, about 5 minutes. Stir in rice and garlic and cook until fragrant, about 30 seconds.

3. ADD BROTH; COOK CHICKEN AND RICE: Stir in broth, scraping up any browned bits. Nestle chicken into rice, browned side up. Cover and cook over medium-low heat until liquid is absorbed and thickest part of chicken registers 160 degrees on instant-read thermometer, about 10 minutes.

4. REST CHICKEN AND FINISH RICE: Transfer chicken to clean plate. Off heat, sprinkle peas and raisins over rice, cover, and let warm through, about 2 minutes. Add cilantro and gently fold into rice. Season with salt and pepper to taste and serve with chicken.

EQUIPMENT: Traditional Skillets

A skillet is the most-used pan in the test kitchen. A slope-sided, flat-bottom skillet is the best choice for sautéing, searing, browning, pan-frying, and just about anything in between. Traditional skillets are good for dishes where browning contributes an essential flavor base, like pan-seared steaks or chicken. We tested eight traditional skillets with 12-inch diameters (or as close as we could find in that manufacturer's line). For its combination of excellent performance, optimum weight and balance, and overall ease of use, the All-Clad was our favorite. But others, such as the Calphalon and Farberware, nearly matched the All-Clad in performance and good handling and did so for less than half the price—thus making these pans our two best buys.

The Best Traditional Skillets

The All-Clad Stainless 12-inch Frypan (top: $125) took top honors in our testing. The Calphalon Tri-Ply Stainless 12-inch Omelette Pan (middle: $65) and the Farberware Millennium 18/10 Stainless 12-inch Covered Skillet (bottom: $70) were rated best buys, costing about half as much as the winning pan.

Spanish-Style Chicken and Rice

SERVES 4

If you can't find chorizo, use tasso, andouille, or linguiça sausage. To use long-grain rice, see "Got Extra Time?" below.

4	boneless, skinless chicken breasts
	Salt and ground black pepper
1/2	cup unbleached all-purpose flour
3	tablespoons vegetable oil
6	ounces chorizo sausage, quartered lengthwise and sliced 1/4 inch thick
1	onion, minced
1	red bell pepper, cored and chopped fine
	Pinch saffron threads, crumbled, or pinch saffron powder
1 1/2	cups instant white rice
3	garlic cloves, minced
1 1/2	cups low-sodium chicken broth
1	cup frozen peas

MAKING THE MINUTES COUNT:

Before cooking, cut the chorizo and mince the onion. While the chicken browns, chop the bell pepper and mince the garlic.

1. SEASON AND BROWN CHICKEN: Pat chicken dry with paper towels and season with salt and pepper. Dredge chicken in flour to coat and shake off excess. Heat 2 tablespoons of oil in 12-inch nonstick skillet over medium-high heat until just smoking. Brown chicken well on one side, about 5 minutes. Transfer chicken to plate and set aside.

2. SAUTÉ CHORIZO, AROMATICS, AND RICE: Add remaining tablespoon oil to skillet and return to medium-high heat until shimmering. Add chorizo, onion, bell pepper, saffron, and 1/2 teaspoon salt and cook until onion is softened, about 5 minutes. Stir in rice and garlic and cook until fragrant, about 30 seconds.

3. ADD BROTH; COOK CHICKEN AND RICE: Stir in broth, scraping up any browned bits. Nestle chicken into rice, browned side up. Cover and cook over medium-low heat until liquid is absorbed and thickest part of chicken registers 160 degrees on instant-read thermometer, about 10 minutes.

4. REST CHICKEN AND FINISH RICE: Transfer chicken to plate. Off heat, sprinkle peas over rice, cover, and let warm through, about 2 minutes. Season with salt and pepper to taste and serve with chicken.

GOT EXTRA TIME?

If you don't have instant rice on hand or if you would like to use long-grain rice in Spanish-Style Chicken and Rice, follow this method:

Substitute 1 1/2 cups long-grain rice and increase broth to 4 1/2 cups. When transferring chicken to plate in step 4, brush any rice off chicken back into skillet, then cover and continue to cook rice over medium-low heat, stirring occasionally, until liquid has been absorbed and rice is tender, about 15 minutes. Then add peas off heat and continue with recipe as directed.

CHICKEN AND COUSCOUS

COUSCOUS, MADE FROM SEMOLINA AND water, is a mainstay on Moroccan tables and has become increasingly popular in recent years. Offering a change from the same old chicken and rice, and naturally quick-cooking, it seemed perfect for an exotic and flavorful meal that could be easily prepared for dinner on a busy weeknight.

First, we browned chicken breasts and transferred them to the oven to finish cooking, which freed up the skillet for the vegetables. Red onion and fennel form the base of the dish, providing body, texture, and a clean vegetal sweetness. We stirred the couscous into the vegetables along with garlic and cayenne for bite. Instead of using straight chicken broth for the cooking liquid, we added orange juice, which is sweet and slightly acidic, helping to pull the fennel flavor to the fore and brighten the entire dish. We then brought the liquid to a simmer and let the mixture sit off the heat until the couscous absorbed the broth and was evenly plump and tender—which took just five minutes! For our final step we made a fragrant oil using orange juice, cayenne, and cilantro—all ingredients we already used in the recipe—and drizzled it over the chicken and couscous before serving. In addition, we also developed a flavor variation with chickpeas, dried apricots, and cinnamon. The dried, chopped apricots soften during cooking and lend a pleasant sweetness to the dish.

> **TEST KITCHEN TIP: Into the Oven**
> Sautéing lightly floured chicken breasts until golden brown on both sides, then transferring them to a low oven to finish cooking, gives us juicy and tender meat and frees up the skillet for the vegetables and couscous.

Chicken and Couscous with Fennel and Orange

SERVES 4

To complete this recipe in 30 minutes, preheat your oven before assembling your ingredients. Be sure to use chicken breasts that are roughly the same size to ensure even cooking. Use regular fine-grained couscous in this dish. Large-grained couscous, often labeled Israeli-style, takes much longer to cook and won't work in this recipe.

4	boneless, skinless chicken breasts
	Salt and ground black pepper
½	cup unbleached all-purpose flour
½	cup olive oil
I	red onion, sliced thin
I	fennel bulb, trimmed, cored, and sliced thin (see page 31)
I	cup couscous (see note)
3	garlic cloves, minced
	Cayenne
I	cup orange juice
¾	cup low-sodium chicken broth
¼	cup minced fresh cilantro

MAKING THE MINUTES COUNT:
While the chicken browns, slice the onion and fennel. While the vegetables cook, mince the garlic and cilantro.

1. **HEAT OVEN:** Adjust oven rack to lower-middle position, place baking dish on rack, and heat oven to 200 degrees.

2. **SEASON, BROWN, AND BAKE CHICKEN:** Pat chicken dry with paper towels and season with salt and pepper. Dredge chicken in flour to coat and shake off excess. Heat 2 tablespoons of oil in 12-inch nonstick skillet over medium-high heat until just smoking. Brown chicken lightly on both sides, about 5 minutes total. Transfer chicken to dish in oven and cook until chicken registers 160 degrees on instant-read thermometer, 10 to 15 minutes.

3. **SAUTÉ AROMATICS AND COUSCOUS:** While chicken bakes, add 1 more tablespoon oil to skillet and return to medium-high heat until shimmering. Add onion, fennel, and ½ teaspoon salt and cook until onion is softened, about 5 minutes. Stir in couscous, garlic, and pinch cayenne, and cook until fragrant, about 30 seconds.

4. **STEAM COUSCOUS:** Stir in ¾ cup of orange juice and broth, scraping up any browned bits. Bring to simmer, cover, and let sit off heat until liquid is absorbed, about 5 minutes.

5. **MAKE DRIZZLING OIL:** Whisk together remaining 5 tablespoons oil, remaining ¼ cup orange juice, 2 tablespoons of cilantro, and pinch cayenne.

6. **FINISH COUSCOUS:** Gently fold remaining 2 tablespoons cilantro into couscous with fork and season with salt and pepper to taste. Drizzle oil over chicken and couscous when serving.

➤ VARIATION

Chicken and Couscous with Chickpeas and Apricots

To complete this recipe in 30 minutes, preheat your oven before assembling your ingredients. To quickly chop the apricots, use clean kitchen scissors and spray them with nonstick spray.

Omit fennel. Substitute ½ teaspoon ground cinnamon for cayenne in step 3. Add 1 (15-ounce) can chickpeas, rinsed, and 1 cup roughly chopped dried apricots with the orange juice in step 4. Substitute a pinch of ground cinnamon for the cayenne in step 5.

ROASTED CHICKEN DINNER

ROASTED CHICKEN AND POTATOES ARE A classic combination, but you can forget about getting them on the table in 30 minutes, right? For starters, a whole chicken needs to see at least one hour of oven time, and potatoes take somewhere in that time range to get golden brown and crispy. Nevertheless, we were determined to turn this tasty dinner into a simple weeknight standby.

We decided early on that bone-in chicken breasts would take the place of a whole chicken. By starting the chicken breasts in a skillet we were able to get the skin nicely browned and crispy. We then transferred the chicken to a baking dish to finish cooking in a hot oven, thereby freeing up the skillet for our potatoes.

We used red potatoes because their tender skin doesn't require peeling. In our initial tests we had trouble getting the potatoes simultaneously golden and crisp on the outside and tender on the inside; there just wasn't enough time. We got a jump-start on the potatoes by microwaving them while the chicken browned, and then adding them to the skillet in a single layer to achieve a deeply caramelized exterior and creamy, moist interior.

As a final flourish, we mimicked the tasty pan juices of a traditional roast chicken by infusing olive oil with lemon juice, garlic, red pepper flakes, and thyme. Drizzled over the chicken and potatoes just before serving, it lent the same moistness and bright flavors of traditional pan juices. In addition, we applied our technique for pan-roasted chicken and potatoes to other tasty combinations, like pan-roasted chicken with baby carrots and pan-roasted chicken with cherry tomatoes and artichokes.

> **TEST KITCHEN TIP:**
> **Microwave Saves the Day**
> We found that by microwaving the potatoes for just 5 to 10 minutes before cooking them in the skillet, we were able to achieve results that mirrored those of oven-roasted potatoes in just half the time.

Pan-Roasted Chicken Breasts with Potatoes
SERVES 4

To complete this recipe in 30 minutes, preheat your oven before assembling your ingredients. If the split breasts are of different sizes, check the smaller ones a few minutes early to see if they are cooking more quickly, and remove them from the oven if they are done.

- 4   bone-in, split chicken breasts
      Salt and ground black pepper
- 6   tablespoons olive oil
- 1½ pounds red potatoes (4 to 5 medium), cut into 1-inch wedges
- 2   tablespoons fresh lemon juice
- 1   garlic clove, minced
- 1   teaspoon minced fresh thyme
      Pinch red pepper flakes

MAKING THE MINUTES COUNT:
While the chicken browns, cut the potatoes.

1. HEAT OVEN: Adjust oven rack to lowest position and heat oven to 450 degrees.

2. SEASON AND BROWN SKIN SIDE OF CHICKEN: Pat chicken dry with paper towels and season with salt and pepper. Heat 1 tablespoon of oil in 12-inch nonstick skillet over medium-high heat until just smoking. Brown chicken well on skin side, about 5 minutes.

3. MICROWAVE POTATOES: Meanwhile, toss potatoes with 1 tablespoon of oil, ½ teaspoon salt, and ¼ teaspoon pepper in microwave-safe bowl. Cover tightly with plastic wrap. Microwave on high until potatoes begin to soften, 5 to 7 minutes, shaking bowl (without removing plastic) to toss potatoes halfway through.

4. BAKE CHICKEN: Transfer chicken, skin side up, to baking dish and bake until thickest part registers 160 degrees on instant-read thermometer, 15 to 20 minutes.

5. BROWN POTATOES: While chicken bakes, pour off any grease in skillet, add 1 more tablespoon oil, and return to medium heat until shimmering. Drain microwaved potatoes, then add to skillet and cook, stirring occasionally, until golden brown and tender, about 10 minutes.

6. MAKE DRIZZLING OIL: Whisk remaining 3 tablespoons oil, lemon juice, garlic, thyme, and red pepper flakes together. Drizzle oil over chicken and potatoes before serving.

Pan-Roasted Chicken Breasts with Baby Carrots

SERVES 4

To complete this recipe in 30 minutes, preheat your oven before assembling your ingredients. If the split breasts are of different sizes, check the smaller ones a few minutes early to see if they are cooking more quickly, and remove them from the oven if they are done.

4	bone-in, split chicken breasts
	Salt and ground black pepper
1	tablespoon vegetable oil
1½	pounds baby carrots
6	tablespoons unsalted butter
1	teaspoon sugar
1	shallot, minced
2	teaspoons minced fresh tarragon

MAKING THE MINUTES COUNT:

While the chicken browns, mince the shallot. While the carrots brown, mince the tarragon.

1. HEAT OVEN: Adjust oven rack to lowest position and heat oven to 450 degrees.

2. SEASON AND BROWN SKIN SIDE OF CHICKEN: Pat chicken dry with paper towels and season with salt and pepper. Heat oil in 12-inch nonstick skillet over medium-high heat until just smoking. Brown chicken well on skin side, about 5 minutes.

3. MICROWAVE CARROTS: While chicken browns, toss carrots with ½ teaspoon salt and ¼ teaspoon pepper in microwave-safe bowl. Cover tightly with plastic wrap. Microwave on high until carrots begin to soften, 5 to 7 minutes, shaking bowl (without removing plastic) to toss carrots halfway through.

4. BAKE CHICKEN: Transfer chicken, skin side up, to baking dish and bake until thickest part registers 160 degrees on instant-read thermometer, 15 to 20 minutes.

5. BROWN CARROTS: While chicken bakes,

pour off any grease in skillet, add 2 tablespoons of butter, and return to medium heat until melted. Drain microwaved carrots, then add to skillet with sugar and cook, stirring occasionally, until golden brown and tender, about 10 minutes.

6. MAKE FLAVORED BUTTER: Microwave remaining 4 tablespoons butter with shallot on 50 percent power until butter has melted and shallots are softened, 30 to 60 seconds. Stir in tarragon. Drizzle butter over chicken and carrots before serving.

Pan-Roasted Chicken Breasts with Artichokes and Cherry Tomatoes

SERVES 4

To complete this recipe in 30 minutes, preheat your oven before assembling your ingredients. If the split breasts are of different sizes, check the smaller ones a few minutes early to see if they are cooking more quickly, and remove them from the oven if they are done. The artichokes will release a significant amount of water in the microwave as they defrost. To ensure that they brown properly, drain them well before adding them to the skillet.

4	bone-in, split chicken breasts
	Salt and ground black pepper
5	tablespoons olive oil
2	(9-ounce) packages frozen artichoke hearts
1	pint cherry tomatoes, halved
2	tablespoons capers, rinsed
2	tablespoons fresh lemon juice
1	garlic clove, minced
1	teaspoon minced fresh oregano
	Pinch red pepper flakes

MAKING THE MINUTES COUNT:

Halve the tomatoes while the chicken browns. Mince the garlic and oregano while the artichokes brown.

1. HEAT OVEN: Adjust oven rack to lowest position and heat oven to 450 degrees.

2. SEASON AND BROWN SKIN SIDE OF CHICKEN: Pat chicken dry with paper towels and season with salt and pepper. Heat 1 tablespoon of oil in 12-inch nonstick skillet over medium-high heat until just smoking. Brown chicken well on skin side, about 5 minutes.

3. MICROWAVE ARTICHOKES: While chicken browns, toss artichokes with ½ teaspoon salt and ¼ teaspoon pepper in microwave-safe bowl. Cover tightly with plastic wrap. Microwave on high until artichokes begin to soften, 5 to 7 minutes, shaking bowl (without removing plastic) to toss artichokes halfway through. Drain artichokes well.

4. BAKE CHICKEN: Transfer chicken, skin side up, to baking dish and bake until thickest part registers 160 degrees on instant-read thermometer, 15 to 20 minutes.

5. BROWN ARTICHOKES: While chicken bakes, pour off any grease in skillet, add 1 more table-spoon oil, and return to medium heat until shimmering. Drain artichokes, then add to skillet and cook, stirring occasionally, until golden brown, about 8 minutes. Stir in tomatoes and capers and cook until tomatoes are lightly wilted, about 2 minutes.

6. MAKE DRIZZLING OIL: Whisk remaining 3 tablespoons oil, lemon juice, garlic, oregano, and red pepper flakes together. Drizzle oil over chicken and vegetables before serving.

Skillet Chicken Pot Pie

MOST RECIPES FOR QUICK CHICKEN POT pie are lousy. The filling is not much more than canned, condensed cream-of-you-name-it soup, leftover chicken, and a paltry amount of vegetables. These versions are far from the comforting dinner that's always been a family favorite. As for the pastry topping, most quick recipes rely on refrigerated pie dough or refrigerated biscuits baked on top of the stew, but even with this shortcut, we had trouble getting this oven-baked dinner on the table in a reasonable amount of time. We knew we could create a quick and fresh-tasting pot pie that relied on neither bad shortcuts nor the talents of an Olympic sprinter. We found that baking a round of refrigerated pie dough or refrigerated biscuits while assembling a flavorful skillet chicken stew allows you to pull this dinner together in record time. Just before serving, simply slide the pie crust right onto the stew (or place the biscuits on top). No one will know the difference.

Skillet Chicken Pot Pie
SERVES 4

To complete this recipe in 30 minutes, preheat your oven before assembling your ingredients. We prefer the flavor of Pillsbury Golden Homestyle Biscuits or Pillsbury Refrigerated Pie Crusts, but you can use your favorite brand (you will need anywhere from 4 to 8 biscuits depending on their size). Because these products all bake at different temperatures, baking times will vary, so bake them according to the package instructions. To make homemade biscuits, see page 116. Serve this pot pie right from the skillet, or transfer the mixture to a large pie dish and top with the pie crust or biscuits.

1	package refrigerated biscuits, or 1 refrigerated pie crust (see note)
1½	pounds boneless, skinless chicken breasts
	Salt and ground black pepper
4	tablespoons unsalted butter
1	onion, minced
1	celery rib, sliced thin
¼	cup unbleached all-purpose flour
¼	cup dry vermouth or dry white wine
2	cups low-sodium chicken broth
½	cup heavy cream
1½	teaspoons minced fresh thyme
2	cups frozen pea-carrot medley, thawed

MAKING THE MINUTES COUNT:
While the chicken browns, mince the onion and slice the celery. When the chicken is returned to the pan to finish cooking, bake the pie crust or biscuits.

1. HEAT OVEN: Adjust oven rack to middle position and heat oven according to pie crust or biscuit package instructions.

2. SEASON AND BROWN CHICKEN: Pat chicken dry with paper towels and season with salt and pepper. Melt 2 tablespoons of butter in 12-inch skillet over medium heat until foaming subsides. Brown chicken lightly on both sides, about 5 minutes total. Transfer chicken to clean plate.

3. **SAUTÉ AROMATICS:** Add remaining 2 tablespoons butter to skillet and return to medium heat until melted. Add onion, celery, and ½ teaspoon salt and cook until onion is softened, about 5 minutes. Stir in flour and cook, stirring constantly, until incorporated, about 1 minute.

4. **ADD VERMOUTH AND BROTH; POACH CHICKEN:** Stir in vermouth and cook until evaporated, about 30 seconds. Slowly whisk in broth, cream, and thyme, and bring to simmer. Nestle chicken into pan, cover, and cook over medium-low heat until thickest part of breast registers 160 degrees on instant-read thermometer, about 10 minutes.

5. **BAKE TOPPING:** While sauce simmers, bake biscuits according to package instructions, or unfold pie dough onto parchment paper–lined baking sheet and bake according to package instructions.

6. **SHRED CHICKEN AND ADD VEGETABLES:** Transfer chicken to plate. Stir peas and carrots into sauce and simmer until heated through, about 2 minutes. When chicken is cool enough to handle, cut or shred into bite-sized pieces and return to skillet.

7. **ADD TOPPING:** Season filling with salt and pepper to taste. If using pie crust, carefully slide onto skillet and serve. If using biscuits, place on top of skillet or place biscuit on individual servings and serve.

GOT EXTRA TIME?

If you have a few extra minutes, these biscuits come together in a flash and require no special equipment.

Quick Homemade Biscuits
MAKES 8 BISCUITS

2	cups unbleached all-purpose flour, plus extra for work surface
2	teaspoons sugar
2	teaspoons baking powder
½	teaspoon salt
1½	cups heavy cream

1. **HEAT OVEN:** Adjust oven rack to upper-middle position and heat oven to 450 degrees.

2. **MAKE DOUGH:** Whisk flour, sugar, baking powder, and salt together in large bowl. Stir in cream with wooden spoon until dough forms, about 30 seconds. Turn dough out onto lightly floured work surface and gather into ball. Knead dough briefly until smooth, about 30 seconds.

3. **CUT BISCUITS:** Pat dough into ¾-inch-thick circle. Cut biscuits into rounds using 2½-inch biscuit cutter or cut into 8 wedges using knife (see illustrations below).

4. **BAKE:** Place biscuits on parchment paper–lined baking sheet. Bake until golden brown, about 15 minutes.

SHAPING BISCUITS

1. Pat the dough on a lightly floured work surface into a ¾-inch-thick circle.

2A. For rounds: Use a biscuit cutter to punch out rounds. Push together the remaining pieces of dough, pat into a ¾-inch-thick round, and punch out more. Discard the remaining scraps.

2B. For wedges: With a sharp knife or bench scraper, cut the dough into 8 wedges.

SKILLET BEEF POT PIE

BEEF POT PIE IS A SLOW-SIMMERED BEEF stew which is transferred to a baking dish, topped with a pastry or biscuit topping, and baked until the crust is golden brown. Certainly there's nothing wrong with such a labor of love, but we wanted a simpler, faster alternative. And we don't mean opening up a can of Dinty Moore and plopping a store-bought biscuit on top. Could a richly flavored beef pot pie—with all the nuance of a slow-simmered beef stew—be made in a fraction of the time?

With the crusty topping on loan from our chicken pot pie recipe, we commenced the testing process with our primary concern: the choice of meat. Beef tenderloin (filet mignon), though pricey, proved to be our best option—other cuts simply needed too long to become tender. We found it best to brown whole steaks, allow them rest while we built the stew, and then cut them into cubes and stir them back in. We used just one pound of beef and supplemented it with hearty mushrooms, along with onions, garlic, and a substantial splash of red wine. We rounded out the filling's flavor with a spoonful of tomato paste—fruity yet densely flavored—and fresh thyme leaves. The result was a surprisingly close approximation of a slow-cooked stew, ready in just 30 minutes.

Skillet Beef Pot Pie

SERVES 4

To complete this recipe in 30 minutes, preheat your oven before assembling your ingredients. We prefer the flavor of Pillsbury Golden Homestyle Biscuits or Pillsbury Refrigerated Pie Crusts, but you can use your favorite brand (you will need anywhere from 4 to 8 biscuits depending on their size). Because these products all bake at different temperatures, baking times will vary so bake them according to the package instructions. To make homemade biscuits, see page 116. Serve this pot pie right from the skillet, or transfer the mixture to a large pie plate and top with the pie crust or biscuits.

1 package refrigerated biscuits, or 1 refrigerated pie crust (see note)
2 (8-ounce) filets mignon
Salt and ground black pepper
2 tablespoons vegetable oil
1 onion, minced
8 ounces white mushrooms, halved if small, quartered if large
¼ cup unbleached all-purpose flour
2 garlic cloves, minced
½ cup dry red wine
2½ cups low-sodium chicken broth
1 tablespoon tomato paste
1½ teaspoons minced fresh thyme
2 cups frozen pea-carrot medley, thawed

MAKING THE MINUTES COUNT:
While the beef browns, mince the onion. While the onion cooks, mince the garlic and thyme. While the sauce simmers, bake the pie crust or biscuits.

1. HEAT OVEN: Adjust oven rack to middle position and heat oven according to biscuit or pie crust package instructions.

2. BROWN STEAKS AND CUT INTO CUBES: Pat beef dry with paper towels and season with salt and pepper. Heat 1 tablespoon of oil in 12-inch skillet over medium-high heat until just smoking. Brown steaks on both sides, leaving centers rare, about 4 minutes total. Transfer to plate, and when cool enough to handle, cut into ½-inch cubes.

3. SAUTÉ AROMATICS AND MUSHROOMS: Add remaining tablespoon oil, onion, mushrooms, and ½ teaspoon salt to skillet and return to medium heat until onion is softened, about 5 minutes. Stir in flour and garlic and cook, stirring constantly, until flour is incorporated, about 1 minute.

4. SIMMER SAUCE: Stir in wine and cook until evaporated, about 30 seconds. Slowly whisk in broth, tomato paste, and thyme, and bring to simmer. Cover and cook over medium-low heat until thickened, 8 to 10 minutes.

5. BAKE TOPPING: While sauce simmers, bake biscuits according to package instructions, or unfold pie dough onto parchment paper–lined baking sheet and bake according to package instructions.

6. ADD VEGETABLES AND BEEF: Stir peas and carrots and beef with accumulated juices into skillet and continue to simmer until heated through, about 2 minutes. Season with salt and pepper to taste.

7. ADD TOPPING: If using pie crust, carefully slide onto skillet and serve. If using biscuits, place on top of skillet or individual servings and serve.

SKILLET SHEPHERD'S PIE

ORIGINALLY, SHEPHERD'S PIE, A RICH LAMB stew blanketed under a mashed-potato crust, was a meal made on Monday with Sunday night's leftovers. In this day and age, few of us have such delicious Sunday dinners, so we aimed to create a quick and easy weeknight shepherd's pie from scratch.

To save on prep time and produce tender meat in just 30 minutes, we used quick-cooking ground lamb. We simmered the lamb with onions, thyme, tomato paste, chicken broth, and Worcestershire sauce. Once the filling was assembled, we were ready to top it off with mashed potatoes. While many quick shepherd's pie recipes call for instant mashed potatoes, we were determined to make ours work with the real thing. By starting the potatoes simmering on the stove before we cooked the filling, we were able to do so. Though we didn't have enough time in our half an hour to make the signature browned potato crust found on most shepherd's pies, tasters were happy with a dollop of creamy mashed potatoes on top—as long as they were made from real spuds.

TEST KITCHEN TIP:
Drain the Meat
Ground lamb releases a great deal of fat as it cooks, so be sure to drain the meat well before simmering it with the other ingredients.

Skillet Shepherd's Pie
SERVES 4

We like the flavor of ground lamb here, but you can substitute 85 percent lean ground beef if you prefer.

1½	pounds russet potatoes (about 3 medium), peeled and cut into 1-inch pieces
1½	pounds ground lamb
1	onion, minced
	Salt and ground black pepper
¼	cup unbleached all-purpose flour
1	tablespoon tomato paste
2	cups low-sodium chicken broth
1½	teaspoons minced fresh thyme
2	teaspoons Worcestershire sauce
2	tablespoons unsalted butter
½	cup half-and-half
2	cups frozen pea-carrot medley, thawed

MAKING THE MINUTES COUNT:
While the potatoes cook, brown the lamb. While the lamb browns, mince the onion.

1. BOIL POTATOES: Cover potatoes with 1 inch water in large saucepan. Bring to boil, then reduce to simmer and cook until tender, about 15 minutes.

2. COOK AND DRAIN LAMB: While potatoes simmer, cook lamb in 12-inch skillet over medium heat, breaking up meat with wooden spoon, until almost cooked through and fat has rendered, about 3 minutes. Drain lamb through fine mesh strainer, discarding all but 1 tablespoon fat.

3. SAUTÉ AROMATICS: Add reserved tablespoon lamb fat to skillet and return to medium heat until shimmering. Add onion and ½ teaspoon salt and cook until onion is softened, about 5 minutes. Stir in flour and tomato paste and cook, stirring constantly, until flour is incorporated, about 1 minute.

4. SIMMER FILLING: Slowly whisk in broth, thyme, and Worcestershire, scraping up browned bits, and bring to simmer. Return drained lamb to skillet, cover, and cook over medium-low heat until sauce is nicely thickened and flavorful, 6 to 8 minutes.

5. MASH POTATOES: Drain potatoes, return to pot, and mash smooth using potato masher. Stir in butter, then half-and-half. Season with salt and pepper to taste. Cover to keep warm.

6. ADD VEGETABLES TO FILLING AND FINISH: Stir peas and carrots into lamb mixture and simmer until heated through, about 2 minutes. Season with salt and pepper to taste. Serve stew in individual bowls and top with mashed potatoes.

GOT EXTRA TIME?

If you have a few minutes to spare, you can make this shepherd's pie more traditional with a browned potato crust.

Preheat the broiler and adjust the rack 6 inches from the heat source. Use an oven-safe skillet or transfer filling to a baking dish. Dollop mashed potatoes evenly over the filling and spread them in a thin layer. Brush with 2 tablespoons melted butter and broil until the potatoes are golden brown, 3 to 5 minutes.

EQUIPMENT: Potato Mashers

For home-style spuds in a hurry, we eschew fancy gadgets and turn to a traditional hand-held potato masher. These come in two forms—wire-looped mashers with a zigzag presser or disk mashers with a perforated round plate. Although elbow grease is the main mashing factor, we found that without exception disk mashers were preferred for achieving a fast and even mash. Our favorite is the Profi Plus Masher ($15.99), whose comfortable grip, small holes, and oval mashing plate turned out mashed potatoes with a minimum of lumps and effort.

The Best Potato Masher

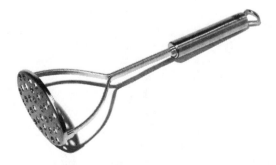

Profi Plus Masher ($15.99) has a comfortable grip, small holes, and an oval mashing plate, for a fast and even mash.

TAMALE PIE

THERE ARE MANY, MANY TRULY AWFUL recipes for quick tamale pie out there. Many feature a can each of chili and creamed corn dumped together and topped with cornbread mix, which is, incidentally, the best part. When the test kitchen prepared various incarnations of this recipe, not a cornbread crumb was left on tasters' plates—but we can't say the same for the fillings we tried. Even recipes that call for fresh ground beef rely on a packet of stale and dusty taco seasoning mix for flavor. We set out to make a quick tamale pie containing a juicy, spicy mixture of meat and vegetables.

For the filling, we found that we liked the flavor and texture of 90 percent lean ground beef. Seasoned with onion, garlic, chili powder, and a little fresh cilantro, the tamale filling tasted fresh and spicy. We then stirred cheddar cheese into the filling not only for flavor and richness, but also to help bind the mixture together.

With the filling in place, we zeroed in on the topping. We had already decided that nothing beats the convenience of cornbread mixes—just pour into a bowl, add milk (and sometimes egg), mix, and bake. As we expected, the moist, tender crumb, subtle sweetness, and corn flavor was the perfect complement to the spicy filling.

Skillet Tamale Pie

SERVES 4

To complete this recipe in 30 minutes, preheat your oven before assembling the ingredients. Cornbread mixes vary from brand to brand; we liked Betty Crocker Golden Corn Muffin and Bread Mix and Jiffy Corn Muffin Mix, but you can use your favorite brand. You may need a few additional ingredients to make this recipe, depending on the cornbread mix you are using. Serve with sour cream.

2	tablespoons vegetable oil
1	onion, minced
2	tablespoons chili powder
	Salt and ground black pepper
2	garlic cloves, minced
1	pound 90 percent lean ground beef

1 (15-ounce) can black beans, rinsed
1 (14.5-ounce) can diced tomatoes, drained
1 (6.5- to 8.5-ounce) package cornbread mix (see note)
1 cup shredded cheddar cheese
2 tablespoons minced fresh cilantro

MAKING THE MINUTES COUNT:
While the filling cooks, mince the cilantro and mix the cornbread batter.

1. **HEAT OVEN:** Adjust oven rack to middle position and heat oven to 450 degrees.

2. **SAUTÉ AROMATICS:** Heat oil in 12-inch skillet over medium heat until shimmering. Add onion, chili powder, and ½ teaspoon salt and cook until onion is softened, about 5 minutes. Stir in garlic and cook until fragrant, about 30 seconds.

3. **MAKE FILLING:** Stir in ground beef, beans, and tomatoes, and bring to simmer, breaking up meat with wooden spoon, about 5 minutes.

4. **MIX TOPPING BATTER:** Meanwhile, mix cornbread batter according to package instructions.

5. **SEASON FILLING AND ADD TOPPING:** Stir cheddar and cilantro into filling and season with salt and pepper to taste. Dollop cornbread batter evenly over filling and spread into even layer.

6. **BAKE PIE:** Bake until cornbread is cooked through in center, 10 to 15 minutes. Serve.

GOT EXTRA TIME?

If you don't have a cornbread mix on hand for Skillet Tamale Pie (or simply want to make the topping from scratch), use this easy recipe instead. It's a bit sweet like the cornbread mixes we recommend, but tasters found its mild sweetness a good complement to the tangy meat filling.

Homemade Cornbread Topping

¾ cup unbleached all-purpose flour
¾ cup yellow cornmeal
3 tablespoons sugar
¾ teaspoon baking powder
¼ teaspoon baking soda
¾ teaspoon salt
¾ cup buttermilk
1 large egg
3 tablespoons unsalted butter, melted and cooled

1. Whisk flour, cornmeal, sugar, baking powder, baking soda, and salt together in large bowl.

2. In separate bowl, whisk buttermilk and egg together. Stir buttermilk mixture into flour mixture until uniform, then stir in butter until just combined. Use as directed in step 5 of Skillet Tamale Pie at left.

SLOPPY JOES

SLOPPY JOES, WHILE POPULAR AND QUICK, are often little more than a can of sweet sauce dumped over greasy, third-rate burger meat. Though the base for Sloppy Joes is pretty constant among most published recipes—ground beef, onion, garlic, spices, something sweet, something sour, and something tomato—many of the recipes we tried were either greasy, dry, crumbly, bland, too sweet, too sour, or even too saucy. The key proved to be finding the right balance.

For the meat, we chose 85 percent lean ground beef, which has just enough fat to yield tender (but not slick) meat. We soon discovered that the way we cooked the meat was just as important as its fat content. For soft, tender meat, it's important to cook it until just pink (no further), then add the remaining ingredients, and finish cooking the meat through.

Because Sloppy Joes are essentially for kids, we wanted to keep the spices to a minimum. Just ½ teaspoon of chili powder and a dash or two of Tabasco added subtle heat. Ketchup combined with tomato puree and a little brown sugar struck the perfect sweet/sour balance. Ten minutes of simmering was all this mixture needed to transform from a runny meat sauce to a nicely thickened, saucy meat dish—ideal for sitting on a soft burger bun.

Sloppy Joes

SERVES 4

Serve this kid-friendly favorite with pickles.

2	tablespoons vegetable oil
1	onion, minced
½	teaspoon chili powder
	Salt
2	garlic cloves, minced
1	pound 85 percent lean ground beef
1	cup tomato puree
½	cup ketchup
¼	cup water
1	teaspoon brown sugar
	Tabasco sauce
4	hamburger buns

1. SAUTÉ AROMATICS: Heat oil in 12-inch skillet over medium heat until shimmering. Add onion, chili powder, and ½ teaspoon salt and cook until onion is softened, about 5 minutes. Stir in garlic and cook until fragrant, about 30 seconds.

2. COOK BEEF: Add beef and cook, breaking up meat with wooden spoon, until almost cooked through, but still slightly pink, about 3 minutes.

3. SIMMER SAUCE: Stir in tomato puree, ketchup, water, brown sugar, and ¼ teaspoon Tabasco. Simmer until sauce is slightly thicker than ketchup, 8 to 10 minutes.

4. SEASON AND ASSEMBLE SANDWICHES: Season with salt and Tabasco to taste. Spoon meat mixture onto hamburger buns and serve.

➤ VARIATIONS

Skinny Joes

This is a slightly lower-fat version of the original.

Substitute 1 pound 93 percent lean ground turkey for ground beef.

Smoky Joes

Try this sweet and smoky version on soft deli-style onion rolls instead of hamburger buns.

Replace ketchup with barbecue sauce.

ITALIAN SAUSAGE SUPPER

HIGHLY SEASONED AND MEATY, ITALIAN sausages shouldn't be relegated to just ballpark fare. When done right, they can be the centerpiece of a hearty dinner. For our quick-cooking dinner, we envisioned two Italian sausage suppers—one with peppers and onions in a savory sauce served on a crusty roll, and another enriched with potatoes that you would eat with a knife and fork.

While you can cook the sausages whole, we found that they cook faster if cut into pieces. First we cut the sausages into 3-inch lengths (a good size for inserting into a bun) and browned them in a skillet. We removed the sausages from the pan and added the bell peppers and onions, which we cooked just until they were beginning to soften. We preferred the red, yellow, and orange bell pepper varieties, which are not only sweeter than green peppers but add visual appeal. Next, we stirred in tomato paste, garlic (fresh, of course), white wine, water, and oregano; nestled the sausages into the pan; and allowed the mixture to simmer just until the sausages were cooked through, the peppers and onions were tender, and the sauce was nicely flavored and thickened. A tablespoon of vinegar added to the savory sauce just before serving lent some bright notes to the finished dish. For our second version, we cut the sausages into smaller pieces (easier to fork) and added potatoes for a heartier meal.

TEST KITCHEN TIP:
Careful Cooking
Be careful not to cook the meat beyond pink in step 2 or it will end up dry and crumbly. The meat will finish cooking once the liquid ingredients are added.

TEST KITCHEN TIP: Knife Cuts
Cutting the sausages into pieces and thinly slicing the peppers and onion ensures the sausages will cook through and the vegetables will become tender in less than half an hour.

Italian Sausage, Pepper, and Onion Hoagies

SERVES 4

We like to use a combination of red, yellow, and orange bell peppers in this dish. Balsamic vinegar can be substituted for the sherry vinegar here.

1	tablespoon olive oil
1½	pounds Italian sausage, cut into 3-inch lengths
3	bell peppers, cored and sliced thin
1	onion, sliced thin
1	tablespoon tomato paste
2	garlic cloves, minced
½	cup dry white wine
½	cup water
1	teaspoon minced fresh oregano, or ½ teaspoon dried
1	tablespoon sherry vinegar
	Salt and ground black pepper
4	submarine sandwich rolls

MAKING THE MINUTES COUNT:

Before cooking, slice the onion. While the sausage browns, slice the peppers. While the peppers and onion cook, mince the garlic.

1. BROWN SAUSAGES: Heat oil in 12-inch skillet over medium-high heat until just smoking. Brown sausages lightly on all sides, about 3 minutes total. Transfer to plate and set aside.

2. SAUTÉ PEPPERS AND ONION: Pour off all but 1 tablespoon fat from skillet. Add bell peppers and onion and return to medium-high heat until peppers begin to soften, about 5 minutes. Stir in tomato paste and garlic and cook until fragrant, about 30 seconds.

3. COOK SAUSAGES: Stir in wine, water, and oregano, scraping up any browned bits, and bring to simmer. Nestle sausages into vegetables, cover, and reduce heat to medium-low. Cook until sausages are no longer pink in center, 10 to 12 minutes.

4. SEASON: Stir in vinegar and season with salt and pepper to taste. Divide sausage mixture among rolls and serve.

Italian Sausages with Peppers, Onions, and Potatoes

SERVES 4

We like to use a combination of red, yellow, and orange bell peppers in this dish. Balsamic vinegar can be substituted for the sherry vinegar here. Serve with crusty bread to sop up the savory sauce.

2	tablespoons olive oil
1½	pounds Italian sausage, cut into 1-inch lengths
1	pound red potatoes, cut into 1-inch wedges
	Salt and ground black pepper
2	bell peppers, cored and sliced thin
1	onion, sliced thin
1	tablespoon tomato paste
2	garlic cloves, minced
½	cup dry white wine
½	cup water
1	teaspoon minced fresh oregano, or ½ teaspoon dried
1	tablespoon sherry vinegar

MAKING THE MINUTES COUNT:

Before cooking, cut the potatoes and slice the onion. While the sausage browns, slice the peppers. While peppers and onion cook, mince the garlic.

1. BROWN SAUSAGES: Heat 1 tablespoon of oil in 12-inch skillet over medium-high heat until just smoking. Brown sausages lightly on all sides, about 3 minutes total. Transfer to plate and set aside.

2. MICROWAVE POTATOES: Meanwhile, toss potatoes with remaining 1 tablespoon olive oil, ½ teaspoon salt, and ¼ teaspoon pepper in microwave-safe bowl. Cover tightly with plastic wrap and microwave on high until potatoes begin to soften, 5 to 7 minutes, shaking bowl (without removing plastic) to toss potatoes halfway through.

3. SAUTÉ PEPPERS AND ONION: Pour off all but 1 tablespoon fat from skillet. Add bell peppers and onion and return to medium-high heat until peppers begin to soften, about 5 minutes. Stir in tomato paste and garlic and cook until fragrant, about 30 seconds.

4. COOK SAUSAGES: Stir in wine, water, and oregano, scraping up any browned bits, and bring to a simmer. Nestle sausages and potatoes into vegetables, cover, and reduce heat to medium-low. Cook until sausages are no longer pink in center and potatoes are tender, 10 to 12 minutes.

5. SEASON: Stir in vinegar and season with salt and pepper to taste. Serve.

BRATWURST AND SAUERKRAUT

WELL-BROWNED, FLAVORFUL BRATWURST nestled into meltingly soft sauerkraut is a classic combination. Unfortunately, the dish traditionally relies on a long list of ingredients and a slow simmer in the oven for its full flavor. Despite these hurdles, we were up to the challenge of turning this dish into a quick skillet supper.

Browning the bratwurst was a key step—just a minute or two per side to intensify flavor and develop a fond (the browned bits on the bottom of the pan). As for the sauerkraut, we started it in the microwave, with bacon, chicken broth, juniper berries, and bay leaves, while the sausages browned—this not only speeds up the total cooking time, but it adds another layer of flavor. Once the sauerkraut comes out of the microwave, it's simmered until tender with conventional flavorings like onion, apple, and brown sugar, which added richness and depth to the dish. We then nestled the browned sausages into the sauerkraut mixture and simmered them in the skillet until they were cooked through and the sauerkraut was intensely flavored and soft. The resulting dish looked and tasted like an all-day affair, but we had it on the table in just 30 minutes.

> **TEST KITCHEN TIP:**
> **Superior Sauerkraut**
> To get a jump on flavoring the sauerkraut, start it in the microwave with the bacon, broth, juniper berries, and bay leaves while the bratwurst browns in the skillet.

Skillet-Braised Bratwurst and Sauerkraut
SERVES 4

Juniper berries can be found in the spice section of the supermarket. Although sauerkraut comes packed in cans and jars, we found sauerkraut packaged in plastic bags (which are found in the refrigerated section) to be superior in flavor and texture.

2	pounds packaged sauerkraut, rinsed
2	slices bacon
I	cup low-sodium chicken broth
I0	juniper berries
2	bay leaves
2	tablespoons unsalted butter
I½	pounds bratwurst, cut into 3-inch lengths
I	onion, sliced thin
	Salt and ground black pepper
I	Granny Smith apple, peeled and grated
4	teaspoons brown sugar

MAKING THE MINUTES COUNT:
While the sausages brown, slice the onion. While the onion cooks, peel and grate the apple.

I. MICROWAVE SAUERKRAUT: Combine sauerkraut, bacon, broth, juniper berries, and bay leaves in microwave-safe bowl. Cover tightly with plastic wrap. Microwave on high until sauerkraut softens, about 10 minutes.

2. BROWN BRATWURST: Meanwhile, melt butter in 12-inch skillet over medium heat until melted and foaming subsides. Brown bratwurst lightly on all sides, about 3 minutes total. Transfer to plate and set aside.

3. SAUTÉ ONION AND SAUERKRAUT: Add onion and ½ teaspoon salt to skillet, and return to medium heat until onion is softened, about 5 minutes. Stir in sauerkraut mixture, apple, and brown sugar, and bring to simmer.

4. COOK BRATWURST: Nestle bratwurst into sauerkraut, cover, and reduce heat to medium-low. Cook until sausages are no longer pink in center, 10 to 12 minutes.

5. SEASON: Discard bay leaves and bacon, and season with salt and pepper to taste. Serve.

PORK AND BRAISED RED CABBAGE

PORK AND CABBAGE ARE BY NO MEANS A NEW combination. We've come across dozens of recipes that combine these ingredients in myriad ways, most of them calling for pork loins to be marinated overnight and cabbage to be slowly braised for hours and hours. What would it take to develop a no-fuss, one-skillet pork and cabbage dinner?

We chose boneless pork chops because they cook quickly and vibrant red cabbage, which, to our delight, is available pre-shredded. First, while we browned the chops in the skillet, we softened the cabbage in the microwave with apple cider—a flavor that is a classic with both pork and cabbage. Once the pork was browned we sautéed an onion until soft and then stirred in the softened cabbage and a grated Granny Smith apple for more fruity tartness. We then returned the pork chops to the skillet to finish cooking. The chops both soaked up some flavor from the cabbage and infused the cabbage with pork flavor while they cooked.

With a basic method in hand, we could start tackling the auxiliary flavors. A few bacon slices added with the onion contributed smokiness and bulked up the pork flavor, while thyme and bay leaves added fresh floral notes. A sprinkling of brown sugar and a hit of cider vinegar at the end added a welcomed sweet-and-sour element and livened up the flavors of the finished dish.

Pork Chops and Braised Red Cabbage

SERVES 4

This recipe will work with any type of pork chop, but the center-cut chop is our favorite. The microwaving time for the cabbage will vary depending on your microwave and how thin the cabbage is shredded.

1½	pounds (6 cups) pre-shredded red cabbage
2	slices bacon
1	cup apple cider
2	bay leaves
4	boneless pork chops, 1 inch thick
	Salt and ground black pepper
2	tablespoons vegetable oil
1	onion, sliced thin
1	Granny Smith apple, peeled and grated
1½	teaspoons minced fresh thyme
	Brown sugar
	Cider vinegar

MAKING THE MINUTES COUNT:
While the pork chops brown, slice the onion. While the onion cooks, peel and grate the apple and mince the thyme.

1. **MICROWAVE CABBAGE:** Combine cabbage, bacon, cider, and bay leaves in microwave-safe bowl. Cover tightly with plastic wrap. Microwave on high until cabbage wilts, about 10 minutes, shaking bowl (without removing plastic) to toss cabbage halfway through.

2. **BROWN CHOPS:** Pat pork dry with paper towels and season with salt and pepper. Heat 1 tablespoon of oil in 12-inch skillet over medium-high heat until just smoking. Brown chops well on one side, about 4 minutes. Transfer chops to plate and set aside.

3. **SAUTÉ ONION AND CABBAGE:** Add remaining tablespoon oil to skillet and return to medium heat until shimmering. Add onion and ½ teaspoon salt, and cook until softened, about 5 minutes. Stir in cabbage mixture, apple, thyme, and 1 tablespoon brown sugar, and bring to simmer.

4. **COOK CHOPS:** Nestle pork chops into cabbage, browned side up. Cover and cook until center of chops registers 140 degrees on instant-read thermometer, 5 to 10 minutes.

5. **REST CHOPS:** Transfer chops to plate, tent with foil, and let rest until pork reaches internal temperature of 150 degrees.

> **TEST KITCHEN TIP:**
> **Better with Bacon**
> In our quick version of this traditionally slow-cooked dish (and in other recipes as well), we find that a few slices of bacon add a deep smokiness and intensify the pork flavor—just be sure to remove the bacon slices before serving.

6. FINISH CABBAGE: Return cabbage to simmer and cook until cabbage is tender and liquid is slightly thickened, about 5 minutes. Discard bacon and bay leaves. Stir in 2 tablespoons vinegar and season with additional vinegar, brown sugar, salt, and pepper to taste. Serve with chops.

SKILLET FAJITAS

FAJITAS, A COMBINATION OF GRILLED MEAT, onions, and peppers tucked into a flour tortilla, are simple at heart and quick-cooking by design. That said, we wanted to develop a fajita recipe that could be made without lugging out the grill.

For the meat, we chose flank steak because it is readily available and relatively low in cost. Traditionally, the steak for fajitas is heavily marinated in lime juice, then grilled. But we were staying indoors. Pan-searing the steak was an obvious choice, but we found that lime-marinated beef had a tendency to steam, not sear. Our solution was to wait until the steak was seared and then toss it with a zesty seasoning mixture of lime juice, cilantro, Worcestershire, and brown sugar.

As the steak rested, we cooked the peppers and onions in the same pan, taking advantage of the flavorful fond left by the meat. As the peppers and onions sautéed, the fond was effectively deglazed and lent the vegetables a full flavor that needed little enhancement. (A little water added to the pan helped this process along.) We did, however, experiment with a variety of spices and settled on chili powder, which added a characteristically Southwestern touch to the mix.

TEST KITCHEN TIP:

Thinner is Better

It's no surprise that the best flour tortillas are freshly made to order. But those of us without a local tortilleria must make do with the packaged offerings at the local supermarket, which can often be too thick and doughy. Our advice is simple: check out what your supermarket offers and choose the thinnest tortillas they have.

Skillet Steak Fajitas

SERVES 4

If you want your fajitas on the spicy side, add a sliced jalapeño with the bell peppers. Serve with salsa, sour cream, chopped avocado, shredded cheese, shredded lettuce, and lime wedges. Leftovers make great sandwich or omelet fillings.

1	(1½-pound) flank steak
	Salt and ground black pepper
3	tablespoons vegetable oil
2	bell peppers, cored and sliced thin
1	red onion, sliced thin
2	tablespoons water
1	teaspoon chili powder
12	(6-inch) flour tortillas
2	tablespoons fresh lime juice
1	tablespoon minced fresh cilantro
1	teaspoon Worcestershire sauce
½	teaspoon brown sugar

MAKING THE MINUTES COUNT:
Before cooking, slice the onion. While the steak browns, slice the bell peppers. While the bell peppers and onion cook, mix the marinade.

1. SEAR STEAK: Pat steak dry with paper towels, then season with salt and pepper. Heat 1 tablespoon of oil in 12-inch skillet over medium-high heat until just smoking. Brown steak on first side, about 5 minutes, reducing heat if pan begins to scorch. Flip steak over and continue to cook to desired doneness (see page 193), 3 to 6 minutes. Transfer steak to clean plate, tent with foil, and let rest for 5 to 10 minutes before slicing.

2. SAUTÉ VEGETABLES: While steak rests, add 1 more tablespoon of oil to skillet and return to medium heat until shimmering. Add bell peppers, onion, water, chili powder, and ½ teaspoon salt and cook until onion is softened, about 5 minutes. Transfer to serving bowl.

3. SOFTEN TORTILLAS: Stack tortillas on plate and cover with plastic wrap. Heat in microwave until soft and hot, 30 seconds to 2 minutes.

4. MAKE SEASONING MIXTURE: Mix remaining tablespoon oil, lime juice, cilantro, Worcestershire, brown sugar, and ¼ teaspoon salt together in large bowl and set aside.

5. SLICE AND MARINATE STEAK: Slice steak very thin across grain, following illustration on page 98, and toss with marinade. Arrange beef on platter and serve with tortillas and vegetables.

➤ VARIATION
Skillet Chicken Fajitas

Substitute 1½ pounds boneless, skinless chicken breasts for flank steak. Adjust oven rack to lower-middle position, place large heatproof dinner plate on rack, and heat oven to 200 degrees. Pat chicken dry with paper towels and season with salt and pepper. Heat 2 tablespoons oil in 12-inch nonstick skillet over medium-high heat until just smoking. Brown chicken lightly on both sides, about 5 minutes total. Transfer chicken to plate in oven and cook until chicken registers 160 degrees on instant-read thermometer, 10 to 15 minutes. Slice chicken into ¼-inch strips before tossing with marinade in step 5.

FRIED FISH SKILLET SUPPER

WE WANTED TO MAKE CORNMEAL-FRIED FISH the center of a quick meal and what better accompaniment than succotash, the classic American vegetable medley of lima beans and corn? The sweet flavor and blend of textures—crisp, starchy, and soft—are ideal complements to fish. With the aid of frozen vegetables, this became an upscale dish with bargain-priced ingredients ready for the table within half an hour.

We started with the succotash. For freshness, we briefly sautéed red bell pepper and onion in butter, which added sweetness and depth. The lima beans also benefited from a bit of sautéing to intensify their mild flavor. Frozen corn, on the other hand, was at its best when just warmed through. For herbs, tasters favored a modest amount of tarragon, finding its mild anise flavor improved the flavor of both the succotash and the fish. We transferred the succotash to a bowl in a

warm oven, dotted it with butter to keep it from drying out, and moved on to the fish.

We wanted fish with a crisp cornmeal coating that was easy to prepare—no three-step breading for this recipe. We found that seasoning the fish with salt and pepper and letting it sit while we prepared the succotash drew out moisture so that our coating could stick. While the oil was heating, we dredged the moistened fillets in a seasoned cornmeal coating. They browned beautifully and cooked through in only a matter of minutes.

Cornmeal Fried Fish and Succotash
SERVES 4

To complete this recipe in 30 minutes, preheat your oven before assembling your ingredients. Trout, flounder, or tilapia fillets make good alternatives to the catfish—if the fillets are small, buy four and do not cut them in half. Serve with lemon wedges or, if you've got a few extra minutes, with Tartar Sauce (page 127).

2	skinless catfish fillets (12 ounces each), cut in half lengthwise
	Salt and ground black pepper
½	cup unbleached all-purpose flour
½	cup fine-ground cornmeal
4	tablespoons unsalted butter
I	onion, minced
I	red bell pepper, cored and chopped fine
I	(10-ounce) package frozen lima beans
I½	cups frozen corn
I	tablespoon minced fresh tarragon
I	cup vegetable oil

I. HEAT OVEN AND SEASON FISH: Adjust oven rack to middle position and heat oven to 200 degrees. Season fish with salt and pepper and set aside. Mix flour and cornmeal together in shallow

> **TEST KITCHEN TIP:**
> **Seasoning Secrets**
> Seasoning fish with salt and pepper while preparing the succotash draws moisture to the surface, giving the cornmeal something to stick to.

dish and set aside.

2. SAUTÉ SUCCOTASH: Melt 2 tablespoons of butter in 12-inch nonstick skillet over medium heat until melted. Add onion, bell pepper, and ½ teaspoon salt and cook until onion is softened, about 5 minutes. Add lima beans and cook until heated through and softened, about 5 minutes. Stir in corn and cook until heated through, about 1 minute. Stir in tarragon and season with salt and pepper to taste.

3. KEEP SUCCOTASH WARM: Transfer vegetables to ovenproof bowl and dot with remaining 2 tablespoons butter. Cover with foil and keep warm in oven until serving time (up to 20 minutes).

4. HEAT OIL AND BREAD FISH: Wipe out skillet with paper towels, add oil, and return to medium-high heat until shimmering. Meanwhile, dredge fish in cornmeal mixture, one piece at a time. Press on breading to make sure it adheres.

5. FRY FISH: Fry fillets until golden on both sides, about 4 minutes total (if fillets are large, you may need to fry in two batches). Remove fried fish from oil and let drain briefly on paper towel–lined plate (if necessary, keep first batch warm in oven). To serve, top succotash with fish on platter or individual plates.

KITCHEN SHORTCUT
DISPOSING OF OIL NEATLY

Fried foods, such as fish, are a real treat, but cleaning up after frying is not. Disposing of the spent oil neatly and safely is a particular challenge. Here's how we do it: First we allow the oil to cool completely. Then we make a quadruple- or quintuple-layered bag using four or five leftover plastic grocery bags. With someone holding the layered bags open over a sink or in an outdoor area, we carefully pour the cooled frying oil from the pot into the innermost bag. We tie the bag handles shut and dispose of the oil in the garbage.

GOT EXTRA TIME?

Our Cornmeal Fried Fish and Succotash is great with just a squeeze of lemon, but tartar sauce is good too. Try our recipe if you've got a few extra minutes.

Tartar Sauce
MAKES ABOUT 1 CUP

This is the classic sauce for fried seafood. If cornichons are not available, substitute 2 tablespoons minced dill pickles. The sauce can be refrigerated in an airtight container for up to 4 days.

- ¾ cup mayonnaise
- 2 tablespoons minced red onion
- 1 tablespoon capers, rinsed and minced
- 3 cornichons, minced
- 1 teaspoon cornichon juice
  Salt and ground black pepper

Mix ingredients together and season with salt and pepper to taste.

FISH TACOS

EVERYONE IS FAMILIAR WITH THE CLASSIC taco, filled with chicken, beef, or pork, but what about fish tacos? Born in the Baja region of Mexico, the standard version is composed of battered white fish tucked into a corn tortilla with shredded cabbage and a tangy white sauce. With few components and little preparation needed, we knew we could pull a 30-minute recipe together.

The fish itself was the natural starting point. We favored sturdy white fish, like cod, halibut, or haddock. We cut skinned fillets into 1-inch-thick pieces about 4 to 5 inches long, or just about the diameter of a small tortilla. A beer batter coating for the fish is traditional, and we could find little reason to change. We discovered that a thin, pourable batter (similar to a crêpe batter) yielded fried fish that was light and crisp. To season the batter, we added chili powder, salt, and pepper—simple seasonings that perked up the mild flavor of the fish. And while we tended to the fish, our tortillas, wrapped in foil, warmed in a low oven. Soft corn tortillas are traditional, but flour tortillas work too.

For our sauce, we doctored up store-bought mayonnaise with chipotle chiles. The heat and smokiness of the chipotles intensified the mayonnaise enough that additional condiments were superfluous. All we needed was a simple garnish of pre-shredded cabbage and diced tomato, and dinner was served.

Baja-Style Fish Tacos

SERVES 4

To complete this recipe in 30 minutes, preheat your oven before assembling your ingredients. Haddock or halibut make good alternatives to the cod. Serve with lime wedges, if desired.

12	(6-inch) corn or flour tortillas
4–5	cups vegetable oil
1	cup unbleached all-purpose flour
1	teaspoon chili powder
	Salt and ground black pepper
1	cup light-colored beer
1½	pounds skinless cod, cut into 4 by 1-inch strips
¾	cup mayonnaise
2	tablespoons minced chipotle chiles in adobo sauce
¼	pound (2 cups) pre-shredded green cabbage
1	tomato, cored and diced

1. **HEAT OVEN AND WARM TORTILLAS:** Adjust oven racks to upper- and lower-middle positions and heat oven to 200 degrees. Wrap tortillas in foil and warm on baking sheet in oven.

2. **HEAT OIL AND MAKE BATTER:** Pour oil into large Dutch oven until it measures 1 inch deep and heat to 375 degrees over medium-high heat. (Use an instant-read thermometer that registers high temperatures or clip a candy/deep fat thermometer onto the side of the pan before turning on the heat.) While oil heats, whisk flour, chili powder, 1 teaspoon salt, and ¼ teaspoon pepper together in large bowl, and set aside. When oil is almost ready, whisk beer into flour mixture until completely smooth.

3. **FRY FISH:** Pat fish dry with paper towels, add half of fish to batter, and stir gently to coat. Using tongs, lift pieces of fish from batter, one by one, allowing excess batter to drip back into bowl. Add battered fish to hot oil and fry, stirring gently to prevent fish from sticking, until golden brown, about 5 minutes. Remove fried fish from oil and let drain briefly on paper towel–lined plate. Transfer drained fish to wire rack set over baking sheet and keep warm in oven. Return oil to 375 degrees and repeat with remaining fish.

4. **MAKE DRESSING AND ASSEMBLE TACOS:** Mix mayonnaise and chipotle together and season with salt and pepper to taste. Smear each warm tortilla with chipotle mayonnaise, then sprinkle with cabbage and diced tomatoes. Add 1 piece fish to each tortilla, fold over, and serve.

PAN-SEARED SALMON WITH COUSCOUS

IT'S NO WONDER SALMON IS SO popular—it's rich, meaty, and satisfying—and almost always available at the fish counter. We wanted to use this hearty and convenient fish as the basis of a skillet supper using a pan-searing method. Recalling Chicken and Couscous (page 111), which was such a hit in the test kitchen, we aimed to develop a similar method for salmon.

We browned the fillets on one side before transferring them to a low oven to cook through. Next into the pan was the couscous, but for this recipe we decided to use Israeli couscous, which is larger than traditional couscous and therefore must be simmered (like pasta). It's got a bit more character than traditional couscous and we thought it would make a worthy partner to the meaty salmon. We found that toasting the small pearls before simmering them kept the grains distinct and added a pleasant nuttiness. But we learned the hard way that it is essential to wipe out the skillet before adding the couscous. If this step is omitted, the fishy oils left in the pan from the salmon overpower the fresh, bright flavors of the couscous. Next we simmered the couscous with a touch of garlic, shallots, and floral lemon zest for depth, and stirred green peas, chives, and lemon juice in at the end for fresh color and flavor.

We were pleased with the distinct elements of the dish, but found the dish as a whole was improved by drizzling a lemon-scented chive oil over the salmon and couscous just before serving for additional moistness and a final burst of freshness.

Salmon and Couscous Skillet Supper

SERVES 4

To complete this recipe in 30 minutes, preheat your oven before assembling your ingredients. Serve with lemon wedges.

4	salmon fillets, 1¼ inches thick
	Salt and ground black pepper
4	tablespoons olive oil
1½	cups Israeli couscous
3	garlic cloves, minced
1	shallot, minced
½	teaspoon grated lemon zest
3	cups water
¼	cup minced chives
2	tablespoons fresh lemon juice
½	cup frozen peas

MAKING THE MINUTES COUNT:
While the salmon browns, mince the garlic and shallot. While the couscous cooks, make the chive oil.

1. PREHEAT OVEN: Adjust oven rack to middle position, place baking dish on oven rack, and heat oven to 200 degrees.

2. BROWN FISH ON ONE SIDE: Pat fish dry with paper towels and season with salt and pepper. Heat 1 tablespoon of oil in 12-inch nonstick skillet over medium-high heat until just smoking. Gently place fish in skillet (flesh side down if fillets are skin-on) and brown well on first side, about 5 minutes.

3. TRANSFER FISH TO OVEN: Gently transfer fish (skin-side down if fillets are skin-on) to baking dish in oven and continue to cook until fish has turned from translucent to opaque, about 15 minutes.

4. SAUTÉ COUSCOUS AND AROMATICS: While fish bakes, wipe out skillet with paper towels, add 1 more tablespoon of oil to skillet, and return to medium-high heat. Add couscous and toast until light golden, about 2 minutes. Stir in garlic, shallot, and lemon zest and cook until fragrant, about 30 seconds.

5. SIMMER COUSCOUS: Stir in water and cook over high heat until liquid is absorbed and couscous is tender, about 12 minutes.

6. MAKE DRIZZLING OIL: Meanwhile, whisk together remaining 2 tablespoons oil along with 2 tablespoons of chives and 1 tablespoon of lemon juice; set aside.

7. FINISH COUSCOUS: Off heat, sprinkle peas over couscous, cover, and let warm through, about 2 minutes. Stir in remaining 2 tablespoons chives and 1 tablespoon lemon juice. Season with salt and pepper to taste. Drizzle chive oil over salmon and couscous when serving.

RISOTTO WITH SEARED SCALLOPS AND TOMATOES

EVERYONE LOVES RISOTTO, BUT IT TAKES nearly an hour to cook—way too much time for a weeknight supper. Instant rice turns mushy when cooked in this manner, so we turned to orzo—pasta that is shaped like rice. The orzo cooked quickly in a skillet and, when stirred frequently as it simmered, released its starches and became creamy, just like real risotto. We treated the orzo just as we would have treated the rice for risotto: We toasted the grains, sautéed the aromatics (garlic and shallot), deglazed the pan with white wine, and even finished the dish with butter. In an effort to turn this simple dish into a sophisticated dinner, we made a quick cherry tomato-caper sauce and added seared scallops to the plate. Because the orzo cooks quickly, we were able to sear the scallops in the skillet first and transfer them to a plate to keep warm while we quickly sautéed the tomatoes, and then cooked the orzo. The result? Creamy orzo risotto, zesty tomato sauce, and rich seared scallops all cooked in just one skillet, and on the table in just 30 minutes.

Orzo Risotto with Seared Scallops and Tomatoes

SERVES 4

Be sure to remove the small crescent-shaped muscle that is sometimes attached to the scallop. It will turn rubbery when cooked. Garnish with minced fresh parsley, if desired.

1½	pounds sea scallops (16 to 20 large)
	Salt and ground black pepper
4	tablespoons olive oil
6	garlic cloves, minced
1	pint cherry tomatoes, quartered
2	tablespoons capers, rinsed
1½	cups orzo
1	shallot, minced
2	teaspoons minced fresh oregano
½	cup dry white wine
3½	cups water
2	tablespoons unsalted butter

MAKING THE MINUTES COUNT:
Before cooking, mince the garlic and shallot. While the scallops brown, cut the cherry tomatoes.

1. **SEASON AND DRY SCALLOPS:** Lay scallops out over dish towel–lined plate, and season with salt and pepper. Press single layer of paper towels flush to surface of scallops and set aside.

2. **SEAR HALF OF SCALLOPS:** Heat 1 tablespoon of oil in 12-inch nonstick skillet over high heat until just smoking. Add half of scallops to skillet and brown well on one side, 1 to 2 minutes (when last scallop is added to pan, first few scallops will be close to done). Reduce heat to medium. Flip scallops over and continue to cook until sides of scallops have firmed up and all but middle third of each scallop is opaque, 30 to 60 seconds longer. Transfer scallops to plate, browned side up, and tent with foil.

3. **SEAR REMAINING SCALLOPS:** Wipe out skillet with wad of paper towels. Add 1 more tablespoon of oil and return to high heat until just smoking. Add remaining scallops and brown well on one side, 1 to 2 minutes. Reduce heat to medium. Flip scallops over and continue to cook until sides of scallops have firmed up and all but middle third of each scallop is opaque, 30 to 60 seconds longer. Transfer scallops to plate with first batch, browned side up, and tent with foil.

4. **COOK TOMATOES:** Add 1 more tablespoon of oil and half of garlic to skillet and cook until fragrant, about 30 seconds. Stir in tomatoes and capers and cook until beginning to soften, about 1 minute. Season with salt and pepper to taste. Transfer to clean bowl and cover to keep warm.

5. **SAUTÉ ORZO AND AROMATICS:** Add remaining tablespoon oil to skillet and return to medium-high heat. Add orzo and toast until light golden, about 2 minutes. Stir in remaining garlic, shallot, and oregano and cook until fragrant, about 30 seconds. Stir in wine and cook until evaporated.

6. **SIMMER ORZO:** Stir in water and cook over high heat, stirring frequently, until liquid is absorbed and orzo is tender, 10 to 12 minutes.

7. **FINISH ORZO:** Off heat, stir in butter and season with salt and pepper to taste. Serve topped with tomatoes and scallops.

Paella

PAELLA, ONCE FOUND PRIMARILY ON restaurant menus, is making a bit of a comeback in the home kitchen. As is true of many classic dishes, however, paella made the traditional Spanish way can take hours of preparation and a laundry list of ingredients, ranging from artichokes and green beans to pork, chicken, lobster, and calamari. And the list doesn't end there. But, with some adjustments to technique and ingredients, we were confident we could make paella within half an hour.

The hallmark of paella is the saffron-infused rice and chorizo, so we weren't going to forgo either. In an attempt to slim down the ingredient list, however, we decided to feature quick-cooking shrimp and clams and save the chicken and lobster for another day. Spanish cuisine uses a trio of onion, garlic, and tomatoes sautéed in olive oil—called a sofrito—as the foundation for its rice dishes, and we followed suit. We also threw in green peas for sweetness and color. And for instant white rice that is flavorful and not mushy, we took a cue from our chicken and rice recipe. We first coated the grains in the oil and aromatics before adding the cooking liquid. Using water for the cooking liquid made the dish taste bland, and chicken broth tasted out of place. Because shrimp and clams were to be the primary flavors in the dish, clam juice proved the best choice.

To serve paella, it is customary to bring the pan to the table and allow diners to serve themselves. Even though our version was less than authentic, it looked the part, and we saw no reason to break with this serving tradition. Plus, you don't dirty a serving bowl!

Skillet Paella

SERVES 4

If you can't find chorizo sausage, use tasso, andouille, or linguiça. If desired, sprinkle the finished dish with minced fresh parsley and serve with lemon wedges.

¾	pound extra-large (21/25) shrimp, peeled and deveined
	Salt and ground black pepper
I	tablespoon olive oil
8	ounces chorizo sausage, halved and sliced ¼ inch thick
I	onion, minced
	Pinch saffron threads, crumbled, or pinch saffron powder
I½	cups instant white rice
3	garlic cloves, minced
I	(8-ounce) bottle clam juice
I	(14.5-ounce) can diced tomatoes, drained
I	dozen clams or mussels, scrubbed
½	cup frozen peas

I. SEASON SHRIMP: Season shrimp with salt and pepper and set aside.

2. SAUTÉ SAUSAGE, AROMATICS, AND RICE: Heat oil in 12-inch skillet over medium heat until shimmering. Add chorizo, onion, saffron, and ½ teaspoon salt and cook until onion is softened, about 5 minutes. Stir in rice and garlic and cook until fragrant, about 30 seconds.

3. STEAM CLAMS: Stir in clam juice and tomatoes and bring to simmer, scraping up browned bits. Nestle clams into pan, cover, and cook over medium-low heat until most of liquid is absorbed, about 5 minutes.

4. COOK SHRIMP: Scatter shrimp over rice and continue to cook, covered, until rice is tender and shrimp are cooked through, about 5 minutes. Off heat, sprinkle peas over rice, cover, and let warm through, about 2 minutes. Season with salt and pepper and serve.

GOT EXTRA TIME?

If you don't have instant rice on hand or if you would like to use long-grain rice in Skillet Paella, follow this method:

Substitute 1½ cups long-grain rice. Add 2½ cups low-sodium chicken broth to skillet with clam broth and tomatoes in step 3, but do not add the clams. Cover and cook rice over medium-low heat, stirring occasionally, until most of the liquid has been absorbed, about 10 minutes. Then add clams and continue with recipe as directed.

TEST KITCHEN TIP:
Sizing Up Saffron

Saffron is available in two forms—threads and powder. Conventional wisdom says that deep, dark red threads are better than yellow or orange threads, and also cautions against using powdered saffron. We held a tasting of broths infused with different saffron samples. The reddest threads yielded intensely flavorful, heady, perfumed broths—so much so that less ardent saffron fans would have been happier with a little less saffron.

We also found that powdered saffron purchased from a reputable source was just as flavorful and fragrant as even the highest quality threads, and easier to measure.

SAFFRON THREADS **POWDERED SAFFRON**

JAMBALAYA

ORIGINATING IN THE BAYOUS OF LOUISIANA, jambalaya has become synonymous with Creole cooking. A hearty mix of spicy andouille sausage and plump shrimp cooked together with rice and vegetables, it seemed like a natural for this chapter. Having already developed a reliable recipe and technique for a similar dish—Skillet Paella (page 131)—we hoped to simply incorporate the ingredients that make jambalaya so distinct and develop a quick rendition of this Creole classic.

To re-create the flavors of jambalaya in a skillet, we added andouille sausage and red bell pepper to sauté with the onion. Tasters complained that they missed the flavor celery contributes to the dish. To keep prep time to a minimum, we added Old Bay Seasoning to the mix, which imparted a subtle celery flavor along with other warm spices. We then stirred in tomato paste, which helped deepen the flavor and color of the rice, giving the illusion of a long-cooked dish. To prevent the instant white rice from becoming mushy, we took a cue from Skillet Paella and coated the grains of rice in the oil and aromatics before adding the cooking liquid. We chose chicken broth as the cooking liquid here because it helped to heighten the flavor of the rice and give the dish its classic meaty undertones. A couple of tablespoons of chopped parsley provided the finishing touch to our Creole classic.

Skillet Jambalaya

SERVES 4

If you can't find andouille, use tasso, chorizo, or linguiça sausage. Serve with plenty of Tabasco. We like Old Bay Seasoning in this recipe, but you can use your favorite Creole spice blend instead.

GOT EXTRA TIME?

If you don't have instant rice on hand or if you would like to use long-grain rice in Skillet Jambalaya, follow this method:

Substitute 1½ cups long-grain rice for instant rice and increase broth amount to 4 cups. Extend rice cooking time in step 3 to about 20 minutes, then add shrimp and continue with recipe as directed.

1	pound extra-large (21/25) shrimp, peeled and deveined
	Salt and ground black pepper
1	tablespoon vegetable oil
8	ounces andouille sausage, halved and sliced ¼ inch thick
1	onion, minced
1	red bell pepper, cored and chopped fine
½	teaspoon Old Bay Seasoning
1½	cups instant white rice
5	garlic cloves, minced
1	tablespoon tomato paste
1¾	cups low-sodium chicken broth
2	tablespoons minced fresh parsley

MAKING THE MINUTES COUNT:
While the andouille and vegetables cook, mince the garlic and parsley.

1. SEASON SHRIMP: Season shrimp with salt and pepper and set aside.

2. SAUTÉ SAUSAGE, AROMATICS, AND RICE: Heat oil in 12-inch skillet over medium heat until shimmering. Add andouille, onion, bell pepper, Old Bay, and ½ teaspoon salt and cook until onion is softened, about 5 minutes. Stir in rice, garlic, and tomato paste and cook until fragrant, about 30 seconds.

3. ADD BROTH AND COOK RICE: Stir in broth and bring to simmer, scraping up browned bits. Cover and cook over medium-low heat until liquid is absorbed, about 5 minutes.

4. COOK SHRIMP: Scatter shrimp over rice and continue to cook, covered, until rice is tender and shrimp are cooked through, about 5 minutes. Off heat, let rice sit for 2 minutes. Stir in parsley, season with salt and pepper to taste, and serve.

TEST KITCHEN TIP:
Seasoning Shrimp
To save time, we thought we'd skip seasoning our shrimp prior to cooking, but tasters noticed a difference. For the best-tasting shrimp, season the raw shrimp with salt and pepper and let sit for 10 minutes before cooking.

7

SKILLET PASTA

Skillet Pasta

Lasagna   137
  Skillet Lasagna
  Skillet Lasagna with Sausage and Red Bell Pepper

Spaghetti and Meatballs   138
  Skillet Spaghetti and Meatballs

Pasta alla Carbonara   139
  Skillet Pasta Carbonara

Baked Ziti   140
  Skillet Baked Ziti
  Skillet Baked Ziti with Vodka-Cream Sauce
  Skillet Baked Ziti with Puttanesca Sauce

Penne Skillet Suppers   141
  Skillet Penne with Sausage and Spinach
  Skillet Penne with Sausage and Broccoli
  Skillet Penne with Cherry Tomatoes, White Beans, and Olives
  Creamy Skillet Penne with Mushrooms and Asparagus

Tuna Noodle Casserole   143
  Skillet Tuna Noodle Casserole
  Skillet Turkey Tetrazzini

Macaroni and Cheese   144
  Skillet Macaroni and Cheese
  Spicy Skillet Macaroni and Cheese
  Skillet Macaroni and Cheese with Ham and Peas
  Skillet Macaroni and Cheese with Broccoli and Garlic
  Skillet Macaroni and Cheese with Kielbasa and Mustard

Pasta Quattro Formaggi   146
  Skillet Pasta Quattro Formaggi

Chili Mac   146
  Skillet Chili Mac
  Skillet Chili Mac with Corn and Green Chiles

EVERY STEP COUNTS WHEN YOU ARE rushing to get dinner on the table in half an hour. And yes, even pasta dishes, many of which are quick-cooking by nature, can become labor intensive when you have to cook the pasta in one pot, prepare a sauce in another, and for some pasta recipes, transfer the mixture to a third where it needs to bake in the oven. We wanted to streamline the process and create tasty suppers with tender, not mushy pasta, fresh vegetables, and juicy meat, all with satisfying sauces. And we wanted to do so with minimal prep and using just one pan—a skillet.

Our most important breakthrough in developing our skillet pasta recipes occurred when we found that we could eliminate the step of boiling pasta in a separate pot. Small amounts of pasta (12 ounces or less) cook very well in a 12-inch skillet with a brothy, creamy, or diluted tomato sauce. And because we were cooking the pasta in the same skillet used to cook the other elements—meat, vegetables, and sauce—it absorbed maximum flavor. (See "While the Pasta Cooks" on page 156 to learn how we streamlined recipes where cooking the pasta the traditional way—in a pot of boiling water—is essential.)

Where did we start? Using our skillet method, we were able to replicate the ultimate baked, layered pasta dish, lasagna, by rethinking the individual elements. To fit bulky lasagna noodles into the skillet, we broke them into pieces and found they were no worse for the wear. For the lasagna's hearty meat sauce we enriched jarred tomato sauce with browned meatloaf mix and aromatics. The result was richly flavored meat sauce that was fresher tasting than any jarred meat sauce and far quicker than any traditionally cooked meat sauce. Instead of spreading the ricotta cheese between the pasta's layers, we dolloped it on top, then covered the skillet to melt and heat it through. Scattered with fresh minced basil, this dish holds a fresher appeal than its baked counterpart.

Many other dishes may surprise you. Who knew you could cook spaghetti and meatballs all in one skillet? But we found that by browning the meatballs in the skillet, removing them to build the sauce, and then adding spaghettini

(a thinner version of spaghetti) into the sauce to cook along with the browned meatballs, we had a respectable version of the original multi-pot dish. And one dish reinvented for the skillet, pasta alla carbonara, actually improves upon the original. Preparing pasta alla carbonara the traditional way—boiling the pasta in one pot, cooking the bacon in another, stirring the eggs and cheese together in a bowl and then tossing the whole together before it all cools off—can be a race against the clock. For our skillet version, we simmered the pasta in broth, then added the sauce and served it piping hot directly from the skillet. This way, the sauce remains silky and smooth—foolproof carbonara.

And we didn't limit our skillet pasta suppers to Italian-style pastas. We also include Asian-style dishes using instant ramen. We ditched the dusty seasoning packets and simmered the noodles in simply flavored broths so they cooked up tender and tasty into dishes such as Kung Pao–Style Shrimp with Ramen and Ramen with Beef, Shiitakes, and Spinach.

Note that you will need either a nonstick or traditional 12-inch skillet for the recipes in this chapter (see pages 5 and 110 for recommended brands of nonstick and traditional skillets). Some recipes require an ovensafe skillet. If you do not have an ovensafe skillet and the recipe requires one, transfer the pasta mixture into a shallow 2-quart casserole dish before baking. Similarly, if a recipe calls for a lid and you don't have one that fits your skillet, simply lay a sheet of foil over the skillet and crimp at the edges to seal.

A final note: When developing these recipes we weighed our pasta, which we find to be the most accurate way to measure it. If you do not have a scale on hand, be sure to measure the pasta using a dry measuring cup, and thoroughly pack it. Using the specified amount of pasta is important to the success of these recipes—if you use more than required, there won't be enough liquid to cook it through. And, conversely, if you use less, the resulting sauce will be too thin or soupy. Pasta shape is important too—use the shape specified (or the alternative that is sometimes given) for best results.

LASAGNA

TRADITIONAL MEAT AND CHEESE LASAGNA requires multiple steps and multiple pots. The meat sauce needs a long simmer and the assembled lasagna requires at least a 30-minute bake in the oven. No wonder this dish is best prepared on a lazy Sunday. We aimed to turn this hearty dish into a quick weeknight supper.

Our first goal was to build a hearty meat sauce with long-simmered flavor. To start, we browned flavorful meatloaf mix (ground beef, pork, and veal) in a skillet, then seasoned the meat with garlic and red pepper flakes. We then added jarred marinara sauce along with water to the meat and let the whole mixture simmer while we moved on to the pasta.

We didn't want to boil the pasta separately—there'd be no time for that in this streamlined dish—so we broke the lasagna sheets into 2-inch lengths and added them to the sauce to cook. We tried no-boil lasagna noodles first, but they turned gummy, so then we turned to regular lasagna noodles, which worked just fine.

Next, we stirred in shredded mozzarella and grated Parmesan for great cheesy flavor. If you can find it, use packaged shredded Italian cheese blend for ease. Once the lasagna noodles were cooked through, we removed the skillet from the heat and dolloped spoonfuls of creamy, rich ricotta on top along with more mozzarella and Parmesan. Then we covered the skillet to trap the heat and melt the cheeses. Just before serving, we scattered minced fresh basil over the top for a hit of lively color and fresh flavor. Only one pot is required for this dish and assembly is a cinch. Even better, you have a hot and hearty dinner on the table in 30 minutes.

TEST KITCHEN TIP:

Keep it Covered

We like to simmer most of our skillet pastas uncovered, so the pan is relatively dry by the time the pasta is tender. Conversely, with the lasagna, which is simmered in watered-down tomato sauce as opposed to a brothy liquid, we like to keep the cover on the skillet, so the lasagna is nice and saucy.

Skillet Lasagna

SERVES 4

For the jarred tomato sauce, we like marinara, but you can use whatever type you like. Any brand of curly-edged lasagna noodles will work here, but do not use no-boil lasagna noodles. If the pasta is especially dry and shattery, you may need to add extra water to the skillet while the pasta cooks. If you can't find meatloaf mix, use ½ pound 85 percent lean ground beef and ½ pound ground pork. Like it spicy? Increase the amount of red pepper flakes up to 1 teaspoon. To make things go even quicker, you can replace the mozzarella and Parmesan with ¾ cup of shredded Italian cheese blend.

1	pound meatloaf mix (see note)
2	garlic cloves, minced
¼	teaspoon red pepper flakes
	Salt and ground black pepper
6	ounces curly-edged lasagna noodles (8 noodles), broken into 2-inch pieces
1	(26-ounce) jar tomato sauce, such as marinara (about 3 cups)
2	cups water
½	cup mozzarella cheese, shredded (see note)
¼	cup grated Parmesan cheese (see note)
¾	cup whole-milk ricotta cheese
¼	cup minced fresh basil

MAKING THE MINUTES COUNT:

Mince the garlic and measure out the pasta while the meat cooks.

1. COOK AND DRAIN MEAT: Cook meat in 12-inch nonstick skillet over high heat, breaking it into pieces with wooden spoon, until fat renders, 3 to 5 minutes. Drain meat and return it to skillet.

2. SAUTÉ AROMATICS: Stir in garlic, pepper flakes, and ½ teaspoon salt and cook over medium-high heat until fragrant, about 30 seconds.

3. SIMMER LASAGNA NOODLES: Sprinkle broken noodles into skillet, then pour in tomato sauce and water over top. Cover and cook, stirring often and adjusting heat as needed to maintain vigorous simmer, until noodles are tender, about 20 minutes.

4. ADD CHEESE: Off heat, stir in half of mozzarella and half of Parmesan. Season with salt and pepper. Dot heaping tablespoons of ricotta over noodles, then sprinkle with remaining mozzarella and Parmesan. Cover and let stand off heat until cheeses melt, 3 to 5 minutes. Sprinkle with basil before serving.

➤ VARIATION

Skillet Lasagna with Sausage and Red Bell Pepper

Substitute 1 pound hot or sweet Italian sausage, casings removed, for meatloaf mix. Add 1 red bell pepper, cored and chopped fine, to skillet with meat in step 1.

SPAGHETTI AND MEATBALLS

TRADITIONAL SPAGHETTI AND MEATBALLS can involve an entire afternoon in the kitchen. Among quick versions we found recipes whose meatballs were dry and flavorless. This just wouldn't do. We aimed to consolidate this classic into one skillet, and get it on the table in just 30 minutes.

We started with the meatballs. As we did in Skillet Lasagna (page 137), we used meatloaf mix (a combination of ground beef, pork, and veal). For flavor, we added garlic, Parmesan, and oregano. Buttermilk-soaked sandwich bread and an egg yolk bound the mixture together and gave our meatballs a tender texture. Meatballs taste best when they're first browned in a skillet, but since time was tight, we browned them on just one side, and then briefly cooked them on the second side just to firm up. We then set the meatballs aside while we focused on the pasta.

We cooked the spaghetti—which we broke in half to fit into the skillet—in a mixture of our favorite jarred tomato sauce diluted with some water. The amount and consistency of the sauce was perfect, but the pasta, time and time again, was just shy of tender at the 30-minute mark. Using thin spaghetti (a slightly thinner noodle sometimes called spaghettini) solved this problem. (We also tried angel hair, but tasters found this

noodle to be too thin for the dish.) After the spaghettini had softened and begun to bend (about eight minutes), we returned the meatballs to the skillet, browned-side up, to cook through and infuse the sauce with rich, meaty flavor. A sprinkling of grated Parmesan and chopped basil, and dinner was served.

~≈~

Skillet Spaghetti and Meatballs
SERVES 4

If you can't find meatloaf mix, use ½ pound 90 percent lean ground beef and ½ pound ground pork. Note that some pasta brands label thin spaghetti as "spaghettini." Measuring 8 ounces of thin spaghetti can be difficult without a scale—when 8 ounces of uncooked thin spaghetti are bunched together, the diameter measures about 1½ inches.

2	slices high-quality white sandwich bread, crusts removed
¼	cup buttermilk or 3 tablespoons plain yogurt thinned with 1 tablespoon milk or water
1	pound meatloaf mix (see note)
⅓	cup grated Parmesan, plus extra for serving
1	large egg yolk
2	garlic cloves, minced
¾	teaspoon fresh minced oregano, or ¼ teaspoon dried Salt and ground black pepper
2	tablespoons olive oil
1	(26-ounce) jar tomato sauce, such as marinara (about 3 cups)
2	cups water
8	ounces thin spaghetti (or spaghettini), broken in half (see page 150)
2	tablespoons minced fresh basil

> **TEST KITCHEN TIP:**
> **Bread Plus Buttermilk**
> Most meatball recipes use dried bread crumbs to help bind the meat and seasoning, but we found that the key to tender, not rubbery, meatballs is to start with a mixture of sandwich bread mashed to a paste with buttermilk (called a *panada* in Italian cooking).

1. **MIX MEATBALL MIXTURE**: Tear bread into small pieces and mash with buttermilk to form wet paste in medium bowl. Add meat, Parmesan, egg yolk, garlic, oregano, ½ teaspoon salt, and ⅛ teaspoon pepper, and mix until uniform.

2. **FORM AND BROWN MEATBALLS**: Heat oil in 12-inch nonstick skillet over high heat until shimmering. Pinch off 2-tablespoon-sized pieces of meat mixture and roll firmly into balls. Add meatballs to skillet (mixture should make 16 meatballs). Brown meatballs on just one side, about 1 minute (when last meatball is added to skillet, first meatball should be browned). Flip meatballs over to cook briefly on second side, then transfer to paper towel–lined plate and set aside.

3. **START SIMMERING SPAGHETTI**: Discard oil in skillet. Add tomato sauce, water, spaghetti, and ½ teaspoon salt and return to medium-high heat. Cover and cook, stirring often and adjusting heat as needed to maintain vigorous simmer, until spaghetti has begun to soften and bend, about 8 minutes.

4. **SIMMER SPAGHETTI WITH MEATBALLS**: Nestle meatballs into spaghetti, browned side facing up. Reduce heat to medium-low, cover, and continue to cook, gently scraping skillet bottom to prevent sticking, until spaghetti is al dente and meatballs are cooked through, about 8 minutes. Sprinkle with basil and Parmesan before serving.

PASTA ALLA CARBONARA

AMONG SIMPLE PASTA DISHES, PASTA ALLA carbonara is at the top of the list; not only is it quick to prepare, but it relies on ingredients most cooks are sure to always have on hand—pasta, bacon, and eggs. We adapted this Italian classic for the skillet and created a sauce that was so rich and creamy, and coated the pasta so well, that we were surprised to discover that our skillet actually made this dish foolproof.

Traditional carbonara starts by browning bacon in a skillet, while at the same time boiling the spaghetti in another pot. When the pasta is al dente, it is drained and tossed with eggs and cheese to make the sauce. The problem is that by the time the pasta is married with the sauce and served, it can quickly congeal to form an unappetizing mess of dry, stodgy noodles strewn with chunks of cheese. The secret to our recipe was to simmer thin spaghetti (also called spaghettini) in the skillet in a garlicky, white wine–flavored broth until tender. Then we stirred the eggs right into the skillet with heavy cream and cheese (we preferred Pecorino Romano to Parmesan). The cream loosened the sauce to the perfect consistency and prevented the eggs from scrambling, and the heat from the pan melted the cheese to thicken the sauce. Add to that some salty, chewy bacon, minced garlic, and a good hit of black pepper and you can't possibly go wrong.

SHORTCUT INGREDIENT:
Supermarket Tomato Sauce

In several of our recipes, jarred tomato sauce can be a real time-saver. But does brand make a difference? To find out, we set out to test a variety of widely available jarred marinara sauces. We found that some jarred sauces rely on tomato paste as their primary tomato ingredient, while others use a fresher product—canned diced or pureed tomatoes—either alone or along with tomato paste. It then came as no surprise that those sauces made with canned or diced tomatoes scored higher in our tests.

The Best Jarred Tomato Sauces

Patsy's Marinara ($8.95 for 24 ounces), which scored highly among tasters, contains fresh garlic instead of garlic powder and had a good, chunky texture (though its high price tag might deter some).

Bertolli Tomato and Basil Pasta Sauce ($3.69 for 26 ounces) also scored highly and was admired for its fresh flavor and texture, which was described as "meaty" with an agreeable balance of tomato chunks and puree.

Barilla Pasta Sauce ($3.59 for 26 ounces), another front-runner, was liked by tasters for its good balance, fresh flavor, and chunky texture.

Skillet Pasta Carbonara

SERVES 4

Note that some pasta brands label thin spaghetti as "spaghettini." Serve this ultra-rich dish with a simple leafy green salad.

6	slices thick-cut bacon, cut into ½-inch pieces
5	garlic cloves, minced
	Salt and ground black pepper
¾	cup dry white wine
3	cups water
3	cups low-sodium chicken broth
12	ounces thin spaghetti (or spaghettini), broken in half (see page 150)
⅓	cup heavy cream
2	large eggs
⅔	cup grated Pecorino Romano cheese

1. **RENDER BACON:** Cook bacon in 12-inch skillet over medium-high heat until fat has rendered, about 4 minutes. Transfer bacon to small bowl with slotted spoon; set aside. Pour off all but 1 tablespoon bacon fat.

2. **SAUTÉ AROMATICS:** Add garlic and ½ teaspoon pepper to skillet and cook until fragrant, about 30 seconds. Stir wine into skillet and simmer until almost dry, about 2 minutes.

3. **SIMMER SPAGHETTI:** Stir water, broth, and spaghetti into skillet. Increase heat to high and cook, stirring often, until spaghetti is tender and liquid has thickened, 15 to 18 minutes. Meanwhile, whisk cream, eggs, and cheese together in small bowl.

4. **ADD EGG MIXTURE:** Off heat, pour egg mixture over pasta and toss to combine. Add bacon and season with salt and pepper to taste. Serve immediately.

BAKED ZITI

BAKED ZITI, LIKE LASAGNA, USUALLY requires lots of pots and pans and lots of time. The pasta and tomato sauce need to be cooked separately, combined with cheese, and baked for up to an hour in the oven. On top of the time issue, baked ziti can sometimes come out dry, bland, and downright unappealing. We knew it was possible to get a good baked ziti on the table; we just had to figure out how to do it in a skillet, and in just 30 minutes.

While ziti is traditional, we found that penne works too. We knew that the pasta cooking liquid would form the basis of the sauce and serve to keep the noodles moist. A combination of crushed tomatoes, water, and heavy cream coated the pasta evenly and thoroughly. To keep the dish saucy and prevent it from drying out, we baked it for just 10 minutes in a 475-degree oven. We chose classic mozzarella to sprinkle over the top of the ziti and make this dish rich and gooey, but it was a little bland on its own. The addition of grated Parmesan perked up the flavor.

We found that this Italian-American dish is best made with some restraint. Just a few really fresh ingredients are all it needs. In addition to the classic version made with tomatoes, mozzarella, and basil, we developed two simple variations—one with vodka and cream and another that combines red wine, olives, and anchovies.

Skillet Baked Ziti

SERVES 4

To complete this recipe in 30 minutes, preheat your oven before assembling your ingredients. If your skillet is not ovensafe, transfer the pasta mixture into a shallow 2-quart casserole dish before sprinkling with the cheese and baking. Packaged pre-shredded mozzarella is a real time-saver here. Penne can be used in place of the ziti.

1	tablespoon olive oil
6	garlic cloves, minced
¼	teaspoon red pepper flakes
	Salt and ground black pepper
1	(28-ounce) can crushed tomatoes
3	cups water
12	ounces ziti (3¾ cups)
½	cup heavy cream
½	cup grated Parmesan cheese
¼	cup minced fresh basil
1	cup shredded mozzarella cheese

MAKING THE MINUTES COUNT:
Measure the water and the pasta before you begin cooking. Prep the Parmesan and basil while the pasta cooks.

1. HEAT OVEN: Adjust oven rack to middle position and heat oven to 475 degrees.

2. SIMMER ZITI: Combine oil, garlic, pepper flakes, and ½ teaspoon salt in 12-inch ovensafe nonstick skillet and sauté over medium-high heat until fragrant, about 1 minute. Add crushed tomatoes, water, ziti, and ½ teaspoon salt. Cover and cook, stirring often and adjusting heat as needed to maintain vigorous simmer, until ziti is almost tender, 15 to 18 minutes.

3. ADD CHEESE AND BAKE: Stir in cream, Parmesan, and basil. Season with salt and pepper to taste. Sprinkle mozzarella evenly over ziti. Transfer skillet to oven and bake until cheese has melted and browned, about 10 minutes. Serve.

➤ VARIATIONS
Skillet Baked Ziti with Vodka-Cream Sauce
Vodka enhances the tomato flavor in this sauce.

Replace ½ cup of water with ½ cup vodka.

Skillet Baked Ziti with Puttanesca Sauce
Anchovies and olives lend zest to this variation.

Add 2 anchovy fillets, rinsed and minced, with garlic in step 2. Replace the cream with red wine. Add ½ cup pitted Kalamata olives, chopped coarse, with basil and Parmesan in step 3.

PENNE SKILLET SUPPERS
HAVING MASTERED SKILLET VERSIONS OF classic Italian pasta dishes, we turned our attention to developing lighter-sauced skillet pasta dishes that were still hearty enough to be a complete meal. For the pasta, penne was our favorite (though other shapes worked as well) because it cooked—in a mixture of broth and water, cream, and/or wine—to a perfect al dente within our allotted time.

We began with the classic combination of penne with sausage and spinach. Pork sausage required that we drain the fat from the skillet, so we turned to less greasy sausage made from turkey (chicken sausage works too). We started by browning the sausage in the skillet and then added garlic, chicken broth, water, and penne. (In an earlier test we found that using all chicken broth made the dish taste too chickeny, which is why we decided to dilute the mixture with water.) We found it necessary to crank the heat to high and really let it simmer so that the pasta absorbed the liquid and became tender. The dish was good, but not as flavorful as we would have liked, so we added minced sun-dried tomatoes to perk things up. Once the pasta was done, we stirred in handfuls of spinach and cooked the mixture briefly just until the spinach wilted. To finish things off, we stirred in grated Parmesan, which not only added flavor, but also mixed with what was left of the pasta cooking liquid to create a light sauce that perfectly coated the pasta. Crunchy toasted pine nuts provided the final touch to this hearty skillet supper.

INGREDIENTS: Sun-Dried Tomatoes
We prefer oil-packed sun-dried tomatoes to their leather-like counterparts; however, we have found that not all oil-packed sun-dried tomatoes taste the same, at least straight from the jar. Our favorite brand, Trader Joe's, is packed in olive oil, garlic, herbs, spices, and sulfur dioxide (to retain color), and has the right balance of flavors and sweetness. Another thing we liked about Trader Joe's tomatoes is that they are available in julienne strips, which saves us time in the kitchen—no cutting required. Many other brands have an overpowering musty, herbal flavor, though we found that we could improve their flavor by rinsing away excess herbs and spices. The rinsed tomatoes won't taste as good as our favorite brand, but they won't taste musty, either.

The Best Sun-Dried Tomatoes
Trader Joe's Sun-Dried Tomatoes, conveniently available in julienne strips, were praised by tasters for their balance of flavors and sweetness.

We then made a version with broccoli in place of spinach and a vegetarian version with olives, cherry tomatoes, and white beans. For a creamy variation we enriched the sauce with heavy cream and incorporated flavorful mushrooms, both white button and dried porcini, as well as a hefty amount of garlic. For this variation, a splash of white wine cuts the richness of the sauce a bit, giving the dish a sophisticated flavor in a short amount of time.

> **TEST KITCHEN TIP:**
> **A Strong Simmer**
> Simmering the pasta vigorously guarantees that the pasta will absorb the cooking liquid and become tender in the allotted time.

Skillet Penne with Sausage and Spinach

SERVES 4

Use either hot or sweet Italian-style turkey (or chicken) sausage here. Pork sausage can be substituted, but you will have to drain off the extra fat before adding the pasta. The spinach may seem like a lot at first, but it wilts down substantially. Ziti can also be used here.

I	tablespoon olive oil
I	pound Italian-style turkey sausage, casings removed
3	garlic cloves, minced
2¼	cups low-sodium chicken broth
2¼	cups water
8	ounces penne (2½ cups)
½	cup oil-packed sun-dried tomatoes, rinsed and chopped fine
	Salt and ground black pepper
I	(6-ounce) bag baby spinach
½	cup grated Parmesan cheese
¼	cup pine nuts, toasted (see page 36)

I. BROWN SAUSAGE: Heat oil in 12-inch non-stick skillet over medium-high heat until just smoking. Add sausage, breaking it up with spoon, and cook until lightly browned, about 3 minutes. Stir in garlic and cook until fragrant, about 30 seconds.

2. SIMMER PENNE: Stir in broth, water, penne, sun-dried tomatoes, and ½ teaspoon salt. Increase heat to high and cook, stirring often, until penne is tender and liquid has thickened, 15 to 18 minutes.

3. WILT SPINACH: Stir in spinach, handful at a time, and cook until wilted. Off heat, stir in Parmesan and pine nuts. Season with salt and pepper to taste. Serve.

➤ VARIATION

Skillet Penne with Sausage and Broccoli
Try using packaged broccoli florets here for ease.

Omit spinach. Add 8 ounces broccoli florets (3 cups) to skillet after penne has cooked for only 12 minutes, then continue to cook until penne and broccoli are both tender, about 5 minutes longer.

Skillet Penne with Cherry Tomatoes, White Beans, and Olives

SERVES 4

While we use vegetable broth here, you can substitute low-sodium chicken broth, if desired.

2	cups low-sodium vegetable broth (see note)
2	cups water
8	ounces penne (2½ cups)
	Salt and ground black pepper
I	pint cherry tomatoes, halved
I	(15-ounce) can cannellini beans, rinsed
½	cup chopped pitted Kalamata olives
½	cup minced fresh basil
½	cup grated Parmesan cheese
2	tablespoons extra-virgin olive oil
	Fresh lemon juice

MAKING THE MINUTES COUNT:
While the pasta cooks, cut the tomatoes and olives. After tomatoes, beans, and olives are added to the skillet, chop the basil.

I. SIMMER PENNE: Cook broth, water, penne, and ½ teaspoon salt in 12-inch nonstick skillet over high heat, stirring often, until penne is tender and liquid has thickened, 15 to 18 minutes.

2. ADD VEGETABLES: Stir in tomatoes, beans,

and olives, and continue to cook until heated through, about 2 minutes.

3. ADD CHEESE: Off heat, stir in basil, Parmesan, and oil. Season with lemon juice, salt, and pepper to taste. Serve.

Creamy Skillet Penne with Mushrooms and Asparagus

SERVES 4

1	tablespoon olive oil
10	ounces sliced white mushrooms
	Salt and ground black pepper
1	shallot, minced
1/2	ounce dried porcini mushrooms, rinsed (see page 4) and minced
1	teaspoon minced fresh thyme, or 1/4 teaspoon dried
6	garlic cloves, minced
1/2	cup dry white wine
3 1/2	cups water
1	cup heavy cream
8	ounces penne (2 1/2 cups)
1	bunch asparagus, trimmed (see page 58) and cut into 1-inch lengths
1/2	cup grated Parmesan cheese

MAKING THE MINUTES COUNT:
Cook the mushrooms right away. Prepare and measure the remaining ingredients while the mushrooms cook.

1. SAUTÉ MUSHROOMS: Heat oil in 12-inch nonstick skillet over medium-high heat until shimmering. Add white mushrooms and 1/2 teaspoon salt and cook until mushrooms are browned, about 8 minutes.

2. SAUTÉ AROMATICS: Stir in shallot, porcini, and thyme and cook until shallot has softened, about 1 minute. Stir in garlic and cook until fragrant, about 30 seconds. Stir in wine and simmer until almost dry, about 1 minute.

3. SIMMER PENNE: Stir in water, cream, and penne. Increase heat to high and cook, stirring often, until penne is almost tender and liquid has thickened, 12 to 15 minutes. Add asparagus and cook until tender, about 3 minutes more.

4. ADD CHEESE: Off heat, stir in Parmesan and season with salt and pepper to taste. Serve.

TUNA NOODLE CASSEROLE

TUNA NOODLE CASSEROLE IS A FAMILY favorite. Most versions aren't exactly complicated to prepare, but we wanted to streamline this dish further. There'd be no boiling the noodles in one pot and cooking the casserole in another—this would be a true one-pot (or skillet) dish. At the same time, we wanted to improve on the flavor, which can often be dull. The most popular version relies on canned cream of mushroom or cream of celery soup mixed with the requisite noodles, tuna, and a few stray vegetables. The mixture is baked for upwards of 30 minutes. We knew we could do better. Ready to give this hard-working classic a well-deserved makeover, we began by shutting the cupboard door to all canned soups and focused on making a sauce from scratch.

We knew that a mushroom-flavored sauce was essential. We found that the key to an intense mushroom flavor was to start out by sautéing thinly sliced white mushrooms until they released all their liquid and began to brown. To round out the flavor of the sauce we added onions. Since we were making the dish entirely in a skillet, the cooking liquid for the noodles would become the bulk of the sauce. A mixture of chicken broth and heavy cream provided the right basic flavor and heft. Four-and-a-half cups of liquid produced enough sauce with the right texture to coat 8 ounces of pasta without being either soupy or thick.

For the vegetable, frozen peas were given the thumbs-up by the test-kitchen staff. We prevented them from turning mushy by adding them along with the tuna and a little minced parsley right before baking. Buttery crushed Ritz crackers made the perfect crumb topping and they toasted nicely in the oven while the casserole baked for just 8 minutes.

Skillet Tuna Noodle Casserole

SERVES 4

To complete this recipe in 30 minutes, preheat your oven before assembling your ingredients. Kids will love this dish as is, but some adults might enjoy it served with lemon wedges.

2	tablespoons unsalted butter
10	ounces sliced white mushrooms
1	onion, minced
	Salt and ground black pepper
3½	cups low-sodium chicken broth
1	cup heavy cream
8	ounces egg noodles (3 cups)
1	cup frozen peas
2	(7-ounce) pouches water-packed solid white tuna, flaked
2	tablespoons minced fresh parsley
20	Ritz crackers, crushed to coarse crumbs (1 cup)

1. **HEAT OVEN**: Adjust oven rack to middle position and heat oven to 475 degrees.

2. **SAUTÉ MUSHROOMS**: Melt butter in 12-inch ovensafe skillet over medium-high heat. Add mushrooms, onion, and ½ teaspoon salt and cook until mushrooms are lightly browned, 5 to 7 minutes.

3. **SIMMER NOODLES**: Stir in broth, cream, and noodles. Increase heat to high and cook, stirring often, until noodles are tender and sauce has thickened, about 8 minutes.

4. **ADD TUNA AND BAKE**: Stir in peas, tuna, and parsley. Season with salt and pepper to taste. Sprinkle cracker crumbs over top. Transfer skillet to oven and bake until lightly browned, about 8 minutes. Serve.

➤ VARIATION

Skillet Turkey Tetrazzini

This post-Thanksgiving classic, similar to tuna noodle casserole, can be made with either turkey or chicken.

Substitute 14 ounces (about 3 cups) shredded cooked turkey for tuna. Stir in 1 tablespoon dry sherry along with turkey.

MACARONI AND CHEESE

WHILE SUPERMARKET MAC AND CHEESE mixes are certainly convenient and a favorite of kids everywhere, this meal-in-a-box just doesn't hold the same allure for adults. And many of the "quick" homemade macaroni and cheese recipes are just as lackluster. Typically, a mixture of shredded cheese and condensed cream soup is stirred into hot, buttered macaroni and heated through—frankly, the flavor is no better than the boxed variety. Using our skillet pasta cooking method, we knew we could do better.

We brought a mixture of water and evaporated milk (which we preferred over whole milk, which curdled, and heavy cream, which was simply too rich) to a simmer in a 12-inch nonstick skillet, stirred in the macaroni, and cooked it until tender. By the time the macaroni was done, there was just enough liquid left in the pan to make a quick sauce. We did so by mixing evaporated milk with cornstarch to thicken it, and for flavor we added dry mustard and Tabasco.

As for the cheese, the star ingredient of this dish, tasters favored a combination of cheddar and Monterey Jack for flavor and meltability. Three cups, gradually stirred in off the heat, provided maximum creaminess and good cheese flavor. A little butter enriched the finished dish, making it smooth and silky. In addition, we came up with a host of flavor variations—one with spicy chipotle chiles, one with ham and peas, another with garlic and broccoli, and a fourth with kielbasa and mustard.

TEST KITCHEN TIP:
Evaporated Milk is Key
In our testing, batches of macaroni and cheese made with nonfat, low-fat, and whole milk curdled a bit, resulting in a chalky, grainy texture. Evaporated milk, which created a silky smooth sauce with a rich, creamy flavor, was the solution.

Skillet Macaroni and Cheese

SERVES 4

Small shells can be substituted for the elbows. Pre-shredded cheese works just fine here.

3½	cups water, plus more as needed
1	(12-ounce) can evaporated milk
12	ounces elbow macaroni (3 cups)
	Salt and ground black pepper
1	teaspoon cornstarch
½	teaspoon dry mustard
¼	teaspoon Tabasco
2	cups shredded cheddar cheese
2	cups shredded Monterey Jack cheese
3	tablespoons unsalted butter

1. SIMMER MACARONI: Bring 3½ cups water, 1 cup of evaporated milk, macaroni, and ½ teaspoon salt to simmer in 12-inch nonstick skillet over high heat, stirring often, until macaroni is tender, 8 to 10 minutes.

2. THICKEN AND AND FLAVOR SAUCE: Whisk remaining ½ cup evaporated milk, cornstarch, mustard, and Tabasco together, then stir into skillet. Continue to simmer until slightly thickened, about 1 minute.

3. ADD CHEESE: Off heat, stir in cheeses, one handful at a time, adding additional water as needed to adjust sauce consistency. Stir in butter and season with salt and pepper to taste. Serve.

➤ VARIATIONS

Spicy Skillet Macaroni and Cheese

Rotel brand tomatoes are diced tomatoes with green chiles and seasonings added.

Add 2 teaspoons minced chipotle chiles in adobo sauce and 1 (10-ounce) can Rotel tomatoes, drained, with cornstarch mixture in step 2.

Skillet Macaroni and Cheese with Ham and Peas

Add 4 ounces deli-style baked ham, diced medium, and ½ cup frozen peas with cornstarch mixture in step 2.

Skillet Macaroni and Cheese with Broccoli and Garlic

Before cooking macaroni in step 1, cook 1 tablespoon olive oil, 3 garlic cloves, minced, and ¼ teaspoon red pepper flakes in skillet over medium-high heat until fragrant, about 1 minute. Proceed as directed. Stir in 1 (10-ounce) package frozen broccoli florets, thawed and squeezed dry, after cheese has been incorporated in step 3.

Skillet Macaroni and Cheese with Kielbasa and Mustard

Before step 1, heat 1 tablespoon oil in skillet over medium-high heat until just smoking. Add 8 ounces kielbasa, halved lengthwise and sliced thin, and cook until lightly browned, 3 to 5 minutes. Transfer kielbasa to paper towel–lined plate and set aside, then continue to simmer macaroni as directed in step 1. Add browned kielbasa and 1 tablespoon whole-grain mustard with cornstarch mixture in step 2.

KITCHEN SHORTCUT
SHREDDING SEMISOFT CHEESE

Semisoft cheeses can stick to a box grater and cause a real mess. Here's how to keep the holes on the grater from becoming clogged.

1. Use nonstick cooking spray to lightly coat the side of the box grater that has large holes.

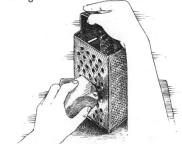

2. Shred the cheese as usual. The cooking spray will keep the cheese from sticking to the surface of the grater.

Pasta Quattro Formaggi

WE LOVE MAC AND CHEESE, ESPECIALLY our skillet adaptation (see page 144), but sometimes we get a hankering for the Italian version, *pasta quattro formaggi*. This hearty dish is a silky-smooth blending of pasta and four cheeses that is rich and sophisticated.

Our goal, therefore, would be to turn this classic dish into a skillet pasta without losing the hallmark silkiness of the sauce. We began by sautéing shallots in butter until softened. Then we added wine to deglaze the pan and cut through the richness of the sauce. Water, heavy cream, and penne were added to the skillet and simmered until the pasta was tender. (We found it important to use a tubular pasta shape so that the sauce coats the pasta inside and out.) And for the paramount ingredients—the cheeses—we remained committed to the traditional Italian favorites: fontina, Gorgonzola, Pecorino Romano, and Parmesan. Together they proved to be the perfect combination. We wanted to cook the cheeses as little as possible for the best flavor, so we stirred them into the skillet off the heat. A quick toss melted the cheeses without cooking them. We had simplified the recipe without any loss in flavor or texture, producing an authentically flavored Italian classic in less than 30 minutes.

Skillet Pasta Quattro Formaggi

SERVES 4

Ziti can be substituted for the penne here.

2	tablespoons unsalted butter
2	shallots, minced
	Salt and ground black pepper
¾	cup dry white wine
4 ¾	cups water
1¼	cups heavy cream
12	ounces penne (3¾ cups)
¾	cup shredded fontina cheese
½	cup crumbled Gorgonzola cheese
⅓	cup grated Pecorino Romano cheese
⅓	cup grated Parmesan cheese

1. **SAUTÉ AROMATICS**: Melt butter in 12-inch nonstick skillet over medium heat. Add shallots and ½ teaspoon salt and cook until softened, about 1 minute. Stir in wine and simmer until almost dry, about 1 minute.

2. **SIMMER PENNE**: Stir in water, cream, and penne. Increase heat to high and cook, stirring often, until penne is tender and liquid has thickened, 15 to 18 minutes.

3. **ADD CHEESE**: Off heat, stir in cheeses, one after another. Season with salt and pepper to taste and serve.

Chili Mac

THERE ARE A LOT OF RECIPES FOR QUICK chili mac out there, though most are a sorry mixture of canned chili and jarred salsa stirred into packaged macaroni and cheese. We wanted a chili mac worth the guilty pleasure—a zesty chili-like meat sauce, real cheese, and perfectly cooked macaroni.

We started with the chili. We found that cooking 90 percent lean ground beef until no longer pink in the skillet with onion, chili powder, cumin, garlic, and brown sugar developed the baseline of flavor for the dish, sealed in the meat's juices, and mellowed the raw bite of the spices.

We then sprinkled in the macaroni and poured in tomato sauce and water, which thickened and bound the dish together as it simmered, while the macaroni became tender. For the finishing touch, we stirred shredded Mexican cheese blend—a combination of shredded cheddar, Monterey Jack, asadero, and queso blanco cheeses—into the chili mac. The cheeses help bind the mixture together and infuse the chili mac with cheesy flavor. Additional cheese sprinkled on top melted into a gooey final layer of flavor. For an even spicier chili mac, we created a variation with green chiles, sweet corn, and cilantro.

Skillet Chili Mac

SERVES 4

For a lighter dish, substitute 93 percent lean ground turkey for the ground beef. If you want to spice things up, add ½ teaspoon red pepper flakes along with the chili powder, or serve with Tabasco. If you can't find shredded Mexican cheese blend, substitute 1 cup shredded Monterey Jack cheese and 1 cup shredded cheddar cheese.

I	tablespoon vegetable oil
I	pound 90 percent lean ground beef
I	onion, minced
I	tablespoon chili powder
I	tablespoon ground cumin
	Salt and ground black pepper
3	garlic cloves, minced
I	tablespoon brown sugar
I	(15-ounce) can tomato sauce
2	cups water
8	ounces elbow macaroni (2 cups)
I	(8-ounce package) shredded Mexican cheese blend (see note)

MAKING THE MINUTES COUNT:

While the beef and onion cook, mince the garlic.

I. COOK BEEF: Heat oil in 12-inch nonstick skillet over medium-high heat until shimmering. Add beef, onion, chili powder, cumin, and ½ teaspoon salt. Cook, breaking beef into pieces with wooden spoon, until beef is no longer pink, about 3 minutes.

2. SIMMER MACARONI: Stir in garlic and brown sugar and cook until fragrant, about 30 seconds. Stir in tomato sauce, water, and macaroni. Cover and cook, stirring often and adjusting heat as needed to maintain vigorous simmer, until macaroni is tender, 10 to 15 minutes.

3. ADD CHEESE: Season with salt and pepper to taste. Stir in 1 cup of cheese and sprinkle remaining 1 cup cheese over top. Cover and let sit off heat until cheese melts, about 2 minutes. Serve.

➤ VARIATION

Skillet Chili Mac with Corn and Green Chiles

Stir in 1 cup frozen corn, 1 (4.5-ounce) can chopped green chiles, drained, and 2 tablespoons minced fresh cilantro with cheese in step 3.

AMERICAN CHOP SUEY

GOOD AMERICAN CHOP SUEY ISN'T ROCKET science—the casserole should be a homey dish of tender macaroni mixed with a simply seasoned ground beef–tomato sauce. Quick versions we came across relied on browned ground beef mixed with canned spaghetti, which tastes as dreadful as it sounds. We knew we could do better.

We started with the ground beef. Most recipes we consulted, quick and traditional, tended to be overly greasy. We rectified the problem by using 90 percent lean ground beef, which we cooked just until no longer pink, then set aside to make

---

SHORTCUT INGREDIENT: Shredded Mexican Cheese Blend

The refrigerator section of our local supermarket practically overflows with varieties of pre-shredded cheese, but the flavorful combination known as cheese blend (a mix of three or four cheeses, often Monterey Jack, cheddar, queso blanco, and asadero) caught our attention. It's both authentic and convenient, perfect in many dishes, including our Skillet Chili Mac (above). Don't confuse this blend with taco cheese blend, which includes both cheese (often cheddar, Colby, and Monterey Jack) and spices (usually chili powder, garlic powder, and cumin). We found these added seasonings to be redundant in most recipes.

Flavorful shredded Mexican cheese blend, a mix of three or so cheeses, such as Monterey Jack, cheddar, queso blanco, and asadero, is a convenient time-saving alternative to shredding your own mix of cheeses.

room in the skillet for the vegetables. When it came to testing vegetables we kept things simple, as is tradition with this dish. Onions and garlic provided the sauce with deep flavor, celery gave the dish much-needed texture, and a red pepper lent both texture and a touch of sweetness.

Once the ground beef and vegetables were cooked, we built the sauce—a combination of canned diced tomatoes, which kept the dish tasting fresh, and canned tomato sauce, which gave the dish some body and distributed the tomato flavor throughout the dish. At the same time, we added the ground beef and vegetables back in with the macaroni and simmered until the pasta was tender and the sauce was reduced. Tasters, however, thought that the tomato flavor was too strong. We tried adding water to help dilute the tomato as we've done in other skillet pasta recipes, but found that chicken broth was even better, as it not only mellowed the acidity of the sauce but gave it a bit of richness too.

Skillet American Chop Suey
SERVES 4

2 tablespoons vegetable oil
1 pound 90 percent lean ground beef
1 onion, minced
1 red bell pepper, cored and chopped medium
1 celery rib, chopped medium
  Salt and ground black pepper
2 garlic cloves, minced
1 (14.5-ounce) can diced tomatoes
1 (15-ounce) can tomato sauce
1½ cups low-sodium chicken broth
8 ounces elbow macaroni (about 2 cups)

MAKING THE MINUTES COUNT:
Before cooking, mince the onion. While the beef cooks, chop the bell pepper and celery. While the vegetables cook, mince the garlic.

1. **COOK BEEF:** Heat 1 tablespoon of oil in 12-inch skillet over medium-high heat until shimmering. Add beef and cook, breaking it into pieces with wooden spoon, until no longer pink, about 3

minutes. Transfer to bowl and set aside.

2. **SAUTÉ VEGETABLES:** Add remaining tablespoon oil to skillet and return to medium-high heat until shimmering. Add onion, bell pepper, celery, and ½ teaspoon salt and cook until vegetables begin to soften, about 4 minutes. Stir in garlic and cook until fragrant, about 30 seconds.

3. **SIMMER MACARONI:** Stir in tomatoes, tomato sauce, chicken broth, macaroni, and browned beef. Cover and cook, stirring often and adjusting heat as needed to maintain vigorous simmer, until macaroni is tender, 10 to 15 minutes. Season with salt and pepper to taste and serve.

PASTITSIO

PASTITSIO, THE GREEK-STYLE BAKED PASTA dish of macaroni in a cinnamon-scented lamb and tomato sauce layered with creamy béchamel and cheese, is comfort food at its finest. Unfortunately, it is not at all cut out for a quick weeknight dinner. The pasta, meat sauce, and béchamel are all cooked in separate pots, and then layered in a casserole and baked in the oven. We set out to turn this classic Greek dish into a weeknight skillet supper.

While some recipes call for ground beef, we preferred the authenticity and earthy flavor of ground lamb, which we cooked and drained of its fat before constructing the dish (if you don't drain the fat, the finished dish will be greasy). We reserved one tablespoon of the lamb fat to sauté the onion and cinnamon, which added sweetness and warmth to the sauce. Garlic was added for bite and oregano for its woodsy undertones. Tomato paste rounded out the sauce. We added macaroni to the skillet next, along with chicken broth and heavy cream, and simmered it until tender. In lieu of preparing béchamel sauce separately, we decided to simply finish the dish with a quick replication: more heavy cream thickened with cornstarch, along with a little Parmesan cheese for flavor. We then slid the skillet into a hot oven to briefly brown the top—and once it came out, no one could tell that this typically time-consuming Greek classic took just 30 minutes.

Skillet-Baked Pastitsio

SERVES 4

Ground lamb is traditional in this dish and we like the flavor, but you can substitute 90 percent lean ground beef if you prefer. If using 90 percent lean ground beef, do not drain the meat in step 2.

I	pound ground lamb
I	onion, minced
1/4	teaspoon ground cinnamon
	Salt and ground black pepper
2	tablespoons tomato paste
6	garlic cloves, minced
2	teaspoons minced fresh oregano, or
	3/4 teaspoon dried
3	cups low-sodium chicken broth
I	cup heavy cream
8	ounces elbow macaroni (2 cups)
I	teaspoon cornstarch
I	cup grated Parmesan cheese

MAKING THE MINUTES COUNT:
While the lamb browns, mince the onion. While the onion cooks, mince the oregano.

I. HEAT OVEN: Adjust oven rack to middle position and heat oven to 475 degrees.

2. COOK AND DRAIN LAMB: Cook lamb in 12-inch skillet over medium heat, breaking it into pieces with wooden spoon until fat renders, 3 to 5 minutes. Drain lamb, reserving 1 tablespoon fat.

3. SAUTÉ AROMATICS: Add tablespoon of reserved fat to skillet and return to medium-high heat until shimmering. Add onion, cinnamon, and ½ teaspoon salt and cook until softened, about 5 minutes. Stir in tomato paste, garlic, and oregano and cook until fragrant, about 30 seconds.

4. SIMMER MACARONI: Stir in broth, ½ cup of cream, macaroni, and drained lamb. Increase heat to high and cook, stirring often, until macaroni is tender, 8 to 10 minutes.

5. THICKEN SAUCE: Whisk remaining ½ cup cream and cornstarch together, then stir into skillet. Continue to simmer until slightly thickened, about 1 minute.

6. ADD CHEESE AND BAKE: Off heat, stir in ½ cup of Parmesan and season with salt and pepper to taste. Sprinkle remaining ½ cup Parmesan over top. Bake until lightly browned, about 5 minutes. Serve.

SOPA SECA

THIS SKILLET SUPPER IS BASED ON THE traditional Mexican dish *sopa seca,* which translates literally as "dry soup." It begins with an aromatic broth built in a skillet (the soup part), which is poured over thin strands of pasta in a baking dish and baked until the liquid is absorbed and the pasta is tender (the dry part). It's not a difficult dish to make, nor is it time-consuming, but we wanted to get rid of the baking time and cook the entire dish on the stovetop. Authentic versions of the dish often require specialty ingredients and frankly aren't substantial enough for a main dish. For our quick version, we wanted a dish that relied on easily accessible ingredients and was hearty enough to make a satisfying meal.

Traditionally, this dish is prepared with *fideos,* thin strands of coiled, toasted noodles, which lend a distinctive background flavor. These noodles are great, but are not found at our local market. We found that vermicelli, toasted in a skillet until golden brown, was the closest match in texture and depth of flavor. After toasting the vermicelli, we browned sliced chorizo—a Mexican sausage that's found in many supermarkets—along with onion, garlic, and a jalapeño chile, which are traditional in sopa seca. But the fresh jalapeños gave this quick-cooking interpretation too much of a raw chile flavor. Instead, we turned to canned chipotles in adobo, which are smoked jalapeños in a vinegary sauce—they were perfect. They still pack a punch in terms of spice, but without the rawness of the fresh chile. We then added canned diced tomatoes with their juices, along with chicken broth, to make a rich base. To add more heft to the dish, canned black beans went into the mixture. Then we added the vermicelli back in and simmered until most of the liquid was absorbed and the pasta was tender. A sprinkling of shredded Monterey Jack cheese melted to form a gooey layer over the noodles, and a little chopped cilantro for freshness, color, and authenticity, put the finishing touches on the dish.

Skillet Vermicelli with Chorizo Sausage and Black Beans

SERVES 4

If you like your food spicy, increase the chipotle in adobo to 1 tablespoon. Serve with sour cream, if desired.

8	ounces vermicelli, broken in half (see below)
2	tablespoons vegetable oil
8	ounces chorizo sausage, halved and sliced ¼ inch thick
1	onion, minced
2	garlic cloves, minced
2	teaspoons minced chipotle chiles in adobo sauce
	Salt and ground black pepper
1	(15-ounce) can black beans, rinsed
1	(14.5-ounce) can diced tomatoes
2	cups low-sodium chicken broth
½	cup shredded Monterey Jack cheese
¼	cup minced fresh cilantro

MAKING THE MINUTES COUNT:
Before cooking, slice the chorizo and mince the onion. While the vermicelli toasts, mince the garlic and chipotle. While the vermicelli simmers, mince the cilantro.

1. **TOAST VERMICELLI:** Cook vermicelli with 1 tablespoon of oil in 12-inch skillet over medium-high heat, stirring frequently, until toasted and golden, about 4 minutes. Transfer to paper towel–lined plate and set aside.

2. **SAUTÉ AROMATICS:** Add remaining tablespoon oil to skillet and return to medium heat until shimmering. Add chorizo, onion, garlic, chipotle, and ½ teaspoon salt and cook until onion is softened, 3 to 5 minutes.

3. **SIMMER VERMICELLI:** Stir in beans, tomatoes, broth, and toasted vermicelli. Cover and cook, stirring often and adjusting heat as needed to maintain vigorous simmer, until all liquid is absorbed and vermicelli is tender, about 10 minutes.

4. **ADD CHEESE:** Season with salt and pepper to taste. Off heat, sprinkle cheese over top. Cover and let sit off heat until cheese melts, about 1 minute. Sprinkle with cilantro before serving.

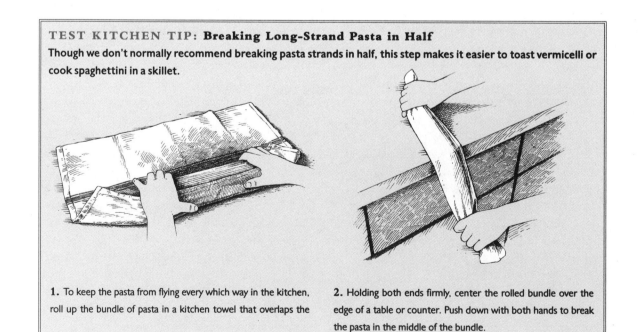

TEST KITCHEN TIP: Breaking Long-Strand Pasta in Half
Though we don't normally recommend breaking pasta strands in half, this step makes it easier to toast vermicelli or cook spaghettini in a skillet.

1. To keep the pasta from flying every which way in the kitchen, roll up the bundle of pasta in a kitchen towel that overlaps the

2. Holding both ends firmly, center the rolled bundle over the edge of a table or counter. Push down with both hands to break the pasta in the middle of the bundle.

RAMEN NOODLE SKILLET SUPPERS

INSTANT RAMEN NOODLE SOUPS ARE CHEAP (under $1 a package) and they cook quickly (in about 10 minutes), making them a convenient dinner for the time-crunched cook (or the starving student). The downside is that packages of ramen often contain seasoning mixes that are loaded with a day's worth of sodium, not to mention stale, dehydrated ingredients that we can't even pronounce. We wanted to take a second look at these quick-cooking noodles and see if we could incorporate them with fresh flavors and turn them into hearty skillet noodle suppers.

To start, we knew we'd need to pitch the flavor packets in the trash. Creating flavorful broths in which to simmer the noodles was easy with fresh garlic and ginger. To enrich our dishes and turn them into hearty meals, we chose a few different paths. Seared shrimp, red bell pepper, and chopped peanuts add richness and heft to our Kung Pao-Style Shrimp with Ramen. Tasters approved of thinly sliced blade steak, shiitake mushrooms, and spinach (a classic Asian combination) with the ramen. And a vegetarian version with tofu features an interpretation of the flavors found in hot and sour soup. These ramen dishes are a bit brothy, but as the noodles stand they soak up the flavorful broth.

Kung Pao-Style Shrimp with Ramen

SERVES 4

The sauce in this dish will seem a bit brothy when finished, but the liquid will be quickly absorbed by the noodles when serving.

3	tablespoons vegetable oil
1	pound extra-large (21/25) shrimp, peeled and deveined
1	red bell pepper, cored and sliced thin
1/2	cup roasted unsalted peanuts
3	garlic cloves, minced
1	tablespoon grated fresh ginger
1	teaspoon red pepper flakes
3 1/2	cups low-sodium chicken broth
4	(3-ounce) packages ramen noodles, seasoning packets discarded
2	tablespoons hoisin sauce
1	tablespoon rice vinegar
2	teaspoons toasted sesame oil
4	scallions, sliced thin

1. **SEAR HALF OF SHRIMP:** Heat 1 tablespoon of oil in 12-inch nonstick skillet over high heat until just smoking. Add half of shrimp to pan in single layer and cook until spotty brown and edges turn pink, about 1 minute. Transfer to clean bowl.

2. **SEAR REMAINING SHRIMP:** Add 1 more tablespoon of oil to skillet and return to high heat until just smoking. Sear remaining shrimp.

3. **SAUTÉ PEPPER AND PEANUTS:** Add remaining tablespoon oil to skillet and return to medium-high heat until shimmering. Add bell pepper and peanuts and cook until pepper is softened, 2 to 3 minutes. Transfer to bowl with shrimp.

4. **SIMMER RAMEN:** Add garlic, ginger, and red pepper flakes to oil left in skillet and return to medium-high heat until fragrant, about 30 seconds. Stir in broth. Break bricks of ramen into small chunks and add to skillet. Bring to simmer and cook, tossing ramen constantly with tongs to separate, until ramen is just tender but there is still liquid in pan, about 2 minutes.

5. **FINISH:** Stir in hoisin, vinegar, and sesame oil and continue to simmer until sauce is thickened, about 1 minute. Stir in shrimp, peppers, and peanuts. Sprinkle with scallions before serving.

Ramen with Beef, Shiitakes, and Spinach

SERVES 4

The sauce in this dish will seem a bit brothy when finished, but the liquid will be quickly absorbed by the noodles when serving. See page 186 for a tip on how to slice shiitake mushrooms quickly.

12	ounces blade steak, sliced into thin strips (see page 98)
8	teaspoons soy sauce
2	tablespoons vegetable oil

8 ounces shiitake mushrooms, stemmed
and sliced thin

3 garlic cloves, minced

1 tablespoon grated fresh ginger

3½ cups low-sodium chicken broth

4 (3-ounce) packages ramen noodles,
seasoning packets discarded

3 tablespoons dry sherry

2 teaspoons sugar

1 (6-ounce) bag baby spinach

MAKING THE MINUTES COUNT:
While the beef browns, slice the shiitakes. While
the shiitakes brown, prep the garlic and ginger.

1. **SAUTÉ BEEF:** Pat beef dry with paper towels
and toss with 2 teaspoons of soy sauce. Heat 1
tablespoon of oil in 12-inch nonstick skillet over
medium-high heat until just smoking. Add beef
and cook, stirring occasionally and breaking up
clumps, until lightly browned, about 3 minutes.
Transfer to clean bowl.

2. **SAUTÉ MUSHROOMS AND AROMATICS:** Add
remaining tablespoon oil to skillet and return to
medium-high heat until shimmering. Add mushrooms and cook until browned, about 4 minutes.
Stir in garlic and ginger and cook until fragrant,
about 30 seconds.

3. **SIMMER RAMEN:** Stir in broth. Break bricks of
ramen into small chunks and add to skillet. Bring
to simmer and cook, tossing ramen constantly
with tongs to separate, until ramen is just tender
but there is still liquid in pan, about 2 minutes.

4. **FINISH:** Stir in remaining 2 tablespoons soy
sauce, sherry, and sugar. Stir in spinach, handful at
a time, until spinach is wilted and sauce is thickened. Stir in beef and serve.

Hot and Sour Ramen with Tofu, Shiitakes, and Spinach

SERVES 4

*If you like your food spicy, add more chili sauce (see page
100 for more information on chili sauce). The sauce will
seem a bit brothy when finished, but it will be quickly
absorbed by the noodles when serving.*

1 (14-ounce) package extra-firm tofu, cut into
1-inch cubes

8 teaspoons soy sauce

2 tablespoons vegetable oil

8 ounces shiitake mushrooms, sliced thin

2 teaspoons Asian chili sauce

3 garlic cloves, minced

1 tablespoon grated fresh ginger

3½ cups low-sodium chicken or vegetable broth

4 (3-ounce) packages ramen noodles, seasoning
packets discarded

3 tablespoons cider vinegar

2 teaspoons sugar

1 (6-ounce) bag baby spinach

MAKING THE MINUTES COUNT:
While the tofu browns, slice the shiitakes. While
the shiitakes brown, prep the garlic and ginger.

1. **SAUTÉ TOFU:** Pat tofu dry with paper towels
and toss with 2 teaspoons of soy sauce. Heat 1
tablespoon of oil in 12-inch nonstick skillet over
medium-high heat until just smoking. Lightly
brown tofu on several sides, about 5 minutes total.
Transfer tofu to clean bowl.

2. **SAUTÉ MUSHROOMS AND AROMATICS:** Add
remaining tablespoon oil to skillet and return to
medium-high heat until shimmering. Add mushrooms and cook until browned, about 4 minutes.
Stir in chili sauce, garlic, and ginger and cook
until fragrant, about 30 seconds.

3. **SIMMER RAMEN:** Stir in broth. Break bricks of
ramen into small hunks and add to skillet. Bring
to simmer and cook, tossing ramen constantly
with tongs to separate, until ramen is just tender
but there is still liquid in pan, about 2 minutes.

4. **THICKEN SAUCE AND FINISH:** Stir in remaining 2 tablespoons soy sauce, vinegar, and sugar.
Stir in spinach, one handful at a time, until spinach is wilted and sauce is thickened. Stir in tofu
and serve.

8

WHILE THE PASTA COOKS

WHILE THE PASTA COOKS

FEW FOODS RIVAL PASTA IN TERMS OF EITHER speed or convenience. Pasta is almost always on hand, it cooks in minutes, and it can serve as the basis for literally hundreds of one-dish meals. And best of all, any variety of tasty sauces, meats, and vegetables can be prepared while the pasta cooks. While there's no disputing the fact that heating a jar of tomato sauce is convenient and quick, there are just so many more interesting options to choose from. For this chapter, we've developed a diverse array of quick pasta meals that can be on the table in 30 minutes. Sometimes we rely on convenience products such as jarred tomato sauce as the base of a richer sauce or packaged ravioli in a cheesy baked casserole; other times we create the components from scratch.

Off the bat, we knew we wanted to create a simple, fresh-flavored tomato pasta sauce. After our tests, we discovered that a short simmer was all this sauce requires. A combination of canned diced and crushed tomatoes gave us the thick, chunky texture we sought and a few simple ingredients like garlic, basil, and a touch of sugar rounded out the sauce's flavors. We were able to create several variations on our simple sauce by adding just a few ingredients. Vodka and cream in one variation turns our simple tomato sauce into something rich and luxurious. Olives, anchovies, and capers in another yields a zesty puttanesca.

We also aimed to develop some quick cream sauces for pasta. Rather than reducing the cream (the traditional way to thicken the sauce), we substituted half-and-half for the cream and combined it with a cornstarch and water mixture, which thickened our sauce in no time. We also infused these cream sauces with distinctive flavors like basil and porcini mushroom by whirring the sauce together in a blender. This technique gave us long-simmered flavor in just a few minutes. We did, however, stick with a traditional cream sauce method in our Fettuccine with Shrimp, Tarragon, and Cream. In this recipe, we reduced the cream in the same skillet used to lightly cook the shrimp. There was just no substitute for the flavor we achieved, and we were still able to prepare this special-occasion dish in under 30 minutes.

In addition to including the utterly simple yet boldly flavored pasta classic, pasta with garlic and olive oil (pasta aglio e olio), we offer variations on the dish. These variations include vegetables like fresh fennel and broccoli for a more well-rounded meal. And to save a pot, we use the same cooking water to boil the pasta as we do to cook the vegetables. A third variation includes frozen artichoke hearts, which, once thawed in the microwave, only require a brief sauté to become lightly browned and flavorful.

In our skillet pasta chapter, we transformed traditional, layered baked lasagna into a skillet supper. It's a delicious dish, but we recognize that sometimes nothing less than a layered, baked version will do. After much trial and error, we found that no-boil noodles, a microwave, and a brief spell in the oven (a step which browns the gooey top layer of cheese), gave us a more than acceptable version of the long-baked original. And while our lasagna is not baked (it cooks in the microwave), no one will know the difference.

We didn't limit our recipes to Italian pasta dishes; Asian noodle dishes are quick cooking too. You'll find a simplified pad thai, which eliminates pesky hard-to-find ingredients that tasters didn't feel were truly essential to the dish. Instead we worked to provide reasonable substitutions. For example, most recipes for pad thai include tamarind paste, which gives the sauce a slightly sour, molasses-like flavor; however, we found a combination of lime juice, water, and brown sugar made a worthwhile stand-in. We weren't always successful—there is simply no substitute for fish sauce in pad thai, so we kept it in the recipe. But fish sauce, we learned, is carried in most well-stocked supermarkets. In addition, we provide recipes for other quick-cooking Asian noodle dishes like Singapore Noodles with Shrimp, Soba Noodles with Pork and Scallions, and both Vegetable and Beef Lo Mein.

Overall, we tried to use as many pantry ingredients as possible to minimize not only kitchen work, but trips to the store as well. We also aimed to keep the shopping lists short for those trips that you do have to make. One last note: To keep these pasta meals within the 30-minute parameter, we recommend that you put the water on to boil before assembling your ingredients.

A TEST KITCHEN CLASSIC

PASTA WITH QUICK TOMATO SAUCE

SURE, IT'S EASY ENOUGH TO POP OPEN A JAR of sauce for a weeknight pasta dinner, but why do so when you can make a far fresher tasting homemade sauce in the time it takes for the pasta to cook? The idea that you need to simmer tomato sauce all day in order to develop good flavor is simply not true. In fact, we've found that most simple tomato sauces taste best when simmered for just 15 to 20 minutes—when they're simmered longer you actually cook out the tomato flavor rather than deepen it.

Given that good fresh tomatoes are a rare commodity, we decided to use canned diced tomatoes in combination with crushed tomatoes. The diced tomatoes add good chunky texture, while the crushed tomatoes provide a nice, smooth foundation. After conducting a number of tests, we determined that the sauce's other crucial ingredients include garlic, fresh basil, olive oil, salt, and a touch of sugar, which balances out the acidity of the tomatoes. As for the simmering time, 15 minutes was all it took.

With our quick, fresh-flavored tomato sauce down, we looked to developing several variations. For two sauces, we added heavy cream during the last three minutes of simmering. One tomato cream sauce contains vodka—a classic combination. The vodka does not give the sauce a boozy flavor as you might expect, but it does enhance the tomato flavor. In the other tomato cream sauce, we incorporated finely chopped jarred roasted red peppers. The peppers' sweet flavor works especially well with tomato. And with our tomato sauce as a base, we were able to create a zesty puttanesca-style sauce by increasing the amount of garlic and red pepper flakes and incorporating the sauce's trademark ingredients—olives, anchovies, and capers. Our tomato sauce also worked well as a platform for more hearty variations, such as a

quick meat sauce that relies on meatloaf mix and a bit of tomato paste, which made for a slightly thicker sauce with deeper flavor. We also developed a take on mussels marinara—tomato sauce enriched with lots of garlic and briny mussels.

Pasta with 20-Minute Tomato Sauce

SERVES 4 TO 6

This basic sauce works well with any type or shape of pasta. Reserve some of the pasta cooking water in case you need to thin the sauce a bit.

3   tablespoons extra-virgin olive oil
3   garlic cloves, minced
1/4   teaspoon red pepper flakes (optional)
1   (28-ounce) can crushed tomatoes
1   (14.5-ounce) can diced tomatoes
1   pound pasta
     Salt and ground black pepper
3   tablespoons minced fresh basil
1/4   teaspoon sugar

1. **BOIL WATER FOR PASTA:** Bring 4 quarts water to boil in large pot.

2. **SAUTÉ AROMATICS:** Cook oil, garlic, and pepper flakes (if using) in medium saucepan over medium heat, stirring often, until fragrant but not browned, 1 to 2 minutes.

3. **SIMMER TOMATOES:** Stir in crushed tomatoes and diced tomatoes and simmer until slightly thickened, 15 to 20 minutes.

4. **COOK AND DRAIN PASTA:** Add pasta and 1 tablespoon salt to boiling water and cook, stirring often, until al dente. Reserve 1/2 cup cooking water, then drain pasta and return pasta to pot.

5. **TOSS PASTA WITH SAUCE:** Remove sauce from heat, stir in basil and sugar, and season with salt and pepper to taste. Stir sauce into pasta and add reserved pasta cooking water as needed to loosen sauce. Serve immediately.

Cooking Pasta 101

Cooking pasta seems simple—just boil water and wait—but cooking perfect pasta takes some finesse. Here's how we do it:

CHOOSING PASTA

You have two basic choices—dried or fresh. Dried pasta is made from high-protein durum wheat flour, so it cooks up springy and firm and is suitable for thick tomato and meat sauces as well as concentrated oil-based sauces. Fresh pasta is made from softer all-purpose flour and is quite delicate. Its rough, porous surface pairs well with dairy-based sauces.

DRIED SEMOLINA PASTA

No longer gummy and bland, American brands of semolina (which is coarsely ground durum wheat) pasta have improved so much that many bested their pricey Italian counterparts in our tasting.

DRIED PASTA WINNER: RONZONI

➤COOKING TIPS:

When cooked to al dente, pasta retains some chew but is neither hard nor gummy at the center.

FRESH EGG PASTA

While your best bet for fresh pasta is still homemade, there are a few serviceable supermarket options. Our favorite brand is found in the refrigerator case, sealed in spoilage-retardant packaging and made from pasteurized eggs.

FRESH PASTA
WINNER: BUITONI

➤COOKING TIPS:

Fresh pasta is easily overcooked, so test early. Drain the pasta a few minutes before it reaches al dente, return it to the empty pot, and then cook with the sauce for another minute or two. The underdone pasta will absorb flavor from the sauce, and the starch from the pasta will help thicken the sauce.

WHOLE WHEAT AND GRAIN PASTAS

Most of the whole wheat pastas we tried were gummy, grainy, or lacking in "wheaty" flavor, but there were a few that we really liked. Our favorite is made from a blend of whole wheat and regular flours. We were less thrilled about the alternative-grain pastas we tried. Made from rice, corn, quinoa, and spelt, these products were plagued by shaggy, mushy textures and off flavors. If you're desperate to avoid wheat, try Tinkyáda Organic Brown Rice Pasta.

➤COOKING TIPS:

Cook and use as you would dried semolina pasta.

WHOLE WHEAT WINNER:
RONZONI HEALTHY HARVEST

MATCHING PASTA SAUCES AND SHAPES

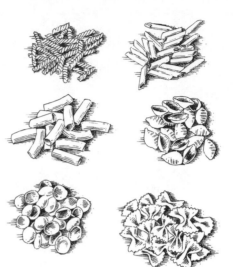

SHORT PASTAS

Short tubular or molded pasta shapes do an excellent job of trapping chunky sauces. Sauces with very large chunks are best with rigatoni or other large tubes. Sauces with small chunks make more sense with fusilli or penne. Clockwise from top right, the shapes shown are: penne, shells, farfalle, orecchiette, rigatoni, and fusilli.

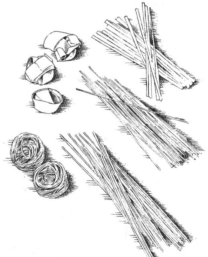

STRAND PASTAS

Long strands are best with smooth sauces or sauces with very small chunks. In general, wider noodles, such as pappardelle and fettuccine, can support slightly chunkier sauces than can very thin noodles. Clockwise from top right, the shapes shown are: fettuccine, linguine, spaghetti, capellini, and pappardelle.

AT A GLANCE: COOKING PASTA

1. Add salt and pasta to water at a rolling boil
2. Stir immediately to prevent sticking.
3. Cover and return to boil, stirring often.
4. Check early and often for doneness.
5. Reserve some cooking water and drain.
6. Sauce, season, and serve immediately.

THE SETUP

Pasta cooks quickly and should be served immediately, so have all the necessary ingredients and utensils assembled before you begin—as well as your family or dinner guests. As the Italians say, "People wait for pasta, not the other way around."

WATER AND POT: You'll need 4 quarts of water to cook 1 pound of dried pasta. Any less and the noodles may stick. Pasta leaches starch as it cooks. Without plenty of water to dilute it, the starch coats the noodles, making them sticky.

The pot should be large, with at least a 6-quart capacity—to guard against boil-overs. But forget expensive metal pots and fancy mesh inserts. A lightweight, inexpensive stockpot with sturdy handles and a lid does the job just fine.

OIL: Unless you're serving a butter- or cream-based sauce, keep some extra-virgin olive oil on hand for drizzling over the sauced pasta for a final burst of flavor. Just don't waste it in the cooking water: It won't prevent the pasta from sticking (not a problem if you use enough water), but it will prevent the sauce from coating the pasta.

PASTA: One pound of dried pasta generally serves four to six people as a main course, depending on whether the sauce is light (tomato sauce), rich (creamy Alfredo or hearty Bolognese), or bulked up with other ingredients such as vegetables or seafood.

LIQUID MEASURING CUP: In that last flurry of activity before saucing the pasta and getting dinner on the table, it's easy to forget to reserve some cooking water to thin the sauce, if needed. We often place a measuring cup in the colander as a reminder when we start to cook.

COLANDER: Once the pasta is drained, give the colander a shake or two, but don't shake the pasta bone-dry. The little bit of hot cooking water clinging to the pasta will help the sauce coat it.

SAUCE: Don't drop the pasta into the water until the sauce is nearly ready. Smooth sauces and sauces with very small bits, such as garlic and oil, are best with long strands of pasta. Chunkier sauces are best matched with short tubular or molded shapes.

SALT: Properly seasoned cooking water is crucial for good flavor—use 1 tablespoon table salt (or 2 tablespoons kosher salt) per 4 quarts of water.

SERVING BOWLS AND LADLE: We like to serve pasta in wide soup bowls, as the edge provides an easy place to twirl noodles on a fork. To warm, before serving the pasta (especially important with cream sauces, which cool quickly and congeal), add a few extra cups of water to the pasta pot. When it boils, ladle about ½ cup of boiling water into each bowl and let stand while the pasta cooks.

PASTA FORK: Of the countless items of pasta paraphernalia we've tested over the years, the only one we recommend is a pasta fork—a long-handled, perforated spoon with ridged teeth. The wood variety is clunky and prone to splitting, but the plastic and stainless-steel versions are great. Not essential—basic tongs work fine—but we're glad we bought one.

QUICK TIP:

WARM THE SERVING BOWL

If you're using a large serving bowl, try placing it underneath the colander while draining the pasta. The hot water heats up the bowl, which keeps the pasta warm longer.

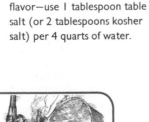

➤ VARIATIONS

Pasta with 20-Minute Tomato, Vodka, and Cream Sauce

Vodka enhances the tomato flavor in this sauce.

Omit diced tomatoes, basil, and sugar. Add ½ cup vodka with crushed tomatoes in step 3. Add ¾ cup heavy cream during final 3 minutes of simmering.

Pasta with 20-Minute Tomato, Roasted Red Pepper, and Cream Sauce

For the results from our tasting of jarred roasted red peppers, see page 13.

Omit diced tomatoes. Add 1 (17-ounce) jar roasted red peppers, rinsed and chopped fine, with crushed tomatoes in step 3. Add ¾ cup heavy cream during final 3 minutes of simmering.

DEBEARDING MUSSELS

Mussels often contain a weedy beard protruding from the crack between the two shells. It's fairly small and can be difficult to tug out of place. Here's how we handle this task.

Trap the beard between the side of a small knife and your thumb and pull to remove it. The flat surface of the paring knife gives you some leverage to extract the pesky beard.

Pasta with 20-Minute Puttanesca

We like Kalamata or niçoise olives in this sauce; avoid canned California black olives, which have little flavor.

Omit basil, increase garlic to 4 cloves, and increase red pepper flakes to ¾ teaspoon. Add 8 anchovy fillets, rinsed and minced, with garlic in step 2. Stir in ½ cup chopped Kalamata olives, ¼ cup minced fresh parsley, and 3 tablespoons capers, rinsed, after sauce has simmered in step 3.

Pasta with 20-Minute Hearty Meat Sauce

If you can't find meatloaf mix, substitute ½ pound ground beef and ½ pound ground pork, or 1 pound sweet or hot Italian sausage removed from its casing and crumbled.

Add 2 tablespoons tomato paste when cooking garlic in step 2. Before adding tomatoes in step 3, add 1 pound meatloaf mix and cook, breaking up meat with wooden spoon, until no longer pink, about 5 minutes.

Pasta with 20-Minute Mussels Marinara

Prepare this sauce in a Dutch oven. Discard any mussels that do not open.

Increase garlic to 6 cloves. After sauce has simmered in step 3, add 2 pounds mussels, rinsed and debearded (see illustration at left). Continue to simmer, covered, until mussels have opened, about 3 minutes. Substitute minced fresh parsley for basil.

PASTA WITH QUICK CREAM SAUCE

THE SILKY RICHNESS OF CREAM SAUCE tossed with pasta can't be beat. It's a quick-cooking sauce, too, making it ideal for weeknight meals. But we wanted to take a second look at the traditional recipe and see if we could streamline things even further.

Typically, a cream sauce requires finely mincing aromatics like garlic or shallots, then sautéing them in butter. Next, heavy cream is added and the mixture is simmered (for about 8 minutes) until it has reduced and thickened to a sauce-like consistency. During the simmering time the sauce not only thickens, but becomes infused with the flavor of the aromatics.

To begin, we sautéed minced shallots in butter, followed by garlic. Our next step was to ditch the sauce's classic reduction method and instead make a quick thickened sauce with a combination of half-and-half and cornstarch mixed with water (this mixture works better than heavy cream and cornstarch). The cornstarch thickens and stabilizes the half-and-half. The sauce only requires a few minutes of simmering (enough time to fully cook the starch until it thickens). Tasters liked the sauce, but thought it was lacking the richness of traditional cream sauce. We then turned to cutting the half-and-half with store-bought chicken broth, which added some necessary depth. But due to the short simmering time, we were still having trouble infusing our sauce with a worthy amount of flavor.

Until now, we'd been adding the half-and-half mixture to the aromatics in the saucepan, then finishing the sauce with our herb of choice, basil. As a time-saving measure we tossed the basil in the blender (borrowing a technique from our creamy salad dressing recipes) instead of finely mincing an entire cup by hand. Going on a suggestion made by one of our tasters, we added the half-and-half mixture to the blender along with the basil. We then simply poured the mixture from the blender right into the saucepan with the aromatics for a brief simmer. This step infused our sauce with bold flavor in a short amount of time.

Once we mastered this cream sauce, we turned to developing a few variations. Our Mushroom-Thyme Cream Sauce relies on deeply flavorful porcini mushrooms and an unusual ingredient—soy sauce—which helps reinforce the mushroom's flavor. Our vibrantly colored Roasted Red Pepper Cream Sauce gets its flavor from two key ingredients: jarred roasted red peppers and balsamic vinegar.

Pasta with Garlic–Basil Cream Sauce

SERVES 4 TO 6

The sauce does not hold well, so it should be served immediately with the pasta. Serve with grated Parmesan, if desired.

1	cup packed fresh basil leaves
1½	cups half-and-half
1	cup low-sodium chicken broth
1	tablespoon cornstarch
2	tablespoons unsalted butter
1	shallot, minced
	Salt and ground black pepper
2	garlic cloves, minced
2	tablespoons minced fresh basil
1	pound linguine or spaghetti

1. BOIL WATER FOR PASTA: Bring 4 quarts water to boil in large pot.

2. BLEND BASIL, HALF-AND-HALF, AND BROTH: Puree basil leaves, half-and-half, chicken broth, and cornstarch together in blender until completely smooth, about 30 seconds.

3. SAUTÉ AROMATICS AND SIMMER SAUCE: Melt butter in medium saucepan over medium heat. Add shallot and ¼ teaspoon salt and cook until softened, about 2 minutes. Stir in garlic and cook until fragrant, about 30 seconds. Briefly re-blend half-and-half mixture to dissolve cornstarch, then stir into saucepan and simmer until thickened, about 2 minutes. Remove sauce from heat, stir in minced basil, and season with salt and pepper to taste.

4. COOK AND DRAIN PASTA: Add pasta and 1 tablespoon salt to boiling water and cook, stirring often, until al dente. Reserve ½ cup cooking water, then drain pasta and return pasta to pot.

5. TOSS PASTA WITH SAUCE: Stir sauce into pasta and add reserved pasta cooking water as needed to loosen sauce. Serve immediately.

Pasta with Mushroom-Thyme Cream Sauce

SERVES 4 TO 6

The sauce does not hold well, so it should be served immediately with the pasta. When rehydrating the mushrooms, use about 1½ cups of boiling water; you will need 1 cup of the leftover rehydrating liquid for the sauce (it replaces the broth). This sauce is thicker than the Garlic-Basil Cream Sauce and yields more, but it is still the right amount to sauce 1 pound of pasta. Serve with grated Parmesan, if desired.

2	tablespoons unsalted butter
I	pound sliced white mushrooms
	Salt and ground black pepper
½	ounce dried porcini mushrooms, rehydrated with I cup liquid reserved (see page 4)
1½	cups half-and-half
I	tablespoon soy sauce
I	tablespoon fresh thyme
I	tablespoon cornstarch
I	shallot, minced
2	garlic cloves, minced
¼	cup dry sherry
I	pound linguine or spaghetti

MAKING THE MINUTES COUNT:
Rehydrate the porcini mushrooms while the white mushrooms brown.

I. BOIL WATER FOR PASTA: Bring 4 quarts water to boil in large pot.

2. SAUTÉ MUSHROOMS: Melt butter in medium saucepan over medium-high heat. Add white mushrooms and ¼ teaspoon salt and cook until browned, about 8 minutes.

3. BLEND PORCINI, HALF-AND-HALF, AND BROTH: While mushrooms cook, puree rehydrated porcini mushrooms, 1 cup reserved porcini liquid (add water if short), half-and-half, soy sauce, thyme, and cornstarch in blender until smooth, about 30 seconds.

4. SAUTÉ AROMATICS AND SIMMER SAUCE: Stir shallot into saucepan with mushrooms and cook until softened, about 2 minutes. Stir in garlic and cook until fragrant, about 30 seconds. Stir in sherry and cook until nearly evaporated, about 1 minute. Briefly re-blend porcini mixture to dissolve cornstarch, then stir into saucepan and simmer until thickened, about 2 minutes. Remove sauce from heat and season with salt and pepper to taste.

5. COOK AND DRAIN PASTA: Add pasta and 1 tablespoon salt to boiling water and cook, stirring often, until al dente. Reserve ½ cup cooking water, then drain pasta and return pasta to pot.

6. TOSS PASTA WITH SAUCE: Stir sauce into pasta and add reserved pasta cooking water as needed to loosen sauce. Serve immediately.

Pasta with Roasted Red Pepper Cream Sauce

SERVES 4 TO 6

This sauce does not hold well, so it should be served immediately with the pasta. Roasted red peppers are sold in jars of different sizes—you will need about 4 to 5 medium roasted red peppers, drained, for this recipe. This sauce is thicker than the Garlic-Basil Cream Sauce and yields more, but it is still the right amount to sauce 1 pound of pasta. Serve with grated Parmesan, if desired.

I	(17-ounce) jar roasted red peppers (see note), rinsed and patted dry
1½	cups half-and-half
I	cup low-sodium chicken broth
I	tablespoon sugar
I	tablespoon fresh oregano
I	tablespoon cornstarch
2	tablespoons unsalted butter
4	garlic cloves, minced
⅛	teaspoon red pepper flakes
I	pound linguine or spaghetti
	Salt and ground black pepper
2	tablespoons balsamic vinegar

I. BOIL WATER FOR PASTA: Bring 4 quarts water to boil in large pot.

2. BLEND PEPPERS, HALF-AND-HALF, AND BROTH: Puree roasted peppers, half-and-half, chicken broth, sugar, oregano, and cornstarch together in blender until smooth, about 30 seconds.

3. SAUTÉ AROMATICS AND SIMMER SAUCE: Melt butter in medium saucepan over medium heat. Add garlic and red pepper flakes and cook until fragrant, about 30 seconds. Briefly re-blend half-and-half mixture to dissolve cornstarch, then stir into saucepan and simmer until thickened, about 2 minutes. Remove sauce from heat, stir in vinegar, and season with salt and pepper to taste.

4. COOK AND DRAIN PASTA: Add pasta and 1 tablespoon salt to boiling water and cook, stirring often, until al dente. Reserve ½ cup cooking water, then drain pasta and return pasta to pot.

5. TOSS PASTA WITH SAUCE: Stir sauce into pasta and add reserved pasta cooking water as needed to loosen sauce. Serve immediately.

A TEST KITCHEN CLASSIC

PASTA WITH GARLIC AND OLIVE OIL

PASTA WITH GARLIC AND OIL, OR AGLIO e olio, is among the most satisfying (and simple) of pasta dishes. Composed of kitchen staples—pasta, olive oil, garlic, red pepper flakes, and often a few gratings of Parmesan cheese—it is also quick to prepare. However, if not made with care, the dish is either dominated by the flavor of burnt garlic or worse, has no garlic presence at all. We headed to the test kitchen to create a recipe that made the most of its simple flavors.

We explored different techniques for imbuing the olive oil with garlic. Tasters didn't care for sautéed whole or slivered garlic, whether ultimately removed from the dish or left in. In fact, no one cared for browned garlic at all—it was acrid and one-dimensional. Uncooked minced or grated garlic alone was too metallic. We needed a third way. In the end, we found that slowly sautéing a large amount of minced garlic (about 3 tablespoons) over a low flame until it turned golden and mellow produced the deep, complex garlic flavor we were after.

We finessed our sauce even more by settling on a set ratio of minced garlic to olive oil. We then finished the sauce with a bit more olive oil and raw minced garlic. While you might think that raw garlic would give the dish a harsh flavor, it does not. The raw garlic, spread into the sauce and tossed with a pound of hot pasta, enlivens the dish, setting it apart from any other version we tried. To finish, a fistful of minced parsley, fresh lemon juice, and a dash of red pepper flakes give a final layer of oomph to this simple pasta dish. Best of all, we discovered that this sauce plays host to a number of easy variations using vegetables like broccoli, fennel, and artichoke hearts.

Spaghetti with Garlic and Olive Oil

SERVES 4 TO 6

This recipe requires 12 minced garlic cloves, which measures 4 tablespoons. Three tablespoons are sautéed and the remaining tablespoon is stirred into the pasta, raw, when finishing the dish.

6	tablespoons extra-virgin olive oil
12	garlic cloves, minced (see note)
	Salt and ground black pepper
1	pound spaghetti
3	tablespoons minced fresh parsley
2	teaspoons fresh lemon juice
¼	teaspoon red pepper flakes
	Grated Parmesan cheese (for serving)

TEST KITCHEN TIP:

Don't Rush the Garlic

In trying to shave time off this already quick recipe, we sautéed the garlic over medium heat until lightly browned, but the flavor was either acrid (from too much browning) or washed out. Instead, we found patience is a true virtue here. The key to success is a combination of three parts slowly sautéed garlic to one part minced raw garlic. (The minced raw garlic gives the dish a welcome bite.) For sautéed garlic with well-developed flavor, sauté it until it foams and turns sticky and straw-colored (about 10 minutes).

MAKING THE MINUTES COUNT:
Prep the remaining ingredients while the garlic is sautéing.

1. BOIL WATER FOR SPAGHETTI: Bring 4 quarts water to boil in large pot.

2. SAUTÉ GARLIC: Cook 3 tablespoons of oil, 3 tablespoons of garlic, and ½ teaspoon salt in 10-inch nonstick skillet over low heat, stirring often, until garlic is sticky, foamy, and straw-colored, about 10 minutes. Remove from heat.

3. COOK AND DRAIN SPAGHETTI: Add spaghetti and 1 tablespoon salt to boiling water and cook, stirring often, until al dente. Reserve ½ cup cooking water, then drain spaghetti and return spaghetti to pot.

4. TOSS SPAGHETTI WITH SAUCE: Stir parsley, lemon juice, red pepper flakes, remaining 3 tablespoons oil, sautéed garlic, and 2 tablespoons reserved pasta cooking water into spaghetti. Season with remaining tablespoon raw garlic, salt, and pepper to taste. Add reserved pasta cooking water as needed to loosen sauce. Serve, passing the Parmesan separately.

➤ VARIATIONS

Spaghetti with Garlic, Olive Oil, and Broccoli

For speed and ease, look for packaged fresh broccoli florets. Do not substitute frozen broccoli florets.

After garlic is sautéed in step 2, transfer it to small bowl. Add ½ cup water and 4 cups fresh broccoli florets (12 ounces) to skillet. Cover and cook over medium-high heat until broccoli is tender but still crisp at center, 5 to 7 minutes. Drain broccoli and stir into spaghetti with sautéed garlic in step 4.

Spaghetti with Garlic, Olive Oil, and Fennel

Fennel's mellow licorice-like flavor is a nice complement to the garlic in this sauce.

After garlic is sautéed in step 2, transfer it to small bowl. Add ¼ cup water, 1 tablespoon olive oil, and 2 fennel bulbs, trimmed, cored, and sliced thin, to skillet. Cover and cook over high heat until fennel is slightly tender, about 3 minutes. Uncover and continue to cook until fennel is lightly browned and fully tender, about 5 minutes. Stir fennel into spaghetti with sautéed garlic in step 4.

SHORTCUT INGREDIENT: Ready-to-Use Garlic

Garlic is a kitchen staple, used in everything from salad dressings to stir-fries and soups. For the time-crunched cook, however, peeling and mincing cloves of garlic can be a hassle. And with all the substitutes for fresh garlic cloves on the market, from handily peeled whole cloves to jars of minced garlic packed in water or oil, and even frozen cubes of garlic puree, we wondered if we could eliminate the tedious task of peeling and mincing fresh garlic from our recipes. We tested a variety of these products against fresh garlic cloves in a wide range of recipes, including Spaghetti with Garlic and Olive Oil (page 163), in which garlic is the main flavor in the dish, and Stir-Fried Tofu (page 101), where garlic plays a complementary role.

Tasters preferred fresh garlic cloves in both applications, though peeled whole cloves were also deemed acceptable. We did, however, find that the freshness of the peeled cloves varied from store to store. Conversely, tasters found minced garlic in a jar and pureed cubes of frozen garlic to be unacceptable. Comments ranged from "plastic-like" to "tasteless" and "gross."

Fresh Garlic
Fresh garlic really doesn't take much prep and it tastes far better than the ready-to-use products we tried.

Jarred Peeled Garlic Cloves
In a pinch, jarred peeled garlic cloves are an option, but we found that freshness varied from store to store.

Minced and Crushed Garlic
Whether packed in jars or frozen in cubes, ready-to-use minced or crushed garlic was deemed unacceptable in all applications.

Spaghetti with Garlic, Olive Oil, and Artichokes

To quickly thaw frozen artichoke hearts, place them in a bowl, cover with plastic wrap, and microwave for about 5 minutes. Drain thoroughly before using.

After garlic is sautéed in step 2, transfer it to small bowl. Add 1 tablespoon olive oil to skillet and return to high heat until shimmering. Add 2 (9-ounce) packages frozen artichoke hearts, thawed and drained (see note), and ¼ teaspoon salt. Cook until artichokes are lightly brown and tender, about 6 minutes. Stir artichokes into spaghetti with sautéed garlic in step 4.

PASTA WITH GREENS

ITALIANS HAVE A KNACK FOR TRANSFORMING humble ingredients into remarkable meals, and a meal of pasta and greens is no exception. But making something out of almost nothing takes finesse—and this is a dish that can certainly be dull if not done right. We were after a really outstanding, speedy pasta-with-greens recipe, one that would rely mainly on boldly flavored ingredients found in most home kitchens. Tasters requested two different styles of quick pasta with greens: one with tender greens and another, heartier, version with sturdy greens.

Starting with the type of greens for our pasta, we all agreed on baby spinach for our tender greens candidate. The spinach wilted nicely when stirred into our pasta at the end of cooking. As for heartier greens, tasters liked either kale or collards, and we found it most efficient to add them to the boiling water along with the pasta, because both cooked in the same amount of time as the pasta. We next looked to the sauce component, concluding that a brothy sauce would work best to carry the mellow, verdant earthiness of the greens. And to give our sauce backbone, we used chicken broth fortified with sautéed bacon and onion: two ingredients commonly on hand in most home kitchens. Their combined complexity seemed a natural fit with the greens (think collard greens with ham hocks). The sauce was still not as rich as we would have liked, so we stirred in grated Italian fontina

cheese, a variety that tasters preferred over a number of others we tested for its creamy texture and nutty flavor. One last touch, and a simple one that added welcome textural contrast and flavor, was a sprinkling of toasted bread crumbs—a classic Italian pasta topping.

Spaghetti with Spinach, Bacon, and Toasted Bread Crumbs
SERVES 4 TO 6

Look for Italian-made fontina that costs about $8 a pound for this recipe; it has a waxy brownish coating and a semi-soft, super-creamy texture. Be aware that the pricier Fontina Val d'Aosta is best eaten out of hand, and that the inexpensive Swedish or Danish fontina has a generic, unremarkable flavor. When adding the spinach, it may look like too much at first, but it will wilt down substantially.

- 2 slices high-quality sandwich bread, torn into quarters
- 2 tablespoons olive oil
- 6 garlic cloves, minced
- Salt and ground black pepper
- 4 slices bacon, chopped fine
- 1 onion, minced
- ¼ teaspoon red pepper flakes
- 2 cups low-sodium chicken broth
- 1 pound spaghetti
- 12 ounces baby spinach (9½ cups)
- 1 cup grated fontina cheese (see note)

TEST KITCHEN TIP:
Getting Even . . . Browning
The bread crumbs are an important element of this dish; therefore, preparing them just right is crucial. What you want to avoid are unevenly cooked crumbs, where some of them are too browned and others are pale and soft. Overly browned crumbs will give a burnt flavor to the dish. Pale and soft crumbs will become mushy once tossed with the pasta and give the dish a clumpy texture. To avoid these pitfalls, make sure to stir the crumbs frequently during toasting and don't be afraid to lower the heat if they seem to be browning too quickly.

MAKING THE MINUTES COUNT:
Chop the bacon and mince the onion while the bread crumbs toast.

1. BOIL WATER FOR PASTA: Bring 4 quarts water to boil in large pot.

2. MAKE AND TOAST BREAD CRUMBS: Pulse bread and oil in food processor to coarse crumbs. Toast crumbs in 12-inch skillet over medium-high heat, stirring frequently, until beginning to brown, about 3 minutes. Stir in half of garlic and continue to cook until crumbs are fragrant and golden, about 1 minute. Season with salt and pepper to taste, transfer to bowl, and set aside. Wipe skillet out with wad of paper towels.

3. MAKE SAUCE: Add bacon to skillet and return to medium-high heat until fat is partially rendered, about 2 minutes. Stir in onion and continue to cook until bacon is crisp and onion is softened and browned, about 6 minutes. Stir in remaining garlic and red pepper flakes and cook until fragrant, about 30 seconds. Stir in broth, scraping up browned bits, and bring to simmer. Remove skillet from heat, cover, and set aside.

4. COOK AND DRAIN PASTA: Add spaghetti and 1 tablespoon salt to boiling water and cook, stirring often, until al dente. Reserve ½ cup cooking water, then drain spaghetti and return spaghetti to pot.

5. TOSS PASTA WITH SAUCE: Stir sauce into spaghetti. Stir in spinach, one handful at a time, until wilted. Stir in fontina and season with salt and pepper to taste. Add reserved cooking water as necessary to loosen sauce. Sprinkle bread crumbs over individual servings, or pass separately.

➤ VARIATION

Spaghetti with Greens, White Beans, Bacon, and Toasted Bread Crumbs
This hearty variation tastes great when drizzled with fruity extra-virgin olive oil before serving.

Add 1 (15-ounce) can cannellini beans, rinsed, to skillet with broth in step 3. Omit spinach. Add 1 bunch kale or collard green leaves, chopped into 1-inch pieces (10 cups), into boiling water with spaghetti in step 4.

PASTA WITH VEGETABLES

CREATED BY A FAMOUS NEW YORK CITY restaurateur in the 1970s, pasta primavera is the ultimate pasta with vegetables dish. The trouble is, this dish is fussy and time-consuming to prepare. The authentic recipe calls for blanching each green vegetable in a separate pot to retain its individual character (an hour-long process when all is said and done). We decided to cast this primavera aside and create our own quick pasta and vegetable dish from scratch.

Our initial tests were geared toward finding a mix of quick-cooking vegetables our tasting panel could agree on. After trying a number of combinations, tasters settled on a mix of zucchini, onion, carrots, and cherry tomatoes. (Numerous taste tests revealed that cherry tomatoes were much more flavorful than other supermarket varieties, which were consistently bland, watery, and mealy.) With the basics in place, we looked to extracting as much flavor as possible from these everyday vegetables.

Lightly browning the vegetables was a must for building big flavor. And sautéing the vegetables in batches was key to ensuring that the vegetables retained their shape and browned properly. With a good backbone of flavor in place from the browning, we looked to sharpen the flavors of the vegetables with a good hit of fresh minced

---

QUICK CHEESY BREAD STICKS
THESE SOFT BREAD STICKS ARE A NICE addition to many of the recipes in this chapter.

Adjust oven rack to middle position and heat oven to 400 degrees. Roll out 1 pound pizza dough into ½-inch-thick rectangle. Cut dough into 1-inch-wide strips and lay on well-oiled baking sheet. Brush with 2 tablespoons olive oil and sprinkle with ½ cup grated Parmesan cheese, ½ teaspoon kosher salt, and ½ teaspoon ground black pepper. Bake until golden brown, about 15 minutes. Let cool slightly on wire rack and serve warm.

garlic, a touch of red pepper flakes, and fresh basil. Chicken broth mixed with a judicious amount of tomato paste added just enough liquid, flavor, and body to bring all the elements together. We tossed our vegetable sauce with rotini, a corkscrew-shaped pasta similar to fusilli—its crevices perfectly grasped the chunky sauce.

Rotini with Summer Garden Vegetables
SERVES 4

Both zucchini and summer squash work well here. Serve with grated Parmesan cheese and a splash of extra-virgin olive oil, if desired.

4	tablespoons extra-virgin olive oil
2	zucchini, halved lengthwise and sliced crosswise 1/2 inch thick
	Salt and ground black pepper
1	pint cherry tomatoes, halved
2	carrots, halved lengthwise and sliced crosswise 1/2 inch thick
1	onion, minced
3	tablespoons tomato paste
3	garlic cloves, minced
1/8	teaspoon red pepper flakes
1 1/2	cups low-sodium chicken broth
1/2	pound rotini or fusilli
1/4	cup minced fresh basil

MAKING THE MINUTES COUNT:
Prep the tomatoes, carrots, and onion while the zucchini cooks.

1. BOIL WATER FOR PASTA: Bring 3 quarts water to boil in large pot.

2. SAUTÉ ZUCCHINI AND CHERRY TOMATOES: Heat 1 tablespoon of oil in 12-inch skillet over high heat until just shimmering. Add zucchini and 1/4 teaspoon salt, and cook, stirring often, until browned, about 5 minutes. Stir in cherry tomatoes and heat through, about 1 minute. Transfer mixture to bowl and set aside.

3. SAUTÉ ONIONS AND CARROTS: Add 2 more tablespoons of oil to skillet and return to medium heat until shimmering. Add carrots, onion, and 1/4 teaspoon salt, and cook until carrots are lightly browned, about 8 minutes.

4. MAKE SAUCE: Stir in tomato paste to coat vegetables and brown lightly, about 30 seconds. Stir in garlic and pepper flakes and cook until fragrant, about 30 seconds. Stir in broth, scraping up any browned bits, and simmer until slightly thickened, about 1 minute. Remove skillet from heat, cover, and set aside.

5. COOK AND DRAIN PASTA: Add rotini and 1 tablespoon salt to boiling water and cook, stirring often, until al dente. Reserve 1/2 cup cooking water, then drain rotini and return rotini to pot.

6. TOSS PASTA WITH VEGETABLES AND SAUCE: Stir zucchini mixture, carrot mixture, basil, and remaining tablespoon olive oil into rotini. Season to taste with salt and pepper, adding reserved pasta cooking water as needed to loosen sauce. Serve immediately.

PASTA ALLA NORMA

THIS TRADITIONAL SICILIAN DISH FEATURES a short tubular pasta, like rigatoni, tossed with a gutsy yet simple tomato sauce studded with chunks of eggplant. A handsome amount of garlic, red pepper flakes, and basil gives this sauce its moxie, and a grating of ricotta salata (ricotta that has been aged and hardened) adds a counterpoint of pungent creaminess. This is not your typical vegetable pasta sauce; the eggplant takes on a meaty quality, making this dish a rich and hearty vegetarian meal.

With sauces as simple as alla Norma—as with most any vegetable pasta sauce—building a good base of flavor is key. We began with the eggplant and focused on extracting as much flavor as possible from the vegetable in a short amount of time. We didn't want to bother with salting the eggplant (salting extracts some of the juices and helps promote browning), because of the time involved. Instead we found that a sauté in a generous amount of olive oil brought out the hearty robustness we were after.

After browning the eggplant, we turned to the rest of the sauce. We stirred minced garlic and red pepper flakes into the eggplant and then added canned diced tomatoes. A five-minute simmer gave us the chunky well-flavored sauce we were looking for. And because the eggplant simmered only briefly in the sauce, it retained its shape, so that our sauce had a pleasantly chunky texture with meaty cubes of eggplant. Tossed with pasta and finished with tangy ricotta salata and fresh basil, this dish makes a hearty meal in no time.

Rigatoni with Eggplant, Tomatoes, and Ricotta Salata

SERVES 4 TO 6

You can either peel the eggplant or leave the skin on. If you can't find ricotta salata, don't substitute regular ricotta—it lacks the sharp tang of the dried cheese. Instead, try ½ cup grated Pecorino Romano.

    6   tablespoons extra-virgin olive oil
    2   medium eggplant (2 pounds), cut into
         ¾-inch cubes
    3   garlic cloves, minced
    ¼   teaspoon red pepper flakes
    2   (14.5-ounce) cans diced tomatoes
         Salt and ground black pepper
    1   pound rigatoni (see note)
    1   cup grated ricotta salata cheese (see note)
    ¼   cup minced fresh basil

MAKING THE MINUTES COUNT:
Prep the remaining ingredients while the eggplant cooks.

1. BOIL WATER FOR PASTA: Bring 4 quarts water to boil in large pot.

2. SAUTÉ EGGPLANT: Heat 4 tablespoons of oil in 12-inch nonstick skillet over medium-high heat until shimmering. Add eggplant and cook until it begins to brown, about 4 minutes. Reduce heat to medium-low and continue to cook until eggplant is tender and lightly browned, about 10 minutes.

3. MAKE SAUCE: Stir in garlic and pepper flakes and cook until fragrant, about 30 seconds. Stir in tomatoes and simmer until slightly thickened, about 5 minutes. Season with salt and pepper to taste.

4. COOK AND DRAIN PASTA: Add rigatoni and 1 tablespoon salt to boiling water and cook, stirring often, until al dente. Reserve ½ cup cooking water, then drain rigatoni and return rigatoni to pot.

5. COMBINE PASTA AND SAUCE: Stir eggplant mixture, ricotta salata, basil, and remaining 2 tablespoons olive oil into rigatoni. Season to taste with salt and pepper, adding reserved pasta cooking water as needed to loosen sauce. Serve immediately.

PENNE WITH CHICKEN AND VEGETABLES

TYPICALLY A QUICK-COOKING RECIPE, THIS pasta-chain classic often goes wrong: dry chicken, overcooked vegetables, and mushy pasta in gloppy sauce that does little except bind these elements together—literally. We aimed to create a quick version with a clean, fresh-flavored sauce, along with crisp broccoli and tender chicken, all tossed with pasta that still had a bit of bite.

Lightly browning chicken breast strips in butter started building flavor. We kept the chicken tender and added more flavor to the meat by cooking the strips through later in the sauce. For the sauce, we decided on building a broth-based sauce, instead of the usual cream-based one. Omitting the cream allowed the flavor of the broccoli and chicken to really come through and gave the pasta a lighter character. We began the sauce by sautéing onion in butter and then added garlic with red pepper flakes and thyme. Next, we added white wine to the pan and cooked it briefly until it just about evaporated. We stirred in low-sodium chicken broth and—to thicken the sauce slightly so that it would lightly coat the pasta—we added a mixture of cornstarch dissolved in water.

With the chicken and sauce down, we turned to the other elements. We boiled the broccoli for just 2 minutes until tender, but still crisp at the center. We then used the same cooking water to boil the pasta. To finish, we simply combined the pasta, broccoli, chicken, and sauce, and stirred in some grated Asiago cheese for richness along with thinly sliced sun-dried tomatoes for a final hit of flavor. With this traditional version down, we came up with a Mediterranean-style variation that relies on olive oil in lieu of butter and features artichoke hearts, red bell peppers, and creamy goat cheese in a garlicky broth-based sauce.

Penne with Chicken, Broccoli, and Sun-Dried Tomatoes

SERVES 4

To complete this recipe in 30 minutes, put the water on to boil before assembling your ingredients. The broccoli is blanched in the same water that is later used to cook the pasta. Remove the broccoli when it is tender at the edges but still crisp at the core.

I	pound boneless, skinless chicken breasts, cut into thin strips (see page 98)
	Salt and ground black pepper
4	tablespoons unsalted butter
I	onion, minced
6	garlic cloves, minced
1/4	teaspoon red pepper flakes
2	teaspoons minced fresh thyme
1/2	cup dry white wine
1 1/2	cups low-sodium chicken broth
2	teaspoons cornstarch, dissolved in I tablespoon water
4	cups broccoli florets (12 ounces)
1/2	pound penne (2 1/2 cups)
I	cup oil-packed sun-dried tomatoes, rinsed and sliced thin
I	cup grated Asiago cheese, plus extra for serving

MAKING THE MINUTES COUNT:
Prep the onion and garlic before cooking the chicken. While the onion cooks, prep the remaining ingredients.

I. BOIL WATER FOR BROCCOLI AND PASTA: Bring 4 quarts water to boil in large pot.

2. SAUTÉ CHICKEN: Season chicken with salt and pepper. Melt 1 tablespoon of butter in 12-inch nonstick skillet over high heat until just beginning to brown. Add chicken, spread into single layer, and cook without stirring for 1 minute. Stir chicken and continue to cook until most, but not all, of pink color has disappeared and chicken is lightly browned around edges, about 2 minutes longer. Transfer chicken to clean bowl and set aside.

3. MAKE SAUCE: Add 1 more tablespoon of butter to skillet and melt over medium-high heat. Add onion and 1/4 teaspoon salt, and cook until softened, about 5 minutes. Stir in garlic, red pepper flakes, and thyme, and cook until fragrant, about 30 seconds. Stir in wine and cook until nearly evaporated, about 2 minutes. Stir in the broth and dissolved cornstarch mixture and simmer until slightly thickened, about 2 minutes. Remove skillet from heat, cover, and set aside.

4. COOK BROCCOLI: Add broccoli and 1 tablespoon salt to boiling water and cook until broccoli is tender but still crisp at center, about 2 minutes. Using slotted spoon, transfer broccoli to large paper towel–lined plate and set aside.

5. COOK AND DRAIN PASTA: Return water to boil, stir in penne, and cook, stirring often, until al dente. Reserve 1/2 cup cooking water, then drain penne and return penne to pot.

6. FINISH COOKING CHICKEN IN SAUCE AND TOSS WITH PASTA: Stir remaining 2 tablespoons butter, sun-dried tomatoes, 1 cup Asiago, and chicken with any accumulated juices into sauce in skillet. Return sauce to simmer and cook until chicken is cooked through, about 1 minute. Stir sauce mixture and broccoli into penne. Season to taste with salt and pepper, adding reserved pasta cooking water as needed to loosen sauce. Serve immediately, passing extra Asiago at table.

Penne with Chicken, Artichokes, Red Bell Pepper, and Goat Cheese

SERVES 4

To thaw the artichoke hearts, remove them from the package and place in a medium bowl. Cover the bowl with plastic wrap, microwave for 5 minutes, and then drain. To complete this recipe in 30 minutes, put the water on to boil before assembling your ingredients.

1   pound boneless, skinless chicken breasts, cut into thin strips (see page 98)
    Salt and ground black pepper
3   tablespoons olive oil
2   (9-ounce) boxes frozen artichoke hearts, thawed and drained (see note)
1   red bell pepper, cored and diced fine
8   garlic cloves, minced
¼   teaspoon red pepper flakes
2   teaspoons minced fresh oregano
½   cup dry white wine
1½ cups low-sodium chicken broth
2   teaspoons cornstarch, dissolved in 1 tablespoon water
½   pound penne (2½ cups)
1   cup crumbled goat cheese

MAKING THE MINUTES COUNT:
While the artichokes are thawing in the microwave, start prepping the chicken. Then, while the artichokes and peppers cook, prep the remaining ingredients.

1. **BOIL WATER FOR PASTA:** Bring 3 quarts water to boil in large pot.

2. **SAUTÉ CHICKEN:** Season chicken with salt and pepper. Heat 1 tablespoon of oil in 12-inch nonstick skillet over high heat until just smoking. Add chicken, spread into single layer, and cook without stirring for 1 minute. Stir chicken and continue to cook until most, but not all, of pink color has disappeared and chicken is lightly browned around edges, about 2 minutes longer. Transfer chicken to clean bowl and set aside.

3. **MAKE SAUCE:** Add remaining 2 tablespoons oil to skillet and return to high heat until shimmering. Add artichokes, red pepper, and ¼ teaspoon salt, and cook until artichokes are lightly browned, about 8 minutes. Stir in garlic, red pepper flakes, and oregano and cook until fragrant, about 30 seconds. Stir in wine and cook until nearly evaporated, about 2 minutes. Stir in broth and dissolved cornstarch mixture and simmer until slightly thickened, about 2 minutes. Remove skillet from heat, cover, and set aside.

4. **COOK AND DRAIN PASTA:** Add penne and 1 tablespoon salt to boiling water and cook, stirring often, until al dente. Reserve ½ cup cooking water, then drain penne and return penne to pot.

5. **TOSS PASTA WITH CHICKEN AND SAUCE:** Stir chicken with any accumulated juices into sauce in skillet, and simmer until chicken is cooked through, about 1 minute. Stir sauce mixture and goat cheese into penne. Season to taste with salt and pepper, adding reserved pasta cooking water as needed to loosen sauce. Serve immediately.

PASTA WITH SAUSAGE AND BROCCOLI RABE

ITALIANS LOVE BROCCOLI RABE AND commonly use this bitter, spicy green in pasta sauces. Broccoli rabe with garlic, spicy red pepper flakes, and sausage is a classic combination often tossed with orecchiette, an ear-shaped pasta. It's a simple dish, but we found that it's important to get the timing and order of things just right; otherwise you wind up with flavorless pasta tossed with drab, overcooked greens and dry sausage. We wanted a dish of well-seasoned pasta tossed with tender greens (with just a bit of a bite at the center) and juicy sausage.

Broccoli rabe can be tricky to cook because it contains thick stalks, tender leaves, and small florets. Our task was to devise a cooking method that would soften the stalks but keep the florets and leaves from becoming mushy. Cutting the rabe into 1½-inch lengths, blanching it for a minute or two, shocking it in a bowl of ice water, and reintroducing it to the sauce at the end to warm it through worked okay. However, the process seemed like a lot of trouble and tasters pointed out that the vegetable didn't really carry any of the other flavors in the sauce. Going on one taster's suggestion, we devised a way to quickly cook the rabe in the sauce itself.

We started by lightly browning the sausage, adding garlic and red pepper flakes, and then adding the broccoli rabe along with some chicken broth (some recipes suggest reserving some of the pasta cooking water to moisten the dish; however, tasters preferred the roundness and depth of the broth). Cooking the rabe for two minutes covered, and then two minutes uncovered produced just what we were looking for—perfectly cooked rabe that was infused with the flavor of the sauce. We timed the pasta to finish around the same time as the sauce and tossed the two together along with olive oil and grated Parmesan for nutty richness.

Orecchiette with Sausage and Broccoli Rabe

SERVES 4 TO 6

If you prefer to use broccoli instead of broccoli rabe in this recipe, use 2 pounds broccoli cut into 1-inch florets and increase the cooking time by several minutes.

8	ounces hot Italian sausage, casings removed
6	garlic cloves, minced
1/2	teaspoon red pepper flakes
1	bunch broccoli rabe (1 pound), trimmed and cut into 1 1/2-inch lengths
1/2	cup low-sodium chicken broth
	Salt and ground black pepper
1	pound orecchiette
1	tablespoon extra-virgin olive oil
1/2	cup grated Parmesan cheese

1. BOIL WATER FOR PASTA: Bring 4 quarts water to boil in large pot.

2. COOK SAUSAGE: Cook sausage in 12-inch nonstick skillet over medium-high heat until lightly browned, breaking meat up with wooden spoon, about 5 minutes. Stir in garlic and red pepper flakes and cook until fragrant, about 30 seconds.

3. COOK BROCCOLI RABE: Stir in broccoli rabe, chicken broth, and 1/4 teaspoon salt, cover, and cook until broccoli rabe turns bright green, about 2 minutes. Uncover and continue to cook until broth is nearly evaporated and broccoli rabe is tender, about 2 minutes. Remove skillet from heat, cover, and set aside.

4. COOK AND DRAIN PASTA: Add orecchiette and 1 tablespoon salt to boiling water and cook, stirring often, until al dente. Reserve 1/2 cup cooking water, then drain orecchiette and return orecchiette to pot.

5. TOSS PASTA WITH SAUSAGE AND BROCCOLI RABE: Stir oil, Parmesan, and sausage mixture into orecchiette. Season to taste with salt and pepper, adding reserved pasta cooking water as needed to loosen sauce. Serve immediately.

PREPARING BROCCOLI RABE

1. The thick stalk ends of broccoli rabe should be trimmed and discarded. Use a sharp knife to cut off the thickest part (usually the bottom 2 inches) of each stalk.

2. Cut the remaining stalks and florets into bite-sized pieces about 1 1/2 inches long.

GOT EXTRA TIME?

If you've got a few extra minutes, try serving this Rosemary-Olive Foccacia with Orecchiette with Sausage and Broccoli Rabe. It's also good with many other recipes in this chapter, as well as soups and salads.

Adjust oven rack to middle position and heat oven to 400 degrees. Press 1 pound pizza dough into well-oiled 13 by 9-inch baking pan or 10-inch pie dish and dimple surface with your fingers. Brush dough liberally with extra-virgin olive oil and sprinkle with 1/4 cup chopped olives, 1/2 teaspoon minced fresh rosemary, 1/2 teaspoon kosher salt, and 1/2 teaspoon cracked black pepper. Bake until golden brown, about 30 minutes. Cool on wire rack and serve warm.

Pasta with Shrimp, Garlic, and Lemon

ALMOST EVERY ITALIAN RESTAURANT MENU in the United States features shrimp scampi. We love the dish for its simplicity and bold flavors: a garlicky, lemony sauce plays as a natural partner to tender shrimp. We wanted to transform this Italian-American seafood staple into a quick pasta meal.

Our initial test was as simple as tossing a pound of al dente linguine with a batch of shrimp scampi. However, this didn't go over so well with the tasting panel, which complained that the dish was bland and dry from a lack of sauce. We tried adding some olive oil, but it just made the dish greasy—and it was still bland.

One taster suggested adding some chicken broth to enrich the sauce. We tested the broth and decided to try clam juice too, which we figured would naturally reinforce the shellfish flavor. Surprisingly, everyone agreed that the chicken broth was the best. The clam juice made a sauce that was just too strong on clams, which masked the subtle complexity of the shrimp. For further flavor, we incorporated sweet sautéed onion, more garlic, and spicy red pepper flakes. And because we wanted the sauce to cling to the pasta and shrimp, we thickened it with a bit of cornstarch dissolved in water—as we've done in other broth-based pasta sauces. To finish, we simply tossed the linguine with the sauce, shrimp, additional butter, fresh lemon juice, and minced fresh parsley.

Linguine with Shrimp, Garlic, and Lemon

SERVES 4 TO 6

The key to moist, tender shrimp is to finish cooking them off the heat, so be sure to follow the visual cues in the recipe.

1¼	pounds large (31/40) shrimp, peeled and deveined
	Salt and ground black pepper
⅛	teaspoon sugar
6	tablespoons unsalted butter
1	onion, minced
8	garlic cloves, minced
¼	teaspoon red pepper flakes
¼	cup dry white wine
1½	cups low-sodium chicken broth
2	teaspoons cornstarch, dissolved in 1 tablespoon water
1	pound linguine
3	tablespoons fresh lemon juice
¼	cup minced fresh parsley

1. BOIL WATER FOR PASTA: Bring 4 quarts water to boil in large pot.

2. SAUTÉ SHRIMP: Pat shrimp dry with paper towels, then season with ¼ teaspoon salt, ¼ teaspoon pepper, and sugar. Melt 2 tablespoons of butter in 12-inch skillet over medium-high heat until just beginning to brown. Add shrimp, spread into single layer, and cook without stirring for 1 minute. Stir shrimp and continue to cook until spotty brown and just pink at edges, about 30 seconds. Transfer shrimp to clean bowl, cover, and set aside.

3. MAKE SAUCE: Add 2 more tablespoons of butter to skillet and melt over medium-high heat. Add onion and ¼ teaspoon salt and cook until softened, about 5 minutes. Stir in garlic and red pepper flakes and cook until fragrant, about 30 seconds. Stir in wine and cook until nearly evaporated, about 2 minutes. Stir in broth and dissolved cornstarch mixture and simmer until slightly thickened, about 2 minutes. Remove skillet from heat, cover, and set aside.

4. COOK AND DRAIN PASTA: Add linguine and 1 tablespoon salt to boiling water and cook, stirring often, until al dente. Reserve ½ cup of cooking water, then drain linguine and return linguine to pot.

5. TOSS PASTA WITH SHRIMP AND SAUCE: Stir remaining 2 tablespoons butter, lemon juice, parsley, sauce, and reserved shrimp, including any accumulated juices, into linguine. Season to taste with salt and pepper, adding reserved pasta cooking water as needed to loosen sauce. Serve immediately.

DEVEINING SHRIMP

1. With a paring knife, make a shallow slit along the back of each shrimp. With the tip of the blade, lift up and loosen the vein.

2. Because the vein is quite sticky, we like to touch the knife blade to a paper towel on the counter. The vein will stick to the towel, and you can devein the next shrimp with a clean knife.

PASTA WITH SHRIMP, TARRAGON, AND CREAM

FOR SPECIAL OCCASIONS, NOTHING BEATS the elegance of pasta and shrimp in a creamy sauce. We headed to the test kitchen with a vision of plump, juicy shrimp in a velvety cream sauce tossed with fresh fettuccine.

As we discovered in our pasta recipes using chicken, it's best to give the protein a quick sauté and remove it from the pan before building the sauce. We lightly cooked the shrimp, which had been seasoned with salt, pepper, and sugar (to promote browning) in butter and then added garlic. The shrimp were cooked until just underdone and beginning to curl. Then we transferred them to a bowl and covered them with foil; the residual heat from the sauté gently finished cooking the interior of the shellfish.

To the same skillet, we added heavy cream and reduced it. The flavorful bits left from the shrimp infused the cream with flavor. After reducing the heavy cream to a velvety texture—one which would cling best to the pasta and shrimp—we looked at how best to finish our dish. We discovered that the last minute of cooking turned out to be crucial. We found it most effective to cook the fresh pasta until not quite al dente, drain it, and then add it back to the pot along with the reserved shrimp, reduced cream, and bit of fresh tarragon. In the last minute, the shrimp warmed through, the tarragon lightly flavored the cream, and the pasta had a chance to finish cooking and absorb the sauce, making for an elegant dish.

Fettuccine with Shrimp, Tarragon, and Cream

SERVES 4 TO 6

The key to moist, tender shrimp is to finish cooking them off the heat, so be sure to follow the visual cues in the recipe. Note that it is important to cook the pasta until not quite al dente, as it will cook further when it is cooked with the sauce. While we prefer fresh fettucine in this dish, you can use substitute 1 pound dried fettucine.

1¼	pounds large (31/40) shrimp, peeled and deveined
	Salt and ground black pepper
⅛	teaspoon sugar
2	tablespoons unsalted butter
2	garlic cloves, minced
2	cups heavy cream
2	(9-ounce) packages fresh fettuccine
2	tablespoons minced fresh tarragon

1. **BOIL WATER FOR PASTA:** Bring 4 quarts water to boil in large pot.

2. **SAUTÉ SHRIMP:** Pat shrimp dry with paper towels, then season with ¼ teaspoon salt, ¼ teaspoon pepper, and sugar. Melt butter in 12-inch skillet over medium-high heat until just beginning to brown. Add shrimp, spread into single layer, and cook without stirring for 1 minute. Stir shrimp and continue to cook until spotty brown and just pink at edges, about 30 seconds. Stir in garlic and cook until fragrant, about 30 seconds more. Immediately transfer shrimp to clean bowl, cover, and set aside.

3. REDUCE CREAM: Add cream to skillet and simmer over medium-high heat until slightly thickened and measures 1½ cups, about 8 minutes. Remove skillet from heat, cover, and set aside.

4. COOK FETTUCCINE: Add fettuccine and 1 tablespoon salt to boiling water and cook, stirring often, until just shy of al dente. Reserve ½ cup cooking water, then drain fettuccine and return fettuccine to pot.

5. TOSS FETTUCCINE WITH CREAM SAUCE AND SHRIMP: Stir tarragon and reduced cream into fettuccine and cook over low heat until sauce clings lightly to pasta, about 1 minute. Stir in shrimp, including any accumulated juices, and season with salt and pepper to taste, adding reserved pasta cooking water as needed to loosen sauce. Serve immediately.

Pasta with Tuna

FOR THE QUICK COOK, PANTRY STAPLES ARE key. And two pantry staples, canned tuna and dry pasta, can be the beginning of a fast, satisfying dinner. We'd already developed a creamy tuna casserole (see page 143), so we turned our attention to developing a zesty Italian-style tuna and pasta dish.

A side-by-side tasting of different types of tuna made into sauces got us going. The line-up comprised water-packed solid white StarKist in the pouch (which won our tasting of leading brands of tuna packed in water), its vegetable-oil-packed counterpart, and Italian-style tuna packed in olive oil. Tasters preferred water-packed tuna for its texture and light, clear flavor in the pasta sauce. Tuna packed in olive oil came in a close second and was admired for its rich flavor. Everyone frowned on the off flavor and mushy texture of the tuna packed in vegetable oil.

With the type of tuna settled, we turned to the other elements in the sauce. We wanted a tomato-based sauce and settled on canned diced tomatoes. We also settled on briny olives and fennel, whose refreshing licorice-like flavor would work well with the tuna. We started the sauce by cooking the fennel until softened, stirring in garlic, red pepper

flakes, and fresh lemon zest. We next added the tuna and olives and cooked the mixture further, then added the tomatoes, simmered them with the other ingredients, and tossed the sauce with the hot pasta. The sauce was a disappointment: The tuna had turned dry and mealy. We decided to switch around the order of things a bit and held off adding the tuna until after the tomatoes had simmered. This did the trick—added to the sauce toward the end of simmering and cooked just long enough to heat through, the tuna remained tender and moist. We also found that adding fresh lemon juice to the sauce, along with minced fresh parsley, gave the dish a lively finish.

Penne with Tuna, Tomatoes, Olives, and Fennel
SERVES 4 TO 6

If you like the stronger flavor of tuna packed in olive oil, be sure to drain the tuna and discard the oil.

6	tablespoons extra-virgin olive oil
1	bulb fennel, trimmed, cored, and chopped fine
	Salt and ground black pepper
6	garlic cloves, minced
¼	teaspoon red pepper flakes
1	teaspoon grated lemon zest
2	(14.5-ounce) cans diced tomatoes
1	(7-ounce) pouch water-packed solid white tuna
¾	cup Kalamata olives, pitted and chopped
1	pound penne
¼	cup minced fresh parsley
2	teaspoons fresh lemon juice

MAKING THE MINUTES COUNT:
Prep the parsley and olives while the fennel is browning. Juice the lemon while the sauce simmers.

1. BOIL WATER FOR PASTA: Bring 4 quarts water to boil in large pot.

2. SAUTÉ FENNEL: Heat 2 tablespoons of oil in large saucepan over medium-high heat until shimmering. Add fennel and ¼ teaspoon salt and cook until softened and lightly browned, about 6 minutes. Stir in garlic, pepper flakes, and lemon zest and cook until fragrant, about 30 seconds.

3. MAKE SAUCE: Stir in tomatoes and simmer until flavors meld, about 10 minutes. Stir in tuna and olives and continue to simmer until heated through, about 2 minutes. Remove saucepan from heat, cover, and set aside.

4. COOK PENNE: Add penne and 1 tablespoon salt to boiling water and cook, stirring often, until al dente. Reserve ½ cup cooking water, then drain penne and return penne to pot.

5. TOSS PENNE WITH SAUCE: Stir remaining 4 tablespoons olive oil, parsley, lemon juice, and sauce mixture into penne. Season to taste with salt and pepper, adding reserved pasta cooking water as needed to loosen sauce. Serve immediately.

STUFFED PASTA DISHES

IT'S A COMMON QUICK DINNER SCENARIO: boil up a couple packages of store-bought tortellini or ravioli and toss with some variety of jarred sauce. Easy and quick? Yes. But, sadly, a little ho-hum. We do appreciate the convenience of store-bought tortellini and ravioli, but we wanted to get creative and come up with some really interesting dishes.

To start, there's the pasta itself. Stuffed pastas are now sold dried, frozen, and fresh in the refrigerator case. We prefer those pastas sold fresh. Tasters found the dried pasta to be inedible, and frozen pasta, while not bad, still wasn't quite as good as fresh. As for the type of stuffed pastas, we decided on cheese, to keep things simple and to allow us free reign in creating sauces. For our first dish, we started with tortellini. We decided on a quick, light cream sauce and a duo of spring vegetables: quick-cooking fresh asparagus spears and frozen peas. To boost the flavors of the cream sauce we relied on garlic, shallot, and dry white wine. Tasters liked the addition of fresh tarragon too, which they felt accentuated the springtime flavors of the dish. Some also liked the dish dusted with grated Parmesan and sprinkled with a few drops of lemon juice to cut through the richness of the sauce and tortellini.

For the ravioli, we aimed to interpret the classic combination of pumpkin or butternut squash ravioli in a sage-butter sauce. Sticking with cheese ravioli, we incorporated the butternut squash element by sautéing the diced vegetable in butter. For ease, we used pre-cut squash. Slivered almonds gave a nice, crunchy contrast to the soft textures of the squash and ravioli. We added minced fresh sage, grated Parmesan, and a few drops of balsamic vinegar, and we had a well-flavored pasta meal in no time.

Tortellini, Peas, and Asparagus with a Creamy Tarragon Sauce
SERVES 4

To complete this recipe in 30 minutes, put the water on to boil before assembling your ingredients. Serve with freshly grated Parmesan. Lemon wedges are also a nice touch. Although we prefer the flavor and more delicate texture of fresh tortellini here, 1 pound of frozen cheese tortellini can be substituted.

2	tablespoons unsalted butter
2	shallots, minced
	Salt and ground black pepper
2	garlic cloves, minced
½	cup dry white wine
1½	cups half-and-half
1	cup frozen peas
1	tablespoon minced fresh tarragon
2	teaspoons cornstarch, dissolved in 1 tablespoon water
1	bunch asparagus, trimmed and cut into ½-inch lengths
2	(9-ounce) packages fresh cheese tortellini

1. BOIL WATER FOR ASPARAGUS AND TORTELLINI: Bring 4 quarts water to boil in large pot.

2. MAKE SAUCE: Melt butter in 12-inch skillet over medium-high heat. Add shallot and ¼ teaspoon salt and cook until softened, about 2 minutes. Stir in garlic and cook until fragrant, about 30 seconds. Stir in wine and cook until nearly evaporated, about 2 minutes. Stir in half-and-half, peas, tarragon, and dissolved cornstarch mixture and simmer until slightly thickened, about 2 minutes. Remove skillet from heat, cover, and set aside.

3. COOK ASPARAGUS: Add asparagus and 1 tablespoon salt to boiling water and cook, stirring often, until asparagus is tender but still crisp at center, about 2 minutes. Using slotted spoon, transfer asparagus to large paper towel–lined plate and set aside.

4. COOK AND DRAIN TORTELLINI: Return water to boil, stir in tortellini, and cook until tender. Reserve ½ cup cooking water, then drain tortellini and return tortellini to pot.

5. TOSS TORTELLINI WITH ASPARAGUS AND SAUCE: Stir sauce and asparagus into tortellini. Season to taste with salt and pepper, adding reserved pasta cooking water as needed to loosen sauce. Serve immediately.

Ravioli with Butternut Squash, Almonds, and Parmesan

SERVES 4

To complete this recipe in 30 minutes, buy pre-peeled, pre-cut squash and put the water on to boil before assembling your ingredients. The sauce in this dish is simply butter and Parmesan loosened with some of the pasta cooking water, so don't forget to reserve some of the cooking water when draining the ravioli. Although we prefer the flavor and more delicate texture of fresh ravioli here, 1 pound of frozen cheese ravioli can be substituted. Fresh sage is essential to this dish; do not use dried.

6	tablespoons unsalted butter
1	pound peeled butternut squash, cut into ½-inch cubes (3½ cups)
1	shallot, minced
2	tablespoons minced fresh sage
	Salt and ground black pepper
2	(9-ounce) packages fresh cheese ravioli
½	cup grated Parmesan cheese, plus extra for serving
½	cup slivered almonds, toasted
	Balsamic vinegar (for serving)

1. BOIL WATER FOR RAVIOLI: Bring 4 quarts water to boil in large pot.

2. SAUTÉ SQUASH: Melt 1 tablespoon of butter in 12-inch nonstick skillet over medium-high heat. Add squash, spread in even layer, and cook without stirring until golden brown on first side, about 5 minutes. Stir squash and continue to cook, stirring occasionally, until tender and browned, about 5 minutes longer. Stir in shallot, sage, ¼ teaspoon salt, and ¼ teaspoon pepper and continue to cook until shallot is softened, about 2 minutes. Remove from heat, cover, and set aside.

3. COOK AND DRAIN RAVIOLI: Add ravioli and 1 tablespoon salt to boiling water and cook, stirring often, until tender. Reserve ½ cup cooking water, then drain ravioli and return ravioli to pot.

4. TOSS RAVIOLI WITH BUTTER AND SQUASH: Stir 2 tablespoons reserved pasta water, remaining 5 tablespoons butter, Parmesan, toasted almonds, and squash mixture into ravioli. Season to taste with salt and pepper, adding reserved pasta cooking water as needed to loosen sauce. Sprinkle with extra Parmesan cheese and several drops of balsamic vinegar before serving.

TEST KITCHEN TIP:

Making the Cut

Buying peeled, pre-cut squash is a big time saver; however, it never comes in small, uniformly cut pieces. We found it important to trim the pre-cut squash down into evenly sized (about ½ inch) pieces before cooking.

RAVIOLI BAKE

IN OUR RESEARCH FOR QUICK PASTA casseroles, we found those that began with purchased ravioli. At first, we rejected these assemble and bake dishes—after all, how good could they be? But after some debate in the test kitchen, we decided to forge ahead and see if we could concoct a worthy ravioli casserole. Our goal was to create a substantial and comforting cheesy baked pasta dish that was quick to assemble. Right off the bat, we knew we wanted to use ricotta-stuffed ravioli, which we thought would add a lasagna-like complexity of noodle and cheese without any of the layering.

We guessed that we'd need two 9-ounce packages of fresh supermarket ravioli to fill a standard 13 by 9-inch baking dish. You can use frozen, but fresh is better. While the ravioli boiled, we turned to the sauce.

We decided to use our recipe for 20-Minute Hearty Meat Sauce (page 160) as a jumping-off point. Tasters preferred a variation of the sauce, which uses crumbled Italian sausage instead of ground beef and pork. We found that both hot and sweet varieties of sausage were equally good. After a number of tests we made a few changes to the original sauce by omitting a can of diced tomatoes because tasters found the sauce too chunky for this casserole. We also added a small amount of heavy cream, which mellowed the flavors and gave the casserole some desirable richness.

With the sauce down, we turned to assembly. We simply tossed the cooked ravioli with the sauce and poured it into the baking dish. We topped the mixture with shredded mozzarella and into the oven it went for just 5 minutes to melt the cheese into a lightly browned gooey layer. With minimal preparation and a total cooking time of roughly 25 minutes, we found that this zippy casserole turned out to be a good framework for a vegetarian-friendly variation flavored with fennel and olives and topped with feta cheese.

Quick Cheesy Ravioli Bake
SERVES 4

To complete this recipe in 30 minutes, boil the water for the ravioli and preheat the oven before gathering your ingredients. We prefer fresh ravioli here; however, 1 pound of frozen cheese ravioli can be substituted.

- 1   pound sweet or hot Italian sausage, casings removed
- 1   tablespoon olive oil
- 3   garlic cloves, minced
- 1   tablespoon tomato paste
- 1   (28-ounce) can crushed tomatoes
- 3   tablespoons minced fresh basil
- 1/4   cup heavy cream
-    Salt and ground black pepper
- 2   (9-ounce) packages fresh cheese ravioli
- 1   cup shredded mozzarella cheese

1. HEAT OVEN AND BOIL WATER FOR RAVIOLI: Adjust oven rack to middle position and heat oven to 475 degrees. Bring 4 quarts water to boil in large pot.

2. COOK SAUSAGE: Cook sausage in 12-inch nonstick skillet over medium-high heat, breaking meat up with wooden spoon, until lightly browned and no longer pink, about 5 minutes. Drain meat and set aside.

3. MAKE SAUCE: Add oil, garlic, and tomato paste to skillet and return to medium heat until fragrant, about 1 minute. Stir in tomatoes and reserved sausage and cook until slightly thickened, 8 to 10 minutes. Stir in basil and cream and continue to simmer until slightly thickened, about 2 minutes. Remove skillet from heat, cover, and set aside.

4. COOK AND DRAIN RAVIOLI: Add 1 tablespoon salt and ravioli to boiling water and cook, stirring often, until tender. Drain ravioli and return to pot.

5. ASSEMBLE AND BAKE CASSEROLE: Stir sauce into ravioli and season with salt and pepper to taste. Spread mixture into 13 by 9-inch baking dish and sprinkle evenly with mozzarella. Bake until cheese is melted and lightly browned, about 5 minutes. Serve.

➤ VARIATION

Quick Cheesy Ravioli Bake with Fennel, Olives, and Feta

To complete this recipe in 30 minutes, boil the water for the ravioli and preheat the oven before gathering your ingredients. We prefer the flavor and more delicate texture of fresh ravioli here; however, 1 pound of frozen cheese ravioli can be substituted.

3	tablespoons olive oil
I	head fennel, trimmed, cored, and sliced thin
	Salt and ground black pepper
3	garlic cloves, minced
I	(28-ounce) can crushed tomatoes
½	cup pitted Kalamata olives, coarsely chopped
3	tablespoons minced fresh basil
¼	cup heavy cream
2	(9-ounce) packages fresh cheese ravioli
I	cup crumbled feta cheese

I. **HEAT OVEN AND BOIL WATER FOR RAVIOLI:** Adjust oven rack to middle position and heat oven to 475 degrees. Bring 4 quarts water to boil in large pot.

2. **SAUTÉ FENNEL:** Heat 2 tablespoons of oil in 12-inch nonstick skillet over medium-high heat until shimmering. Add fennel and ¼ teaspoon salt and cook until lightly browned, about 6 minutes.

3. **MAKE SAUCE:** Stir in garlic and cook until fragrant, about 30 seconds. Stir in tomatoes and cook until slightly thickened, 8 to 10 minutes. Stir in olives, basil, and cream and continue to simmer until slightly thickened, about 2 minutes. Remove skillet from heat, cover, and set aside.

4. **COOK AND DRAIN RAVIOLI:** Add 1 tablespoon salt and ravioli to boiling water and cook, stirring often, until tender. Drain ravioli and return to pot.

5. **ASSEMBLE AND BAKE CASSEROLE:** Stir sauce into ravioli and season with salt and pepper to taste. Spread mixture into 13 by 9-inch baking dish, sprinkle evenly with feta, and drizzle with remaining tablespoon oil. Bake until cheese is melted and lightly browned, about 5 minutes. Serve.

LASAGNA

WHILE WE'VE ALREADY CREATED A QUICK skillet version of lasagna, there are some of us who still have a hankering for the traditional layered baked version. Ready for a challenge, we headed to the test kitchen to see if we could find enough shortcuts to make a baked lasagna in less than 30 minutes.

Among a number of issues we were facing, cooking the lasagna noodles seemed the most pressing. We ran a battery of tests using our noodle of choice—no-boil lasagna noodles. But we knew that even no-boil noodles would not cook through in 30 minutes, so we needed to find a way to give these noodles a head start. We tried methods to quickly soften the noodles (soaking the noodles in hot water and microwaving them in water), but the results were spotty at best. Sometimes the softening simply took too long and sometimes the noodles became gummy and hard to handle. After a lengthy discussion we changed tack, wondering if we could simply build a lasagna with dry no-boil noodles and cook the whole thing in the microwave.

After deciding on the best cooking vessel, an 8 by 8-inch baking dish (the best size for a standard microwave and enough to serve four), we began to layer the no-boil noodles, store-bought jarred tomato sauce, and a cheese filling (ricotta, Parmesan, basil, and egg yolks for richness and to bind the mixture together). We topped the lasagna with shredded mozzarella and covered it with plastic wrap (to prevent the lasagna from drying out), then cooked it in the microwave on high. Our results proved promising; the intensity of the microwave had rendered the noodles soft, and they soaked up the sauce and flavors of the lasagna as they would have if they were baked. This was a huge step in the right direction, but we still needed to find the best way to cook the noodles

> **TEST KITCHEN TIP: Under Cover**
> Make sure that the top layer of no-boil noodles is well covered with sauce before the lasagna goes into the microwave. Otherwise that top layer will dry out and turn leathery.

evenly and consistently, as some parts of our test lasagna were underdone.

Another series of tests, which focused on number of layers, amount of sauce, and cooking time, yielded the results we were looking for. During the process, we found it was also important to make sure the top layer of noodles was sufficiently covered with sauce, or else the noodles tended to dry out and become chewy. We also held back on adding the top layer of cheese until the lasagna came out of the microwave. Then we sprinkled the cheese over the top and baked the lasagna in a hot oven for just five minutes to evenly brown and melt the cheese—giving our quick lasagna the traditional homey look of the long-baked original.

Easy Cheese Lasagna

SERVES 4

To complete this recipe in 30 minutes, preheat the oven before assembling your ingredients. Be sure the top layer of noodles is completely covered by the sauce, so that the noodles cook evenly and don't dry out. And, take care when peeling back the plastic wrap in step 5—the steam will be quite hot.

1¼	cups ricotta cheese
¾	cup grated Parmesan cheese
¼	cup minced fresh basil
2	large egg yolks
	Salt and ground black pepper
3	cups jarred tomato sauce
8	no-boil lasagna noodles
2	cups shredded mozzarella cheese

1. HEAT OVEN: Adjust oven rack to middle position and heat oven to 475 degrees.

2. MAKE FILLING: Mix ricotta, ½ cup of Parmesan, basil, egg yolks, ¼ teaspoon salt, and ¼ teaspoon pepper together until well combined.

3. ASSEMBLE LASAGNA: Spread ½ cup of tomato sauce over bottom of 8 by 8-inch baking dish. Place 2 noodles on top of sauce. Spread ¼ cup ricotta mixture evenly over each noodle. Sprinkle ½ cup mozzarella over noodles, then top with ½ cup more sauce. Repeat this layering twice more. For final layer, lay remaining 2 noodles on top and cover completely with remaining 1 cup sauce.

4. MICROWAVE LASAGNA: Wrap dish tightly with plastic wrap and microwave on high power until noodles are soft and tender when poked using fork, 10 to 14 minutes.

5. BAKE LASAGNA: Remove plastic wrap and sprinkle remaining ¼ cup Parmesan and remaining ½ cup mozzarella over top. Bake until cheese is melted and lightly browned, about 5 minutes. Let lasagna stand for several minutes before serving.

⏱ GOT EXTRA TIME?

If you have an extra few minutes, you can add browned sausage to your lasagna for a heartier meal.

Heat 1 tablespoon olive oil in a large nonstick skillet over medium-high heat until shimmering. Add 1 pound sweet or hot Italian sausage, casings removed, and cook until sausage is lightly browned, breaking meat up with wooden spoon, about 5 minutes. Drain sausage and divide evenly among lasagna layers.

SHORTCUT INGREDIENT:
Pre-Shredded Mozzarella

There's no disputing the fact that pre-shredded cheese saves time in the kitchen, but does flavor suffer? When you open a pack of pre-shredded mozzarella, you'll notice that the shreds are dry and separate—that's because an anti-caking agent is added (usually potato or rice starch and/or powdered cellulose). To find out if this adversely affects flavor, we tasted seven pre-shredded mozzarellas, all commonly found in supermarkets nationwide. We tasted both part-skim and whole milk varieties and we tasted them raw and melted on pizza. What did we find? Some cheeses simply didn't melt well and had a plasticky texture. Others, whether tasted raw or melted, were sometimes overly salty or chalky. One brand, however, stood apart from the rest: Kraft Shredded Part-Skim Mozzarella, which was noted for its rich and tangy flavor.

The Best Pre-Shredded Mozzarella

Kraft Shredded Part-Skim Mozzarella was the clear winner of our test. Rich and tangy, it's a convenient, time-saving alternative to shredding your own cheese.

Pad Thai

WHEN PREPARED RIGHT, PAD THAI IS A symphony of flavors and textures, balancing sweet, salty, and sour. The tender, glutinous rice noodles ensnare curls of shrimp, crisp strands of bean sprouts, and soft curds of fried egg. And even better, this dish cooks in minutes. Home cooks, however, rarely make pad thai because of its imposing ingredient list, instead resorting to take-out versions. The quality of take-out pad thai, however, varies by establishment. Without compromising the flavor of the dish, we aimed to eliminate ingredients that required trips to specialty markets and turn this dish into an accessible weeknight meal.

For the noodles, thick rice sticks are essential. Most well-stocked supermarkets sell them in the Asian foods aisle. These noodles are soaked in hot water to soften them and then stir-fried briefly until tender. While we soaked the noodles, we turned to the other elements in the dish.

We knew our pad thai would consist of sautéed shrimp, scrambled eggs, chopped peanuts, bean sprouts, and scallions. Obscure ingredients like dried shrimp and Thai salted preserved radish fell by the wayside. But two ingredients that give pad thai its distinctive sweet, salty, sour flavor—tamarind and fish sauce—had us stumped. Eventually, we worked out a reasonable substitution for the tamarind: equal parts lime juice and water plus a bit of brown sugar. After extensive testing, there just is no substitution for the salty-sweet pungency of fish sauce. But as it turns out, fish sauce is more readily available than we had thought—we found it in the Asian section of the supermarket.

Simplified Pad Thai
SERVES 4

Be sure to use the wide, fettuccine-style rice noodles here. There is no need to season the shrimp before cooking them because the sauce is so flavorful. And note that the key to moist, tender shrimp is to finish cooking them off the heat, so be sure to follow the visual cues in the recipe. Serve this dish with lime wedges and fresh cilantro. For spicy noodles, add a pinch of cayenne to the finished dish or serve with Tabasco.

8	ounces thick rice stick noodles (see note)
1/4	cup fresh lime juice
1/3	cup water
3	tablespoons fish sauce
1	tablespoon rice vinegar
3	tablespoons brown sugar
4	tablespoons vegetable oil
3/4	pound medium (40/50) shrimp, peeled and deveined
3	garlic cloves, minced
2	large eggs, beaten lightly
	Salt
6	tablespoons chopped unsalted roasted peanuts
3	cups bean sprouts, well rinsed
5	scallions, sliced thin
1	lime, cut into wedges (for serving)

DRIED RICE NOODLES

In our recent research we found dried rice noodles sold in two different styles: a thick, flat, fettuccine-width noodle and a very thin, thread-like noodle. It's confusing to try to buy these noodles by name. Because they are used in several Asian cuisines (including Chinese, Thai, and Vietnamese), they're marketed under several different Asian names. The English names are no more helpful because they're not standardized. You'll find the thicker noodles sold as "rice sticks" and the thread-like noodles sold as both "rice sticks" and "vermicelli." So don't bother with the names, just look for the shape of the noodle—all the packages we've seen have been obligingly transparent.

THIN RICE VERMICELLI

THICK RICE STICK

MAKING THE MINUTES COUNT:
Prep all the ingredients while the noodles soak. Be sure to have everything prepared before you begin cooking because this dish comes together quickly.

1. SOAK NOODLES: Cover noodles with hot tap water in large bowl and soak until softened, pliable, and limp but not fully tender, about 20 minutes. Drain noodles and set aside.

2. MAKE SAUCE: While noodles soak, stir lime juice, water, fish sauce, rice vinegar, brown sugar, and 2 tablespoons of oil together and set aside.

3. COOK SHRIMP: Pat shrimp dry with paper towels. Heat 1 more tablespoon of oil in 12-inch nonstick skillet over high heat until just smoking. Add shrimp, spread into single layer, and cook without stirring for 1 minute. Stir shrimp and continue to cook until spotty brown and just pink around the edges, about 30 seconds. Transfer shrimp to clean bowl, cover, and set aside.

4. COOK EGGS: Add remaining tablespoon oil and garlic to skillet and return to medium heat until fragrant, about 30 seconds. Add eggs and ¼ teaspoon salt and cook, stirring vigorously until eggs are scrambled, about 20 seconds.

5. COOK NOODLES AND SAUCE: Stir soaked noodles into eggs. Add fish sauce mixture, increase heat to high, and cook, tossing constantly, until noodles are evenly coated. Add ¼ cup of peanuts,

bean sprouts, all but ¼ cup of scallions, and cooked shrimp. Continue to cook, tossing constantly, until noodles are tender, about 2 minutes (if not yet tender add 2 tablespoons water to skillet and continue to cook until tender).

6. GARNISH: Transfer noodles to serving platter and sprinkle with remaining scallions and peanuts. Serve, passing lime wedges separately.

SINGAPORE NOODLES

HAVING MASTERED A STREAMLINED VERSION of pad thai, we sought to master another rice noodle dish—Singapore noodles—sometimes referred to as curry noodles. This dish relies on the thinner rice stick noodles called thin rice vermicelli (see page 180).

After sifting through our library, we turned up a number of recipes for Singapore noodles. The use of curry powder and thin rice stick noodles were the defining threads of the dish, and the sauce seemed to always have three major components: something salty, something sweet, and a base that provided moisture and flavor. For a salty ingredient we settled on soy sauce, a traditional ingredient. As for the sweet element, we agreed on mirin (sweetened Japanese rice wine), as tasters felt that it provided a desirable, subtle sweetness that didn't overpower the nuances of the dish as

SOAKING THE NOODLES

STIFF NOODLES
Soaking the rice sticks in room-temperature water yields hard noodles that take too long to stir-fry.

STICKY NOODLES
Fully cooking the rice sticks in boiling water results in soft, sticky, gummy, overdone noodles.

PERFECT NOODLES
Soaking the rice sticks in hot water yields softened noodles. When stir-fried, they are tender but resilient.

granulated sugar did. Chicken broth, a common inclusion, worked best as a base for our sauce (better than coconut milk and water, as some recipes instructed) to flavor and moisten our noodles.

With our sauce completed, we addressed the other ingredients in our Singapore noodles. Taking some cues from our pad thai recipe, we found it best to soak our noodles in hot tap water. Because these noodles are thinner than the ones used for pad thai, they take only 15 minutes to soften. Tossing shrimp—a traditional addition—with a scant amount of curry powder before sautéing them enhanced the flavor of the dish greatly. The shrimp also helped transform our recipe into a light, satisfying one-dish meal. Shallots added a mellow onion flavor, red bell pepper lent its sweetness, and a handful of bean sprouts contributed a fresh crunch.

Singapore Noodles with Shrimp

SERVES 4

The key to moist, tender shrimp is to finish cooking them off the heat, so be sure to follow the visual cues in the recipe. If you like spicy noodles, add a pinch of cayenne to the finished dish or serve with Tabasco. If you can't find thin rice vermicelli, substitute 6 ounces capellini.

6	ounces thin rice vermicelli
I	pound medium (40/50) shrimp, peeled and deveined
2½	teaspoons curry powder
2	tablespoons vegetable oil
3	shallots, sliced thin
I	red bell pepper, cored and sliced thin
2	garlic cloves, minced
I	cup bean sprouts, well rinsed
¾	cup low-sodium chicken broth
¼	cup soy sauce
2	tablespoons mirin
4	scallions, sliced thin

MAKING THE MINUTES COUNT:
Prep the remaining ingredients while the noodles soak.

I. SOAK NOODLES: Cover rice vermicelli with hot tap water in large bowl and soak until softened, pliable, and limp but not fully tender, about 15 minutes. Drain noodles and set aside.

2. COOK SHRIMP: While noodles soak, pat shrimp dry with paper towels, then toss with ½ teaspoon of curry powder. Heat 1 tablespoon of oil in 12-inch nonstick skillet over medium-high heat until just smoking. Add shrimp, spread into single layer, and cook without stirring for 1 minute. Stir shrimp and continue to cook until spotty brown and just pink around the edges, about 30 seconds. Transfer shrimp to clean bowl, cover, and set aside.

3. COOK VEGETABLES: Add remaining tablespoon oil to skillet and return to medium heat until shimmering. Add shallots, bell pepper, and remaining 2 teaspoons curry powder, and cook until vegetables have softened, about 2 minutes. Stir in garlic and cook until fragrant, about 30 seconds.

4. COOK NOODLES: Stir in soaked vermicelli, shrimp with their accumulated juices, bean sprouts, broth, soy sauce, mirin, and scallions. Cook, tossing constantly, until noodles and vegetables are heated through, about 2 minutes. Serve.

KEEPING BEAN SPROUTS CRISP AND FRESH

The bagged bean sprouts sold in supermarkets often contain more than enough for a single recipe. Once you open the bag, however, the sprouts are liable to lose their crunch. To keep leftover sprouts crisp, submerge the sprouts in a container of cold water. The sprouts will stay crisp for up to five days.

SOBA NOODLES WITH PORK AND SCALLIONS

JAPANESE SOBA NOODLES ARE MADE WITH a mix of wheat and buckwheat flour, or sometimes all buckwheat flour. The buckwheat adds a hearty nuttiness and springy chew to the noodles. Soba is typically served in a simple broth along with vegetables or meat. We sought to make a quick, substantial meal out of this hearty noodle.

With a number of soba noodles styles on the market, we headed to the test kitchen to try them all. While we like the strong flavor of 100 percent buckwheat noodles, they do take longer to cook, so we settled on soba made with part buckwheat and part wheat flour. Tasters found this noodle to have a good balance of flavor and chew.

With the noodle issue ironed out, we looked to choosing other ingredients to add to our soba meal. We decided on a simple pork stir-fry, which we'd simply toss with the boiled noodles. The supple texture and quick-cooking quality of pork tenderloin made it a natural choice for the protein element of our dish. Quickly cooking the pork, removing it from the pan, setting it aside, and reintroducing it to finish the dish ensured tender, moist slices of pork. And sticking with the Japanese theme, we settled on full-flavored shiitake mushrooms, combined with a light sauce composed of soy sauce, mirin (sweetened Japanese rice wine), rice vinegar, and grated fresh ginger. Bean sprouts add texture and crunch and sliced scallions finish the dish with fresh allium flavor and vibrant color.

Soba Noodles with Pork and Scallions

SERVES 4

For this dish, avoid the darker colored sobas made from 100 percent buckwheat, as they take twice the amount of time to cook as the lighter colored soba, which are made with part buckwheat and part regular wheat.

MAKING THE MINUTES COUNT:
Prep the mushrooms before cooking the pork. Then prep the remaining ingredients while the mushrooms brown.

3	tablespoons vegetable oil
1½	pounds pork tenderloin, cut into thin strips (see page 98)
10	ounces shiitake mushrooms, stemmed and quartered
6	garlic cloves, minced
1	tablespoon grated fresh ginger
3	cups bean sprouts, well rinsed
½	cup soy sauce
¼	cup mirin
¼	cup rice vinegar
8	ounces soba noodles (see note)
	Salt
4	scallions, sliced thin

1. BOIL WATER FOR NOODLES: Bring 3 quarts water to boil in large pot.

2. STIR-FRY PORK: Heat 1 tablespoon of oil in 12-inch nonstick skillet over high heat until just smoking. Add pork, spread into single layer, and cook without stirring for 1 minute. Stir pork and continue to cook until most, but not all, of pink color has disappeared and pork is lightly browned around edges, about 3 minutes longer. Transfer pork to clean bowl, cover, and set aside.

3. STIR-FRY MUSHROOMS: Add remaining 2 tablespoons oil to skillet and return to medium-high heat until shimmering. Add mushrooms and cook until browned, about 4 minutes.

4. COMBINE PORK, MUSHROOMS, AND SAUCE: Stir garlic and ginger into mushrooms and cook until fragrant, about 30 seconds. Stir in bean sprouts, soy sauce, mirin, rice vinegar, and pork with any accumulated juices. Cook until pork is just heated through, about 1 minute. Remove from heat, cover, and set aside.

5. BOIL AND DRAIN NOODLES: Add soba and 1 tablespoon salt to boiling water and cook, stirring often, until al dente, about 4 minutes. Reserve ½ cup of cooking water, then drain soba and return soba to pot.

6. TOSS NOODLES WITH PORK, MUSHROOMS, AND SAUCE: Stir pork-mushroom mixture and scallions into noodles. Add reserved cooking water as necessary to moisten, and serve.

LO MEIN

LO MEIN IS A SIMPLE DISH—BASICALLY A stir-fry with boiled noodles. So why is it so often poorly executed? The lo mein served in many Chinese restaurants is frequently oily and uninteresting; the noodles are often a tasteless mass. We aimed to create a quick dish of flavorful noodles and vegetables coated in a light, tangy sauce.

Addressing the noodle component first, we found it best to stick with the traditional fresh Chinese egg noodles. A soft, wheat-based pasta, these egg noodles are notorious for sticking and clumping together after cooking. But we found by boiling our noodles less and draining them about a minute before they were al dente, we could avoid the sticky mass problem. In addition to undercooking the noodles slightly, we rinsed the drained noodles with cold water and tossed them with a little bit of sesame oil. Sure enough, rinsing the noodles rid them of excess starch, and tossing them with sesame oil further prevented the noodles from sticking together. The oil also enhanced the flavor of the completed dish.

Now that we had solved the noodle problems, we moved on to the sauce. We aimed to generate the greatest flavor with the fewest ingredients. We also wanted to keep the sauce light and therefore improve on the goopy Chinese take-out sauces. A pungent mix of garlic, ginger, scallions, and chicken broth made for a vibrant, light sauce; fresh shiitake mushrooms (the common choice in many recipes) turned out to be a crucial foundation of flavor. Common varieties of mushrooms, such as white button and portobello, were odd additions and didn't add the deep, authentic flavor to our sauce like the shiitakes. Soy sauce was another essential component, and to finish the dish, we chose oyster-flavored sauce. While not exactly a household staple, it was listed in most of the recipes we consulted. We found, and tasters agreed, that the oyster-flavored sauce gave the lo mein an interesting brininess and an appealing gloss.

Vegetable Lo Mein
SERVES 4

Look for fresh Chinese egg noodles (lo mein) in the produce section of your supermarket. Vegetable broth can be substituted for the chicken broth to make this dish vegetarian. Be careful when seasoning this dish with salt, as the sauce is fairly salty on its own.

2	tablespoons vegetable oil
10	ounces shiitake mushrooms, stemmed and sliced thin (see page 186)
1	small head Napa cabbage, sliced crosswise into 1/4-inch-wide shreds
1	red bell pepper, cored and sliced thin
1	tablespoon grated fresh ginger
2	garlic cloves, minced
1/4	cup low-sodium chicken broth
3	tablespoons soy sauce
3	tablespoons oyster-flavored sauce
1	(9-ounce) package fresh Chinese egg noodles
	Salt and ground black pepper
1	tablespoon toasted sesame oil
4	scallions, sliced thin

MAKING THE MINUTES COUNT:
Prep the remaining ingredients while the mushrooms are browning,

1. BOIL WATER FOR NOODLES: Bring 3 quarts water to boil in large pot.

2. STIR-FRY VEGETABLES: Heat oil in 12-inch nonstick skillet over high heat until shimmering. Add mushrooms and cook until browned, about 4 minutes. Stir in cabbage and bell pepper and cook until cabbage wilts, about 2 minutes.

3. MAKE SAUCE: Stir ginger and garlic into vegetables and cook until fragrant, about 30 seconds. Stir in broth, soy sauce, and oyster-flavored sauce and bring to simmer. Remove from heat, cover, and set aside.

4. COOK, DRAIN, AND RINSE NOODLES: Add egg noodles and 1 tablespoon salt to boiling water and cook, stirring often, until noodles are slightly underdone, about 2 minutes. Drain noodles, then rinse under cold running water and drain again. Return noodles to pot and toss with sesame oil.

5. TOSS NOODLES WITH VEGETABLES AND SAUCE: Add cabbage mixture to pot, return to medium-high heat, and cook until noodles are heated through, about 1 minute. Stir in scallions, season with salt and pepper to taste, and serve.

Beef Lo Mein

SERVES 4

Boneless, skinless chicken or pork tenderloin, sliced into strips, can be substituted for the beef if you like.

3	tablespoons vegetable oil
12	ounces blade steak, sliced into thin strips (see page 205)
10	ounces shiitake mushrooms, stemmed and sliced thin (see page 186)
1	small head Napa cabbage, sliced crosswise into 1/4-inch-wide shreds
1	red bell pepper, cored and sliced thin
1	tablespoon grated fresh ginger
2	garlic cloves, minced
1/4	cup low-sodium chicken broth
3	tablespoons soy sauce
3	tablespoons oyster-flavored sauce
1	(9-ounce) package fresh Chinese egg noodles
	Salt and ground black pepper
1	tablespoon toasted sesame oil
4	scallions, sliced thin

MAKING THE MINUTES COUNT:

Prep the remaining ingredients while the mushrooms are browning,

1. BOIL WATER FOR NOODLES: Bring 3 quarts water to boil in large pot.

2. STIR-FRY BEEF AND VEGETABLES: Heat 1 tablespoon of oil in 12-inch nonstick skillet over high heat until just smoking. Add beef and cook, stirring occasionally, until no longer pink, about 3 minutes. Transfer beef to clean bowl and cover with foil to keep warm. Heat remaining 2 tablespoons oil in skillet over high heat until shimmering. Add mushrooms to skillet and cook until browned, about 4 minutes. Stir in cabbage and bell pepper and cook until cabbage wilts, about 2 minutes.

3. MAKE SAUCE: Stir ginger and garlic into vegetables and cook until fragrant, about 30 seconds. Stir in broth, soy sauce, and oyster-flavored sauce and bring to simmer. Remove from heat, cover, and set aside.

4. COOK, DRAIN, AND RINSE NOODLES: Add egg noodles and 1 tablespoon salt to boiling water and cook, stirring often, until noodles are slightly underdone, about 2 minutes. Drain noodles, then rinse under cold running water and drain again. Return noodles to pot and toss with sesame oil.

5. TOSS NOODLES WITH BEEF, VEGETABLES, AND SAUCE: Add reserved beef and cabbage mixture to pot, return to medium-high heat, and cook until noodles are heated through, about 1 minute. Stir in scallions, season with salt and pepper to taste, and serve.

SHREDDING CABBAGE

1. Cut a whole head of cabbage into quarters. Cut away the hard piece of the core attached to each quarter. Separate the cored cabbage quarters into stacks of leaves that flatten when pressed lightly.

2. Use a chef's knife to cut each stack of cabbage diagonally into long, thin pieces. Alternatively, roll the stacked leaves crosswise to fit them into the feed tube of a food processor fitted with the shredding disk.

ASIAN NOODLES WITH WINTER GREENS

THE SHARP, PEPPERY FLAVOR OF WINTER greens is a perfect match for the mild, wheaty flavor and silken texture of Asian udon noodles. We wanted to find a way to combine greens and noodles with a simple sauce to create a quick meal.

Blanching turned out to be the optimal method for cooking the greens; this technique maintained the vibrant color of the greens but tamed their bitterness. When we started testing, we had three pots going—one for greens, one for noodles, and one for the sauce. After a few experiments, we found that it worked fine to cook the greens with the noodles. This approach cut one pot and two steps from the recipe. We didn't have to worry about removing the greens from the boiling water or about running them under cold water to stop them from cooking, because once the noodles and greens are done, they are simply drained together and added to the sauce.

We found that fresh noodles should go into the pot after the greens, but that dried noodles will need a head start on the greens. See the recipe headnote for more detailed cooking instructions.

Mustard Greens and Udon Noodles with Shiitake-Ginger Sauce

SERVES 4

You can find fresh Japanese udon noodles in the produce section of many supermarkets. If they are not available, use dried udon and add them to the pot in step 3 first. Cook the noodles for 3 minutes, then add the greens and continue cooking until both the noodles and greens are tender, another 2 or 3 minutes.

1½	cups low-sodium chicken broth
2	tablespoons rice vinegar
¼	cup mirin
½	pound shiitake mushrooms, stemmed and sliced thin
1	(2-inch) piece fresh ginger, peeled and cut into ¼-inch coins
½	teaspoon Asian chili sauce
2	tablespoons soy sauce
1	teaspoon toasted sesame oil
	Salt and ground black pepper
1½	pounds mustard greens (1 large bunch), leaves trimmed from stalks; stalks discarded and leaves cut into 2-inch pieces
14	ounces fresh udon noodles

1. BOIL WATER FOR GREENS AND NOODLES: Bring 5 quarts water to boil in large pot.

2. HEAT AND REDUCE BROTH MIXTURE: Bring broth, vinegar, mirin, mushrooms, ginger, chili sauce, soy sauce, and sesame oil to boil in medium saucepan over high heat. Simmer briskly until liquid thickens and reduces by half, 8 to 10 minutes. Off heat, remove ginger using a slotted spoon. Season broth with salt and pepper to taste and cover to keep warm.

3. COOK GREENS AND NOODLES: Meanwhile, add 1 tablespoon salt and greens to boiling water. Cook until greens are almost tender, 2 to 4 minutes. Add noodles, stir to separate, and cook until both greens and noodles are tender, about 2 minutes longer. Reserving ¼ cup noodle cooking water, drain noodles and greens, and return to pot.

4. TOSS GREENS AND NOODLES WITH SAUCE: Add sauce and reserved water and cook over medium-low heat, stirring to meld flavors, about 1 minute. Adjust seasonings with salt and pepper to taste. Serve immediately.

KITCHEN SHORTCUT
MAKING SHORT WORK OF SHIITAKES

To slice up the stemmed mushrooms more quickly, stack 4 or 5 at a time instead of slicing them individually.

9

FLASH IN THE PAN

FLASH IN THE PAN

A WELL-SEARED STEAK OR SAUTÉED FISH fillet makes the centerpiece to a delicious and quick meal. Like stir-frying, both pan-searing and sautéing rely on high heat and a small amount of fat to cook foods quickly. While the principles of these methods are straightforward, they're not one-size-fits-all methods. Meats vary—fish is delicate and chicken won't cook exactly like steak or pork chops—therefore, they all require slightly different handling. Likewise, the same meat should be handled differently depending on how it's cut; thinner cuts like chicken cutlets cook faster than chicken breasts, and thick, bone-in pork chops take longer to cook than thin, boneless chops. While the technique may vary slightly from one dish to the other, the ultimate goals are the same—a well-seared crust and a moist, juicy interior.

Mention pan-seared meat and most people think of steak. We found that choosing the right steak for searing is important (see page 206 for recommended steaks for pan-searing). And although it might seem elementary, the size of the steak is important as well. Crowding oversized steaks into a pan will cause the meat to stew, rather than sear, resulting in the loss of the flavorful crust. Therefore, choose the size of your steaks accordingly and don't try to cram too many into the same pan—if necessary, use two pans to cook them. Pan-searing bone-in pork chops is similar—choosing the right chops makes a difference, as well as being sure they're not crowded into the pan.

Boneless chops, however, pose more of a challenge. Overcooked pork is tough, leathery, and tasteless. Because boneless chops are so thin, they can easily overcook by the time the exterior has seared. We found it important to partially brown boneless chops in the pan, then let them finish cooking in a glaze or browned onions—each helps ensure juicy meat.

Mild-flavored chicken can play host to a variety of flavors. So, in addition to the simple sauté, we've included several recipes featuring chicken. Rich and crunchy breaded chicken cutlets can be served with just a squeeze of lemon or used as a springboard for another dinner option, like your favorite recipe for chicken Parmesan. We found

it was essential to choose cutlets of even thickness so that the chicken cooked at the same rate. Using enough oil and ensuring that the oil is hot (it should be just smoking) is also key. If you've ever eaten a cutlet with a sodden crust, you can bet the cooking oil hadn't been hot enough. We've also included a recipe for chicken teriyaki using bone-in chicken thighs. We were able to give the thighs a super-crisp crust by using high heat and weighting down the chicken with a heavy pot.

Fish fillets take well to sautéing. Preventing the fish from sticking to the skillet (and falling apart) is the primary challenge we faced. A nonstick skillet helps, as does using a wide, thin spatula to turn the fillets—in some cases, using two spatulas is helpful (see page 215). Because fish cooks so quickly, overcooking can easily occur. For thicker fillets, we found that it was best to slightly undercook the fish and then let it rest before serving. While the fillets rested, their residual heat gently finished cooking them. Shellfish, too, is prone to overcooking. We pan-sear shrimp until just pink around the edges, then remove the shrimp from the heat to allow the residual heat to gently finish the job. We take a similar tack with scallops.

An added bonus to sautéing and pan-searing are the browned bits, called *fond,* left behind in the skillet. They are the perfect building block for making a quick, delicious pan sauce. Pan sauces provide endless variety, turning a simple sautéed piece of meat or fish into something truly special. But there are other options as well. In addition to pan sauces, we've included recipes for compound butters (butters flavored with aromatics, herbs, and sometimes cheese), which add a quick burst of flavor to a simple pan-seared steak or fish fillet. Compound butters can be mixed together quickly and served straightaway or stored in the refrigerator or freezer.

To round out a pan-seared steak, sautéed fish fillet, or any of the recipes in this chapter, you needn't turn to the freezer for side dish options. With recipes like quick roasted potatoes and skillet-steamed vegetables, you can have fresh side dishes on the table in 30 minutes, too.

A TEST KITCHEN CLASSIC

SAUTÉED AND PAN-SEARED CHICKEN

BONELESS, SKINLESS CHICKEN BREASTS are like a blank canvas, just waiting to be transformed into a quick, convenient dinner, but they are not without challenges. We've all been on the receiving end of poorly cooked chicken breasts. As innocuous as they may look, if cooked poorly, no amount of pan sauce can camouflage their dry, leathery meat.

To cook chicken breasts correctly, the first thing to consider is size. Be sure to select chicken breasts of equal size, so they will cook evenly, at the same rate. Chicken cutlets (thinner than chicken breasts) are prone to overcooking. The key to cutlets is to use high heat and cook them quickly. Whether cooking breasts or cutlets, we found that flouring the chicken prior to sautéing served to protect the meat from drying out and helped prevent it from sticking to the skillet. Turning the heat down when browning the second side of the chicken is crucial to prevent the pan from scorching while the chicken cooks through and helps to prevent a leathery, stringy exterior.

Simple Sautéed Chicken Breasts

SERVES 4

If you like, serve the chicken with a pan sauce—see the recipes on pages 196–197.

- 1/2 cup unbleached all-purpose flour
- 4 boneless, skinless chicken breasts
  Salt and ground black pepper
- 2 tablespoons vegetable oil

I. SEASON AND FLOUR CHICKEN: Spread flour in shallow dish. Pat chicken dry with paper towels and season with salt and pepper. Dredge chicken in flour to coat and shake off excess.

2. SEAR CHICKEN ON ONE SIDE: Heat oil in 12-inch skillet over medium-high heat until just smoking. Carefully lay chicken in skillet and brown well on one side, 6 to 8 minutes.

3. FLIP CHICKEN AND COOK THROUGH: Flip chicken over, reduce heat to medium-low, and continue to cook until thickest part of breasts registers 160 degrees on instant-read thermometer, 6 to 8 minutes longer.

4. REST CHICKEN: Transfer chicken to plate, cover with foil, and let rest for at least 5 minutes (or while making pan sauce) before serving.

Simple Sautéed Chicken Cutlets

SERVES 4

Don't confuse chicken cutlets with boneless, skinless chicken breasts. Cutlets are thin, about 1/4 to 1/2 inch thick. If your cutlets are of uneven thickness, lightly pound them to an even thickness, so they cook at the same rate. Be careful not to overcook the cutlets—they really do cook through in just 4 minutes. This recipe will also work with turkey, pork, or veal cutlets. If you like, serve the cutlets with a pan sauce—see the recipes on pages 196–197.

- 1/2 cup unbleached all-purpose flour
- 8 boneless chicken cutlets (see note)
  Salt and ground black pepper
- 1/4 cup vegetable oil

I. SEASON AND FLOUR CUTLETS: Spread flour in shallow dish. Pat cutlets dry with paper towels and season with salt and pepper. Dredge cutlets in flour to coat and shake off excess.

2. COOK HALF OF CUTLETS: Heat 2 tablespoons of oil in 12-inch skillet over medium-high heat until just smoking. Carefully lay half of cutlets in pan and brown lightly on both sides, about 4 minutes total. Transfer to plate and tent loosely with foil.

3. COOK REMAINING CUTLETS: Add remaining 2 tablespoons oil to skillet and return to medium-high heat until just smoking. Cook remaining cutlets and serve.

Pan-Searing and Sautéing 101

Pan-searing and sautéing are not difficult but they do require some know-how for successful results. Follow our equipment recommendations and these tips for preparing browned, juicy cutlets, well-seared steaks and chops, and golden fish fillets.

EQUIPMENT

COOKWARE: Pans designed for sautéing come in two distinct styles: straight-sided and slope-sided. Through testing, we have found that straight sides inhibit moisture evaporation, allowing foods to "stew." Depending on the manufacturer, a sloped-sided pan may be called everything from an omelette pan to a skillet to a fry pan. For the sake of standardization, we refer to any slope-sided shallow pan as a skillet. For a list of our favorite skillets—both traditional and nonstick—see pages 110 and 5.

ILL-SUITED FOR SAUTÉING
Straight-sided pans inhibit evaporation. They are best used for pan-frying and shallow braising.

PERFECT FOR SAUTÉING
Sloped sides allow for quick evaporation of moisture—preventing foods from stewing in exuded juices.

MEASURING A SKILLET
The industry may not agree on what to call a slope-sided pan, but there is agreement on sizing conventions. All skillets are measured outer lip to outer lip.

THE RIGHT TOOLS: To maneuver food in a skillet as it sautés, you need the following tools:

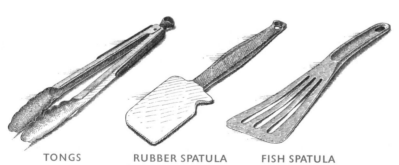

TONGS   RUBBER SPATULA   FISH SPATULA

TONGS are a heatproof extension of your hand and are invaluable whether moving cutlets or stirring vegetables (when closed, they work like a spoon or spatula). After testing a variety of brands and styles, we found models from Oxo and Edlund to be our favorites because they opened wide, had a firm yet comfortable spring tension, and had scalloped—not serrated—tips that gripped securely without damaging food. Medium-length (12-inch) tongs are the most versatile size.

HEATPROOF RUBBER SPATULAS do a great job of scraping up stuck-on bits of food. After testing 10 popular brands of heatproof spatulas (through baking tasks, general scraping chores, and an abuse test), we found Rubbermaid's High Heat Scraper and Le Creuset's Heatproof Spatula to be the best of the bunch. That said, the decidedly low-tech wooden spatula (see page 194) works well too.

FISH SPATULAS maneuver delicate foods with ease. Matfer's Slotted Pelton Fish Spatula was our favorite in a recent test.

4 KEY STEPS TO SUCCESSFUL SAUTÉING

1. PAT THE MEAT DRY
Always pat the meat (or fish) dry with paper towels just before cooking. If you bypass this step, the excess moisture on the surface of the meat will prevent a flavorful brown crust from forming.

2. GET THE SKILLET HOT
To determine when a skillet is ready for sautéing, we use the term "just smoking." When wisps of smoke begin to rise from the oil in the skillet, that is when you should add your meat, chicken, or fish. If the pan is not hot enough, food will stick and not brown as well.

3. DON'T TOUCH!
Leave the meat undisturbed while it cooks, flipping it just once in order to brown the second side. If you constantly flip or move the food around the pan as it cooks, you will both inhibit the meat from browning and mar any crust that is forming.

4. LET CARRYOVER COOKING FINISH THE JOB
Don't cook the food through completely in the pan, or else the residual heat will render it overcooked and dried out by the time you serve it. By slightly undercooking everything and letting it rest for 5 to 10 minutes before serving, you will ensure properly cooked and juicy meat every time. See "Two Ways to Determine Doneness" on page 193 for more information.

OIL

BEST CHOICE: After sautéing chicken (as well as meat and fish) in a variety of different oils, from $48 per liter extra-virgin olive oil to cheap canola oil, we found flavor differences to be virtually imperceptible. That said, we avoid unrefined oils such as extra-virgin olive oil because they have a low smoke point and are thus an inaccurate guide to the skillet's temperature. Butter, too, burns fairly easily unless mixed with oil.

SAUTÉ TROUBLESHOOTING

Over the years, we've found that the following problems are most likely to cause poor results when sautéing:

WARPED SKILLET: It's nearly impossible to brown meat or fish evenly in a skillet with an uneven, warped bottom. If you are unsure of your skillet's evenness, rest the pan on a flat surface. Does it rock to and fro? Does water pool in a particular spot? Adding extra oil to the skillet will help "level" the pan and can improve browning, but it's no guarantee. Warped pans, however, are fine for sautéing vegetables because they are moved frequently.

UNEVEN HEATING: Make sure your pan is properly sized to the burner and vice versa. If the skillet is too big for the burner, only the center will fully heat; if it's too small, the pan may become excessively hot.

THIN PANS: Thin, inexpensive pans heat and cool more rapidly than thicker, heavy-bottomed pans and thus demand more attention. Gauge the browning speed and adjust the burner temperature accordingly.

OVERCROWDING: Avoid overcrowding the pan, which will cause food to steam and thereby affect flavor, color, and texture. Choose the right pan size and allow some space between the food (as shown at right).

STUCK-ON FOODS: If your meat or fish fuses to the skillet, try this tip for freeing them: Dip a flexible spatula into cold water and slide the inverted spatula blade underneath the piece of meat. The cool, wet spatula blade breaks the bond between skillet and meat.

TWO WAYS TO DETERMINE DONENESS

Knowing when to pull the food out of the skillet is one of the most important keys to sautéing. An instant-read thermometer is the most reliable method for checking the doneness of chicken, beef, and pork (below left), while a simple nick-and-peak test works best for thick pieces of fish. That said you can, in a pinch, use the nick-and-peek method (below right). Cutlets, thin fish fillets, shrimp, and scallops all cook too quickly for an actual doneness test and you should rely more on the visual cues and cooking times.

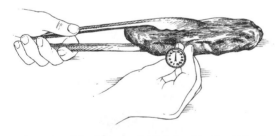

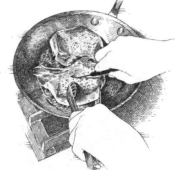

Insert an instant-read thermometer through the side of a chicken breast, steak, or pork chop for the most accurate reading. Refer to the chart below for the temperatures at which the meat should be remove from the pan (the temperature of the meat will continue to climb between 5 and 10 degrees as it rests before serving).

When you think the food is nearing doneness, make a small nick halfway through the meat with a paring knife. If there is a bone, nick next to the bone for an accurate reading (the area along the bone takes the longest to cook).

WHEN IS IT DONE?		
MEAT	COOK UNTIL IT REGISTERS	SERVING TEMPERATURE
CHICKEN BREASTS	160 to 165 degrees	160 to 165 degrees
CHICKEN THIGHS	175 to 180 degrees	175 to 180
PORK	140 degrees	150 degrees
BEEF		
Rare	110 to 115 degrees	120 degrees
Medium-Rare	115 to 120 degrees	125 to 130 degrees
Medium	125 to 130 degrees	135 to 140 degrees
Medium-Well	135 to 140 degrees	145 to 150 degrees
Well Done	145 to 150 degrees	155 to 160 degrees

Pan Sauces 101

THE SETUP

Because pan sauces cook quickly, before you begin to cook it is essential to complete your *mise en place*—that is, have all necessary ingredients and utensils collected and ready to use.

JUST-SEARED MEAT

After searing the meat, transfer it to a plate and tent it loosely with foil while making the sauce. A loose seal will keep any crust that has formed from turning soggy.

SMALL BOWL

Have ready a small empty bowl or container to catch excess fat that might have to be poured off before you begin the sauce.

AROMATICS

Aromatics include garlic and onions, but are most often shallots—their flavor is mild, sweet, and complex. If "minced" is specified, make sure they are fine and even; this will cause them to release maximum flavor, and their texture will be less obtrusive in the finished sauce.

LIQUIDS

Leave liquid ingredients (such as wine, broth, juices) in a measuring cup. Once emptied, keep the measuring cup close at hand; the reduced liquid can be poured back into the measuring cup toward the end of simmering to assess its final volume and to gauge if it is adequately reduced.

WOODEN UTENSIL

A wooden utensil (or heatproof spatula, see page 192) works best to scrape up the fond while deglazing because it is rigid and does not scratch (like metal on metal). Either spatula is ideal because it

can cover more of the surface area of the pan than the rounded tip of a spoon.

HERBS AND FLAVORINGS

Herbs are sometimes used in sprig form, to be removed from the sauce before serving. Delicate herbs such as parsley and tarragon are usually chopped and added to the sauce at the end so they do not discolor. Other flavorings such as mustard, lemon juice, capers, and chopped olives are often added at the end for maximum flavor impact.

WHISK

For maximum efficiency and easy maneuverability, use a medium-size whisk with flexible wires that can get into the rounded sides of the skillet.

BUTTER

Cut the butter into tablespoon-size chunks so that it will melt quickly into the sauce. Cold butter is easier to incorporate into a sauce than softened butter, and it makes a sturdier emulsion that is more resistant to separation. Butter can be omitted, but the sauce will be thinner, with little silkiness.

SALT AND PEPPER

Tasting for and correcting seasoning is the last step before serving. Keep salt in a ramekin so that it is easy to measure out in small amounts.

THE EXECUTION

Here's how to make a pan sauce step-by-step:

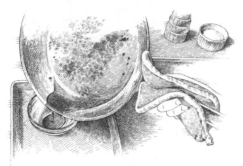

1. DISCARD ANY EXCESS FAT

Sometimes seared meat will leave behind too much fat. After removing the seared or sautéed items from the skillet, discard excess fat, leaving just enough (several teaspoons) to cook the aromatics. With most steaks and chicken, this step is not necessary; but with fatty chops, it probably is.

2. SAUTÉ THE AROMATICS

Add the aromatics to the skillet and cook them until they soften slightly, usually no more than a couple of minutes, adjusting the heat if necessary. Be sure not to let the fond scorch, or the finished sauce will taste burnt and bitter.

3. DEGLAZE AND THICKEN

Add the liquid to the skillet—it will sizzle and steam on contact—and scrape up the fond on the bottom of the skillet. Thicken the sauce with the cornstarch-broth mixture.

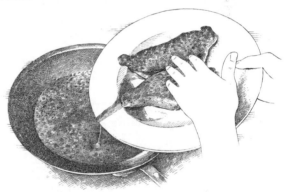

4. RETURN THE JUICES TO THE SKILLET

As the meat rests, it will likely release juices; add these juices back to the skillet. If the juices should thin the sauce, allow it to simmer an additional minute or two to restore proper consistency.

5. WHISK IN THE BUTTER

Whisk in the cold butter, one piece at a time. Grab hold of the butter with the whisk and swirl it around in the skillet until it is melted and incorporated into the sauce. Taste for seasoning before serving.

Whisks come in all sorts of shapes and sizes. Is there one particular style that's best for making pan sauces? To find out, we rounded up 12 models—from balloon whisks (super skinny to large) to square-headed models and coil whisks. We ended up settling on the skinnier balloon whisk as having the best shape for pan sauces. When tilted on its side, this whisk covers a wide swath for efficient deglazing. Its relatively straight sides and flexible tines also come in handy when scraping a sauce from the sides of the pan. Of the models we tried, our favorite brand was the Best Manufacturers 12-inch Standard French Whip.

BEST WHISK FOR PAN SAUCES

The Best Manufacturers 12-inch Standard French Whip ($9.95) boasts an ideal shape and agile set of tines that are perfect for preparing pan sauces.

Quick Pan Sauces and Relishes

THE BASE OF A PAN SAUCE IS THE FOND, or browned bits, clinging to the bottom of the skillet after sautéing or searing meat, poultry, or fish. Once the protein is removed from the skillet, aromatics such as minced shallots can be sautéed; and then, in a process called deglazing, liquid—usually wine, broth, or both—is added to help dissolve the fond into a flavorful sauce. The sauce is then simmered to concentrate flavors and thicken. We made sure that these sauces yield plenty, so that you have a little extra to drizzle over potatoes or rice. We also thickened some of them with cornstarch (rather than simply letting them simmer and reduce) to help speed things up. For more information on preparing pan sauces, see pages 194–195.

Red Wine Sauce

MAKES ABOUT 1¼ CUPS

For a white wine pan sauce, substitute ½ cup dry white wine or vermouth for the red wine.

1	shallot, minced
	Salt and ground black pepper
½	cup dry red wine
1½	cups low-sodium chicken broth
1	tablespoon light brown sugar
1	teaspoon cornstarch
3	tablespoons unsalted butter, cut into 3 pieces and chilled
1	teaspoon minced fresh thyme

1. SAUTÉ SHALLOT: After removing cooked protein from skillet, add shallot and ¼ teaspoon salt to oil left in skillet, return to medium-high heat, and cook until softened, about 2 minutes.

2. DEGLAZE AND SIMMER: Stir in wine, scraping up any browned bits. Stir in 1¼ cups of broth and brown sugar and simmer until sauce measures 1 cup, about 5 minutes.

3. THICKEN: Whisk remaining ¼ cup broth and cornstarch together until smooth, then whisk into sauce. Add any accumulated meat juices and continue to simmer until sauce is thickened, about 2 minutes.

4. FINISH: Reduce heat to low and whisk in butter, one piece at a time. Off heat, stir in thyme and season with salt and pepper to taste.

Worcestershire and Butter Sauce

MAKES ABOUT 1¼ CUPS

Serve this sauce with beef or pork.

2	shallots, minced
	Salt and ground black pepper
2	cups low-sodium chicken broth
1	teaspoon cornstarch
1	tablespoon Worcestershire sauce
½	teaspoon Dijon mustard
3	tablespoons unsalted butter, cut into 3 pieces and chilled
1	tablespoon minced fresh parsley

1. SAUTÉ SHALLOTS: After removing cooked protein from skillet, add shallots and ¼ teaspoon salt to oil left in skillet, return to medium-high heat, and cook until softened, about 2 minutes.

2. DEGLAZE AND SIMMER: Stir in 1¾ cups of broth, scraping up any browned bits. Bring to simmer and cook until sauce measures 1 cup, about 5 minutes.

3. THICKEN: Whisk remaining ¼ cup broth and cornstarch together until smooth, then whisk into simmering sauce. Stir in any accumulated meat juices, Worcestershire, and mustard, and simmer until thickened, about 2 minutes.

4. FINISH: Turn heat to low and whisk in butter, one piece at a time. Off heat, stir in parsley and season with salt and pepper to taste.

Marsala Sauce

MAKES 1½ CUPS

This sauce tastes best with poultry or pork. The key to this sauce is using sweet Marsala (not dry), and omitting the broth. Pancetta is Italian bacon that has been cured but not smoked. If you can't find pancetta, substitute 3 slices bacon, chopped fine.

3 ounces pancetta, chopped fine (see note)
1 tablespoon vegetable oil
8 ounces white button mushrooms, sliced thin
1 garlic clove, minced
1½ cups sweet Marsala
1 teaspoon cornstarch
3 tablespoons unsalted butter, cut into 3 pieces and chilled
1½ tablespoons fresh lemon juice
2 tablespoons minced fresh parsley
    Salt and ground black pepper

1. SAUTÉ MUSHROOMS AND AROMATICS: After removing cooked protein from skillet, add pancetta and oil to oil left in skillet, return to medium-high heat, and cook until pancetta begins to render, about 2 minutes. Stir in mushrooms and continue to cook until mushrooms are browned, about 8 minutes. Stir in garlic and cook until fragrant, about 30 seconds.

2. DEGLAZE: Stir in 1¼ cups of Marsala, scraping up any browned bits.

3. THICKEN: Whisk remaining ¼ cup Marsala and cornstarch together until smooth, then whisk into simmering sauce. Add any accumulated meat juices and continue to simmer sauce until thickened, about 2 minutes.

4. FINISH: Turn heat to low and whisk in butter, one piece at a time. Off heat, stir in lemon juice and parsley. Season with salt and pepper to taste.

Cognac and Mustard Sauce
MAKES ABOUT 1¼ CUPS
This sauce tastes best with beef or pork.

2 shallots, minced
    Salt and ground black pepper
½ cup cognac or brandy
1½ cups low-sodium chicken broth
1 teaspoon cornstarch
2 tablespoons whole-grain mustard
2 tablespoons unsalted butter, cut into 2 pieces and chilled
1 tablespoon fresh lemon juice
2 teaspoon minced fresh tarragon

1. SAUTÉ SHALLOTS: After removing cooked protein from skillet, add shallots and ¼ teaspoon salt to oil left in skillet, return to medium-high heat, and cook until softened, about 2 minutes.

2. DEGLAZE AND SIMMER: Stir in cognac, scraping up browned bits. Add 1¼ cups of broth and simmer until sauce measures 1 cup, about 5 minutes.

3. THICKEN: Whisk remaining ¼ cup broth and cornstarch together until smooth, then whisk into simmering sauce. Stir in any accumulated meat juices and mustard and simmer until thickened, about 2 minutes.

4. FINISH: Turn heat to low and stir in butter, one piece at a time. Off heat, stir in lemon juice and tarragon. Season with salt and pepper to taste.

Chipotle Chile and Orange Sauce
MAKES ABOUT 1¼ CUPS
This sauce tastes best with pork, poultry, or fish.

1 shallot minced
    Salt and ground black pepper
2 garlic cloves, minced
1 teaspoon minced chipotle chiles in adobo sauce
½ cup low-sodium chicken broth
1½ cups orange juice
1 teaspoon cornstarch
2 tablespoons unsalted butter, cut into 2 pieces and chilled
1 orange, peeled, quartered, and cut crosswise into ¼-inch pieces
1 tablespoon minced fresh cilantro

1. SAUTÉ AROMATICS: After removing cooked protein from skillet, add shallot and ¼ teaspoon salt to oil left in skillet, return to medium-high heat, and cook until softened, about 2 minutes. Stir in garlic and chipotle and cook until fragrant, about 30 seconds.

2. DEGLAZE AND SIMMER: Stir in broth and 1¼ cups of orange juice, scraping up any browned bits. Bring to simmer and cook until sauce measures 1 cup, about 5 minutes.

3. THICKEN: Whisk remaining ¼ cup orange juice and cornstarch together until smooth, then whisk into simmering sauce. Stir in any accumulated meat juices and simmer until thickened, about 2 minutes.

4. FINISH: Turn heat to low and stir in butter, one piece at a time. Off heat, stir in orange pieces and cilantro. Season with salt and pepper to taste.

Warm Roasted Red Pepper Relish

MAKES ABOUT I CUP

This relish tastes best with pork, poultry, or fish. Roasted red peppers are sold in jars of different sizes. If you can only find jars of peppers larger than 12 ounces, note that you will need 3 to 4 medium peppers, drained.

I	shallot, minced
	Salt and ground black pepper
I	garlic clove, minced
I	(12-ounce) jar roasted red peppers, rinsed, patted dry, and chopped fine
2	tablespoons red wine vinegar
2	tablespoons unsalted butter, cut into 2 pieces and chilled
I	tablespoon minced fresh basil

I. SAUTÉ AROMATICS: After removing cooked protein from skillet, add shallot and ¼ teaspoon salt to oil left in skillet, return to medium-high heat, and cook until softened, about 2 minutes. Stir in garlic and cook until fragrant, about 30 seconds.

2. SAUTÉ PEPPERS: Add peppers and vinegar and cook, scraping up any browned bits, until peppers are warmed through, about 2 minutes.

3. FINISH: Stir in any accumulated meat juices. Turn heat to low and stir in butter, one piece at a time. Off heat, stir in basil and season with salt and pepper to taste.

Warm Cherry Tomato Relish

MAKES ABOUT I ¾ CUP

Serve with pork, poultry, or fish.

I	teaspoon grated lemon zest
2	garlic cloves, minced
½	teaspoon minced fresh rosemary
I	pint cherry tomatoes, halved
¼	cup pitted Kalamata olives, chopped coarse
2	tablespoons extra-virgin olive oil
	Salt and ground black pepper

I. SAUTÉ AROMATICS: After removing cooked protein from skillet, add lemon zest, garlic, and rosemary to oil left in skillet, return to medium-high heat, and cook until fragrant, about 30 seconds.

2. SAUTÉ TOMATOES: Add tomatoes and olives and cook, scraping up any browned bits, until tomatoes are hot and lightly wilted, about 4 minutes.

3. FINISH: Stir in any accumulated meat juices and olive oil. Season with salt and pepper to taste.

CRISPY BREADED CHICKEN CUTLETS

CRISPY CHICKEN CUTLETS ARE QUICK AND delicious. They can be made into a Parmesan-style casserole, with tomato sauce and cheese, made into a sandwich, or served simply with a wedge of lemon. But we've had our share of bad cutlets, ones so soggy and greasy that no amount of tomato sauce and cheese could rescue them. We wanted a quick, foolproof method for preparing cutlets with moist meat and a crisp, well-browned crust.

Choose your cutlets carefully. They should all be of the same thickness (¼ to ½ inch is ideal) so that they cook at the same rate. If they're of varying thicknesses, you can simply pound them to an even thickness (see page 200). The next step is breading the cutlets. Breading is not a daunting task. Once you get the procedure down, the assembly-line prep can go pretty quickly. Standard breading procedure involves flour, then egg, then bread crumbs, in that order. We use one hand for dredging the cutlets in flour and using tongs to dip them in beaten egg. We use the other hand to press the dry crumbs into the cutlets.

As for cooking the cutlets, there are a few key points to keep in mind. First, there must be enough vegetable oil in the skillet to allow the cutlets to float on a thin layer of hot oil. Too little oil will result in splotchy browning. Next, make sure that the oil is hot enough before placing the cutlets in the pan—it should be just smoking. If the oil is not hot enough, the bread crumbs will absorb the oil. And last, don't crowd the pan. Trying to fit too many cutlets in the skillet will prevent the cutlets from browning properly.

Crispy Breaded Chicken Cutlets
SERVES 4

This recipe will also work with thin-sliced turkey, veal, or pork cutlets. If the cutlets are of uneven thickness, pound the meat between two sheets of plastic wrap to an even thickness (see illustration on page 200). Serve with lemon wedges, if desired.

I	cup unbleached all-purpose flour
2	large eggs
3	cups panko (Japanese-style bread crumbs) or fresh bread crumbs (page 200)
8	chicken cutlets (¼ to ½ inch thick) Salt and ground black pepper
¾	cup vegetable oil

MAKING THE MINUTES COUNT:
To make the breading procedure go faster, line all of your ingredients up assembly-line style and use tongs when coating with the egg.

I. HEAT OVEN: Adjust oven rack to middle position and heat oven to 200 degrees.

2. PREP BREADING: Spread flour in shallow dish. Beat eggs in second shallow dish. Spread panko in third shallow dish.

3. SEASON AND BREAD CUTLETS: Pat cutlets dry with paper towels and season with salt and pepper. Working with one cutlet at a time, dredge in flour, then dip into egg, and finally coat with panko. Press on panko to make sure it adheres.

4. COOK HALF OF CUTLETS: Heat oil in 12-inch nonstick skillet over medium-high heat until just smoking. Add half of cutlets and brown thoroughly on both sides, 4 to 6 minutes total.

5. COOK REMAINING CUTLETS: Drain cutlets briefly on paper towels, then transfer to paper towel–lined plate and keep warm in oven. Return skillet with oil to medium-high heat until just smoking. Cook remaining breaded chicken.

BREADING CUTLETS

1. Coat the cutlet evenly with flour, then shake to remove any excess.

2. Coat the floured chicken thoroughly with egg, then let the excess drip back into the dish. Use tongs to keep your hands clean.

3. Coat the cutlet thoroughly with the bread crumbs, pressing firmly on the bread crumbs to make sure they adhere to the chicken.

➤ VARIATIONS

Crispy Chicken Cutlets Milanese

These cheese-flavored cutlets go well with pasta with 20-Minute Tomato Sauce on page 157.

Stir ¼ cup finely grated Parmesan cheese into bread crumbs.

Crispy Deviled Chicken Cutlets

Serve these highly seasoned cutlets with lemon wedges.

Season each cutlet with generous pinch cayenne in addition to salt and pepper. Whisk 3 tablespoons Dijon mustard, 1 tablespoon Worcestershire, and 2 teaspoons minced fresh thyme into eggs.

Crispy Chicken Fingers

Serve with Honey Mustard Dipping Sauce (recipe follows) or your favorite store-bought barbecue sauce.

Slice cutlets into strips or 1½-inch pieces, then bread and fry as directed in steps 3 through 4.

HONEY MUSTARD DIPPING SAUCE
MAKES ABOUT 1 CUP

This sauce is an excellent dipping sauce for Crispy Chicken Fingers (at left). If you like your honey-mustard sweeter or spicier, increase the amount of honey or mustard, respectively. The sauce can be refrigerated in an airtight container for up to 1 week.

½	cup Dijon mustard
6	tablespoons honey
	Salt and pepper

Mix mustard and honey together until smooth, then season with salt and pepper to taste.

TEST KITCHEN TIP: Freezing Chicken Fingers and Breaded Cutlets
Instead of relying on subpar frozen breaded chicken cutlets and chicken fingers, freeze your own. Our recipe for breaded chicken cutlets and chicken fingers can be frozen in zipper-lock freezer bags, where they will keep for up to one month. Reheat on a paper towel–lined plate in microwave on high heat for 1 to 1½ minutes or on a baking sheet in a 425-degree oven for 12 to 15 minutes.

TEST KITCHEN TIP: Crumbs with Crunch
Our top choice for bread crumbs when breading and frying are Japanese-style bread crumbs, called panko. They provide the lightest, crispiest coating. Our second favorite are fresh homemade bread crumbs made from white sandwich bread (the crumbs are not dried). To make fresh bread crumbs, tear pieces of white sandwich bread (including crusts) into quarters and pulse in a food processor to coarse crumbs, about eight pulses.

POUNDING CUTLETS

Place the cutlets, smooth-side down, on a large sheet of plastic wrap. Cover with a second sheet of plastic wrap and pound gently. The cutlets should already be thin; you simply want to make sure that they have the same thickness from end to end.

Nut-Crusted Chicken Breasts

A SIMPLE BREADED CHICKEN BREAST CAN be quickly transformed into a richer dish with the addition of nuts to the breading. Yet, for the transformation to be a success, we had to uncover a few key tricks. Using boneless, skinless chicken breasts, we began by adapting our standard breading technique: dredging the chicken in flour and then an egg wash, and, finally, bread crumbs. We first tried replacing the bread crumbs with sliced almonds, but the thin almond slices refused to stick to the chicken. We had more success when the almonds were processed into fine crumbs in the food processor. Testing various ratios of nuts to bread crumbs, we landed on equal amounts of each. We found that light Japanese-style bread crumbs, called panko, worked especially well. We also added 2 teaspoons cinnamon for flavor and 1 teaspoon cornstarch to help keep the nuts crisp. You can also substitute pecans for the almonds, but note the crust will be dark colored.

Cooking the chicken turned out to be fairly straightforward. The important factors were to use a skillet large enough to comfortably cook four pieces of chicken and to use plenty of oil. While the chicken is delicious on its own, some tasters felt that a brightly flavored chutney or relish was in order to balance the richness of the nutty crust, so we developed an easy cranberry-orange relish to serve alongside.

Almond-Crusted Chicken Breasts with Cranberry-Orange Relish
SERVES 4

Don't process the nuts longer than directed or they will turn pasty and oily. You can substitute an equal amount of whole pecans for the sliced almonds, but note that the crust will be darker colored. Store-bought dried bread crumbs taste very disappointing here; if you cannot find panko, process two slices of high-quality sandwich bread into coarse crumbs in a food processor, then spread them out onto a baking sheet and let them dry in a 250-degree oven for about 20 minutes.

1 cup unbleached all-purpose flour
2 large eggs
¾ cup sliced almonds (see note)
¾ cup panko (Japanese bread crumbs)
2 teaspoons ground cinnamon
1 teaspoon cornstarch
4 boneless, skinless chicken breasts
  Salt and ground black pepper
1 cup vegetable oil
¾ cup dried cranberries
½ cup orange marmalade
½ cup orange juice
2 tablespoons minced fresh chives
1 teaspoon fresh lemon juice

MAKING THE MINUTES COUNT:
Line the flour, egg, and bread crumbs up in a row for efficient breading. Also, start to heat the oil while breading the chicken.

1. HEAT OVEN: Adjust oven rack to middle position and heat oven to 200 degrees.

2. PREP BREADING: Spread flour in shallow dish. Beat eggs in second shallow dish. Process almonds into fine crumbs in food processor, about 10 seconds, then toss with panko, cinnamon, and cornstarch in third shallow dish.

3. SEASON AND BREAD CHICKEN: Pat chicken dry with paper towels and season with salt and pepper. Working with one piece of chicken at a time, dredge in flour, then dip into egg, and finally coat with nut mixture. Press on nuts to make sure they adhere.

4. COOK CHICKEN: Heat oil in 12-inch nonstick skillet over medium heat until shimmering. Add chicken and brown thoroughly on both sides, 6 to 8 minutes total. Drain chicken briefly on paper towels, then lay on wire rack set over baking sheet and keep warm in oven.

5. MAKE RELISH: Pour hot oil out of pan and wipe pan clean with wad of paper towels. Add cranberries, marmalade, and orange juice to skillet and simmer over medium-high heat until mixture is thick and glossy, 3 to 5 minutes. Off heat, stir in chives and lemon juice and season with salt and pepper to taste. Spoon cranberry relish over chicken before serving.

SALTIMBOCCA

ITS NAME LITERALLY MEANING "JUMP IN THE mouth," saltimbocca is a simple variation on veal scaloppine that hails from Rome. Thinly sliced pieces of prosciutto and leaves of sage are pressed into the cutlet and secured with a toothpick before the cutlets are quickly sautéed. The simple combination of these three flavors is so good that the cutlets jump into your mouth. While using veal is traditional, we've found that chicken is equally tasty and better suited toward weeknight cooking. Turkey or even pork cutlets are good substitutions too.

Although many recipes for this dish pound the prosciutto and sage into the cutlets, we found this didn't work very well. The pounding tore the thin prosciutto and fragile sage to shaggy pieces. Instead, we simply pressed the tacky prosciutto into the already pounded cutlet with our hands. Laying the sage leaf on top of the prosciutto, we secured the trio with a toothpick.

Just like our other cutlet recipes, these cutlets browned better when they were floured, and they cooked quickly—in 4 minutes. While you can serve them with a pan sauce, tasters thought these cutlets were flavorful enough on their own or with just a wedge of lemon—we leave the choice up to you.

MAKING SALTIMBOCCA

Using a toothpick as if it were a stickpin, secure the sage and prosciutto to the cutlets by poking the toothpick down through the layers, then back out again. The toothpick should be parallel to the cutlet and as flat as possible.

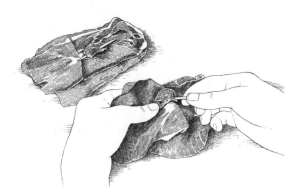

Saltimbocca

SERVES 4

You will need eight sturdy toothpicks for this recipe. Prosciutto can be quite salty, so be careful when seasoning with extra salt. If the cutlets are of uneven thickness, pound the meat to an even ¼ to ½-inch thickness to ensure even cooking. Eight thinly sliced turkey, veal, or pork cutlets can be substituted for the chicken. You can serve these with either lemon wedges, White Wine Sauce (a variation of Red Wine Sauce), or Marsala Sauce (page 196). Don't forget to remove the toothpicks before serving (or, at the very least, alert your diners).

½	cup unbleached all-purpose flour
8	thin chicken cutlets (see note)
	Salt and ground black pepper
8	thin slices prosciutto (6 ounces)
8	large fresh sage leaves
¼	cup vegetable oil

1. HEAT OVEN: Adjust oven rack to middle position and heat oven to 200 degrees. Spread flour in shallow dish.

2. ASSEMBLE SALTIMBOCCA: Pat cutlets dry with paper towels, then season with salt and pepper. Lay 1 slice prosciutto on top of each cutlet (folded over to fit if needed), and lay 1 sage leaf in center. Following illustration at left, secure prosciutto and sage to cutlet using sturdy, wooden toothpick. Dredge cutlets in flour to coat, and shake off any excess.

3. COOK HALF OF CUTLETS: Heat 2 tablespoons of oil in 12-inch skillet over medium-high heat until just smoking. Carefully lay half of cutlets in pan and brown lightly on both sides, about 4 minutes total. Transfer to plate and tent loosely with foil.

4. COOK REMAINING CUTLETS: Add remaining 2 tablespoons oil to skillet and return to medium-high heat until just smoking. Cook remaining cutlets. Remove toothpicks and serve.

GLAZED CHICKEN BREASTS

BONELESS CHICKEN BREASTS ARE QUICK-cooking crowd pleasers, but finding interesting ways to prepare them can be a challenge. Looking at the multitude of chicken breast recipes out there, we were struck by the idea of a simple glazed chicken. In testing a number of different recipes for glazes, the problems we encountered centered around dry, flavorless chicken in a glaze that was either overly sweet and gloppy or too thin. We wanted a browned and moist chicken breast with a fresh-flavored glaze just thick enough to cling to the meat.

We tested several different cooking methods including baking, sautéing, and braising, and found that the ideal method for a great glazed chicken breast requires a combination of sautéing and braising. First we browned the chicken, and then we prepared the glaze in the same skillet. We then let the chicken and glaze simmer together for several minutes in order to blend the flavors and allow the glaze to thicken. Using this method, we concocted several different glazes—but your options are really only limited to the confines of your pantry and your imagination.

Pineapple Glazed Chicken

SERVES 4

Be sure to buy pineapple chunks packed in juice, not syrup. This dish can also be garnished with freshly minced parsley, cilantro, scallions, or chives before serving.

4	boneless, skinless chicken breasts
	Salt and ground black pepper
1	tablespoon vegetable oil
1	(20-ounce) can pineapple chunks in juice
1/4	cup honey
1	tablespoon soy sauce
2	teaspoons curry powder
	Pinch cayenne
1	teaspoon cornstarch
1	tablespoon cider vinegar
1/4	cup sliced almonds, toasted (see page 36)

1. **BROWN CHICKEN:** Pat chicken dry with paper towels and season with salt and pepper. Heat oil in 12-inch skillet over medium-high heat until just smoking. Brown chicken lightly on both sides, about 4 minutes total.

2. **ASSEMBLE GLAZE:** Drain pineapple chunks, reserving 1/2 cup juice. Whisk reserved pineapple juice, honey, soy sauce, curry powder, and cayenne together.

3. **SIMMER CHICKEN IN GLAZE:** Add pineapple juice mixture and pineapple chunks to skillet and bring to simmer. Reduce heat to low, cover, and cook until chicken is no longer pink in center and thickest part registers 160 degrees on instant-read thermometer, 8 to 12 minutes.

4. **REST CHICKEN AND SIMMER GLAZE:** Transfer chicken to serving platter, cover with foil, and let rest for 5 to 10 minutes. Return glaze to simmer and cook, uncovered, until thickened slightly and glossy, about 8 minutes.

5. **FINISH GLAZE:** Add accumulated chicken juices to glaze. Whisk cornstarch and vinegar together until smooth, then whisk into glaze. Continue to simmer glaze until thick and syrupy, about 1 minute. Season with salt and pepper to taste. Pour glaze over chicken, sprinkle with toasted almonds, and serve.

➤ VARIATIONS

Cranberry-Orange Glazed Chicken

Substitute 1 (16-ounce) can whole berry cranberry sauce and 3/4 cup orange juice for pineapple and reserved pineapple juice. Whisk cranberry sauce and orange juice into saucepan with glaze mixture in step 2.

Apricot-Orange Glazed Chicken

Use a clean pair of scissors sprayed with nonstick spray to cut the apricots.

Substitute 1/2 cup chopped dried apricots, 2/3 cup apricot preserves, and 1/2 cup orange juice for pineapple and reserved pineapple juice. Whisk dried apricots, apricot preserves, and orange juice into saucepan with glaze mixture in step 2.

TERIYAKI

AFTER SORTING THROUGH LOTS OF misguided, Americanized recipes—including everything from over-marinated, pre-formed chicken breast patties to skewered beef chunks shellacked in a corn-syrupy sauce—we decided it was time to reclaim this classic recipe and make it taste good again.

Teriyaki consists of pan-fried, grilled, or broiled meat with a sweet-salty sauce which is added during the final stages of cooking. Figuring out which cut of meat to use and how to cook it was fairly easy (see the Test Kitchen Tips below and on page 205). For the chicken teriyaki we preferred bone-in chicken thighs, and for the beef teriyaki we liked thinly sliced blade steak.

Getting the sauce right required some serious testing. Our tasters unanimously rejected bottled teriyaki sauce (see the tasting on page 205) in favor of a homemade sauce, which consists of a handful of ingredients and takes just five minutes to prepare. Tinkering with various amounts of

soy sauce, sugar, and mirin (the core ingredients in a traditional teriyaki), we found that the best balance of sweetness and saltiness was achieved with near equal amounts of soy sauce and sugar, flavored by a smaller amount of mirin (Japanese cooking wine), garlic, and fresh ginger. In terms of consistency, we found the ideal texture hard to attain without the help of a little cornstarch. (The amount of cornstarch depends on the type of meat and its cooking method.)

Chicken Teriyaki
SERVES 4

Small thighs work best here. If the thighs are large, you may need to extend the browning time in step 1. A splatter screen (or a large, inverted strainer/colander) is helpful for reducing the mess when browning the second side of the chicken. There is a fair amount of soy sauce used in this dish, so there is no need to season it with extra salt. Serve with rice.

8	small bone-in, skin-on chicken thighs
	Ground black pepper
1	tablespoon vegetable oil
1/2	cup soy sauce
1/2	cup sugar
2	tablespoons mirin, sherry, or white wine
2	teaspoons grated fresh ginger
1	garlic clove, minced
1/2	teaspoon cornstarch
1/8	teaspoon red pepper flakes
2	scallions, sliced thin

1. BROWN CHICKEN UNDER WEIGHT: Pat chicken dry with paper towels and season with pepper. Heat oil in 12-inch nonstick skillet over medium-high heat until shimmering. Add chicken, skin-side down. Following illustration at left, weight chicken down with heavy pot. Cook until skin is deep mahogany brown and very crisp, about 15 minutes. (Chicken should be moderately brown after 10 minutes. Reduce heat if very brown, or increase heat if pale.)

2. FLIP CHICKEN AND COOK THROUGH: Flip chicken over and continue to cook, without replacing weight, until chicken registers 175 on

---

TEST KITCHEN TIP:

The Crispest Skin

Super-crisp skin is a fundamental component of a good chicken teriyaki. After trying numerous methods, we found it easiest to use bone-in, skin-on thighs and cook them in a nonstick pan under the weight of a heavy pot. We found that cooking the chicken thighs to an internal temperature of 175 to 180 degrees ensured tender, evenly cooked dark meat. The nonstick surface ensures that the crisp, browned skin sticks to the chicken rather than the pan, and the heavy pot presses the skin of the chicken into the skillet for a serious sear.

instant-read thermometer, 5 to 10 minutes.

3. **ASSEMBLE SAUCE:** While chicken cooks, whisk soy sauce, sugar, mirin, ginger, garlic, cornstarch, and pepper flakes together.

4. **SIMMER CHICKEN WITH SAUCE:** Transfer chicken to plate. Pour off all fat from skillet. Whisk sauce to recombine, then add to skillet and return to medium heat. Return chicken to skillet, skin-side up, and spoon sauce over top. Continue to simmer until sauce is thick and glossy, about 2 minutes longer. Transfer chicken and sauce to plate. Sprinkle with scallions before serving.

Beef Teriyaki

SERVES 4

If you cannot find blade steak, substitute 1½ pounds of flank steak sliced thin against the grain. Do not season the meat with salt because the sauce is plenty salty. For the best flavor, be sure to get the skillet smoking hot, and cook the beef in a single layer so that all the pieces brown properly. Garnish with toasted sesame seeds and serve with plenty of steamed white rice.

TEST KITCHEN TIP: The Right Cut

To prevent the beef from becoming overly tough or chewy in the teriyaki, we found it is important to buy the right steak and slice it as thin as possible. Blade steak is our number one choice for teriyaki because it is inexpensive, has a full beefy flavor, and becomes quite tender when cooked. Its one drawback is a line of gristle that runs down the middle—which in this case, we use to our advantage. We found it easy to slice the steak into thin strips running parallel to the line of gristle, and then simply discard the gristle.

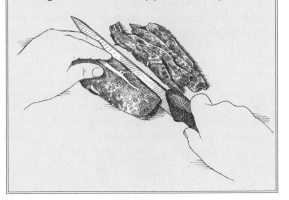

2	pounds top blade steak, sliced thin
	Ground black pepper
2	tablespoons vegetable oil
½	cup soy sauce
½	cup sugar
2	tablespoons mirin, sherry, or white wine
2	teaspoons cornstarch
2	teaspoons grated fresh ginger
1	garlic clove, minced
⅛	teaspoon red pepper flakes
2	scallions, sliced thin

MAKING THE MINUTES COUNT:
Prep the sauce ingredients and assemble the sauce while the beef browns.

1. **BROWN MEAT:** Pat steak dry with paper towels and season with pepper. Heat 1 tablespoon of oil in 12-inch nonstick skillet over medium-high heat until just smoking. Brown half of steak on both sides, about 5 minutes total. Transfer steak to clean bowl. Repeat with remaining tablespoon oil and remaining steak, then transfer to bowl.

2. **ASSEMBLE AND SIMMER SAUCE:** While steak cooks, whisk soy sauce, sugar, mirin, cornstarch, ginger, garlic, and red pepper flakes together. Add sauce to skillet, return to medium-high heat, and simmer, scraping up any browned bits, until thickened, about 2 minutes.

3. **SIMMER MEAT WITH SAUCE:** Add steak and any accumulated juices to skillet and continue to simmer until steak is heated through and sauce has thickened, about 1 minute. Transfer to serving platter and sprinkle with scallions. Serve.

SHORTCUT INGREDIENT:
Store-Bought Teriyaki Sauce

Considering that a great teriyaki sauce can be prepared quickly, bottled sauces can hardly boast convenience. But how do they taste? We sampled seven leading brands to find out. Annie Chun's All-Natural received top marks. But in a second tasting pitting Annie Chun's against our own homemade, judges were less impressed. The panel deemed Annie Chun's harsh in comparison to the brighter tasting homemade sauce. We suggest taking the time to make your own.

Choosing a Steak

The array of steaks at the supermarket can be overwhelming, and the steak you choose can make all the difference in terms of cost, flavor, and texture. In choosing steak, look for meat that has a bright, lively color. Beef normally ranges in color from pink to red, but dark meat probably indicates an older, tougher animal. The external fat as well as the fat that runs through the meat (called intramuscular fat or marbling) should be as white as possible. The marbling should be smooth and fine, running all through the meat, rather than showing up in clumps; smooth marbling melts into the meat during cooking, while knots remain as fat pockets. Stay away from packages that show a lot of red juice (known as purge). The purge may indicate a bad job of freezing; as a result, the steak will be dry and cottony.

Below we've listed the steaks we recommend for pan-searing. Boneless steaks will rest flush against the pan and are easier to pan-sear than bone-in steaks. Steaks sport different names depending on locale. We've used industry names that we feel best describe where the steaks lie on the animal; you'll find some other common names also listed. We also provide a brief description of flavor and tenderness. And, as the price of steak varies widely depending on the cut, we provide an indication of cost ($$$$ being the most expensive).

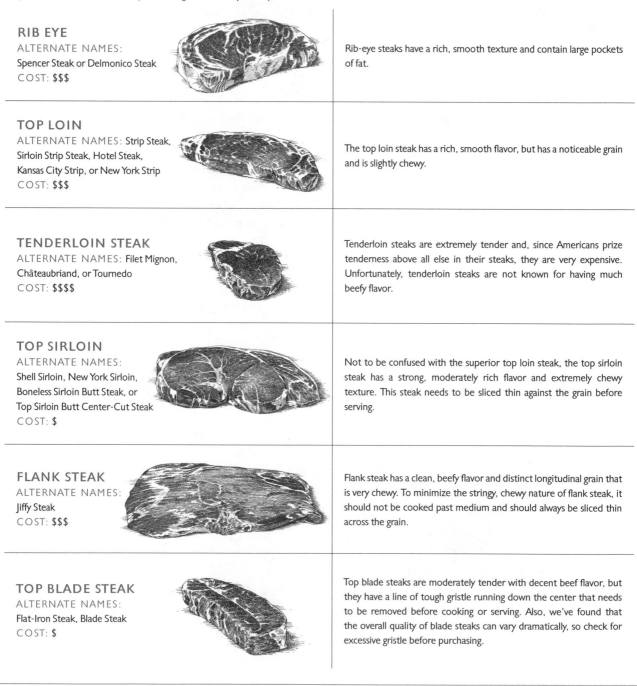

RIB EYE
ALTERNATE NAMES:
Spencer Steak or Delmonico Steak
COST: $$$

Rib-eye steaks have a rich, smooth texture and contain large pockets of fat.

TOP LOIN
ALTERNATE NAMES: Strip Steak, Sirloin Strip Steak, Hotel Steak, Kansas City Strip, or New York Strip
COST: $$$

The top loin steak has a rich, smooth flavor, but has a noticeable grain and is slightly chewy.

TENDERLOIN STEAK
ALTERNATE NAMES: Filet Mignon, Châteaubriand, or Tournedo
COST: $$$$

Tenderloin steaks are extremely tender and, since Americans prize tenderness above all else in their steaks, they are very expensive. Unfortunately, tenderloin steaks are not known for having much beefy flavor.

TOP SIRLOIN
ALTERNATE NAMES:
Shell Sirloin, New York Sirloin, Boneless Sirloin Butt Steak, or Top Sirloin Butt Center-Cut Steak
COST: $

Not to be confused with the superior top loin steak, the top sirloin steak has a strong, moderately rich flavor and extremely chewy texture. This steak needs to be sliced thin against the grain before serving.

FLANK STEAK
ALTERNATE NAMES:
Jiffy Steak
COST: $$$

Flank steak has a clean, beefy flavor and distinct longitudinal grain that is very chewy. To minimize the stringy, chewy nature of flank steak, it should not be cooked past medium and should always be sliced thin across the grain.

TOP BLADE STEAK
ALTERNATE NAMES:
Flat-Iron Steak, Blade Steak
COST: $

Top blade steaks are moderately tender with decent beef flavor, but they have a line of tough gristle running down the center that needs to be removed before cooking or serving. Also, we've found that the overall quality of blade steaks can vary dramatically, so check for excessive gristle before purchasing.

PAN-SEARED STEAK

A GREAT PAN-SEARED STEAK HAS A DEEPLY colored, crisp brown crust and a rosy, juicy interior; the kind of steak you expect from a top-notch steak house. To get that same professional quality steak in your own home, there are a few things to remember. The first is choosing the right steak to ensure success in the skillet. The thickness, shape, and size of the steaks is important because this will determine how well they fit into the skillet and how evenly they will cook. If the steaks are too thin, you will not be able to fit 2 pounds of meat into the skillet at the same time. If the steaks are too large or oddly shaped, you may need to cut them in half in order to make them fit.

Using a large, heavy skillet is key for even heat distribution, as is the right level of heat. To achieve the perfect crust, make sure that the skillet is smoking before you add the steaks and don't crowd the skillet. If it's not hot enough, or the steaks are jammed too tightly together, the steaks will cool the pan down and end up stewing, rather than searing. Allow the steaks to get a deep brown crust on the first side. Remember not to move the steaks. Then, flip the steaks over to finish cooking to the desired doneness. Always undercook the steaks a bit to allow for carryover cooking as the steaks rest.

Purists won't want to adorn their steak with anything other than a sprinkle of salt and grind of pepper, but a compound butter or pan sauce (each of which are easy and quick to prepare) add another flavor dimension and richness that some diners will appreciate.

Simple Pan-Seared Steaks

SERVES 4

Follow the box on page 206 to choose a steak to your liking. Consider serving these steaks with a pan sauce (pages 196–198), or compound butter (pages 216–218).

2   pounds boneless beef steaks, 1 to 1¼ inches thick
    Salt and ground black pepper
1   tablespoon vegetable oil

1. BROWN STEAKS ON ONE SIDE: Pat steaks dry with paper towels and season with salt and pepper. Heat oil in 12-inch skillet over medium-high heat until just smoking. Carefully lay steaks in pan and cook until nicely browned on first side, about 5 minutes.

2. FLIP STEAKS AND COOK THROUGH: Flip steaks over and continue to cook to desired doneness (see page 193), 3 to 6 minutes, reducing heat if pan begins to scorch.

3. REST STEAKS: Transfer steaks to clean plate, tent with foil, and let rest for 5 minutes before serving.

PAN-SEARED PORK CHOPS

WHEN DONE RIGHT, PAN-SEARED PORK chops are moist and meaty. Too often, however, chops turn out dry and leathery. Why? Overcooking is one obvious culprit and choosing the wrong chop is another.

Start by choosing bone-in chops. For simple pan searing, they have better flavor (from the bone). Next, choose rib chops, which will be juicier than the leaner center-cut chops—and don't forget to check the thickness of the chops. They should be about one inch thick, so that you can get a good sear, giving the chop a flavorful browned crust while still allowing a moist, pink interior. Purchasing chops of even thickness is key too (see "Choose the Right Chop" on page 208).

As for cooking chops, brown them on one side in a very hot skillet. Then flip the chops, reduce the heat, and cook just until the temperature registers 140 degrees on an instant-read thermometer. Remove the chops from the heat and cover with aluminum foil for 5 minutes. During this resting period, the chops' temperature will gently rise to 150 degrees. This period also allows the juices in the meat to redistribute, ensuring tender, juicy pork chops.

Simple Pan-Seared Pork Chops

SERVES 4

This recipe will work with any type of pork chop, including boneless, but for the best flavor, we prefer bone-in rib chops. Consider serving these steaks with a pan sauce (pages 196–198).

4   bone-in rib pork chops, 1 inch thick
     Salt and ground black pepper
2   teaspoons vegetable oil

1. BROWN CHOPS ON ONE SIDE: Pat chops dry with paper towels and season with salt and pepper. Heat oil in 12-inch skillet over medium-high heat until just smoking. Carefully lay chops in pan and brown well on first side, about 4 minutes.

2. FLIP CHOPS AND COOK THROUGH: Flip chops over, reduce heat to medium, and continue to cook until center of chop (away from the bone) registers 140 degrees on instant-read thermometer, 5 to 10 minutes.

3. REST CHOPS: Transfer chops to clean plate, tent with foil, and let rest until center of chop reaches 150 degrees, 5 to 10 minutes, before serving.

TEST KITCHEN TIP:
Choose the Right Chop
Many supermarket chops are cut thick at the bone and thinner at the outer edge, like the one at left below. With such chops, the thinner periphery will overcook before the thicker meat near the bone is finished. Make sure you get chops that are of even thickness, like the one at right below.

Uneven Chop   **Even Chop**

30-MINUTE ROASTED RED POTATOES

SERVES 4

To complete this recipe in 30 minutes, preheat your oven before assembling your ingredients.

2   pounds red potatoes (6 medium), cut
     into 1-inch wedges
3   tablespoons olive oil
     Salt and ground black pepper

1. HEAT OVEN: Adjust oven rack to middle position and heat oven to 475 degrees.

2. COOK POTATOES: Toss potatoes with 1 tablespoon of oil, ½ teaspoon salt, and ¼ teaspoon pepper in microwave-safe bowl. Cover bowl tightly with plastic wrap and microwave on high until potatoes begin to soften, 5 to 7 minutes, shaking bowl (without removing plastic) to toss potatoes halfway through.

3. HEAT BAKING SHEET: While potatoes cook, coat rimmed baking sheet with remaining 2 tablespoons oil and heat in oven until just beginning to smoke, about 6 minutes.

4. DRAIN POTATOES: Carefully transfer microwaved potatoes to colander (be careful of scalding steam), and let drain for several minutes.

5. ROAST POTATOES ON HOT BAKING SHEET: Spread drained potatoes over hot baking sheet, cut sides facing down. Roast until potatoes are crusty and golden, about 15 minutes, flipping them over halfway through. Season with salt and pepper to taste before serving.

➤ VARIATIONS
30-Minute Roasted Red Potatoes with Garlic and Rosemary
During final 3 minutes of roasting, sprinkle potatoes with 1 tablespoon minced fresh rosemary. Toss with 1 minced garlic clove before serving.

SCRUBBING POTATOES

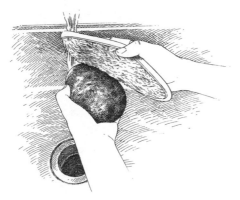

Buy a rough-textured bathing or exfoliating bath glove especially for use in the kitchen. The glove cleans dirt away from potatoes and other root vegetables, but it's relatively gentle and won't scrub away the skin.

OPENING A BAKED POTATO

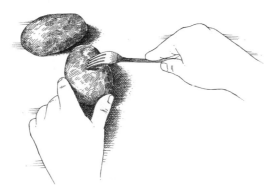

1. Use the tines of a fork to make a dotted X on the top of each potato.

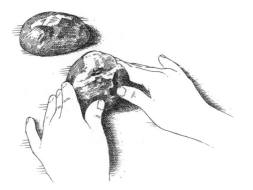

2. Press in at the ends of the potato to push the flesh up and out. Besides releasing steam quickly, this method helps to trap and hold on to bits of butter.

FAST BAKED POTATOES

MOST OF US DON'T HAVE AN HOUR AFTER work to bake the perfect, fluffy baked potato. Many recipes use the microwave exclusively to speed things up, resulting in gummy, unevenly cooked potatoes. After baking a sack of potatoes (literally), we found that microwaving the potatoes (to give them a head start) before placing them in a hot oven (450 degrees) resulted in potatoes with fluffy flesh and a crisp crust in less than half the time of traditional baking methods.

30-Minute Baked Potatoes

SERVES 4

To complete this recipe in 30 minutes, preheat your oven before assembling your ingredients. Look for evenly sized russet potatoes with firm, unblemished skin. You can substitute sweet potatoes for the russets. Once the potatoes are cooked, cut them open as soon as possible because the longer a potato sits after being removed from the oven, the denser the flesh becomes (see illustrations at left).

4   russet potatoes
    Butter (for serving)
    Salt and ground black pepper
    (for serving)

I. HEAT OVEN: Adjust oven rack to middle position and heat oven to 450 degrees.

2. MICROWAVE POTATOES: Poke several holes in each potato with fork and microwave on high until slightly soft to touch, 6 to 10 minutes, turning them over halfway through.

3. BAKE POTATOES: Carefully transfer potatoes to oven and cook directly on hot oven rack until skewer glides easily through flesh, about 20 minutes.

4. RELEASE STEAM FROM POTATOES: Remove potatoes from oven and, following illustration at left, make dotted X on top of each potato with tines of fork. Press in at ends of each potato to push flesh up and out. Serve immediately with butter, salt, and pepper.

MAPLE-GLAZED PORK CHOPS

WHILE WE LIKE THICK, BONE-IN CHOPS for simple pan-searing, we wondered what could be done with the thin, boneless chops found in almost every supermarket. Was there a way to give this convenient cut of meat great flavor? Off the bat, we thought of glazed chops—specifically maple-glazed pork chops. Rich, sweet maple pairs well with pork, and since maple syrup is a pantry item most households are likely to have on hand, it made sense to develop a glaze around it.

To begin, we researched recipes for maple-glazed pork chops and found, after cooking up several skillets of chops, that this dish often falls short of its sweet-savory promise. Not surprisingly, dry, overcooked chops were the norm. The glazes were disappointing too—they varied from sticky and sweet glazes to glazes so thin they pooled around the chop, rather than clinging to the meat.

First, we focused on developing a foolproof method for cooking boneless chops. We decided to go for boneless loin chops that were 1 inch thick, so that we could get a good sear and yield enough fond (flavorful browned bits left in the pan from the sear) to build our glaze. We first cooked the chops in a hot skillet to brown them on both sides. Once they reached 140 degrees on an instant-read thermometer, we removed them to a dish and covered them with foil while we built our glaze.

It was important that our maple glaze not be too sweet so we included ingredients like Dijon mustard and cayenne for savory balance. Once the glaze had simmered and reduced, we returned the chops to the pan (off the heat) and turned them in the glaze to coat. Timing, however, was an issue—this method took well over 30 minutes. And flavor? While tasters liked our meaty and moist pork chops and sweet and savory glaze, they thought the two were a bit disconnected.

For our next test, we browned the chops on one side only. Then we removed them from the pan briefly to build our glaze. We diluted the glaze with chicken broth so that the chops would have enough liquid in which to braise—the chicken broth also lent our glaze a nice, savory

note. We returned the chops to the skillet to finish cooking in the glaze. Once the chops were done, we removed them from the skillet and continued to simmer the glaze until it reduced to a dark, glossy sheen. We then poured the glaze over the chops and served them to tasters. Everyone agreed that these were truly great chops. Because all the flavors in the glaze and the pork had a chance to meld, the dish tasted like a unified whole. And the dish took less time to accomplish than other quick-cooking versions, to boot. We also developed two easy flavor variations—one with star anise and another with orange zest.

TEST KITCHEN TIP:

Pork and Safety Concerns

Guidelines for cooking pork to temperatures as high as 190 degrees originated decades ago when pork quality was inconsistent and fears of trichinosis ran high. Today, the risk of trichinosis is nearly nonexistent in the United States. According to the Centers for Disease Control and Prevention, only 13 human cases of trichinosis were confirmed in 2002, and the source of contamination for eight of those cases was wild game and for two of them privately raised pigs. What's more, even when the trichina parasite is present, it is killed when the temperature of the meat rises to 137 degrees.

Both the U.S. Department of Agriculture and the National Pork Board recommend cooking pork to a final internal temperature of 160 degrees. The Pork Board advises removing larger cuts from the oven at 150 degrees, resting the meat, and serving it at 160. Unfortunately, given the leanness of today's pork, these recommendations result in dry, tough meat. In the test kitchen, we have found cooking modern pork beyond 150 degrees to be a waste of time and money. We cook pork to 140 degrees; the temperature will climb about 10 degrees as the meat rests. (Be sure to check the final temperature before serving to make certain that it does reach 150 degrees.) If you are concerned about contamination from salmonella (which is possible in any type of meat, including beef), you must cook the pork to 160 degrees to be certain that all potential pathogens are eliminated.

Quick Maple-Glazed Pork Chops

SERVES 4

Be sure to buy chops of similar size and thickness so that they will cook at the same rate.

4	boneless pork loin chops, 1 inch thick
	Salt and ground black pepper
1	tablespoon vegetable oil
1	shallot, minced
1	cup low-sodium chicken broth
1/2	cup pure maple syrup
2	tablespoons cider vinegar
1	teaspoon minced fresh rosemary
1/8	teaspoon cayenne
1	teaspoon Dijon mustard
2	tablespoons unsalted butter

MAKING THE MINUTES COUNT:
Measure and prep the sauce ingredients while the chops brown.

1. BROWN CHOPS ON ONE SIDE: Pat chops dry with paper towels and season with salt and pepper. Heat oil in 12-inch skillet over medium-high heat until just smoking. Brown chops well on one side, about 4 minutes. Transfer chops to plate and set aside.

2. MAKE GLAZE: Add shallot and 1/4 teaspoon salt to fat left in skillet, return to medium-high heat, and cook until softened, about 2 minutes. Stir in broth, maple syrup, vinegar, rosemary, and cayenne, scraping up any browned bits.

3. SIMMER CHOPS IN GLAZE: Return chops to skillet, browned side up. Reduce heat to medium, cover, and continue to cook until center of chop registers 140 degrees on instant-read thermometer, 5 to 10 minutes.

4. REST CHOPS AND SIMMER GLAZE: Transfer chops to clean plate, tent with foil, and let rest until center of chop reaches 150 degrees, 5 to 10 minutes. Meanwhile, return glaze to simmer and cook, uncovered, until darkly colored and thickened, about 7 minutes.

5. FINISH GLAZE: Add accumulated pork juice and mustard to glaze. Reduce heat to low and whisk in butter, one piece at a time. Season with salt and pepper to taste. Pour glaze over chops and serve.

VARIATIONS

Quick Maple-Glazed Pork Chops with Star Anise
Omit rosemary and mustard. Add 4 star anise to skillet along with broth in step 2. Remove star anise before serving.

Quick Maple-Glazed Pork Chops with Orange Essence
Omit rosemary. Add 1 tablespoon grated fresh orange zest to skillet with broth in step 2.

SMOTHERED PORK CHOPS WITH APPLE CIDER

ONCE WE TACKLED BONELESS PORK CHOPS in a glazed guise, we thought of other moist-heat methods of cooking boneless chops. Smothered pork chops came to mind. The typical method for preparing smothered pork chops requires long, slow cooking. The pork chops need to be browned, the onions need to be slowly cooked until caramelized, and then the two components need to be combined and simmered for at least 30 minutes. We aimed to bring this long-cooking recipe in under the 30-minute wire.

Following our method for glazed chops, we browned the boneless chops on just one side, then turned to the onion. We started the caramelization process by covering the onion slices in the skillet for five minutes to sweat them. This five-minute sweating period gives the caramelization a head start. We removed the skillet cover to brown the onion. Partway through, we add the pork back to the skillet along with apple cider. We covered the skillet and simmered the mixture until the chops reached 140 degrees on an instant-read thermometer, then removed the chops to a dish and tented them with foil. Meanwhile, finishing the sauce required just a brief simmer and the addition of water and cornstarch (for thickening) and mustard (for flavor). A final addition of cider vinegar lent the onion some zip and reinforced the cider flavor in the sauce. We spooned the onion mixture over the chops, and they were ready to serve—great smothered pork chops in just 30 minutes.

Simplified Smothered Pork Chops with Apple Cider

SERVES 4

Try to buy chops of similar size so that they will cook evenly.

4	boneless pork loin chops, 1 inch thick
	Salt and ground black pepper
1	tablespoon vegetable oil
2	slices bacon, minced
1	onion, halved and sliced thin
2	teaspoons sugar
2	bay leaves
1	sprig fresh thyme
1½	cups apple cider
2	tablespoons water
2	teaspoons cornstarch
2	teaspoons Dijon mustard
2	teaspoons cider vinegar

MAKING THE MINUTES COUNT:
Slice the onion while the chops are browning.

1. BROWN CHOPS ON ONE SIDE: Pat chops dry with paper towels and season with salt and pepper. Heat oil in 12-inch skillet over medium-high heat until just smoking. Brown chops well on one side, about 4 minutes. Transfer chops to plate and set aside.

2. COOK ONION: Add bacon to skillet and cook over medium-high heat until fat begins to render, about 2 minutes. Stir in onion, sugar, bay leaves, thyme, and ½ teaspoon salt, scraping up any browned bits. Cover and cook, stirring often, until onion is softened and lightly browned, 5 minutes. Uncover skillet and continue to cook until onion is well browned, about 5 minutes.

3. COOK CHOPS WITH ONION: Stir in cider, scraping up browned bits. Nestle chops into onion, browned side up. Reduce heat to medium, cover, and cook until center of chop registers 140 degrees on instant-read thermometer, 5 to 10 minutes.

4. REST CHOPS: Transfer chops to clean plate, tent with foil, and let rest until center of chop reaches 150 degrees, 5 to 10 minutes.

5. FINISH SAUCE: As pork rests, return onion and sauce to simmer. Whisk water, cornstarch, and mustard together until smooth, then whisk into sauce. Continue to simmer sauce, adding any accumulated pork juices, until slightly thickened, about 2 minutes. Discard thyme sprig and bay leaves. Stir in vinegar and season with salt and pepper to taste. Pour onion sauce over chops and serve.

LAMB PATTIES WITH YOGURT SAUCE

WHETHER YOU KNOW THEM AS KEFTA, KIBBE, kofta, or simply ground meat patties, ground lamb patties appear all over the Middle East and are an ideal recipe for an exotic weeknight dinner. After looking at numerous ingredient lists, we broke down the patties into three components—the meat, the binding, and the seasoning—and focused on making them tasty and fast.

In contrast to meatballs, most Middle Eastern recipes for lamb patties do not contain much binding, relying instead on packing the meat tightly or occasionally using a handful of bulgur or bread crumbs along with the meat. Most tasters, however, found the authentic texture on the dense side so we added a bread and yogurt binder (similar to the bread and buttermilk binder we use in our meatballs). As for flavor, many recipes include as many as 20 different spices and herbs. Fortunately, we found that just a few basic flavorings—including cumin, cilantro, and cayenne—add plenty of flavor.

Lamb patties are traditionally grilled on skewers, but we opted to pan-fry them for convenience's sake. Broiling may seem like the logical indoor replacement for grilling, but pan-frying offered more control, and the patties developed a crisper crust—a definite bonus, according to most tasters. All of the patties could fit into a large skillet at one time and were cooked through in less than 10 minutes. After a quick blot on paper towels, they were ready to eat. Finished off with a quick yogurt sauce, these patties taste great on their own, but are equally good tucked into a pita sandwich.

Middle Eastern Lamb Patties with Yogurt Sauce
SERVES 4

Mint can be substituted for the cilantro. Serve these patties with a green salad and slices of tomato and cucumber, or tucked into a pita sandwich.

LAMB PATTIES
2   slices high-quality white sandwich bread, crusts removed
3   tablespoons plain yogurt
1   pound ground lamb
2   tablespoons minced fresh cilantro
    Salt and ground black pepper
1   teaspoon ground cumin
    Pinch cayenne
3   tablespoons vegetable oil

YOGURT SAUCE
1   cup plain yogurt
2   tablespoons minced fresh cilantro
1   tablespoon fresh lemon juice
½   garlic clove, minced
    Salt and ground black pepper

1. MAKE LAMB PATTIES: Tear bread into small pieces and mash with yogurt to form wet paste in medium bowl. Add lamb, cilantro, 1 teaspoon salt, ¼ teaspoon pepper, cumin, and cayenne, and mix until uniform. Pinch off 3-tablespoon-sized pieces of meat mixture, roll firmly into balls (12 balls), then flatten into small patties about 1½ inches thick.

2. BROWN PATTIES: Heat oil in 12-inch non-stick skillet over high heat until shimmering. Brown patties on just one side, about 2 minutes. Flip patties over, reduce heat to medium, and continue to cook until well browned on second side, about 6 minutes. Transfer patties to paper towel–lined plate.

3. MAKE YOGURT SAUCE: While patties cook, mix sauce ingredients together and season with salt and pepper to taste. Serve patties with sauce.

PAN-SEARED AND SAUTÉED FISH FILLETS

A PERFECTLY COOKED FISH FILLET WITH a delicate, golden brown crust and moist interior can't be beat. But sautéing fish can be intimidating—especially if the fish sticks to the pan or falls apart. We wanted to establish a consistent method that could be used for a variety of fish fillets, both thick and thin style. Thick fillets (about 1 to 1½ inches thick) include salmon, halibut, cod, sea bass, and tilapia. Thin fillets (¼ to ½ inch thick) include flounder, sole, and perch.

To start, we found the choice of pan to be key. Nonstick pans work best. Avoid cheap, flimsy nonstick pans—a heavy pan that conducts heat evenly is best here. (See page 5 for more information on choosing a pan.) For the cooking fat, we like vegetable oil: Its mild flavor and high smoke point work well for sautéing fish.

Preparing thick fillets for sautéing was easy. We patted the fillets dry and seasoned them with salt and pepper. We heated the vegetable oil until just smoking and carefully slid the fillets in the pan. After just a few minutes, the first side was well browned. We carefully turned the fillets to lightly brown the other side. We didn't, however, want to cook the fish through entirely, because while it rested it would continue cooking.

Thin fillets were trickier. Because they were so thin, they cooked quickly—too quickly for us to achieve a crust. They were also difficult to turn over, even when we used two spatulas to gently turn them. We solved the problem by lightly dredging the fillets in flour. The flour helped promote a thin crust in short order and it helped prevent the fillets from sticking to the pan. The crust also aided in holding the fillet together.

We still advise using two thin spatulas to turn them—just in case.

Pan-Seared Thick Fish Fillets
SERVES 4

Be sure to use a nonstick skillet here. Serve with a wedge of lemon or lime, a compound butter (pages 216–218), or one of the pan sauces on pages 196–198.

4	fish fillets, 1 to 1½ inches thick
	Salt and ground black pepper
1	tablespoon vegetable oil
1	lemon or lime, cut into wedges (for serving)

1. **BROWN FISH ON ONE SIDE**: Pat fish dry with paper towels and season with salt and pepper. Heat oil in 12-inch nonstick skillet over medium-high heat until just smoking. Gently lay fish in skillet (flesh side down if fillets are skin-on) and brown well on first side, about 5 minutes.

2. **FLIP FISH AND COOK THROUGH**: Gently flip fish and continue to cook until all but very center of fish has turned from translucent to opaque, about 3 minutes, reducing heat if pan begins to smoke heavily.

3. **REST FISH**: Transfer fish to plate, tent with foil, and let rest for 5 minutes before serving with lemon wedges.

Sautéed Thin Fish Fillets
SERVES 4

Flounder and sole work well in this recipe. Do not use fillets thinner than ¼ inch, or they will fall apart while cooking. Serve the thin fish fillets with lemon or a compound butter (pages 216–218). If you want to serve the fish with a pan sauce, we recommend the variation with browned butter and parsley sauce on the following page.

½	cup unbleached all-purpose flour
6–8	boneless, skinless fish fillets, ¼ to ½ inch thick
	Salt and ground black pepper
3	tablespoons vegetable oil
1	lemon, cut into wedges (for serving)

1. **SEASON AND FLOUR FISH**: Spread flour in shallow dish. Pat fish dry with paper towels and season with salt and pepper. Dredge fish in flour to coat and shake off excess.

2. **BROWN HALF OF FILLETS**: Heat 2 tablespoons of oil in 12-inch nonstick skillet over medium-high heat until shimmering but not smoking. Add half of fish and brown lightly on first side, 2 to 3 minutes.

3. **FLIP FILLETS AND COOK THROUGH**: Following illustrations on page 215, use two spatulas to gently flip fillets. Continue to cook on second side until thickest part of fillets is firm to touch and fish flakes easily, 30 to 60 seconds. Transfer fillets to platter and tent with foil.

REMOVING PINBONES FROM SALMON

Pinbones are small white bones that run through the center of a side of fish or a fish fillet. Most salmon is sold with the pinbones removed, but it never hurts to check one more time.

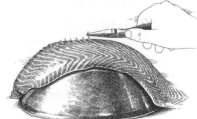

A. For fish fillets, run your fingers firmly over the salmon to feel for any bones, and use a clean pair of needle-nose pliers or tweezers to grab and remove.

B. For a large piece of salmon, drape it over an inverted bowl and use a clean pair of needle-nose pliers or tweezers to remove the pinbones. The curve of the bowl forces the pinbones to stick up and out, so they are easier to spot and remove.

4. BROWN AND COOK REMAINING FILLETS: Wipe out skillet with wad of paper towels. Add remaining 1 tablespoon oil and return to medium-high heat until shimmering. Cook remaining fish. Serve with lemon wedges.

➤ VARIATION

Sautéed Thin Fish Fillets with Browned Butter and Parsley Sauce

Transfer second batch of cooked fish to plate with first batch and cover with foil. Add 4 tablespoons unsalted butter to skillet and return to medium-high heat. Cook, swirling skillet constantly, until butter has melted and turned golden brown with nutty aroma, 2 to 3 minutes. Off heat, add 1½ tablespoons fresh lemon juice and 1 tablespoon minced fresh parsley. Season with salt and pepper to taste and pour over fish before serving.

FLIPPING FISH FILLETS

To easily turn fish fillets over without breaking them, use two spatulas. Use one spatula to get underneath the fish, while using the other to both hold the fish in place, and "catch" the fish after it's been flipped over. An extra-wide spatula especially designed for fish works well on the "catching" end.

PATTING FISH DRY

To ensure even cooking, limit splatter, and promote a crisp crust, make sure the fish is thoroughly blotted dry between paper towels.

TEST KITCHEN TIP:
Choosing Fish Fillets
Getting the fish you want is no easy task. Fish may be sold in small pieces and called "fillets," or they may be sold by the whole side and still be referred to as "fillets." Armed with a little knowledge, you can pick out the right catch of the day with ease. Here are descriptions of the white fish (appropriate for our recipe) that you are likely to encounter at the market, along with tips for buying them.

THE CUT: If possible, have the fishmonger cut out the fillets from the whole side. Usually, the center part of the side will yield at least 4 fillets. Most markets will cut and weigh fillets to your specifications.

THE THICKNESS: To ensure evenly cooked fillets, order and buy fillets that are the same thickness. A panful of thin fillets will cook more evenly than a pan containing a mix of thick and thin.

ABOUT THIN FILLETS: If the fish selection is limited, you can "cheat" by folding paper-thin fish fillets (often flounder or sole) in half. Their larger girth will cook more evenly alongside thicker fillets.

FLAVOR KEY: Flavor can run from mild to downright fishy. Here's how to buy fish that matches your personal preference.

FISH	THICKNESS	FLAVOR
Catfish	1 – 1½"	Assertive
Cod	¾ – 1½"	Medium
Flounder	¼ – ½"	Mild
Grouper	¾ – 1¼"	Medium
Haddock	¾ – 1½"	Medium
Hake	¾ – 1½"	Medium
Halibut	1 – 1½"	Medium
Orange Roughy	¾ – 1½"	Assertive
Red Snapper	¾ – 1"	Assertive
Salmon	1 – 1½"	Assertive
Sea Bass	¾ – 1½"	Assertive
Sole	¼ – ½"	Mild
Tilapia	¾ – 1"	Assertive

COMPOUND BUTTERS

Compound butters are both versatile and easy. They can be whipped together at a moment's notice and are an easy way to add flavor to fish, poultry, and meat. Compound butters can also add flavor to vegetables or rice.

Tarragon–Lime Butter

MAKES ENOUGH FOR 8 SERVINGS OF
MEAT, POULTRY, OR FISH

Leftovers can be stored in the freezer. See instructions at right on rolling the butter into a log and storing.

8	tablespoons unsalted butter, softened
2	scallions, minced
2	tablespoons minced fresh tarragon
4	teaspoons fresh lime juice
	Salt and ground black pepper

Beat butter with large fork in medium bowl until light and fluffy. Mix in scallions, tarragon, and lime juice until combined; season with salt and pepper to taste. Dollop 1 tablespoon butter per portion of fish, poultry, or meat and serve.

Garlic–Herb Butter

MAKES ENOUGH FOR 8 SERVINGS OF
MEAT, POULTRY, OR FISH

Leftovers can be stored in the freezer. See instructions at right on rolling the butter into a log and storing.

8	tablespoons unsalted butter, softened
2	garlic cloves, minced
2	tablespoons minced fresh sage
1	tablespoon minced fresh parsley
1	tablespoon minced fresh thyme
	Salt and ground black pepper

Beat butter with large fork in medium bowl until light and fluffy. Mix in garlic and herbs until combined; season with salt and pepper to taste. Dollop 1 tablespoon butter per portion of fish, poultry, or meat and serve.

PREPARING COMPOUND BUTTER FOR THE FREEZER

1. Place the compound butter on top of a piece of waxed paper.

2. Roll the butter into a long, narrow cylinder. Transfer the paper-wrapped cylinder to a zipper-lock plastic bag and freeze.

3. When you need it, take the butter out of the freezer, unwrap it, and cut off rounds about ½ inch thick. Place the rounds on top of freshly cooked hot foods and let them melt as you carry plates to the table.

Parsley-Caper Butter

MAKES ENOUGH FOR 8 SERVINGS OF
MEAT, POULTRY, OR FISH

Leftovers can be stored in the freezer. See page 216 for instructions on rolling the butter into a log and storing.

8	tablespoons unsalted butter, softened
1/4	cup minced fresh parsley
4	teaspoons grated lemon zest
4	teaspoons capers, rinsed and minced
	Salt and ground black pepper

Beat butter with large fork in medium bowl until light and fluffy. Mix in parsley, lemon zest, and capers; season with salt and pepper to taste. Dollop 1 tablespoon butter per portion of fish, poultry, or meat and serve.

Blue Cheese Butter

MAKES ENOUGH FOR 8 SERVINGS OF
MEAT, POULTRY, OR FISH

Leftovers can be stored in the freezer. See page 216 for instructions on rolling the butter into a log and storing.

8	tablespoons unsalted butter, softened
1/2	cup crumbled blue cheese
2	teaspoons brandy
	Salt and ground black pepper

Beat butter with large fork in medium bowl until light and fluffy. Mix in cheese and brandy until combined; season with salt and pepper to taste. Dollop 1 generous tablespoon butter per portion of fish, poultry, or meat and serve.

Rosemary-Parmesan Butter

MAKES ENOUGH FOR 8 SERVINGS OF
MEAT, POULTRY, OR FISH

Leftovers can be stored in the freezer. See page 216 for instructions on rolling the butter into a log and storing.

8	tablespoons unsalted butter, softened
6	tablespoons grated Parmesan cheese
4	teaspoons minced fresh rosemary
2	garlic cloves, minced
1/4	teaspoon red pepper flakes
	Salt and ground black pepper

Beat butter with large fork in medium bowl until light and fluffy. Mix in cheese, rosemary, garlic, and red pepper flakes until combined; season with salt and pepper to taste. Dollop 1 generous tablespoon butter per portion of fish, poultry, or meat and serve.

Tapenade Butter

MAKES ENOUGH FOR 8 SERVINGS OF
MEAT, POULTRY, OR FISH

Leftovers can be stored in the freezer. See page 216 for instructions on rolling the butter into a log and storing.

8	tablespoons unsalted butter, softened
10	oil-cured black olives, pitted and chopped fine
2	teaspoons minced fresh thyme
2	garlic cloves, minced
1	anchovy fillet, rinsed and minced
1	tablespoon brandy
1/4	teaspoon grated fresh orange zest
	Salt and ground black pepper

Beat butter with large fork in medium bowl until light and fluffy. Mix in chopped olives, thyme, garlic, anchovy, brandy, and orange zest until combined; season with salt and pepper to taste. Dollop 1 generous tablespoon butter per portion of fish, poultry, or meat and serve.

Anchovy-Garlic Butter

MAKES ENOUGH FOR 8 SERVINGS OF
MEAT, POULTRY, OR FISH

Leftovers can be stored in the freezer. See page 216 for instructions on rolling the butter into a log and storing.

8	tablespoons unsalted butter, softened
1/4	cup minced fresh parsley
2	garlic cloves, minced
2	anchovy fillets, rinsed and minced
1	tablespoon fresh lemon juice
	Salt and ground black pepper

Beat butter with large fork in medium bowl until light and fluffy. Mix in parsley, garlic, anchovies, and lemon juice until combined; season with salt and pepper to taste. Dollop 1 tablespoon butter per portion of fish, poultry, or meat and serve.

Mustard-Garlic Butter

MAKES ENOUGH FOR 8 SERVINGS OF
MEAT, POULTRY, OR FISH

Leftovers can be stored in the freezer. See page 216 for instructions on rolling the butter into a log and storing.

8   tablespoons unsalted butter, softened
¼   cup Dijon mustard
4   garlic cloves, minced
4   teaspoons minced fresh thyme
    Salt and ground black pepper

Beat butter with large fork in medium bowl until light and fluffy. Mix in mustard, garlic, and thyme until combined; season with salt and pepper to taste. Dollop 1 generous tablespoon butter per portion of fish, poultry, or meat and serve.

Chipotle-Cilantro Butter

MAKES ENOUGH FOR 8 SERVINGS OF
MEAT, POULTRY, OR FISH

Leftovers can be stored in the freezer. See page 216 for instructions on rolling the butter into a log and storing.

8   tablespoons unsalted butter, softened
5   teaspoons minced chipotle chiles in
    adobo sauce
4   teaspoons minced fresh cilantro
2   garlic cloves, minced
2   teaspoons honey
2   teaspoons grated fresh lime zest
    Salt and ground black pepper

Beat butter with large fork in medium bowl until light and fluffy. Mix in chipotle, cilantro, garlic, honey, and lime zest until combined; season with salt and pepper to taste. Dollop 1 tablespoon butter per portion of fish, poultry, or meat and serve.

PAN-SEARED SCALLOPS

SCALLOPS ARE A TERRIFIC CHOICE FOR THE busy cook. Naturally rich and sweet, scallops require little embellishment beyond a squeeze of lemon. We've found pan searing to be the ideal cooking method for scallops because the method caramelizes the exterior to a concentrated, nutty-flavored brown-and-tan crust. This crust greatly enhances the natural sweetness of the scallops and provides a nice, crisp contrast with the tender interior.

But achieving a browned crust without overcooking the interior can be tricky. We uncovered a few basic rules. By law, processed scallops must be identified at the wholesale level so ask your fishmonger. You can also simply look at the scallops. Scallops are naturally ivory or pinkish tan; processing turns them bright white. Processed scallops are slippery and swollen and usually sitting in a milky white liquid at the store. Unprocessed scallops (also called dry scallops) are sticky and flabby. If they are surrounded by any liquid (often they are not), the juices are clear, not white.

Next we found that a nonstick 12-inch skillet was a must. But even in a 12-inch skillet, 1½ pounds of scallops must be cooked in two batches, or they will steam instead of sear. We needed to develop a technique that neither overcooked the scallops nor let half of them turn cold while the other half finished cooking. To prevent overcooking, we seared the first batch of scallops on one side and then removed them from the pan. We then cooked the second batch of scallops on one

REMOVING TENDONS FROM SCALLOPS

The small crescent-shaped muscle that is sometimes attached to the scallop will be incredibly tough when cooked. Use your fingers to peel this muscle away from the side of each scallop before cooking.

side and then returned the first batch of scallops to the pan to finish cooking alongside them. This worked like a charm.

To preserve the creamy texture of the flesh, we cooked the scallops to medium-rare, which means the scallop is hot all the way through but the center still retains some translucence. As a scallop cooks, the soft flesh firms and you can see an opaqueness that starts at the bottom of the scallop, where it sits in the pan, and slowly creeps up toward the center. The scallop is medium-rare when the sides have firmed up and all but about the middle third of the scallop has turned opaque.

Simple Pan-Seared Sea Scallops

SERVES 4

Be sure to remove the small crescent-shaped muscle that is sometimes attached to the scallops. It will turn rubbery when cooked. Serve the scallops right away because they will cool off quickly.

1½   pounds sea scallops (16 to 20 large)
      Salt and ground black pepper
4   tablespoons vegetable oil
1   lemon, cut into wedges (for serving)

1. **SEASON AND DRY SCALLOPS:** Lay scallops out over dish towel–lined plate and season with salt and pepper. Press single layer of paper towel flush to surface of scallops and set aside.

2. **SEAR HALF OF SCALLOPS:** Heat 2 tablespoons of oil in 12-inch nonstick skillet over high heat until just smoking. Add half of scallops to skillet and brown well on one side, 1 to 2 minutes (when last scallop is added to pan, first few scallops will be close to done). Transfer scallops to plate, browned side up, and set aside.

3. **SEAR REMAINING SCALLOPS:** Wipe out skillet with wad of paper towels. Add remaining 2 tablespoons oil and return to high heat until just smoking. Add remaining scallops and brown well on one side, 1 to 2 minutes.

4. **COOK ALL SCALLOPS THROUGH TOGETHER:** Reduce heat to medium. Flip second batch of scallops over and return first batch of scallops to skillet, browned side up. Continue to cook until sides of scallops have firmed up and all but middle third of scallop is opaque, 30 to 60 seconds longer. Transfer all scallops to individual plates or serving platter. Serve immediately with lemon wedges.

PAN-SEARED SHRIMP

HAVING PREPARED LITERALLY TONS OF SHRIMP in the test kitchen and in our own home kitchens, we have found that pan searing produces the ultimate combination of a well-caramelized exterior and a moist, tender interior. If executed properly, this cooking method also preserves the shrimp's plumpness and trademark briny sweetness.

That being said, a good recipe for pan-seared shrimp is hard to find. Of the handful of recipes we uncovered, the majority resulted in shrimp that were variously dry, flavorless, pale, tough, or gummy—hardly appetizing. It was time to start some serious testing.

We quickly uncovered a few basic rules. First, tasters unanimously favored shrimp that were peeled before being cooked. Peeled shrimp are easier to eat, and unpeeled shrimp fail to pick up the delicious caramelized flavor that pan searing provides. Second, the shrimp were best cooked in a 12-inch skillet; its large surface area kept the shrimp from overcrowding the pan and steaming—a surefire way to prevent caramelization. Third, oil was the ideal cooking medium, favored over both a dry pan (which made the shrimp leathery and metallic-tasting) and butter (which tended to burn).

Next, when pan-searing the shrimp, we found that in the time it took to get the shrimp to brown, they turned out tough and overcooked. Looking for another way to promote browning, we thought to add a pinch of sugar to the shrimp. Not only did the sugar caramelize into a nice brown crust, it also accentuated the shrimp's natural sweetness, nicely setting off its inherent sea-saltiness.

Even in a 12-inch skillet, 1½ pounds of shrimp must be cooked in two batches, or they will steam instead of sear. The trick was to develop a technique that neither overcooked the shrimp nor let half of them turn cold while the other half finished cooking. To prevent overcooking, we tried searing the shrimp on one side, removing the pan from the flame, and then allowing the residual heat to finish cooking the other side of the shrimp. This worked like a charm. Better yet, the residual heat solved the cold shrimp problem. As soon as the second batch finished cooking (the first batch was now near room temperature), we tossed the first batch back into the pan, covered it, and let the residual heat work its magic once again. After about a minute, all of the shrimp were both perfectly cooked and piping hot.

Now all we needed were a few ideas for some quick sauces. Unlike scallops, which have a rich, distinct flavor, shrimp are milder and benefit from additional flavoring. A parsley-lemon butter perfectly complemented the sweet, briny shrimp. And we came up with two glazes made with assertive ingredients: one made with ginger and hoisin and another with chipotle chiles and lime—each are a perfect foil to the shrimp's richness.

Pan-Seared Shrimp with Parsley-Lemon Butter

SERVES 4

Either a nonstick or traditional skillet will work for this recipe, but a nonstick skillet will simplify cleanup. Serve with steamed rice or couscous.

2	tablespoons unsalted butter, softened
1	tablespoon fresh lemon juice
1	tablespoon minced fresh parsley
1½	pounds extra-large (21/25) shrimp, peeled and deveined
	Salt and ground black pepper
⅛	teaspoon sugar
2	tablespoons vegetable oil

1. MAKE FLAVORED BUTTER: Mix butter, lemon juice, and parsley together, and set aside. Pat shrimp dry with paper towels and season with ¼ teaspoon salt, ¼ teaspoon pepper, and sugar.

2. SEAR HALF OF SHRIMP: Heat 1 tablespoon of oil in 12-inch nonstick skillet over high heat until smoking. Add half of shrimp to pan in single layer and cook until spotty brown and just pink around the edges, about 1 minute. Off heat, use tongs to quickly flip over each shrimp and let stand until all but very center is opaque, about 30 seconds. Transfer shrimp to plate and cover with foil.

3. SEAR REMAINING SHRIMP: Add remaining tablespoon oil to skillet and return to high heat until just smoking. Sear remaining shrimp.

4. WARM SHRIMP THROUGH WITH BUTTER: After second batch has stood off heat, return first batch to skillet and toss to combine. Add butter mixture, cover, and let stand until butter melts, about 1 minute. Toss shrimp to coat and serve.

SHRIMP SIZES

Shrimp are sold by size (extra large, large, medium, and small), as well as by the number needed to make a pound, usually given in a range. Choosing shrimp by the numerical rating is more accurate than choosing by a size label, which varies from store to store. Here's how the two sizing systems generally line up.

Small	**Medium**	**Large**	**Extra-Large**
51 to 60 shrimp per pound	40 to 50 shrimp per pound	31 to 40 shrimp per pound	21 to 25 shrimp per pound

➤ VARIATIONS
Pan-Seared Shrimp with Ginger-Hoisin Glaze

Either a nonstick or traditional skillet will work for this recipe, but a nonstick skillet will simplify cleanup. Serve this Asian-style shrimp with steamed rice.

2	tablespoons hoisin sauce
1	tablespoon rice vinegar
2	teaspoons grated fresh ginger
2	teaspoons water
2	scallions, thinly sliced
1½	teaspoons soy sauce
	Pinch red pepper flakes
1½	pounds extra-large (21/25) shrimp, peeled and deveined
	Salt and ground black pepper
⅛	teaspoon sugar
2	tablespoons vegetable oil

1. MAKE GLAZE AND SEASON SHRIMP: Whisk together hoisin sauce, rice vinegar, ginger, water, scallions, soy sauce, and red pepper flakes in a small bowl and set aside. Pat shrimp dry with paper towels and season with ¼ teaspoon salt, ¼ teaspoon pepper, and sugar.

2. SEAR HALF OF SHRIMP: Heat 1 tablespoon of oil in 12-inch nonstick skillet over high heat until smoking. Add half of shrimp to pan in single layer and cook until spotty brown and just pink around the edges, about 1 minute. Off heat, use tongs to quickly flip over each shrimp and let stand until all but very center is opaque, about 30 seconds. Transfer shrimp to plate and cover with foil.

3. SEAR REMAINING SHRIMP: Add remaining tablespoon oil to skillet and return to high heat until just smoking. Sear remaining shrimp.

4. WARM SHRIMP THROUGH WITH GLAZE: After second batch has stood off heat, return first batch to skillet and toss to combine. Add glaze, cover, and let stand to warm through glaze, about 1 minute. Toss shrimp again to coat and serve.

Pan-Seared Shrimp with Chipotle-Lime Glaze

Either a nonstick or traditional skillet will work for this recipe, but a nonstick skillet will simplify cleanup. Serve this spicy shrimp with rice or warm corn tortillas.

2	tablespoons fresh lime juice
2	tablespoons chopped fresh cilantro
1	tablespoon minced chipotle chile in adobo sauce, plus 2 teaspoons adobo sauce
4	teaspoons brown sugar
1½	pounds extra-large (21/25) shrimp, peeled and deveined
	Salt and ground black pepper
⅛	teaspoon sugar
2	tablespoons vegetable oil

1. MAKE GLAZE AND SEASON SHRIMP: Whisk together lime juice, cilantro, chipotle chile and adobo sauce, and brown sugar in small bowl and set aside. Pat shrimp dry with paper towels and season with ¼ teaspoon salt, ¼ teaspoon pepper, and sugar.

2. SEAR HALF OF SHRIMP: Heat 1 tablespoon of oil in 12-inch nonstick skillet over high heat until smoking. Add half of shrimp to pan in single layer and cook until spotty brown and just pink around the edges, about 1 minute. Off heat, use tongs to quickly flip over each shrimp and let stand until all but very center is opaque, about 30 seconds. Transfer shrimp to plate and cover with foil.

3. SEAR REMAINING SHRIMP: Add remaining tablespoon oil to skillet and return to high heat until just smoking. Sear remaining shrimp.

4. WARM SHRIMP THROUGH WITH GLAZE: After second batch has stood off heat, return first batch to skillet and toss to combine. Add glaze, cover, and let stand to warm through glaze, about 1 minute. Toss shrimp again to coat and serve.

EASIER STEAMED VEGETABLES

COOKING FRESH VEGETABLES FOR A SIDE dish while the rest of dinner is in the works can be a serious hassle in terms of timing. We wanted to come up with an easy, versatile method that could be done either at the last minute (no waiting for quarts of water to come to a boil), or up to 30 minutes ahead of time. Our answer was found in using a 12-inch skillet. The skillet's wide bottom allows for small amounts of water to come to a boil quickly, and when covered with a lid, the skillet of boiling water turns into a steaming vessel. The other benefit of the skillet is its shape—the wide bottom makes it easy to spread the vegetables in a single layer for more even cooking, while the short sides makes the vegetables more accessible for checking their doneness. Using just ½ cup of water, we found that we could cook a wide variety of vegetables until they were perfectly crisp-tender, in as little as seven minutes.

If you want to get the vegetables out of the way ahead of time, we found you can simply undercook them in the skillet by a few minutes and then hold them in a 200-degree oven. They will hold beautifully for about 30 minutes, leaving time to focus on the rest of the meal. As an added time saver, you can just wipe out the same skillet and use it for cooking the rest of your meal.

Skillet Steamed Vegetables

Bring ½ cup water to boil in a 12-inch skillet over high heat. Add vegetables, cover, and cook for time listed in chart. If holding the vegetables, transfer them to an ovenproof bowl, cover with foil, and hold in a 200-degree oven until needed—no longer than 30 minutes. To serve, drain water and toss with 1 to 2 tablespoons butter or extra-virgin olive oil. For more flavoring ideas, see below. Season with salt and pepper to taste before serving.

STEAMING VEGETABLES		
VEGETABLE	IF SERVING IMMEDIATELY, COOK FOR	IF HOLDING IN 200-DEGREE OVEN, COOK FOR
Green Beans, stem ends trimmed	4 to 5 minutes	2 to 4 minutes
Asparagus, tough ends snapped off and discarded	5 to 7 minutes	3 to 5 minutes
Cauliflower, cored and florets cut into 1-inch pieces	5 to 7 minutes	3 to 5 minutes
Broccoli, florets cut into 1 to 1½-inch pieces and stalks peeled and cut into ¼-inch pieces	5 to 7 minutes	3 to 5 minutes
Baby Carrots	7 to 9 minutes	5 to 7 minutes
Brussels Sprouts, stem ends trimmed, discolored leaves removed, and halved through the stem	7 to 9 minutes	5 to 7 minutes

ADDING FLAVOR TO STEAMED VEGETABLES

Here are a few easy and quick ways to add more flavor to steamed vegetables before serving:

- Dot with a compound butter (pages 216–218) and toss to coat.
- Toss with a vinaigrette (pages 20–22).
- Toss with butter (or extra-virgin olive oil) and fresh lemon juice.
- Sprinkle with toasted sesame seeds, soy sauce, and toasted sesame oil.

10

HOT FROM THE OVEN

HOT FROM THE OVEN

"STUFFED" CHICKEN BREASTS   227
   Un-Stuffed Chicken Breasts with Dijon, Ham, and Gruyère
   Un-Stuffed Chicken Breasts with Prosciutto, Sage, and Porcini

CHICKEN PIZZAIOLA   229
   Chicken Pizzaiola with Mozzarella and Pepperoni
   Chicken Pizzaiola With Provolone and Capicola

OVEN-BARBECUED CHICKEN   230
   Fast Oven-Barbecued Chicken

PAN-ROASTED CHICKEN   231
   Pan-Roasted Chicken Parts with Lemon-Thyme Jus
   Pan-Roasted Chicken Parts with Apricot-Ginger Glaze
   Pan-Roasted Chicken Parts with Chipotle-Orange Glaze

MEATLOAF   234
   All-American Mini Meatloaves
   Southwestern Mini Meatloaves

BREADED PORK CHOPS   236
   Quick and Crunchy Breaded Pork Chops
   Quick and Crunchy Sesame Pork Chops

PAN-ROASTED GLAZED PORK TENDERLOIN   238
   Pan-Roasted Pork Tenderloin with Mustard-Maple Glaze
   Pan-Roasted Pork Tenderloin with Tart Cherry Glaze
   Pan-Roasted Pork Tenderloin with Chipotle-Orange Glaze

GLAZED SALMON   240
   Broiled Maple-Soy Glazed Salmon Fillets with Toasted Sesame Seeds
   Broiled Mustard and Brown Sugar Glazed Salmon Fillets with Dill
   Broiled Honey-Lime Glazed Salmon Fillets with Scallions

CRUNCHY BAKED COD   242
   Fast and Crunchy Baked Cod
   Fast and Crunchy Baked Cod with Capers, Tarragon, and Potato Chips
   Fast and Crunchy Baked Cod with Horseradish, Garlic, and Bread Crumbs

BAKED SOLE FLORENTINE 243
Streamlined Sole Florentine

OTHER RECIPES IN THIS CHAPTER

FOR MANY OF US, THE PROSPECT OF PULLING A great dinner out of our oven on a weeknight seems on par with pulling a rabbit out of a hat—virtually impossible. While the latter is done with sleight of hand, we had to come up with our own tricks to make magic in the kitchen. To begin with, we knew we'd have to use a very hot oven in order to get dinner on the table in 30 minutes or less. But we also had to go even further. To that end, we borrowed a technique often used in restaurants: starting our dishes on the stovetop and then finishing them in a hot oven. This two-fold approach gave our dishes a much-needed jump start. Instead of hitting the oven stone cold, the pre-browned meats now went into the oven already piping hot and, in many cases, in a pan that was also hot.

This technique had added benefits, as well. Stovetop browning not only adds flavor to meat, but also yields flavorful bits in the skillet (called fond) to build a no-fuss sauce. In the case of our inside-out take on stuffed chicken breasts, a flavorful sauce virtually makes itself while the dish bakes in the oven. And no-cook glazes for our pan-roasted pork tenderloin can be effortlessly stirred together while the meat is in the oven.

We were surprised at the success we had with some of the dishes in this chapter. Who would have thought you could serve meatloaf on a weeknight—without leaving work early? Our answer was to divide and conquer. We made mini meatloaves that are started in a skillet to get the characteristic browned crust and then finished them in a hot oven to caramelize the sweet glaze. Sole Florentine, typically a company-worthy (read time-consuming) dish, can be on the table in 30 minutes by taking just a few simple shortcuts. Frozen chopped spinach allowed us to skip the fussy cleaning and cooking of fresh spinach, and a tasty cornstarch-thickened white wine sauce replaced the longer cooking roux-based sauce the dish typically requires.

To round out the main courses in this chapter, you'll find easy side dishes—pan-roasted asparagus, skillet green beans, and glazed carrots—sprinkled throughout. These recipes are so simple and quick that they can easily be pulled together while the main course is in the oven, and all of them can be dressed up with minimal effort.

There are a few things to keep in mind to ensure that recipes will be done within the 30-minute time limit. First, preheating your oven is essential (see "A Note on Preheating Your Oven" below). We also found it important to choose cuts of poultry, meat, or fish that are of equal size (and thickness), so that they all finish cooking at the same time. It also pays to be mindful of size overall. These days, some supermarkets are carrying pork tenderloins that are upwards of 1½ pounds, and those just won't cook in the time given—so pay attention to the sizes specified in each recipe and shop accordingly.

Organization is crucial here, too. Try to have all of your ingredients and utensils within arm's reach before you begin so there will be no last-minute running around for the salt and pepper, whisk, tongs, or potholders. And on matters of safety, please take note: Obviously, skillets will be scorching hot when they come out of the oven and reaching for a potholder to remove a hot pan may be second nature. That said, you may forget where that skillet has been once it's on the stovetop and you've turned your attention to side dishes. We like to wrap (or hang) a potholder or dish towel over the handle of the pan to remind us of the hot handle—just in case.

A NOTE ON PREHEATING YOUR OVEN

With the oven being the focal point of this chapter, there are a few things you will need to remember to ensure success. First, preheating the oven is essential. Most ovens need at least 15 minutes to heat fully, so plan accordingly. (If you don't heat your oven fully, your food will require more time in the oven and will likely turn out dry and overcooked.) Also, position the racks in the oven as directed to ensure even browning. It's also a good idea to have your oven equipped with a thermometer to ensure reliable cooking temperatures, and therefore, times.

"Stuffed" Chicken Breasts

MAKING STUFFED CHICKEN BREASTS IS A nice way to dress up chicken, but the laborious preparation makes them an unlikely candidate for a 30-minute meal. Typically, the chicken needs to be pounded thin, stuffed, and then rolled. Many stuffed chicken breasts are also breaded and fried, a concept that we like—but again, too time-consuming. And some recipes we found also require a sauce to serve with the chicken. To make the whole process more efficient, we decided to streamline the steps. Instead of stuffing the chicken breasts, we decided to top the breasts with the stuffing—an inside-out approach.

We started with boneless, skinless chicken breasts—no pounding required. We lightly browned them in a skillet on one side and turned to the topping. The classic combination of Dijon mustard, thin-sliced ham, and shredded Gruyère cheese came to mind. We first tried slices of Gruyère, but they tended to slide off the chicken—shredded cheese adhered better. To assemble our toppings, we brushed the browned chicken with the mustard, over which we layered the ham and cheese. We then mounded crushed buttery cracker crumbs on top and pressed down to help them stick. The crumbs add the flavor (and illusion) of a breaded and fried stuffed chicken breast.

Next, we built a sauce for the chicken by whisking together heavy cream, white wine, and chopped fresh dill. We carefully poured the mixture into the skillet around the chicken, being careful not to disturb the crumbs. We then set the skillet over medium-high heat and brought the sauce to a simmer. To finish, we transferred the skillet back to the oven to cook the chicken through, heat the topping, and thicken the sauce.

We tested oven temperatures ranging from 400 to 475 and quickly discovered that the higher oven temperature of 475 was best. Initially, we were concerned that the chicken would dry out at such a high temperature, but the sauce served to keep the chicken moist and tender, bubbling down to the perfect consistency by the time the chicken

had cooked through. For a variation, we incorporated Italian flavors, swapping in prosciutto and sharp provolone for the ham and Gruyère and flavoring the sauce with dried porcini mushrooms and fresh sage.

Un-Stuffed Chicken Breasts with Dijon, Ham, and Gruyère
SERVES 4

If the sauce becomes too thick, thin it to the desired consistency with hot low-sodium chicken broth or hot water before serving.

4	boneless, skinless chicken breasts
	Salt and ground black pepper
2	teaspoons vegetable oil
2	tablespoons Dijon mustard
4	slices baked deli ham
I	cup shredded Gruyère or Swiss cheese
15	Ritz crackers, crushed coarse (¾ cup)
I	cup heavy cream
½	cup dry white wine
I	tablespoon minced fresh dill or parsley

MAKING THE MINUTES COUNT:
While the chicken is browning, shred the cheese and crush the crackers.

I. HEAT OVEN: Adjust oven rack to upper-middle position and heat oven to 475 degrees.

2. SEASON AND BROWN CHICKEN: Pat chicken dry with paper towels and season with salt and pepper. Heat oil in 12-inch nonstick skillet over medium-high heat until just smoking. Brown chicken lightly on one side, about 3 minutes.

3. TOP CHICKEN AND BAKE: Off heat, turn chicken over. Spread 1 teaspoon of mustard over each breast, then lay 1 slice ham on top. Mound ¼

TEST KITCHEN TIP:
No-Slide Cheese
Don't be tempted to use slices of cheese. Mounding shredded cheese on top of the chicken ensures that the cheese adheres to the chicken and will not slide off as it melts.

cup of cheese over ham. Sprinkle cracker crumbs over cheese and press on crumbs to adhere.

4. ADD CREAM MIXTURE, BRING TO SIMMER, AND BAKE: Whisk cream, wine, and dill together in 2-cup liquid measuring cup and pour into skillet around chicken, without disturbing crumbs. Return skillet to medium-high heat and bring to simmer. Immediately transfer to oven. Bake until thickest part of chicken breast registers 160 degrees on instant-read thermometer, 12 to 15 minutes.

5. FINISH SAUCE: Transfer chicken to individual plates. Whisk remaining 2 teaspoons mustard into sauce and season with salt and pepper to taste. Spoon sauce over chicken and serve.

TEST KITCHEN TIP:

Quick Crunchy Toppings

Crushed crackers and chips are often the quickest way to give a casserole or other food a flavorful crunchy topping. Some of the toasts (such as Melba) turned out to be our preferred crumb for oven-fried foods (as in our Quick and Crunchy Breaded Pork Chops, page 237). For some dishes, we like to use fattier crackers and sturdier chips, each adding their distinct flavor to the dish (such as Ritz crackers on un-stuffed chicken breasts, and kettle potato chips over Fast and Crunchy Baked Cod, page 242). Be sure to take the salt level of these products into consideration and adjust seasoning accordingly.

~≈
Un-Stuffed Chicken Breasts with Prosciutto, Sage, and Porcini
SERVES 4

There is no need to rehydrate the porcini mushrooms here because they will soften in the oven. If the sauce becomes too thick, thin it with hot low-sodium chicken broth or hot water before serving.

4	boneless, skinless chicken breasts
	Salt and ground black pepper
2	teaspoons vegetable oil
4	slices prosciutto
I	cup shredded sharp provolone cheese
15	Ritz crackers, crushed coarse (¾ cup)
I	cup heavy cream
½	cup dry white wine
¼	ounce dried porcini mushrooms, rinsed and chopped fine
I	tablespoon minced fresh sage

MAKING THE MINUTES COUNT:
While the chicken is browning, shred the cheese and crush the crackers.

1. HEAT OVEN: Adjust oven rack to upper-middle position and heat oven to 475 degrees.

2. SEASON AND BROWN CHICKEN: Pat chicken dry with paper towels and season with salt and pepper. Heat oil in 12-inch nonstick skillet over medium-high heat until just smoking. Brown chicken lightly on one side, about 3 minutes.

3. TOP CHICKEN AND BAKE: Off heat, turn chicken over. Lay 1 slice prosciutto over each breast, then top with ¼ cup of cheese. Sprinkle cracker crumbs over cheese and press on crumbs to adhere.

4. ADD CREAM MIXTURE, BRING TO SIMMER, AND BAKE: Whisk cream, wine, porcini, and sage together in 2-cup liquid measuring cup and pour into skillet around chicken, without disturbing crumbs. Return skillet to medium-high heat and bring to simmer. Immediately transfer to oven. Bake until thickest part of breast registers 160 degrees on instant-read thermometer, 12 to 15 minutes. Spoon sauce over chicken and serve.

CHICKEN PIZZAIOLA

CHICKEN PIZZAIOLA IS AKIN TO A CRUST-LESS chicken pizza. It combines the ease and simplicity of baked chicken breasts with toppings that would typically be found on the menu of your favorite pizzeria. In lieu of browning chicken breasts in a skillet, we found we could save time without sacrificing flavor by simply baking them in a cheesy coating.

We began by spreading tomato sauce in the bottom of a baking dish. We coated boneless, skinless chicken breasts with grated Parmesan cheese and placed them in the sauce. (The sauce seasons the chicken and helps prevent it from drying out.) Then we topped the chicken with mozzarella and sliced pepperoni and slid the dish into the oven to bake. Unfortunately, by the time the chicken was cooked through, the mozzarella had overbrowned and the pepperoni had curled and dried up. We took a step back and decided the toppings needed to spend less time in the oven.

For our next try, we partially baked the Parmesan-coated chicken. We then added the toppings and returned the dish to the oven for the chicken to cook through. This did the trick: the chicken was flavorful and moist, the cheese was melted and gooey, and the pepperoni was heated through but not dry. We also include a variation with spicy capicola (an Italian-style ham) along with provolone cheese. This is a family-friendly recipe that can accommodate your favorite pizza toppings like cooked crumbled sausage, sautéed peppers, onions, or mushrooms, or sliced olives.

TEST KITCHEN TIP:

Temp Your Chicken

We've all had boneless chicken breasts that are over-cooked, dry, and chewy. We depend on an instant-read thermometer inserted into the thickest portion of the breast to eliminate any guesswork. Breasts cooked to 160 degrees will be perfect every time.

Chicken Pizzaiola with Mozzarella and Pepperoni

SERVES 4

You will need one 24- to 26-ounce jar of tomato sauce for this recipe (or substitute 3 cups of 20-Minute Tomato Sauce, page 157). Almost any of your favorite pizza toppings can be substituted for the pepperoni. This dish is great served over pasta or with a salad and a loaf of crusty bread.

3	cups tomato sauce (see note)
1	cup grated Parmesan cheese
4	boneless, skinless chicken breasts
	Salt and ground black pepper
1	cup shredded mozzarella cheese
20	slices pepperoni (2 ounces)

1. HEAT OVEN AND PREPARE BAKING DISH: Adjust oven rack to middle position and heat oven to 450 degrees. Spread tomato sauce into 13 by 9-inch baking dish.

2. COAT CHICKEN WITH PARMESAN: Spread Parmesan into shallow dish. Pat chicken dry with paper towels and season with salt and pepper. Working with one breast at a time, dredge in Parmesan. Press on Parmesan to make sure it adheres. Lay chicken in baking dish, smooth side facing up.

3. BAKE CHICKEN: Place chicken in oven and bake 15 minutes.

4. INCREASE OVEN TEMPERATURE, ADD TOPPINGS, AND FINISH: Increase oven temperature to 475 degrees. Mound ¼ cup of mozzarella on top of each chicken breast, then shingle 5 slices pepperoni over cheese. Continue to bake until cheese melts and until thickest part of breast registers 160 degrees on instant-read thermometer, 5 to 7 minutes. Serve.

VARIATION

Chicken Pizzaiola With Provolone and Capicola

Capicola is an Italian-style, thin-sliced spicy deli ham found in most supermarkets.

Substitute 1 cup shredded sharp provolone for mozzarella and 4 slices capicola for pepperoni.

PAN-ROASTED ASPARAGUS
SERVES 4 TO 6

This recipe works best with asparagus that is at least ½ inch thick near the base. Do not use pencil-thin asparagus because it cannot withstand the heat and will overcook too easily.

I	tablespoon olive oil
I	tablespoon unsalted butter
2	pounds thick asparagus, trimmed (see page 58)
	Salt and ground black pepper
½	lemon

I. MELT BUTTER AND ADD ASPARAGUS: Heat oil and butter in 12-inch skillet over medium-high heat. When butter has melted, add half of asparagus to skillet with tips pointed in one direction and remaining spears with tips pointed in opposite direction. Using tongs, distribute spears in even layer (spears will not quite fit into single layer).

2. COOK ASPARAGUS COVERED: Cover and cook until spears are bright green and still crisp, about 5 minutes.

3. COOK ASPARAGUS UNCOVERED: Uncover, increase heat to high, and continue to cook until spears are tender and well browned along one side, 5 to 7 minutes, using tongs to move spears from center of pan to edge of pan to ensure all are browned.

4. FINISH: Transfer asparagus to serving dish, season with salt and pepper to taste, and squeeze lemon half over spears.

➤ VARIATION

Pan-Roasted Asparagus with Toasted Garlic and Parmesan

Before cooking asparagus in step 1, cook 3 sliced garlic cloves with 2 tablespoons olive oil over medium heat until crisp and golden, about 5 minutes. Transfer garlic to paper towel–lined plate and proceed with step 1, adding butter to oil left in skillet. Sprinkle toasted garlic and 2 tablespoons grated Parmesan cheese over asparagus before serving.

OVEN-BARBECUED CHICKEN

OVEN-BARBECUED CHICKEN IS RARELY AS well flavored as the grilled version. For oven-barbecued chicken, chicken parts are usually slathered with barbecue sauce and baked. The recipes we tried that followed this method were lackluster at best. Skin-on parts became flabby and the sauce sometimes slid off the chicken and burned. We knew we could do better. We aimed to develop a quick recipe for well-seasoned chicken in a tangy barbecue sauce.

To crisp the skin, we tried browning the chicken first in a skillet. No matter how crispy we got the skin, it turned flabby once we brushed on the barbecue sauce and finished cooking the chicken. We decided to abandon skin-on chicken parts and go with the more convenient boneless, skinless chicken breasts.

To begin, we browned the chicken in a skillet on the stovetop. We removed the chicken from the skillet, leaving behind the flavorful browned bits (called fond) to flavor our barbecue sauce. (While many quick recipes for oven-barbecued chicken rely on store-bought barbecue sauce, we wanted to develop a tasty and quick homemade sauce.) Relying strictly on pantry ingredients, we whisked together ketchup, cider vinegar, molasses, grated onion, Worcestershire sauce, Dijon mustard, maple syrup, chili powder, and cayenne and added the mixture to the pan to simmer together and thicken. We then returned the chicken to the skillet to bake it through in the oven.

We tested high oven temperatures of 450 and 475 degrees, but were unhappy with the results—the chicken was not as flavorful as we'd hoped. We switched to a more moderate, 325-degree oven and found that the chicken had a longer period of time to simmer in the sauce and soak up the rich barbecue flavor. Once the chicken reached 130 degrees, we switched the oven temperature to broil to mimic the intense heat of the grill. Under the high heat of the broiler, the sugars in the barbecue sauce caramelized for that characteristic slightly charred exterior that clung perfectly to the chicken. When the chicken reached 160 degrees, it was perfectly done—as moist and flavorful as we'd anticipated.

⤚ Fast Oven-Barbecued Chicken
SERVES 4

Real maple syrup is preferable to imitation syrup for the sauce, and mild or original molasses is preferable to the darker kind.

4	boneless, skinless chicken breasts
	Salt and ground black pepper
I	tablespoon vegetable oil
I	cup ketchup
3	tablespoons cider vinegar
3	tablespoons mild molasses
2	tablespoons grated onion
2	tablespoons Worcestershire sauce
2	tablespoons Dijon mustard
2	tablespoons pure maple syrup
I	teaspoon chili powder
¼	teaspoon cayenne

MAKING THE MINUTES COUNT:
Whisk together the sauce ingredients while the chicken browns.

I. HEAT OVEN: Adjust oven rack 6 inches from broiler element and heat oven to 325 degrees.

2. SEASON AND BROWN CHICKEN: Pat chicken dry with paper towels and season with salt and pepper. Heat oil in 12-inch nonstick skillet over medium-high heat until just smoking. Brown chicken lightly on both sides, about 5 minutes total. Transfer chicken to plate.

3. MAKE SAUCE: Whisk ketchup, vinegar, molasses, onion, Worcestershire, mustard, maple syrup, chili powder, and cayenne together. Discard any oil left in skillet and add sauce mixture. Return skillet to medium heat and cook, scraping up any browned bits, until sauce is thick and glossy and spatula leaves clear trail in sauce, about 4 minutes.

4. BAKE CHICKEN WITH SAUCE: Off heat, return chicken to skillet, discarding any accumulated chicken juices, and coat chicken well with sauce. Turn chicken smooth-side up and spoon extra sauce over top to create thick coating. Bake until thickest part of breast registers 130 degrees on instant-read thermometer, about 10 minutes.

5. BROIL CHICKEN: Turn oven to broil and continue to cook until thickest part of breast registers 160 degrees on instant-read thermometer, about 5 minutes. Transfer chicken to platter and transfer remaining sauce to small bowl. Season extra sauce with salt and pepper to taste and serve, passing sauce separately.

PAN-ROASTED CHICKEN

NOTHING CAN BEAT THE COMFORTING simplicity of roast chicken. Its crisp skin and tender, juicy meat make it a perennial favorite. The problem is that a whole 3- to 4-pound chicken takes well over an hour to cook, relegating it to weekend fare. To make roast chicken accessible for a weeknight supper, we knew we had to break the chicken down into more manageable-sized pieces, and then figure out a cooking technique that would jump-start the roasting process. We turned to pan-roasting chicken parts (rather than a whole chicken), and then borrowed a restaurant technique of finishing the browned chicken in a hot oven. (We'd already fine-tuned this technique in Pan-Roasted Chicken Breasts and Potatoes on page 113).

This dual cooking method of both pan-searing and high-heat roasting gave us the crispy, golden skin we were seeking that was every bit as good as a slow-roasted whole chicken. An added bonus was the beautiful browned bits left in the skillet. While the chicken was resting, we made a quick, flavorful jus (a pan sauce made from pan juices), to pour over the chicken. (We also developed flavor variations with glazes in place of the jus). All in all, we think this technique is almost better than roasting a whole chicken. There is no messy carving to deal with before you sit down to the table, and everyone can choose the crispy, juicy parts they like the best.

Pan-Roasted Chicken Parts with Lemon-Thyme Jus

SERVES 4

Be very careful of the searing hot skillet handle in steps 4 and 5; we drape a towel or pot holder over the handle to warn others nearby (and to remind the cook) that the handle is hot. Feel free to substitute minced fresh rosemary for the thyme. If pieces of chicken are dramatically different sizes, they may need to be removed from the oven at different times—use an instant-read thermometer to check doneness. We like to cut the split breasts in half in order to speed up the cooking time, however, you can leave them whole if you prefer (the roasting time may be a bit longer).

CHICKEN

3–3½	pounds bone-in, skin-on chicken pieces such as halved split breasts, thighs, and/or drumsticks
	Salt and ground black pepper
1	teaspoon vegetable oil
6	garlic cloves, peeled and smashed

JUS

1	shallot, minced
1	cup low-sodium chicken broth
½	teaspoon minced fresh thyme
2	tablespoons unsalted butter, cut into 2 pieces and chilled
1	tablespoon fresh lemon juice

1. **HEAT OVEN:** Adjust oven rack to lowest position and heat oven to 450 degrees.

2. **SEASON AND BROWN CHICKEN:** Pat chicken parts dry with paper towels and season with salt and pepper. Heat oil in 12-inch skillet over medium-high heat until just smoking. Brown chicken well on both sides, about 10 minutes total.

3. **ROAST CHICKEN IN SKILLET:** Flip chicken parts skin-side down. Scatter smashed garlic cloves around chicken and stir to coat with oil. Transfer skillet to oven and roast chicken until thickest part of breast registers 160 degrees on instant-read thermometer and thighs or drumsticks register 175 degrees, 8 to 10 minutes.

4. **REST CHICKEN:** Remove skillet from oven. Transfer chicken parts to platter and tent with foil.

Pour off all but 1 teaspoon fat from skillet (leave garlic in skillet).

5. **MAKE JUS:** Return skillet with garlic to medium-high heat and heat until fat is shimmering. Add shallot and cook until softened, about 2 minutes. Stir in broth, thyme, and any accumulated chicken juices, scraping up any browned bits. Simmer until sauce has reduced to about ¾ cup, about 5 minutes. Turn heat to low and whisk in butter, one piece at a time. Off heat, stir in lemon juice and season with salt and pepper to taste. Serve, pouring sauce over chicken or passing separately.

EQUIPMENT: Oven Mitts

We tested nine types of oven mitts made from a variety of materials. Mitts were evaluated for heat protection, ease of manipulation while transferring pans to and from the oven and the stovetop (and while using tongs during grilling), and durability (how well they resisted structural damage and staining). The mitts are listed in order of preference.

The Best Oven Mitts:
Kool-Tek Protective Apparel
$21.95 per mitt (12 inches)
$24.95 per mitt (15 inches)
Everything we want in a mitt—except maybe the price. Mostly Nomex (heat resistant to 450 degrees) with a "racing stripe" of Kevlar (heat resistant to 1,000 degrees), the Kool-Tek won fans for its natural grip, easy dexterity, and stay-cool comfort.

Parvin Flameguard Oven Mitt
$8.40 per pair (17 inches)
A less expensive option, this mitt had almost as many fans as the winner—especially for its comfortable dexterity and "just the right amount of padding"—but some found the length "a bit cumbersome." Unlike the Kool-Tek mitt, these mitts are flammable, so use caution over open flames.

➤ VARIATIONS

Pan-Roasted Chicken Parts with Apricot-Ginger Glaze

Be very careful of the searing hot skillet handle in steps 4 and 5; we drape a towel or pot holder over the handle to warn others nearby (and to remind the cook) that the handle is hot.

- 1   shallot, minced
- 2   tablespoons grated fresh ginger
- 1   cup apricot preserves
- 1/2 cup orange juice
- 1/8 teaspoon red pepper flakes
- 1   tablespoon fresh lime juice
       Salt and ground black pepper
- 2   scallions, sliced thin

Follow recipe for Pan-Roasted Chicken Parts through step 4. Return skillet with garlic and 1 teaspoon fat to medium-high heat until fat is shimmering. Add shallot and cook until softened, about 2 minutes. Stir in ginger and cook until fragrant, about 30 seconds. Stir in apricot preserves, orange juice, red pepper flakes, and any accumulated chicken juices, scraping up any browned bits. Simmer until sauce is thickened, about 2 minutes. Off heat, stir in lime juice and season with salt and pepper to taste. Before serving, pour sauce over chicken and sprinkle with scallions.

Pan-Roasted Chicken Parts with Chipotle-Orange Glaze

Be very careful of the searing hot skillet handle in steps 4 and 5; we drape a towel or pot holder over the handle to warn others nearby (and to remind the cook) that the handle is hot.

- 1   shallot, minced
- 1   cup orange marmalade
- 1/2 cup orange juice
- 1   tablespoon minced chipotle chiles in adobo sauce
- 1   tablespoon fresh lime juice
- 1   tablespoon minced fresh cilantro
       Salt and ground black pepper
- 2   scallions, sliced thin

Follow recipe for Pan-Roasted Chicken Parts through step 4. Return skillet with garlic and 1 teaspoon fat to medium-high heat until fat is shimmering. Add shallot and cook until softened, about 2 minutes. Stir in marmalade, orange juice, chipotle, and any accumulated chicken juices, scraping up any browned bits. Simmer until thickened, about 2 minutes. Off heat, stir in lime juice and cilantro and season with salt and pepper to taste. Before serving, pour sauce over chicken and sprinkle with scallions.

TEST KITCHEN TIP:
Prepping Green Beans
To make the task of preparing green beans for cooking less tedious, try this easy technique. Line the beans up in a row and trim off the inedible stem ends with just one cut.

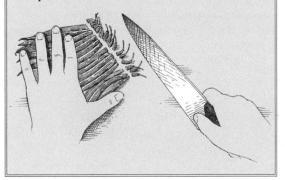

SKILLET GREEN BEANS
SERVES 4

- 1   tablespoon olive oil
- 1   shallot, minced
- 1/2 teaspoon minced fresh thyme
- 3/4 cup low-sodium chicken broth
- 1   pound green beans, trimmed
       Salt and ground black pepper

Heat oil in 12-inch skillet over medium heat until shimmering. Add shallot and cook until lightly browned, about 4 minutes. Stir in thyme and broth and add beans. Cover, reduce heat to low, and simmer until beans are tender, 15 to 20 minutes. Season with salt and pepper to taste and serve.

MEATLOAF

A GREAT MEATLOAF IS AS CLOSE TO THE definition of down-home comfort food as you can get. But who has the time to get their mother's Sunday meatloaf on the table mid-week? With the traditional loaf weighing in at over 2 pounds on average and taking over an hour to cook, we knew we'd have to make some significant changes to make this recipe work.

In terms of meatloaf ingredients, we stuck to the tried and true. For the meat, we used meatloaf mix (a combination of ground beef, pork, and veal) for best flavor and tenderness. For the binder, we liked crushed saltine crackers for their mild flavor. Milk and an egg also helped bind together the meat and added richness, moisture, and tenderness. Worcestershire sauce, Dijon mustard, garlic powder, onion powder, and fresh parsley all served to make a well-seasoned loaf.

A typical meatloaf is baked in a 9 by 5-inch loaf pan. To scale down our meatloaf to quick-cooking size, we ditched the loaf pan and made four individual loaves. First, we browned the loaves in a skillet—all four loaves fit comfortably in a 12-inch skillet. To get the familiar tangy-sweet top crust that goes with a long-baked loaf, we topped the browned loaves with a tomato–brown sugar glaze and high-roasted them at 500 degrees. With this unorthodox approach, we were able to make terrific meatloaf with great flavor in short order. Having tackled the classic version of meatloaf, we turned to one with Southwestern flavors—adding smoky chipotle chiles in adobo sauce, canned green chiles, and swapping in fresh cilantro for the parsley.

TEST KITCHEN TIP: Meatloaf Mix
When making meatloaf, it is important to use a combination of different ground meats for their various flavors and textures. Using just ground beef will make these mini meatloaves simply taste like hamburgers. Often, supermarkets will sell packages of ground "meatloaf mix" made from ground beef, pork, and veal—we prefer to use this. If you can't find meatloaf mix, substitute a combination of half 90 percent lean ground beef and half ground pork.

All-American Mini Meatloaves
SERVES 4

MEATLOAVES
17	saltine crackers, crushed fine (about ⅔ cup)
¼	cup whole milk, plus extra as needed
⅓	cup minced fresh parsley
3	tablespoons Worcestershire sauce
1	large egg
1½	tablespoons Dijon mustard
1	teaspoon onion powder
1	teaspoon garlic powder
	Salt and ground black pepper
1½	pounds meatloaf mix
2	teaspoons vegetable oil

GLAZE
½	cup ketchup
¼	cup packed light brown sugar
4	teaspoons cider vinegar

MAKING THE MINUTES COUNT:
Mix together the glaze ingredients while the meatloaves brown in step 3.

1. HEAT OVEN: Adjust oven rack to middle position and heat oven to 500 degrees.

2. MIX AND SHAPE MEATLOAVES: Stir cracker crumbs, milk, parsley, Worcestershire, egg, mustard, onion powder, garlic powder, 1 teaspoon salt, and ½ teaspoon pepper together in large bowl. Add meatloaf mix and combine until uniform. Following illustrations on page 235, press mixture into four oval loaves.

3. BROWN MEATLOAVES: Heat oil in 12-inch nonstick skillet over medium-high heat until just smoking. Brown meatloaves well on one side, 3 to 5 minutes. Carefully flip loaves over and tidy up edges using a spatula, following illustrations on page 235.

4. TOP WITH GLAZE AND BAKE: Meanwhile, mix glaze ingredients together until smooth, then spoon over top of loaves. Transfer skillet to oven and bake until centers of loaves register 160 on instant-read thermometer, about 15 minutes. Serve.

➤ VARIATION
Southwestern Mini Meatloaves

Substitute ⅓ cup minced fresh cilantro for parsley and add 1 (7-ounce) can chopped green chiles, drained, and 1 tablespoon minced chipotle chiles in adobo sauce to meatloaf mixture in step 2.

MAKING MINI MEATLOAVES

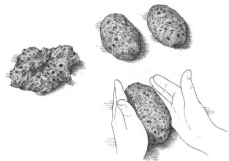

1. Divide the meatloaf mixture into 4 portions. Cup each portion with your hands to form 4 oval loaves.

2. While browning the second side of the loaves in the skillet, use a spatula to tidy up the edges so they maintain their oval shape.

TEST KITCHEN TIP:
Slicing Carrots on the Bias

Cutting carrots on the bias here is not just for looks (although they do look prettier this way). The bias slice makes sure that all the pieces are about the same size (roughly ¼ inch thick) so that they will cook quickly and evenly.

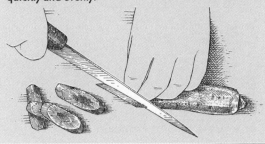

Easy Glazed Carrots
SERVES 4

We like using a nonstick skillet here because it makes clean-up a breeze; however, a regular 12-inch skillet will also work. If you don't have a lid that fits your skillet, use a baking sheet or cover the skillet with a large sheet of foil and crimp it carefully around the edge of the skillet.

1	pound carrots, sliced ¼ inch thick on bias
½	cup low-sodium chicken broth
3	tablespoons sugar
	Salt and ground black pepper
1	tablespoon unsalted butter
2	teaspoons fresh lemon juice

1. COOK CARROTS COVERED: Bring carrots, broth, 1 tablespoon sugar, and ½ teaspoon salt to simmer, covered, in 12-inch nonstick skillet over medium-high heat. Reduce heat to medium and cook until carrots are almost tender when pierced with tip of paring knife, about 5 minutes.

2. COOK CARROTS UNCOVERED: Uncover, increase heat to high, and simmer rapidly until liquid is reduced to about 2 tablespoons, 1 to 2 minutes.

3. FINISH GLAZE: Stir butter and remaining 2 tablespoons sugar into skillet and continue to cook, stirring frequently, until carrots are completely tender and glaze is light gold, about 3 minutes. Off heat, stir in lemon juice. Season with salt and pepper to taste and serve.

➤ VARIATION
Easy Glazed Carrots with Ginger and Rosemary

Add 1-inch piece fresh ginger, peeled and cut into ¼-inch-thick coins, to skillet along with carrots. Add 1 teaspoon minced fresh rosemary along with butter. Discard ginger pieces before serving.

BREADED PORK CHOPS

MOST SUPERMARKETS CARRY BONELESS pork chops, making them a convenient choice for a weeknight supper. They are tasty, too—especially in our pan-seared recipes, Quick Maple-Glazed Pork Chops (page 211) and Simplified Smothered Pork Chops with Apple Cider (page 212). But we wanted a baked pork chop with a well-seasoned, crunchy crumb coating, something we could pop into the oven and bake while we turned our attention to other parts of the meal. The shake-and-bake-style pork chop was what we had in mind, but without the sandy texture and artificial flavors of those breading mixes—and we also wanted to master a technique for baking the chops so they turn out juicy and moist. And, we wanted to pull this off with minimal effort.

We began with the crunchy coating. We tried crushed cornflakes and all kinds of bread crumbs, but time and time again, the coatings were too thin and gummy. We realized we'd need a sturdier, coarser crumb. With this in mind, we turned to crackers. With a heavy-duty freezer bag and mallet, we could turn any cracker into crumbs quickly and easily. Using this low-tech method of crushing the crackers also allowed us to control the coarseness of the crumbs. We tried a variety of cracker crumbs from buttery Ritz crackers to saltines, oyster crackers, and Melba toast. Melba toast won tasters over with its dense, hearty crunch and subtle, toasted flavor. Seasoning the crumbs was easy. Pantry staples such as garlic powder, onion powder, paprika, and thyme did the trick.

Packaged breading mixes call for moistening the chops with water then slipping them into the bag full of crumbs to shake and coat. We didn't find this method very effective—too many crumbs fell off even when we pressed the crumbs to the chops to adhere. We needed to find something stickier than water to hold our crumbs in place. We tried beaten eggs, buttermilk, milk, and heavy cream. Each was flavorful, but none helped the crumbs adhere well enough to make a thick and crunchy coating. We next tried vegetable oil, thinking that an all-fat binder would help—and it did, but our crust was still too thin. Rummaging through our refrigerator in search of another candidate, our eyes landed on a jar of mayonnaise. Mayonnaise was perfect—it stuck to the meat like frosting on a cake and allowed us to pile on the crumbs without them falling off. (We also added a little mayonnaise to our bread-crumb mixture for binding.) As for the shake-and-bake bag method, we found that simply dredging the chops in a dish of the crumb mixture was best for a thick, even coating.

Now we turned to our cooking method. Following the advice of packaged breading mixes, we placed the breaded pork chops on a baking sheet and slid them into a 425-degree oven. This advice turned out to be almost perfect. When we pulled the chops out they were crunchy on the outside, juicy on the inside. The only problem was that the undersides had turned soggy in the

---

DOCTORED APPLESAUCE

NOTHING GOES BETTER WITH PORK CHOPS than applesauce. Breathe new life into store-bought brands with these simple recipes that rely on two unlikely ingredients: Red Hot cinnamon candies and Chinese five-spice powder. Both recipes can be served immediately or refrigerated for up to three days.

Sweet and Hot Cinnamon Applesauce

MAKES 3 CUPS

Plain applesauce, rather than cinnamon-flavored, works best here.

3   cups applesauce
8   Red Hot candies

Cook applesauce and Red Hots in covered, medium saucepan over low heat, stirring often, until candies have completely dissolved and applesauce has turned light pink, about 15 minutes. Serve warm or at room temperature.

➤   VARIATION
Five-Spice Applesauce
Substitute ¼ teaspoon Chinese five-spice powder for Red Hot candies.

oven. To solve the problem, we placed the chops on a wire rack set over the baking sheet. This did the trick and gave us crunchy pork chops all the way around.

Quick and Crunchy Breaded Pork Chops

SERVES 4

Don't crush the Melba toasts too fine—the crumbs should range in size from sand to small pebbles. These chops are a natural match for applesauce (see page 236). Try to find chops that are 1 inch thick. If using larger chops, you will need to cook them a bit longer.

I	(5-ounce) box Melba toast, crushed coarse
	Salt and ground black pepper
½	teaspoon garlic powder
½	teaspoon onion powder
½	teaspoon paprika
I	teaspoon minced fresh thyme or
	½ teaspoon dried
⅛	teaspoon sugar
6	tablespoons mayonnaise
4	boneless, center-cut pork chops, I inch thick

I. HEAT OVEN: Adjust oven rack to middle position and heat oven to 425 degrees.

2. PREPARE CRUMB COATING: Mix Melba crumbs, ½ teaspoon salt, garlic powder, onion powder, paprika, thyme, and sugar in shallow dish. Add 2 tablespoons of mayonnaise and work evenly into crumbs.

3. SEASON AND COAT PORK CHOPS: Pat chops dry with paper towels and season with salt and pepper. Cover chops completely with remaining ¼ cup mayonnaise, then dredge thoroughly with Melba crumbs (including sides). Press on crumbs to make sure they adhere. Transfer breaded chops to wire rack set on rimmed baking sheet.

4. BAKE PORK CHOPS: Bake chops until coating is golden brown and centers of chops register 140 degrees on instant-read thermometer, 18 to 22 minutes. Remove chops from oven and let rest on rack until centers of chops reach 150 degrees before serving, 5 to 10 minutes.

Quick and Crunchy Sesame Pork Chops

Serve this variation with Five-Spice Applesauce.

Substitute sesame-flavored Melba toast for regular Melba toast and add ¼ cup toasted sesame seeds to Melba crumb mixture in step 1.

SAUTÉED CHERRY TOMATOES

SERVES 4

If the cherry tomatoes are especially sweet, you may want to reduce or omit the sugar. Don't toss the tomatoes with the sugar before cooking or they will release too much of their juice.

I	tablespoon olive oil
4	cups cherry tomatoes, halved
2	teaspoons sugar
I	garlic clove, minced
2	tablespoons coarsely chopped fresh basil
	Salt and ground black pepper

Heat oil in 12-inch skillet over medium-high heat until shimmering. Add tomatoes and sugar and cook, tossing frequently, until tomatoes are hot, about 1 minute. Stir in garlic and cook until fragrant, about 30 seconds. Off heat, stir in basil and season with salt and pepper to taste. Serve.

VARIATIONS

Sautéed Cherry Tomatoes with Curry and Mint

Add 1½ teaspoons curry powder to skillet with garlic. Substitute 1 tablespoon coarsely chopped mint leaves for basil. Stir in 2 tablespoons plain yogurt just before serving.

Sautéed Cherry Tomatoes with Brown Butter and Herbs

Substitute 1 tablespoon unsalted butter for oil and heat butter until it begins to brown before adding tomatoes and sugar. Substitute 2 tablespoons fresh herbs such as minced chives, dill, parsley, and/or tarragon for basil.

Pan-Roasted Glazed Pork Tenderloin

FOR WEEKNIGHT COOKING, PORK TENDERLOIN is a quicker alternative to the heftier pork loin, which can take over an hour to cook through. We sought to develop a recipe for pan-roasted pork tenderloin flavored with easy-to-prepare glazes.

After trimming away the silver skin (a thin, very tough membrane found on the surface of the tenderloin) we browned two pork tenderloins (enough to serve 4) in a skillet, then finished cooking them in a hot oven, using the same method we had used for pan-roasted chicken parts on page 232.

The initial step of stove-top browning enabled us to dramatically speed up the cooking time and get great roasted color on the pork. Instead of the pork hitting the oven in a cold roasting pan, the stove-top browning meant the skillet was already hot when it went into the oven. While the pork roasted, we had ample time to prepare a simple glaze to serve with it.

We aimed to develop glazes that would require no cooking to thicken and reduce and could be spooned over the pork at the table. For our first glaze, we chose flavors of maple syrup and whole-grain mustard. The mustard tempers the maple's sweetness and both flavors go well with pork. We also added balsamic vinegar for a bit of sweet bite. The prep is nothing more than whisking together the ingredients and seasoning with salt and pepper.

We then turned to two other glazes, each relying on jarred preserves: in one, cherry teams up with balsamic vinegar and thyme, and in another orange marmalade pairs with spicy canned chipotle chiles in adobo sauce. For these chunkier mixtures, a quick whir in a blender (or food processor) yields a smooth, glaze-like consistency. While heating the glaze is not required, a quick heating in the microwave can take the chill off if your glaze ingredients have been refrigerated prior to mixing.

Pan-Roasted Pork Tenderloin with Mustard-Maple Glaze
SERVES 4

Try to find small pork tenderloins of equal size so that they will cook quickly and evenly. If the tenderloins you find are larger than 1 pound, you will need to increase the roasting time accordingly. The glaze requires no cooking, but if you would like to warm the glaze, place it in a microwave-safe container, cover, and microwave on high for 30 seconds to 1 minute.

2 pork tenderloins (1 pound each), trimmed
   Salt and ground black pepper
1 tablespoon vegetable oil

MUSTARD-MAPLE GLAZE
½ cup pure maple syrup
⅔ cup whole-grain mustard
1 tablespoon balsamic vinegar
   Salt and ground black pepper

MAKING THE MINUTES COUNT:
Trim, pat dry, and season the tenderloins while the skillet heats up. Prepare the glaze while the pork roasts.

1. **HEAT OVEN:** Adjust oven rack to upper-middle position and heat oven to 475 degrees.

2. **SEASON AND BROWN PORK:** Pat tenderloins dry with paper towels and season with salt and pepper. Heat oil in 12-inch nonstick skillet over medium-high heat until just smoking. Brown tenderloins on all sides, about 5 minutes total.

3. **ROAST PORK:** Transfer skillet to oven and roast pork until thickest part of tenderloins register 140 degrees on instant-read thermometer, 18 to 20 minutes.

4. **PREPARE GLAZE:** Whisk maple syrup, mustard, and vinegar together and season with salt and pepper to taste. Set aside.

5. **REST PORK BEFORE SERVING:** Transfer tenderloins to carving board, tent with foil, and let rest until thickest parts of tenderloins reach 150 degrees, about 5 minutes. Cut tenderloins crosswise into thin slices and serve with glaze.

➤ VARIATIONS

Pan-Roasted Pork Tenderloin with Tart Cherry Glaze

The glaze requires no cooking, but if you would like to warm it, place it in a microwave-safe container, cover, and microwave on high for 30 seconds to 1 minute.

Follow recipe for Pan-Roasted Pork Tenderloin with Maple-Mustard Glaze. In place of glaze, prepare Tart Cherry Glaze as follows: In step 4, process 1 cup cherry preserves, 1 tablespoon balsamic vinegar, and 1 teaspoon minced fresh thyme in blender (or food processor) until smooth. Season with salt and pepper to taste.

Pan-Roasted Pork Tenderloin with Chipotle-Orange Glaze

The glaze requires no cooking, but if you would like to warm it, place it in a microwave-safe container, cover, and microwave on high for 30 seconds to 1 minute.

Follow recipe for Pan-Roasted Pork Tenderloin with Maple-Mustard Glaze. In place of glaze, prepare Chipotle-Orange Glaze as follows: In step 4, process 1 cup orange marmalade and 1 tablespoon minced chipotle chiles in adobo sauce in blender (or food processor) until smooth. Season with salt and pepper to taste.

KITCHEN SHORTCUT
TRIMMING SILVER SKIN

To quickly remove the silver skin from a pork tenderloin (it is tough and chewy), simply slip the tip of a sharp paring or boning knife under the silver skin, angle it slightly upward, and use a gentle sawing motion to remove it.

EASY MASHED POTATOES

MASHED POTATOES ARE EVERYONE'S favorite side dish. While they are simple to prepare, we've found a couple of secrets to making the best mashed potatoes. First, make sure the butter and half-and-half are warm before adding them to the potatoes so that the mash doesn't become gluey. Second, stir the butter into the potatoes first and then the half-and-half. This technique makes for smoother, more velvety mashed potatoes.

Easy Mashed Potatoes
SERVES 4

2 pounds russet potatoes (4 medium), peeled and cut into 1-inch chunks
8 tablespoons (1 stick) unsalted butter, melted
1 cup half-and-half, warmed
   Salt and ground black pepper

1. SIMMER POTATOES: Cover potatoes by 1 inch water in large saucepan and bring to boil. Reduce to simmer and cook until dinner fork can be slipped easily into center of potatoes, about 15 minutes.

2. DRAIN AND MASH POTATOES: Drain potatoes, tossing to remove excess water. Wipe saucepan dry. Add potatoes back to pot and mash to uniform consistency (or process through food mill or ricer back into pot).

3. STIR IN BUTTER, THEN HALF-AND-HALF: Using flexible rubber spatula, fold melted butter into potatoes until just incorporated. Fold in ¾ cup of hot half-and-half, adding remaining ¼ cup as needed to adjust consistency. Season with salt and pepper to taste. Serve immediately.

GLAZED SALMON

SWEET GLAZES GO WELL WITH RICH, MEATY salmon. The sugars in the glaze caramelize, creating a glossy, sweet crust. In addition, the glaze also flavors the fish so you get a bit of sweetness in every bite. But glazes can also be finicky—they can go from caramelized to burnt and acrid in a flash.

At first, we thought we'd take the approach we used with pan-roasted glazed pork tenderloins (page 238), where we mix together the glaze and spoon it over the pork after it's cooked. Prepared this way, the salmon was disappointing. It lacked the sweet crust from the glaze caramelizing as it cooked. A number of recipes we consulted instruct the cook to liberally brush the salmon with the glaze and slide it under the broiler, but we had a hard time preventing the glaze from burning on the fish. And often, the glaze was so thin it pooled around the fish, rather than clinging to it.

First, we decided to tackle the viscosity of the glaze—it need to be thick enough to cling to the fish. The first glaze we developed was based on soy sauce and maple syrup. We reduced the mixture on the stovetop before brushing it on the fish. The glaze formed a thin, but substantial coating that clung to the salmon—it was good, but not as flavorful as we'd hoped. Tasters wanted more glaze, but we were wary of the glaze burning.

Instead, on our next test, we tried a trick we picked up from barbecuing chicken. Brushing all the barbecue sauce on the chicken at the outset of grilling will cause the meat to char. Many recipes suggest slathering the chicken with sauce during the last few minutes of cooking and again, just before serving. Following this technique, we brushed the fish with a little glaze partway through cooking, a bit more glaze a few minutes later, then after the fish had been removed from the oven, a final coat of glaze. This worked like a charm. In addition to boosting flavor, the rich coating of glaze also provided some welcome moisture to the fish. We also garnished the salmon with toasted sesame seeds, which lent some crunch and a nutty flavor that worked well with the soy in the glaze.

In addition to our Maple-Soy Glaze, we developed two other variations: Mustard and Brown Sugar Glaze and Honey-Lime Glaze. These glazes are already thick, so they do not need to be reduced on the stovetop, just simply mixed together.

Broiled Maple-Soy Glazed Salmon Fillets with Toasted Sesame Seeds

SERVES 4

Try to find fillets that are of similar size (about 6 ounces each) for even cooking times. If the fillets are thinner than 1¼ inches, they will cook much more quickly and won't have enough oven time to glaze nicely. This recipe will work with both skin-on and skinless fillets.

½	cup pure maple syrup
¼	cup soy sauce
4	salmon fillets, 1¼ inches thick
	Salt and ground black pepper
2	teaspoons sesame seeds, toasted

MAKING THE MINUTES COUNT:
Prepare the glaze while the broiler heats.

I. HEAT OVEN AND PREP BROILER PAN: Adjust oven rack 6 inches from broiler element and heat broiler. Line broiler pan bottom with foil, set broiler pan rack on top, and spray rack with vegetable oil spray.

2. PREPARE GLAZE: Simmer maple syrup and soy sauce together in small saucepan over medium heat until mixture is syrupy and measures roughly ½ cup, 3 to 5 minutes.

3. SEASON AND GLAZE SALMON: Pat salmon dry with paper towels and season with salt and pepper. Lay salmon skin-side down on broiler pan (spaced about 1 inch apart). Reserve 2 tablespoons of glaze in clean bowl for serving, then brush half of remaining glaze evenly over salmon.

4. BROIL SALMON: Broil until all but very center of fish has turned from translucent to opaque, 10 to 12 minutes, brushing salmon again with remaining glaze halfway through broiling.

5. ADD RESERVED GLAZE AND GARNISH: Drizzle reserved glaze over salmon and sprinkle with sesame seeds before serving.

Broiled Mustard and Brown Sugar Glazed Salmon Fillets with Dill

SERVES 4

Try to find fillets that are of similar size (about 6 ounces each) for even cooking times. If the fillets are thinner than 1¼ inches, they will cook much more quickly and won't have enough oven time to glaze nicely. This recipe will work with both skin-on and skinless fillets.

¼	cup packed light brown sugar
3	tablespoons cider vinegar
3	tablespoons whole-grain mustard
1	tablespoon vegetable oil
2	garlic cloves, minced
4	salmon fillets, 1¼ inches thick
	Salt and ground black pepper
1	tablespoon minced fresh dill

MAKING THE MINUTES COUNT:
Prepare the glaze while the broiler heats.

1. HEAT OVEN AND PREP BROILER PAN: Adjust oven rack 6 inches from broiler element and heat broiler. Line broiler pan bottom with foil, set broiler pan rack on top, and spray rack with vegetable oil spray.

2. PREPARE GLAZE: Stir brown sugar, vinegar, mustard, oil, and garlic together until sugar dissolves.

3. PREP AND GLAZE SALMON: Pat salmon dry with paper towels and season with salt and pepper. Lay salmon skin-side down on broiler pan (spaced about 1 inch apart). Reserve 2 tablespoons of glaze in clean bowl for serving, then brush half of remaining glaze evenly over salmon.

4. BROIL FISH: Broil until all but very center of fish has turned from translucent to opaque, 10 to 12 minutes, brushing salmon again with remaining glaze halfway through broiling.

5. ADD RESERVED GLAZE AND GARNISH: Drizzle reserved glaze over salmon and sprinkle with dill before serving.

Broiled Honey-Lime Glazed Salmon Fillets with Scallions

SERVES 4

Try to find fillets that are of similar size (about 6 ounces each) for even cooking times. If the fillets are thinner than 1¼ inches, they will cook much more quickly and won't have enough oven time to glaze nicely. This recipe will work with both skin-on and skinless fillets.

¼	cup honey
1	tablespoon fresh lime juice
1	teaspoon chili powder
⅛	teaspoon cayenne
4	salmon fillets, 1¼ inches thick
	Salt and ground black pepper
2	scallions, minced

MAKING THE MINUTES COUNT:
Prepare the glaze while the broiler heats.

1. HEAT OVEN AND PREP BROILER PAN: Adjust oven rack 6 inches from broiler element and heat broiler. Line broiler pan bottom with foil, set broiler pan rack on top, and spray rack with vegetable oil spray.

2. PREPARE GLAZE: Stir honey, lime juice, chili powder, and cayenne together.

3. PREP AND GLAZE SALMON: Pat salmon dry with paper towels and season with salt and pepper. Lay salmon skin-side down on broiler pan (spaced about 1 inch apart). Reserve 2 tablespoons of glaze in clean bowl for serving, then brush half of remaining glaze evenly over salmon.

4. BROIL FISH: Broil until all but very center of fish has turned from translucent to opaque, 10 to 12 minutes, brushing salmon again with remaining glaze halfway through broiling.

5. ADD RESERVED GLAZE AND GARNISH: Drizzle reserved glaze over salmon and sprinkle with scallions before serving.

CRUNCHY BAKED COD

MANY RECIPES FOR SIMPLE BAKED BREADED fish fillets consist of little more than a mild white fish, like cod or haddock, brushed with butter and rolled in store-bought bread crumbs. Quick? Yes, but hardly better than the frozen variety. We wanted well-seasoned fish in a tasty, crunchy coating and we wanted to keep the prep quick and easy.

We started with the crumbs. Crushed Melba toast crumbs, our choice for Quick and Crunchy Pork Chops (page 237), were too sturdy and hearty for the delicate fish. Panko (Japanese-style bread crumbs) were crisp, but their flavor wasn't as rich as we would have liked. Crushed Ritz cracker crumbs, however, turned out to be perfect. Simple, buttery, and flavorful, these rich crumbs made a perfect crunchy coating for the tender fish. We found it was important not to crush the crumbs too much—they should be coarse.

Picking up a tip from our pork chop recipe, we turned to mayonnaise to help a thick coating of the crumbs adhere. Before coating the fish, we seasoned the mayonnaise with fresh herbs, Dijon mustard, lemon juice, and cayenne. Topping the fish with the crumbs, we pressed them lightly to adhere. We then baked the fish in the oven until the crumbs were golden brown and crunchy and the fish was cooked through but still moist.

This flavorful fish is great on its own but some diners might like a wedge of lemon or Tartar Sauce (page 127). Once we nailed down this classic version, we turned to two others. One recipe flavors the mayonnaise with briny capers and sports a crushed potato chip–tarragon coating and the other adds horseradish and garlic to the mayonnaise and replaces the Ritz cracker crumbs with fresh bread crumbs.

Fast and Crunchy Baked Cod
SERVES 4

Try to find cod fillets that are of similar size (about 6 ounces each) so that they will cook evenly. If some of the fillets are much thinner, they should be folded over in order to make them thicker (see below). Haddock, halibut, orange roughy, or bluefish fillets are good alternatives to the cod. Fresh bread crumbs (page 200) or crushed potato chips can be substituted for the Ritz crackers. Instead of serving the fish with lemon wedges, try Tartar Sauce, on page 127.

MAKING THIN FISH FILLETS THICKER
If some of your fillets are thin (such as the tail piece), you can make them thicker so that they will cook at the same rate as the others.

1. With a sharp knife, cut halfway through the flesh crosswise 2 to 3 inches from tail end. This will create a seam to fold tail under.

2. Fold tail end under to create a fillet of relatively even thickness.

4   skinless cod fillets, I¼ inches thick
      Salt and ground black pepper

20   Ritz crackers, crushed to coarse crumbs
      (I cup)

2   tablespoons minced fresh dill or parsley

¼   cup mayonnaise

I   tablespoon Dijon mustard

I   tablespoon fresh lemon juice
      Pinch cayenne
      Lemon wedges, for serving

I. HEAT OVEN AND PREPARE DISH: Adjust oven rack to middle position and heat oven to 450 degrees. Coat 13 by 9-inch baking dish with vegetable oil spray.

2. SEASON FISH: Pat cod dry with paper towels and season with salt and pepper. Lay cod in baking dish (space about ½ inch apart).

3. COAT FISH: Toss cracker crumbs with 1 tablespoon of dill. In separate bowl, mix remaining tablespoon dill, mayonnaise, mustard, lemon juice, and cayenne together. Spread mayonnaise mixture over top and sides of fish. Press crumbs into mayonnaise, making sure they adhere.

4. BAKE: Bake until crumbs are golden brown and all but very center of fish has turned from translucent to opaque, about 15 minutes. Serve with lemon wedges.

➤   VARIATIONS

Fast and Crunchy Baked Cod with Capers, Tarragon, and Potato Chips
Substitute 4 ounces kettle-cooked potato chips, crushed coarse (1 cup), for Ritz crackers, and 2 tablespoons minced fresh tarragon for dill. Add 2 tablespoons capers, rinsed and minced, to mayonnaise mixture.

Fast and Crunchy Baked Cod with Horseradish, Garlic, and Bread Crumbs
Substitute 1 cup fresh bread crumbs (page 200) for Ritz crackers. Add 2 tablespoons drained prepared horseradish and 1 small garlic clove, minced, to mayonnaise mixture.

BAKED SOLE FLORENTINE

STUFFED SOLE FLORENTINE MAKES AN impressive main course. The traditional dish features sole that has been stuffed (usually with a spinach mixture and sometimes crabmeat), rolled into an elegant shape, and then covered in a delicately flavored white sauce. Guests will assume you've spent hours in the kitchen and, with most recipes for this classic dish, they'd be right. We wanted to find a way to make sole Florentine hassle-free for the cook, yet still impressive enough for company.

We started with the filling. While some recipes include crabmeat, we decided to omit it and create a solely spinach-based stuffing. In lieu of cooking fresh spinach, which would involve washing, drying, sautéing, and then squeezing it dry, we turned to frozen spinach. Using frozen chopped spinach cut out most of the laborious spinach preparation; all we had to do was make sure it was thawed and thoroughly squeezed dry.

For the white sauce, most recipes start with a roux—a combination of butter and flour. The problem we found was that after cream was added to the roux, the sauce needed to be simmered at least 10 minutes for it to thicken. It also took this long for the flour to lose its raw flavor. To solve the problem, we turned to cornstarch to thicken the sauce. Cornstarch lost its raw flavor and thickened our sauce in only two minutes, a great time-saver.

For the filling, we combined the spinach with some of the sauce (setting aside the remainder to pour over the fillets). We lined up the fish fillets, mounded the filling on each, and folded the end of each fillet over the filling. We then arranged the stuffed fillets seam-side down in a baking dish and poured the remaining white sauce over them. Finished with a quick, buttery cracker topping and baked for 15 minutes, this streamlined version of sole Florentine will give the cook time to enjoy the party too.

Streamlined Sole Florentine

SERVES 4

Try to buy fish fillets of equal size to ensure even cooking. Be sure to squeeze as much moisture out of the frozen spinach as possible or the sauce will be too watery. To check the doneness of the fish, use the tip of a paring knife to gently prod the fish—the flesh should be opaque and flaky, but still juicy.

2	tablespoons unsalted butter
I	shallot, minced
I	garlic clove, minced
2	cups half-and-half
2	teaspoons minced fresh thyme
4	teaspoons cornstarch
	Salt and ground black pepper
1/2	cup grated Parmesan cheese
2	(10-ounce) packages frozen chopped spinach, thawed and squeezed dry
8	boneless, skinless sole fillets, 1/4 to 1/2 inch thick
15	Ritz crackers, crushed fine (3/4 cup)
	Lemon wedges, for serving

MAKING THE MINUTES COUNT:
Prep the spinach and get the fish ready for filling while the sauce cooks.

I. HEAT OVEN AND PREPARE BAKING DISH: Adjust oven rack to middle position and heat oven to 475 degrees. Coat 13 by 9-inch baking dish with 1 tablespoon of butter.

2. MAKE SAUCE: Melt remaining tablespoon butter in medium saucepan over medium-high heat. Add shallot and cook until softened, about 2 minutes. Stir in garlic and cook until fragrant, about 30 seconds. Stir in 1¾ cups of half-and-half and thyme and bring to simmer. Whisk remaining ¼ cup half-and-half and cornstarch together to dissolve cornstarch, then stir into saucepan. Continue to simmer until thickened, about 2 minutes. Season with salt and pepper to taste.

3. MAKE FILLING AND PREP FISH: Stir 1 cup of sauce and Parmesan into spinach and season with salt and pepper to taste. Pat fish dry with paper towels and season with salt and pepper.

4. MAKE FISH BUNDLES: Following illustration below, place fish on cutting board, skinned-side down. Divide spinach filling among fish fillets, mounding it in middle of each fillet. Fold tapered end of fish tightly over filling and then fold thicker end of fish over top to make tidy bundle.

5. ASSEMBLE DISH AND BAKE: Arrange fish bundles in baking dish, seam-side down (leaving space between each roll). Pour remaining sauce evenly over fish, then sprinkle with Ritz cracker crumbs. Bake until all but very center of fish turns from translucent to opaque, 12 to 15 minutes. Serve with lemon wedges.

MAKING FISH BUNDLES

1. Lay the fillets out on a cutting board, skinned sides down. Divide the spinach filling evenly among the fillets and mound it in the center of each fillet. Tightly fold the tapered end of each fillet over the filling, then fold the thicker end of the fillet over the top.

2. Flip the bundles over, transfer them to the baking dish, and press on them lightly to flatten, leaving a small space between each bundle. Pour the sauce evenly over the fish, then sprinkle with Ritz crumbs.

11

STARTING WITH LEFTOVERS

Starting With Leftovers

WE KNOW THAT FOR TIME-CRUNCHED cooks, leftovers are a real saving grace. But admit it, who really wants to eat warmed-over sliced chicken or pork? It's one thing to heat up a savory stew or casserole, but another thing altogether to transform leftover meat from your Sunday roast into another dish entirely. So while we don't generally plan our cooking around recipes that incorporate leftovers, we think some of the ones in this chapter merit roasting an extra chicken on the weekend or sautéing a few extra chicken breasts with your Tuesday night supper—just so you can make Cheesy Chicken and Rice Casserole or a fast Chicken Tortilla Casserole.

We approached this chapter in the most practical of ways, with the goal of providing specific recipes for leftover chicken, pork, beef, and even fish, as well as recipes where you might use any kind of leftover meat.

That said, we found that there are two key points to keep in mind when devising a new meal using leftover meat. The first trick is to make sure you have enough leftovers to work with. Although we've come across some recipes that claim you can stretch a 4-ounce piece of leftover steak into dinner for four, it's just not true. All of the recipes in this chapter are based on 2 cups of shredded or thinly sliced meat (about 10 ounces), which is plenty for three to four people.

The second, and arguably most important, trick is to understand that leftover meat has already been cooked once, and additional cooking will only dry it out and ruin its flavor. Therefore, always add the leftover meat to the new dish just to warm it through before serving.

Note that while some recipes in this chapter specify a cut of meat, such as steak, many do not, calling for simply chicken, beef, pork, or lamb. This gives you the option of using what you have on hand—whether it be Sunday's roast beef or Tuesday night's steak.

CHICKEN SALADS

MAKING CHICKEN SALAD IS THE OBVIOUS way to use up leftover chicken—our goal was to come up with some inspired flavors. One trick we found to making good chicken salad is to shred the meat rather than cut it up into cubes. The shreds of chicken get nicely coated with the dressing so that the salad is more cohesive and flavorful, while the cubes taste dry and boring. Also, we found that letting the salad sit for 10 minutes before serving helped the flavors to blend.

For our first three salads, we stuck with a mayonnaise base and adjusted each with vibrant seasonings. Spicy curry powder, sweet grapes, and crunchy cashews team up in one salad. Our second salad incorporates classic Southwestern flavors like smoky chipotle chiles, avocado, and fresh lime juice. We go Italian in the third with fennel, pine nuts, basil, and Parmesan. And for our fourth salad, we swap in a spicy Asian-style vinaigrette for the mayonnaise base and toss in shredded cabbage, fresh cilantro, and peanuts.

MAKING LEFTOVERS WORK
Here are a few tips to help you make the most out of your leftovers.

Tip #1	Tip #2	Tip #3
Keep your pantry (and freezer) full of staples. Chicken broth, canned beans, canned tomatoes, and pasta, as well as frozen peas and broccoli, are some of the obvious staples, while specialty flavorings such as chipotles, chutneys, or unusual vinegars play an equally important role.	Always include at least one fresh ingredient in a leftover dish. An herb, a vegetable, or even a squeeze of fresh lemon juice can make all the difference. Merely tossing leftover meat with canned pantry ingredients will wind up tasting as dull as it sounds.	Figure out your flavors and stick to them. There is nothing worse than leftovers gussied up with everything but the kitchen sink. We often find it helpful to consider a region or culture around which to base the dish's flavor and any accompanying side dishes.

Curried Chicken Salad

SERVES 3 TO 4

Curry powders tend to be salty, so season this salad carefully.

- ½ cup mayonnaise
- 2 teaspoons curry powder
  Salt and ground black pepper
- 2 cups shredded cooked chicken
- I cup grapes, halved
- I celery rib, chopped fine
- 2 tablespoons minced red onion
- 2 tablespoons minced fresh parsley
- ¼ cup chopped cashews

Mix together mayonnaise, curry powder, ⅛ teaspoon salt, and ⅛ teaspoon pepper in large bowl. Stir in chicken, grapes, celery, onion, and parsley until combined. Season with salt and pepper to taste. Let sit 10 minutes to allow flavors to meld. Sprinkle with cashews and serve.

Spicy Chicken Salad with Chipotle and Avocado

SERVES 3 TO 4

Use less chipotle to make this salad milder.

- I ripe avocado, halved and pitted
- ¼ cup mayonnaise
- 2 teaspoons minced chipotle chiles in adobo sauce
- 2 tablespoons fresh lime juice
  Salt and ground black pepper
- 2 cups shredded cooked chicken
- ½ red bell pepper, cored and chopped fine
- 2 scallions, sliced thin
- 2 tablespoons minced fresh cilantro

Mash half of avocado into paste and dice other half into small pieces. Mix mashed avocado, mayonnaise, chipotle, lime juice, ⅛ teaspoon salt, and ⅛ teaspoon pepper together in large bowl. Stir in diced avocado, chicken, bell pepper, scallions, and cilantro until combined. Season with salt and pepper to taste. Let sit 10 minutes to allow flavors to meld, and serve.

Chicken Salad with Fennel, Lemon, and Parmesan

SERVES 3 TO 4

We like this salad when seasoned heavily with freshly ground black pepper.

- ½ cup mayonnaise
- ¼ cup grated Parmesan cheese
- 2 tablespoons fresh lemon juice
- ¼ teaspoon grated lemon zest
  Salt and ground black pepper
- 2 cups shredded cooked chicken
- ½ fennel bulb, trimmed, cored, and chopped fine
- 2 tablespoons minced red onion
- 2 tablespoons minced fresh basil
- ¼ cup pine nuts, toasted

Mix mayonnaise, Parmesan, lemon juice, lemon zest, ⅛ teaspoon salt, and ⅛ teaspoon pepper together in large bowl. Stir in chicken, fennel, onion, and basil until combined. Season with salt and pepper to taste. Let sit 10 minutes to allow flavors to meld. Sprinkle with pine nuts and serve.

INGREDIENT: Mayonnaise

Is one brand of mayonnaise better than another? To find out, we tasted our way through seven nationally available brands. Hellmann's Real Mayonnaise took top honors with its clear flavor and touch of acidity that balances the fat from the oil. Kraft Real Mayonnaise came in second and was described as "flavorful, but not overpowering." And what about light mayonnaise? Again, Hellmann's Light Mayonnaise, which had bright, balanced flavors similar to Hellmann's full-fat version, finished ahead of its light counterparts.

The Best Mayonnaise
Hellmann's (left), which is known as Best Foods west of the Rockies, took top honors in our tasting. Among the reduced-fat mayonnaises we tested, Hellmann's Light (right) was the clear winner.

~❧~

Southeast Asian Chicken Salad with Cabbage, Carrots, and Peanuts

SERVES 4

For more information on fish sauce and Asian chili sauce, see page 100. Asian chili sauce can vary in spiciness depending on the brand. If you have some red bell peppers, fresh basil, or fresh mint on hand, feel free to chop and add them to the salad. While our other chicken salads can be served sandwich style, this one is best served over salad greens.

12	ounces (6 cups) pre-shredded cabbage
2	cups shredded cooked chicken
1/2	cup minced fresh cilantro
5	tablespoons rice vinegar
3	tablespoons vegetable oil
2	tablespoons sugar
2	tablespoons fish sauce
2	teaspoons Asian chili sauce
1/4	cup chopped unsalted roasted peanuts

Toss cabbage, chicken, and cilantro together in large bowl. In separate bowl, whisk vinegar, oil, sugar, fish sauce, and chili sauce together. Pour dressing over cabbage mixture and toss to coat. Let sit 10 minutes to allow flavors to meld. Sprinkle with peanuts before serving.

COLD SESAME NOODLES WITH SHREDDED CHICKEN

WHETHER YOU'RE MAKING THESE NOODLES with leftover chicken or starting from scratch, the problems can be the same: gluey noodles and a gloppy sauce with a too-strong peanut flavor that overwhelms the sesame. We found that rinsing the noodles under cool, running water washes away excess starch and helps prevent them from sticking together. Tossing the noodles with sesame oil not only flavors the noodles but also further ensures that they don't stick. As for the sauce, we found that a little brown sugar helps mellow the flavors while chunky peanut butter gives it a fuller,

fresher flavor than the creamy variety. Toasted sesame seeds further reinforce the distinctive nutty flavor of this easy-to-prepare noodle dish.

~❧~

Cold Sesame Noodles with Shredded Chicken

SERVES 4

You can substitute 8 ounces of dried spaghetti or linguine for the fresh Chinese egg noodles, but increase the pasta cooking time to 10 minutes. Shredded carrots and thinly sliced bell pepper are also good in this dish.

1/4	cup sesame seeds
1/4	cup chunky peanut butter
5	tablespoons soy sauce
2	tablespoons rice vinegar
2	garlic cloves, minced
1	tablespoon grated fresh ginger
1	teaspoon Tabasco
2	tablespoons packed light brown sugar
1	(9-ounce) package fresh Chinese egg noodles
	Salt
2	tablespoons toasted sesame oil
2	cups shredded cooked chicken
4	scallions, sliced thin

1. **BOIL WATER FOR NOODLES AND TOAST SESAME SEEDS**: Bring 3 quarts water to boil in large pot. Toast sesame seeds in medium skillet over medium heat until lightly browned and fragrant, about 8 minutes.

2. **PUREE SAUCE**: Puree 3 tablespoons sesame seeds, peanut butter, soy sauce, vinegar, garlic, ginger, Tabasco, and brown sugar together in food processor (or blender) until smooth, about 30 seconds; set aside.

3. **COOK NOODLES**: Stir noodles and 1 tablespoon salt into boiling water and cook until tender, about 4 minutes. Drain noodles and rinse with cold running tap water until cool to touch; drain again.

4. **COMBINE AND GARNISH**: In large bowl, toss noodles with sesame oil until evenly coated. Add shredded chicken, scallions, and sauce and toss to combine. Sprinkle with remaining tablespoon sesame seeds and serve.

CHINESE NOODLES WITH BEEF

THERE ARE SEVERAL WAYS TO PREPARE CHINESE egg noodles; however, this method produces noodles with a bit of brothy sauce—sort of a soupy stir-fry. The key to this dish is using authentic ingredients, such as five-spice powder and chili sauce. And fresh ginger is absolutely essential—without it, the dish is much too bland. This recipe uses a favorite shortcut from our stir-fries which is to incorporate pre-shredded vegetables from the produce section. Here, pre-shredded carrots give the dish some bulk, color, and flavor and they pair nicely with both the beef and the baby spinach. If you don't happen to have fresh Chinese egg noodles on hand, feel free to substitute four 3-ounce packets of instant ramen noodles. Just be sure to discard the seasoning packets because they are overly salty and artificial tasting.

Asian Spicy Noodles with Beef and Spinach

SERVES 4

Any type of cooked steak will work here. Serve this brothy dish in large flat soup bowls. Four 3-ounce packets of instant ramen noodles (seasoning packets discarded), can be substituted for the Chinese egg noodles.

I	(9-ounce) package fresh Chinese egg noodles (see note)
	Salt
2	tablespoons vegetable oil
1/4	teaspoon Chinese five-spice powder
3	garlic cloves, minced
I	tablespoon grated fresh ginger
3/4	cup low-sodium chicken broth
2	tablespoons soy sauce
2	teaspoons Asian chili sauce
2	cups pre-shredded carrots
I	(6-ounce) bag baby spinach
10	ounces thinly sliced cooked steak

I. BOIL WATER FOR PASTA: Bring 3 quarts water to boil in large pot. Stir in noodles and 1 tablespoon salt and cook, stirring often, until noodles are tender,

about 3 minutes. Drain noodles and set aside.

2. MAKE SAUCE: Add oil and five-spice powder to same pot and return to medium heat until fragrant, about 1 minute. Add garlic and ginger and cook until fragrant, about 30 seconds. Stir in broth, soy sauce, and chili sauce and bring to simmer; add carrots and simmer 1 minute.

3. COMBINE AND HEAT THROUGH: Turn heat to medium-low and stir in cooked noodles, spinach, and meat. Cover and cook until spinach is wilted and steak is heated through, about 1 minute, and serve.

PASTA WITH CHICKEN

MOST QUICK CHICKEN AND PASTA DISHES rely on jarred cream sauces or a powdery packet from a chicken and pasta "kit," which just don't taste very good. But cream sauces complement chicken better than, say, tomato sauce and we were determined to develop easy-to-prepare creamy sauces with really fresh flavor. Having developed some easy and creamy blender sauces for other fast pasta dishes, we thought we could put a similar style of sauce to use here. Using just cheese, milk, and some aromatics, we made our sauce while the pasta boiled, then simply combined everything over low heat until the chicken warmed through and the sauce thickened slightly. And rather than use the same old tired Italian flavorings, we spruced up these recipes with some untraditional ingredients, including goat cheese in one and feta cheese in another.

Pasta with Chicken, Peas, and Radicchio in Creamy Goat Cheese Sauce

SERVES 4

Orecchiette and farfalle are other pasta shapes that work well in this dish.

3/4	cup crumbled goat cheese
1/2	cup grated Parmesan cheese
3/4	cup heavy cream
2	tablespoons fresh lemon juice
2	garlic cloves, minced

1 teaspoon minced fresh thyme
   Salt and ground black pepper
8 ounces penne (2 cups)
2 cups shredded cooked chicken
2 cups (12 ounces) frozen peas, thawed
1 small head radicchio, shredded

1. **BOIL WATER FOR PASTA**: Bring 3 quarts water to boil in large pot.

2. **PUREE SAUCE**: Puree goat cheese, Parmesan, cream, lemon juice, garlic, thyme, ½ teaspoon salt, and ¼ teaspoon pepper in blender until smooth, adding water as needed, 1 tablespoon at a time, to facilitate blending.

3. **COOK PASTA**: Stir pasta and 1 tablespoon salt into boiling water and cook until pasta is al dente. Reserve ½ cup of cooking water, then drain pasta.

4. **COMBINE AND HEAT THROUGH**: Return drained pasta to pot over low heat. Stir in sauce, chicken, peas, and radicchio and cook until radicchio has wilted and sauce has warmed through, about 2 minutes. Add reserved pasta cooking water as needed to adjust sauce consistency. Season to taste with salt and pepper and serve.

Pasta with Chicken, Spinach, and Cherry Tomatoes in Creamy Feta Sauce

SERVES 4

Orecchiette and farfalle are other pasta shapes that work well in this dish.

¾ cup crumbled feta cheese
¾ cup heavy cream
3 tablespoons fresh lemon juice
2 teaspoons minced fresh oregano
2 garlic cloves, minced
   Salt and ground black pepper
8 ounces penne (2 cups)
2 cups shredded cooked chicken
1 (6-ounce) bag baby spinach
1 pint cherry tomatoes, halved

1. **BOIL WATER FOR PASTA**: Bring 3 quarts water to boil in large pot.

2. **PUREE SAUCE**: Puree feta, cream, lemon juice, oregano, garlic, ½ teaspoon salt, and ¼ teaspoon pepper in blender until smooth, adding water as needed, 1 tablespoon at a time, to facilitate blending.

3. **COOK PASTA**: Stir pasta and 1 tablespoon salt into boiling water and cook until pasta is al dente. Reserve ½ cup of cooking water, then drain pasta.

4. **COMBINE AND HEAT THROUGH**: Return drained pasta to pot over low heat. Stir in sauce, chicken, spinach, and tomatoes and cook until the spinach has wilted and sauce has warmed through, about 2 minutes. Add reserved pasta cooking water as needed to adjust sauce consistency. Season to taste with salt and pepper and serve.

PASTA WITH SALMON

ONE OF THE EASIEST WAYS TO TRANSFORM last night's salmon into a second meal is to incorporate it into a pasta dish. The recipes we tried from other books, however, tasted incredibly bland or felt unfinished. These recipes usually toss flaked salmon with hot pasta, peas, and ricotta, which isn't all that appealing (or tasty). We found that all it took to elevate this easy dish to an elegant meal was to make a very simple cream reduction and then add peas and fresh tarragon to it along with the pasta and salmon. To keep the salmon from breaking up too much, gently stir it into the pasta toward the end of cooking.

Fettuccine with Salmon, Peas, Tarragon, and Cream

SERVES 4

Fresh tarragon is key to this dish—don't substitute dried. Boil the pasta until it is just shy of your preferred doneness, as it will continue to cook for a few minutes with the sauce. While you might be tempted to use canned salmon here, don't—it won't taste nearly as good as fresh.

1 tablespoon unsalted butter
1 shallot, minced
1 cup heavy cream

8   ounces linguine or fettuccine
    Salt and ground black pepper
I   cup frozen peas, thawed
I   tablespoon minced fresh tarragon (see note)
2   cups flaked cooked salmon (see note)

I. BOIL WATER FOR PASTA: Bring 3 quarts water to boil in large pot.

2. MAKE SAUCE: Melt butter in small saucepan over medium heat. Add shallot and cook until softened, about 2 minutes. Stir in cream, bring to simmer, and cook until thickened and reduced to about ¾ cup, about 6 minutes. Set sauce aside off heat.

3. COOK PASTA: Stir pasta and 1 tablespoon salt into boiling water and cook until pasta is just shy of al dente. Reserve ½ cup of cooking water, then drain pasta.

4. COMBINE AND HEAT THROUGH: Return drained pasta to pot over low heat. Stir in cream mixture, peas, and tarragon. Gently fold in salmon and cook, stirring until sauce clings to pasta and salmon and peas have heated through, about 1 minute. Add reserved pasta cooking water as needed to adjust sauce consistency. Season with salt and pepper to taste and serve.

SALMON CAKES

MOST QUICK SALMON CAKE RECIPES ARE a greasy conglomeration relying on canned salmon. We wanted to create a recipe for fresh-tasting salmon cakes using leftover salmon—the kind that inspire you to cook an extra fillet the night before. We decided to give our salmon cakes a Southwestern spin, so we flavored them with finely chopped red bell pepper and corn. We also added green chiles to pack a little heat, scallions to add bite, and cilantro for herby freshness. To bind our cakes together and keep them moist, we used a combination of bread crumbs, mayonnaise, and egg. We then dredged the cakes in additional bread crumbs and lightly fried them to a crispy golden brown.

Southwestern-Style Salmon Cakes
SERVES 4

Depending on how the salmon was cooked, you may need to season the salmon mixture with additional salt and pepper before forming the cakes. Handle the salmon cakes carefully when coating them in the bread crumbs, as they are very soft. Panko (Japanese bread crumbs) also work here.

2   cups flaked cooked salmon
I   red bell pepper, cored, seeded, and chopped fine
¾   cup frozen corn, thawed
I   (4-ounce) can chopped green chiles
4   scallions, minced
2   tablespoons minced fresh cilantro
I   cup dried plain bread crumbs
¼   cup mayonnaise
I   large egg
    Salt and ground black pepper
¼   cup vegetable oil
    Lemon wedges, for serving

I. COMBINE INGREDIENTS: Gently toss salmon, bell pepper, corn, chiles, scallions, and cilantro together in medium bowl. Stir together ¼ cup bread crumbs, mayonnaise, egg, ½ teaspoon salt, and ¼ teaspoon pepper in small bowl, then add to salmon mixture. Using rubber spatula, gently combine mixture until uniform. If mixture is very wet, add 1 to 2 more tablespoons bread crumbs.

2. FORM CAKES: Divide salmon mixture into four equal portions and pack each tightly into 3½-inch-wide patties. Dredge each cake in remaining bread crumbs.

3. BROWN CAKES: Heat oil in 12-inch non-stick skillet over medium heat until shimmering. Gently lay cakes in skillet and cook until golden brown and crisp, 8 to 10 minutes, turning cakes halfway through. Drain on paper towels and serve with lemon wedges.

CHICKEN AND RICE CASSEROLES

MOST FAST CHICKEN AND RICE CASSEROLES use canned soups or powdered soup packets—and they taste awful. We wanted to find a recipe that was just as easy to prepare but actually tasted good. After testing several possibilities, we found that using instant rice and a quick sauce made from chicken broth, cream, sautéed onion, and some garlic was the way to go. Bringing the sauce to a simmer on the stovetop before mixing it with the rice and vegetables, and spreading it into the baking dish sped up the baking time significantly. Another trick we learned was to stir the leftover chicken into the casserole toward the end of the baking time so it doesn't dry out.

Cheesy Chicken and Rice Casserole

SERVES 4

Cooked shredded turkey can be substituted for the chicken. Don't add the chicken to the casserole until step 3, otherwise the chicken will dry out. This recipe is based on instant rice—regular rice requires a different amount of liquid and a longer cooking time and should not be substituted here.

1	tablespoon vegetable oil
1	onion, minced
3	garlic cloves, minced
1	teaspoon minced fresh thyme
1	cup low-sodium chicken broth
1/2	cup heavy cream
1	cup instant rice
2	cups (8 ounces) frozen pea-carrot medley, thawed
	Salt and ground black pepper
2	cups shredded cooked chicken
1	cup shredded cheddar cheese
20	Ritz crackers, crushed to coarse crumbs (1 cup)

1. HEAT OVEN, SAUTÉ AROMATICS, AND MAKE SAUCE: Adjust oven rack to middle position and heat oven to 450 degrees. Heat oil in 12-inch nonstick skillet over medium-high heat until shimmering. Add onion and cook until softened, about 3 minutes. Stir in garlic and thyme and cook until fragrant, about 30 seconds. Add broth and cream and bring to simmer.

2. ADD RICE AND VEGETABLES AND BAKE: Stir in rice and pea-carrot medley. Season with salt and pepper to taste. Pour mixture into 8-inch baking dish. Bake for 10 minutes.

3. ADD CHICKEN, CHEESE, CRACKER CRUMBS, AND BAKE: Stir in chicken. Sprinkle cheddar evenly over top, then sprinkle with cracker crumbs. Continue to bake until edges are bubbling and crumbs are toasted, about 5 minutes. Serve.

Fiesta Chicken Casserole

SERVES 4

Cooked shredded turkey can be substituted for the chicken. Don't add the chicken to the casserole until step 3, otherwise the chicken will dry out. This recipe is based on instant rice—regular rice requires a different amount of liquid and a longer cooking time and should not be substituted here. Tasters liked Fritos corn chips, but you can use your favorite brand.

1	tablespoon vegetable oil
1	onion, minced
3	garlic cloves, minced
1	cup low-sodium chicken broth
1/2	cup store-bought salsa, drained
1	cup instant rice
1/2	cup canned black beans, rinsed
1/2	cup frozen corn, thawed
	Salt and ground black pepper
2	cups shredded cooked chicken
1/4	cup minced fresh cilantro
1	cup shredded cheddar cheese
1	cup coarsely crushed Fritos corn chips

> **TEST KITCHEN TIP:**
> **No-Fuss Crumb Toppings**
> Because most crackers and chips already contain fat, they're a better option than using store-bought bread crumbs, which you almost always have to season and enrich with melted butter.

1. HEAT OVEN, SAUTÉ AROMATICS, AND MAKE SAUCE: Adjust oven rack to middle position and heat oven to 450 degrees. Heat oil in 12-inch non-stick skillet over medium-high heat until shimmering. Add onion and cook until softened, about 3 minutes. Stir in garlic and cook until fragrant, about 30 seconds. Add broth and salsa and bring to simmer.

2. ADD RICE AND VEGETABLES AND BAKE: Stir in rice, beans, and corn. Season with salt and pepper to taste. Pour mixture into 8-inch baking dish. Bake for 10 minutes.

3. ADD CHICKEN AND REMAINING INGREDIENTS AND HEAT THROUGH: Stir in chicken and cilantro. Sprinkle cheddar evenly over top, then sprinkle with crushed corn chips. Continue to bake until edges are bubbling and crumbs are toasted, about 5 minutes. Serve.

TORTILLA CASSEROLE

WE FOUND LOTS OF FAST RECIPES FOR tortilla casserole in our cookbook library; however, most of them turned out bone dry, or tasted "canned" because they simply tossed jarred or canned ingredients together. We wanted a moist filling with fresh ingredients. We found that using a broth-based sauce was key for moistness. To keep the prep in this casserole to a minimum, we found that canned beans and tomatoes, tortilla chips, and pre-shredded cheddar cheese were helpful shortcuts. But to prevent the casserole from tasting stale, we discovered that it was essential to use fresh onion, garlic, and cilantro.

Chicken Tortilla Casserole
SERVES 4

We like to use pre-shredded Mexican-blend cheese in this casserole since it's easy (and creamy), but any shredded cheddar cheese works fine.

1	tablespoon vegetable oil
1	onion, minced
3	garlic cloves, minced
1	cup low-sodium chicken broth

1	(15.5-ounce) can pinto beans, rinsed
1	(14.5-ounce) can diced tomatoes, drained
1	tablespoon minced chipotle chiles in adobo sauce
2	cups shredded cooked chicken
¼	cup minced fresh cilantro
	Salt and ground black pepper
5	cups tortilla chips (3 ounces)
2	cups shredded Mexican cheese blend (see note)

1. HEAT OVEN, SAUTÉ AROMATICS, AND MAKE SAUCE: Adjust oven rack to middle position and heat oven to 450 degrees. Heat oil in 12-inch nonstick skillet over medium heat until shimmering. Add onion and cook until softened, about 3 minutes. Stir in garlic and cook until fragrant, about 30 seconds. Add chicken broth and bring to simmer.

2. ADD VEGETABLES, CHICKEN, AND HERBS: Stir beans, tomatoes, and chipotle into sauce and simmer until heated through, about 2 minutes. Stir in chicken, 3 tablespoons cilantro, ¾ teaspoon salt, and ¼ teaspoon pepper.

3. ASSEMBLE CASSEROLE: Spread 1 cup tortilla chips over bottom of 8-inch baking dish and top with 1 cup chicken mixture. Spread 2 more cups tortilla chips into dish and sprinkle with 1 cup cheese. Spread remaining chicken mixture into dish and top with remaining tortilla chips. Sprinkle remaining 1 cup cheese over top.

4. BAKE: Bake until cheese is golden brown and casserole is bubbling, about 10 minutes. Sprinkle with remaining cilantro before serving.

ENCHILADAS

TWO ISSUES AROSE WHEN WE TRIED TO streamline our favorite enchilada recipe with leftover meat. The first issue we encountered was that the enchiladas looked seriously skimpy using the amount of meat most people are likely to have left over—about 2 cups. The second issue was that our initial attempt took us nearly 50 minutes—just too long for a quick recipe.

To bulk up the filling of these meager-looking enchiladas, we found a great, zero-prep solution in canned beans. Sure, it's a bit untraditional to put meat and beans in the same enchilada, but it tasted good. We tested the difference between adding canned whole beans and canned refried beans to the filling. Tasters preferred the refried beans because they had more flavor and their texture helped bind the filling together.

Our timing problem was easily solved when we got the microwave involved. A more traditional enchilada recipe requires about 30 minutes of baking time in order to heat the filling inside the enchiladas. By microwaving the filling before rolling it up in the tortillas we shaved about 15 minutes off the baking time. Finally, we found that placing all of the tortillas out on the counter and filling them assembly-line style was the most efficient way to fill them fast. Canned enchilada sauce is a must if you want to slide in under the 30-minute wire, but our easy homemade sauce on page 257 is good too.

TEST KITCHEN TIP:
No More Torn Tortillas
Simply rolling the filling in cold tortillas left us with piles of broken and torn enchiladas. To solve this problem, we warmed the tortillas in the microwave to make them more pliable. We then sprayed the tops of the enchiladas with vegetable oil spray, which stopped them from splitting when they were baked.

Cool and Stiff: Straight from the fridge, a corn tortilla is too stiff to roll and will tear at the edges.

Warm and Pliable: Heating the tortillas in the microwave and spraying them with vegetable oil will make them pliable and easy to work with.

Easy Enchiladas
SERVES 4

To complete this recipe in 30 minutes, preheat your oven before assembling your ingredients. Enchilada sauce is sold in cans of various sizes—you'll need 20 ounces of sauce for this recipe. Cooked shredded turkey is also good in these enchiladas.

2	cups finely shredded cooked chicken, beef, or pork (see note)
¾	cup refried beans
2½	cups enchilada sauce (see note)
1	(4-ounce) can chopped green chiles, drained
½	cup minced fresh cilantro
3	cups shredded cheddar cheese
12	(6-inch) soft corn tortillas
	Lime wedges, for serving

MAKING THE MINUTES COUNT:
Heat the remaining cup of enchilada sauce while the enchiladas bake.

1. HEAT OVEN AND PREP BAKING DISH: Adjust oven rack to middle position and heat oven to 450 degrees. Lightly spray 13 by 9-inch baking dish with vegetable oil spray and set aside.

2. MIX AND HEAT FILLING: Combine meat, beans, ½ cup enchilada sauce, and chiles together in microwave-safe bowl and cover with plastic wrap. Microwave on high until hot, 1 to 3 minutes. Stir cilantro and 1½ cups cheese into chicken mixture; set aside.

3. MICROWAVE TORTILLAS: Stack tortillas on microwave-safe plate, cover with plastic wrap, and microwave on high until warm and pliable, 40 to 60 seconds.

4. ASSEMBLE ENCHILADAS: Arrange warm tortillas on clean work surface. Divide meat mixture evenly among tortillas, about ¼ cup of filling per enchilada, and spread evenly down center of each. Tightly roll tortilla around filling. Place seam-side down in prepared baking dish.

5. TOP ENCHILADAS: Lightly spray enchiladas with vegetable oil spray. Pour 1 cup more enchilada sauce over enchiladas to coat. Sprinkle remaining cheese over enchiladas.

FAST ENCHILADA SAUCE
MAKES ABOUT 2½ CUPS

If you don't have canned enchilada sauce on hand, or just prefer to make your own, try this quick home-made sauce.

1   tablespoon vegetable oil
1   onion, minced
     Salt and pepper
3   garlic cloves, minced
3   tablespoons chili powder
2   teaspoons ground cumin
2   teaspoons sugar
2   (8-ounce) cans tomato sauce
½   cup water

Heat oil in 12-inch skillet over medium heat until shimmering. Add onion and ½ teaspoon salt and cook until softened, about 5 minutes. Stir in garlic, chili powder, cumin, and sugar. Cook until fragrant, about 30 seconds. Stir in tomato sauce and water. Bring to simmer and cook until slightly thickened, about 5 minutes. Season with salt and pepper to taste, and strain through fine-mesh strainer for smoother sauce, if desired.

6. BAKE AND SERVE: Cover baking dish with foil and bake until enchiladas are heated through, 10 minutes. Remove foil and continue to bake until cheese is completely melted, about 5 minutes longer. Heat remaining 1 cup enchilada sauce in a covered, microwave-safe container on high for 1 to 2 minutes, or until hot. Serve enchiladas with warmed sauce and lime wedges.

CURRY

MAKING A QUICK CURRY IS A PERFECT way to turn leftover chicken, beef, pork, or lamb into a flavorful meal. While you could use one of those jarred curry sauces from the supermarket and be done with it, we don't recommend taking this route—its flavor is less than fresh. It's quite easy to create your own curry sauce and it needn't require a laundry list of spices and seasonings. In this curry we focused on the most vital flavorings necessary to pack the most flavor. Of course we used curry powder, but in addition we found that the fresh bite of garlic and ginger was a must. Yogurt provided the curry with its characteristic tang, tempered the heat of the spices, and married all the flavors of the dish. The sweetness of plump raisins added another necessary flavor dimension, and minced fresh cilantro added brightness and color to the finished dish.

Curry in a Hurry
SERVES 4

The brand of curry powder you use will change the flavor and spiciness of this dish (see page 88 for more information). Don't substitute low-fat or nonfat yogurt here, or the sauce will be too thin and have an off flavor.

¼   cup vegetable oil
1   onion, sliced thin
1   tablespoon curry powder (see note)
     Salt
4   garlic cloves, minced
1   tablespoon grated fresh ginger
½   cup water
2   cups shredded or thinly sliced cooked chicken, beef, pork, or lamb
1   (15-ounce) can chickpeas, rinsed
1   cup frozen peas
¼   cup raisins
½   cup plain whole-milk yogurt
¼   cup minced fresh cilantro

1. BUILD CURRY BASE: Heat oil in 12-inch skillet over medium-high heat until shimmering. Add onion, curry powder, and ½ teaspoon salt and cook until onion is browned, 5 to 7 minutes. Stir in garlic and ginger and cook until fragrant, about 30 seconds.

2. ADD WATER, MEAT, VEGETABLES, AND COOK: Stir in water, meat, chickpeas, peas, and raisins. Cook, stirring frequently, until heated through, 3 to 5 minutes.

3. GARNISH AND SERVE: Off heat, stir in yogurt and cilantro and serve.

FRIED RICE

FRIED RICE SHOULD BE A SIMPLE dish—after all, it relies on leftover rice and naturally quick-cooking ingredients like eggs, frozen peas, and bean sprouts—but all too often it falls short. We've eaten our fair share of bad fried rice, from takeout containers of bland greasy rice with rubbery meat and a meager amount of vegetables, to recipes that rely on an overdose of soy sauce to flavor the often mushy rice and an everything-but-the-kitchen-sink approach to meat and vegetables. We wanted simple, fresh, and flavorful fried rice. To do so, we found it best to cook all the ingredients very quickly in stages over high heat, much like a stir-fry. To prevent the rice from being mushy, we made sure that it was completely chilled before it went into the pan, and then cooked it just until heated through. Garlic, soy sauce, and oyster-flavored sauce gave the rice complexity, while bean sprouts and scallions, stirred into the pan in the last minute, added freshness. This recipe comes together in under 10 minutes—even faster than takeout and much fresher tasting.

Simple Fried Rice

SERVES 4 TO 6

Don't try to make this dish with hot or even warm rice—it will turn out incredibly mushy. Use only cold or slightly chilled rice.

- 3 tablespoons vegetable oil
- 2 large eggs, beaten lightly
- I cup (6 ounces) frozen peas, thawed
- 2 garlic cloves, minced
- 4 cups cooked white rice, chilled
- 2 cups shredded or thinly sliced cooked chicken, pork, or beef
- 3 tablespoons low-sodium soy sauce
- 3 tablespoons oyster-flavored sauce
- I cup bean sprouts
- 5 medium scallions, sliced thin

I. **COOK EGGS:** Heat 1½ teaspoons oil in 12-inch nonstick skillet over medium heat until shimmering. Add eggs and cook without stirring until just beginning to set, about 20 seconds. Continue to cook eggs, stirring constantly, until eggs are cooked through but not browned, about 1 minute; transfer to small bowl and set aside.

2. **STIR-FRY VEGETABLES, RICE, MEAT, AND SAUCE:** Add remaining 2½ tablespoons oil to skillet and return to high heat until just smoking. Add peas and garlic and cook until fragrant, about 30 seconds. Add rice, meat, soy sauce, and oyster-flavored sauce and cook, stirring constantly, until mixture is heated through, about 3 minutes.

3. **ADD SPROUTS, SCALLIONS, EGGS AND HEAT THROUGH:** Stir in bean sprouts, scallions, and reserved cooked eggs and cook until heated through, about 1 minute. Serve.

MOO SHU PORK

MOO SHU IS A STIR-FRIED DISH OF PORK, shredded cabbage, and other vegetables, which is eaten rolled up in a thin crepe. While it is certainly easy enough to call in an order from your local Chinese takeout, why not make your own—especially if you've got some leftover pork in the fridge? Shredded cabbage is a given in moo shu, and conveniently, the preshredded options at the supermarket work well here. We found that we liked the cabbage best when it still had a slightly crisp texture, so we added it with the pork and cooked it just until it began to wilt.

To intensify the flavor of the dish, we sautéed thinly sliced shiitake mushrooms and also included the classic Chinese combination of ginger, garlic, and scallions. A common problem with moo shu is that it is often oversauced, making the crepes soggy. Wary of this, we made just enough sauce to coat the vegetables—a simple mixture of chicken broth, soy sauce, cornstarch, and a little hoisin sauce for sweetness and depth. While Chinese crepes are available at specialty Asian markets, we were happy to roll our moo shu up in easy-to-find flour tortillas, which we quickly softened in the microwave while preparing the filling.

Moo Shu Pork

SERVES 4

Shredded carrots, beans sprouts, or thinly sliced bamboo shoots can be stirred into the pan with the cabbage. This recipe also works well with thinly sliced cooked chicken or beef.

1/3	cup low-sodium chicken broth
6	tablespoons hoisin sauce
2	tablespoons soy sauce
2	teaspoons cornstarch
2	tablespoons vegetable oil
8	ounces shiitake mushrooms, sliced thin
8	(6-inch) flour tortillas
3	garlic cloves, minced
I	tablespoon grated fresh ginger
10	ounces cooked pork, sliced into thin strips (see note)
8	ounces (4 cups) pre-shredded cabbage
5	scallions, sliced thin

I. **MAKE SAUCE**: Mix chicken broth, 2 tablespoons hoisin sauce, soy sauce, and cornstarch together; set aside.

2. **BROWN MUSHROOMS**: Heat 1 tablespoon oil in 12-inch nonstick skillet over high heat. Add mushrooms and cook until lightly browned, about 4 minutes.

3. **HEAT TORTILLAS**: Stack tortillas on plate and cover with plastic wrap. Heat in microwave until soft and hot, 30 seconds to 2 minutes.

4. **COOK FILLING**: Clear center of pan and add remaining 1 tablespoon oil, garlic, and ginger. Cook, mashing garlic mixture into pan with back of spatula, until fragrant, about 30 seconds. Stir in pork, cabbage, and scallions and cook until cabbage begins to wilt, about 1 minute.

5. **ADD SAUCE AND HEAT THROUGH**: Whisk sauce to recombine, add to pan, and bring to simmer. Cook until sauce thickens, 1 to 2 minutes, and mixture is hot. Serve with warm tortillas and remaining hoisin sauce.

CALZONES

CALZONES ARE USUALLY TOO BREADY—THESE aren't. Each bite has the perfect ratio of tender crust to cheesy filling. However, with so much filling packed into the dough, our challenge was to prevent the crust from getting soggy. We found that by using pesto instead of the traditional runny red sauce, we were able to pack flavor into the filling and keep it dry. (You can serve tomato sauce on the side.) Add to that chopped broccoli, shredded mozzarella, and thinly sliced chicken, turkey, or sausage, and a complete meal is served. Store-bought pizza dough, dough from your local pizzeria, or one 12-ounce pop-up canister of pizza dough all work here, making this recipe quick and easy.

Chicken, Cheese, and Broccoli Calzone

SERVES 4

Store-bought pizza dough, dough from your local pizzeria, or one 12-ounce pop-up canister of pizza dough all work here. Serve with a simple tomato sauce on the side. You can also use cooked turkey or cooked and sliced sausage in place of the chicken.

I	(10-ounce) package frozen broccoli, thawed and chopped coarse
2	cups shredded part-skim mozzarella
2	cups shredded cooked chicken (see note)
1/4	cup pesto
	Salt and ground black pepper
	Flour for counter
I	pound pizza dough (see note)
2	tablespoons olive oil
	Kosher salt (optional)

I. **HEAT OVEN AND COMBINE FILLING**: Adjust oven rack to middle position and heat oven to 450 degrees. Pat broccoli dry and toss with mozzarella, chicken, and pesto. Season with salt and pepper to taste.

2. **ROLL DOUGH AND FILL CALZONE**: On floured counter, roll out dough to 12-inch round, about ¼ inch thick. Mound filling over half of dough, leaving 1-inch border around edge. Brush edges of

dough with water. Fold other half of dough over filling and press edges to seal.

3. BAKE CALZONE: Grease baking sheet with 1 tablespoon oil. Slide wide spatula under calzone and transfer to baking sheet. Use sharp knife or kitchen shears to cut 5 slits diagonally across top. Brush remaining tablespoon oil over top and sprinkle with coarse salt (if using). Bake until golden, 15 to 20 minutes. Cool briefly, cut into slices, and serve.

CUBANOS

THE CUBAN SANDWICH, OR CUBANO, IS south Florida's most popular sandwich. Made with a combination of roast pork, ham, Swiss cheese, and pickles, and sometimes mustard and mayonnaise, it is brushed with melted butter, pressed, and grilled. The bread should be golden brown and crisp and the filling hot, its ingredients melded together. Cubanos are the perfect way to use leftover roast pork.

Cubanos are cooked with a heavy cast-iron sandwich press that heats the sandwich from the top as it compresses the contents. While this item is standard issue in sandwich shops, it's rarely found in home kitchens. To mimic the effects of a sandwich press, we used a preheated heavy pot or Dutch oven to weight the sandwiches. These

---

TEST KITCHEN TIP:
Pressed to Perfection
Toasted pressed sandwiches like cubanos take on a luxurious texture and deep, even crust when weighted with a sandwich press. But if you don't own a press, don't despair. We've had excellent results by improvising with this method. Preheat your skillet and use the bottom of a preheated heavy pot to weight down the sandwich. We like to use a Dutch oven, but you can also use a teakettle filled with water.

---

sandwiches were so popular in the test kitchen that our tasters actually looked forward to these "leftovers."

Cuban Sandwiches
SERVES 4

If you can't fit all four sandwiches in the skillet at once, cook them in batches and hold the first batch in a warm oven. (Or you can use a nonstick griddle.) Yellow mustard can be used here instead of spicy brown mustard, and soft potato rolls can be used instead of sub rolls. Jarred banana peppers can be found in the pickle aisle at the supermarket.

4	(6-inch) soft submarine rolls, halved lengthwise
2	tablespoons mayonnaise
4	teaspoons spicy brown mustard
¼	pound thinly sliced ham, preferably Virginia or Black Forest
10	ounces thinly sliced roast pork
⅓	cup chopped dill pickles
⅓	cup chopped jarred banana peppers
¼	pound deli-sliced Swiss cheese
2	tablespoons unsalted butter, melted

I. ASSEMBLE SANDWICHES: Spread top half of each roll with mayonnaise and bottom half with mustard. Layer ham, pork, pickles, peppers, and cheese on bottom half of each roll. Place top halves of rolls on sandwiches and press down to flatten.

2. HEAT SKILLET AND DUTCH OVEN: Heat both 12-inch nonstick skillet and large Dutch oven over medium-low heat for 4 minutes.

3. COOK SANDWICHES: Brush tops of sandwiches with melted butter and place in skillet, top-side down. Brush bottoms of sandwiches with remaining butter and, using preheated pot, press down on sandwiches for 15 to 20 seconds. Continue to cook with pot on sandwiches (but not pressing down), until first side is golden brown, 4 to 5 minutes. Remove pot, flip sandwiches over, and continue to cook with pot on sandwiches (but not pressing down) until second side is golden brown, 3 to 4 minutes. Serve.

PULLED PORK SANDWICHES

MAKING AUTHENTIC PULLED BARBECUE TAKES an entire day of work. The cheater's version of pulled barbecue is far quicker, and although it doesn't taste as deep and complex as the authentic version, it still satisfies a basic barbecue craving. The idea is to simply shred the cooked meat, toss it with some hot barbecue sauce, and pile it on a toasted bun with some pickles. The only key to the cheater's version is to use a good tasting barbecue sauce, or make your own sauce.

SHORTCUT INGREDIENT:
Store-Bought Barbecue Sauce

In just one local supermarket, we found more than 30 varieties of barbecue sauce! To make sense of all these options, we conducted a blind taste test of eight leading national brands.

We chose tomato-based sauces that were labeled "original" and tasted them as a dipping sauce for homemade chicken fingers. While tasters' personal preferences varied, we found a few sauces that were universally liked and a few that were universally disliked. Sauces that tasted like tomatoes rather than tasting just plain sweet were the clear favorites. A good balance of smoke and spice was also appreciated. Texture was another important issue, with tasters objecting to very thin sauces as well as sauces with an overly thick, gloppy consistency. Odd colors (one sauce was bright red from the use of food dye) and weird flavors (one sauce reminded us of spicy red hot candies) were not appreciated. Our conclusion: You don't have to make your own barbecue sauce, but it should taste—and look—like homemade.

THE BEST STORE-BOUGHT BARBECUE SAUCES

Texas Best Barbecue Sauce, Original Rib Style (left), topped the charts because of its emphasis on tomatoes. Tasters liked the "thick, coarse texture." They also praised the "good sweet/tart balance" with "lots of spices." Leaning heavier on the smoke, second-place Bull's Eye Original BBQ Sauce (right) was still deemed "well balanced," although a few tasters thought the heavy smoke "hit you in the back of the throat." Bull's Eye gained points for its "great dark color" and "thick consistency."

Cheater's Pulled Pork Sandwiches
SERVES 4

While pork is traditional, shredded cooked chicken or beef is good here, too. If you don't want to use store-bought barbecue sauce, see our quick homemade sauce below.

- ¾   cup store-bought barbecue sauce
- 2   cups shredded cooked pork (see note)
- 4   sandwich or hamburger rolls, toasted
      Sliced pickles for serving

Heat barbecue sauce in large saucepan until warm, about 1 minute. Stir in meat and cook, stirring frequently, until meat is warmed through, about 2 minutes. Serve on toasted rolls, passing pickles separately.

QUICK BARBECUE SAUCE
MAKES ABOUT 1½ CUPS
This recipe can easily be doubled or tripled.

- 2   tablespoons vegetable oil
- 1   onion, minced
- 1   garlic clove, minced
- 1   teaspoon chili powder
- ¼   teaspoon cayenne
- 1   cup ketchup
- 2   tablespoons cider vinegar
- 2   tablespoons Worcestershire sauce
- 2   tablespoons Dijon mustard
- 5   tablespoons mild or dark molasses
- 1   teaspoon Tabasco
      Salt and ground black pepper

1. SAUTÉ AROMATICS: Heat oil in large saucepan until shimmering. Add onion and cook until softened, about 5 minutes. Stir in garlic, chili powder, and cayenne. Cook until fragrant, about 15 seconds.

2. SEASON AND SIMMER SAUCE: Stir in vinegar, Worcestershire sauce, mustard, molasses, and Tabasco. Simmer, stirring occasionally, until sauce is thickened, about 25 minutes. Season with salt and pepper to taste.

TACOS

FORGET THE TACO KIT—THESE TASTE FAR better. After all, why would you want tacos made with stale, dusty, salty spice blends when it's just as easy to make bright, fresh tasting ones? Instead of dumping a laundry list of raw spices onto the meat, we first "bloomed" our spices (chili powder and cumin) with the onion and garlic in oil to bring out their complex flavors. A can of chopped green chiles conveniently provided heat, and a hefty amount (¼ cup) of minced fresh cilantro added the fresh flavor and color that's missing from taco kits.

PREVENTING SPILLED TACO FILLING

Once a taco shell is filled, it inevitably shatters—if not at first bite, then soon after. To prevent taco fillings and toppings from landing in your lap, we found that this preventive measure helps.

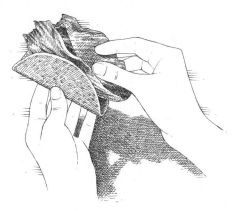

Line the taco shell with a lettuce leaf, then add filling and toppings. When the shell shatters, the lettuce leaf contains the filling.

SHORTCUT INGREDIENT: Store-Bought Taco Shells

Frying your own taco shells from fresh corn tortillas can't be beat, but when you're in a hurry, store-bought taco shells are a quick and convenient alternative. We tasted our way through six brands of taco shells (warmed according to package instructions). Old El Paso Taco Shells came out ahead.

The Best Store-Bought Taco Shells

Old El Paso Taco Shells finished first among the brands we tested.

Tacos

SERVES 4

There are many possible accompaniments for tacos; however, we think that shredded iceberg lettuce, shredded cheese, salsa, and sour cream are essential.

1	tablespoon vegetable oil
1	onion, minced
2	garlic cloves, minced
1	teaspoon chili powder
¼	teaspoon cumin
2	cups shredded or thinly sliced cooked chicken, beef, or pork
¼	cup minced fresh cilantro
2	tablespoons canned chopped green chiles
8	store-bought taco shells, warmed

Heat oil in 12-inch nonstick skillet over medium high heat until shimmering. Add onion and cook until softened, about 5 minutes. Stir in garlic, chili powder, and cumin and cook until fragrant, about 30 seconds. Stir in meat and cook until heated through, about 2 minutes. Stir in cilantro and chiles. Spoon filling into taco shells and serve with desired accompaniments.

QUESADILLAS

IN RECENT YEARS QUESADILLAS HAVE evolved into a version of bad Mexican pizza, becoming stale and soggy and unable to contain their oozing filling. We wanted to make quesadillas that were authentic in spirit (if not quite in substance) yet also quick enough to make for a weeknight dinner. We kept the tortillas crisp by lightly toasting them in a dry skillet. We then filled them, lightly coated them with oil and a sprinkling of salt, and returned them to the skillet until they were well browned and the cheese fully melted. Using 8-inch tortillas and folding them in half around the filling allowed us to cook two at one time in the same skillet, and the fold also kept our generous cheese filling from leaking out.

Quesadillas

MAKES FOUR 8-INCH QUESADILLAS

The skillet should be fairly hot, but it should never smoke; if it does, reduce the heat to medium-low. Larger-grained kosher salt is preferred here, but regular table salt works fine too. Let the quesadillas cool for 3 minutes after cooking so the cheese will not ooze out when cutting them. Serve the quesadillas with salsa, guacamole, and sour cream, if desired. Serve either 1 or 2 quesadillas per person.

 4 (8-inch) flour tortillas
 2 cups shredded or thinly sliced cooked chicken, beef, pork, or sausage
 1⅓ cups shredded Monterey Jack or cheddar cheese
 4 teaspoons minced pickled jalapeños (optional)
 4 teaspoons minced fresh cilantro
   Vegetable oil
   Kosher salt

I. HEAT OVEN: Adjust oven rack to middle position and heat oven to 200 degrees.

2. TOAST TORTILLAS: Heat 10-inch nonstick skillet over medium heat until hot, about 2 minutes. Toast tortillas in skillet, one by one, until soft and slightly puffed on both sides, about 1½ minutes per side; slide toasted tortillas onto cutting board. Begin to assemble first quesadilla while toasting remaining tortillas.

3. ASSEMBLE QUESADILLAS: Sprinkle ½ cup meat, ⅓ cup cheese, 1 teaspoon jalapeños, if using, and 1 teaspoon cilantro over half of tortilla, leaving ½-inch border around edge. Fold tortilla in half and press to flatten. Brush top generously with oil and sprinkle lightly with salt; set aside.

4. COOK QUESADILLAS: Place two quesadillas in skillet, oiled-sides down. Cook over medium heat until crisp and well-browned, 1 to 2 minutes. Brush tops with oil and sprinkle lightly with salt. Flip quesadillas over and continue to cook until second sides are crisp and browned, 1 to 2 minutes longer. Transfer quesadillas to baking sheet and keep warm in oven (they can be held for up to 20 minutes). Repeat with remaining quesadillas. Let quesadillas cool for 3 minutes before cutting and serving.

TOSTADAS

TOSTADAS, COMMONLY SERVED AS AN appetizer in Mexico, can easily be turned into a tasty weeknight supper when bulked up with left-over chicken, beef, pork, or sausage. This version is nothing like the greasy, overloaded, soggy tortillas that pass themselves off as tostadas in many restaurants. We brushed the tortillas with oil and toasted them so they'd be crisp and dry enough to provide a sturdy and flavorful base for toppings. Refried beans provided a creamy layer for the meat to adhere to, and cheese melted over the top held it all together. For the perfect finishing touch, contributing color and freshness, we added a sprinkling of fresh cilantro.

Tostadas

MAKES 4

Serve either 1 or 2 tostadas per person. This recipe can easily be doubled if desired. Canned refried beans work well. Serve with sour cream and salsa.

 4 (6-inch) corn tortillas
   Vegetable oil
 ½ cup canned refried beans
 2 cups shredded or thinly sliced cooked chicken, beef, pork, or sausage
 ½ cup shredded Monterey Jack or cheddar cheese
 2 tablespoons minced fresh cilantro

I. TOAST TORTILLAS: Adjust oven rack to middle position and heat oven to 400 degrees. Brush tortillas liberally with oil and arrange in single layer on baking sheet. Bake until light brown and crisp, 10 to 12 minutes. Remove tortillas from the oven.

2. TOP AND BAKE TOSTADAS: Spread 2 tablespoons refried beans over each toasted tortilla, then top with ½ cup meat and 2 tablespoons cheese. Return topped tortillas to oven and bake until cheese is melted and meat is hot, about 5 minutes. Sprinkle with cilantro before serving.

INDEX

A NOTE ON CONVERSIONS

SOME SAY COOKING IS A SCIENCE AND AN art. We would say that geography has a hand in it, too. Flour milled in the United Kingdom and elsewhere will feel and taste different from flour milled in the United States. So we cannot promise that the loaf of bread you bake in Canada or England will taste the same as a loaf baked in the States, but we can offer guidelines for converting weights and measures. We also recommend that you rely on your instincts when making our recipes. Refer to the visual cues provided. If the bread dough hasn't "come together in a ball," as described, you may need to add more flour—even if the recipe doesn't tell you so. You be the judge. For more information on conversions and ingredient equivalents, visit our Web site at www.cooksillustrated.com and type "conversion chart" in the search box.

The recipes in this book were developed using standard U.S. measures following U.S. government guidelines. The charts below offer equivalents for U.S., metric, and Imperial (U.K.) measures. All conversions are approximate and have been rounded up or down to the nearest whole number. For example:

1 teaspoon = 4.9292 milliliters, rounded up to 5 milliliters

1 ounce = 28.3495 grams, rounded down to 28 grams

Volume Conversions

U.S.	METRIC
1 teaspoon	5 milliliters
2 teaspoons	10 milliliters
1 tablespoon	15 milliliters
2 tablespoons	30 milliliters
¼ cup	59 milliliters
⅓ cup	79 milliliters
½ cup	118 milliliters
¾ cup	177 milliliters
1 cup	237 milliliters
1¼ cups	296 milliliters
1½ cups	355 milliliters
2 cups	473 milliliters
2½ cups	592 milliliters
3 cups	710 milliliters
4 cups (1 quart)	0.946 liter
1.06 quarts	1 liter
4 quarts (1 gallon)	3.8 liters

Weight Conversions

OUNCES	GRAMS
½	14
¾	21
1	28
1½	43
2	57
2½	71
3	85
3½	99
4	113
4½	128
5	142
6	170
7	198
8	227
9	255
10	283
12	340
16 (1 pound)	454

Conversions for Ingredients Commonly Used in Baking

Baking is an exacting science. Because measuring by weight is far more accurate than measuring by volume, and thus more likely to achieve reliable results, in our recipes we provide ounce measures in addition to cup measures for many ingredients. Refer to the chart below to convert these measures into grams.

INGREDIENT	OUNCES	GRAMS
1 cup all-purpose flour*	5	142
1 cup whole-wheat flour	5½	156
1 cup granulated (white) sugar	7	198
1 cup packed brown sugar (light or dark)	7	198
1 cup confectioners' sugar	4	113
1 cup cocoa powder	3	85
Butter†		
4 tablespoons (½ stick, or ¼ cup)	2	57
8 tablespoons (1 stick, or ½ cup)	4	113
16 tablespoons (2 sticks, or 1 cup)	8	227

*U.S. all-purpose flour, the most frequently used flour in this book, does not contain leaveners, as some European flours do. These leavened flours are called self-rising or self-raising. If you are using self-rising flour, take this into consideration before adding leavening to a recipe.

† In the United States, butter is sold both salted and unsalted. We generally recommend unsalted butter. If you are using salted butter, take this into consideration before adding salt to a recipe.

Oven Temperatures

FAHRENHEIT	CELSIUS	GAS MARK (IMPERIAL)
225	105	¼
250	120	½
275	130	1
300	150	2
325	165	3
350	180	4
375	190	5
400	200	6
425	220	7
450	230	8
475	245	9

Converting Temperatures from an Instant-Read Thermometer

We include doneness temperatures in many of our recipes, such as those for poultry, meat, and bread. We recommend an instant-read thermometer for the job. Refer to the table at left to convert Fahrenheit degrees to Celsius. Or, for temperatures not represented in the chart, use this simple formula:

Subtract 32 degrees from the Fahrenheit reading, then divide the result by 1.8 to find the Celsius reading.

EXAMPLE:
"Roast until the juices run clear when the chicken is cut with a paring knife or the thickest part of the breast registers 160 degrees on an instant-read thermometer." To convert:

160° F − 32 = 128°
128° ÷ 1.8 = 71° C (rounded down from 71.11)